Fighting to a Finish

A book in the series

CORNELL STUDIES IN SECURITY AFFAIRS

edited by Robert J. Art *and* Robert Jervis

A complete list of series titles appears at the end of the book.

Fighting to a Finish

THE POLITICS OF WAR TERMINATION IN
THE UNITED STATES AND JAPAN, 1945

LEON V. SIGAL

Cornell University Press

ITHACA AND LONDON

First published 1988 by Cornell University Press.
First published, Cornell Paperbacks, 1989.

International Standard Book Number 0-8014-2086-5 (cloth)
International Standard Book Number 0-8014-9607-1 (paper)
Library of Congress Catalog Card Number 87-24876
Printed in the United States of America
Librarians: Library of Congress cataloging information
appears on the last page of the book.

The paper in this book is acid-free and meets the guidelines for permanence
and durability of the Committee on Production Guidelines for
Book Longevity of the Council on Library Resources.

To Meg

Contents

Preface

This book begins with two puzzles: how do wars end and why do states take so long to end them?

I address these puzzles in the context of a particular war, the one between the United States and Japan, the end of which has been the source of enduring historical controversy. That controversy has turned less on issues of war termination itself than on the question of whether the atomic bombings of Hiroshima and Nagasaki were necessary. The way the controversy has been joined nonetheless reflects the perspective and power of the dominant analytical assumptions in the study of war. Orthodox analysts of the war's end have argued that the United States acted as it did in order to bring about the unconditional surrender of Japan as soon as possible. Revisionist accounts have pointed to contradictions and anomalies in American behavior that call this goal or interest into question and have suggested, instead, that relations with the Soviet Union, not Japan, motivated American use of the bomb. Yet orthodox and revisionist accounts alike proceed from the same premises, that American behavior was, by and large, internally consistent, motivated by national interests, and oriented to external relations.

I first became interested in the topic of war termination nearly two decades ago, as the United States was struggling to end another war. I was struck then by the lack of attention that the issue had received in the scholarly literature on war. More work has appeared since, but still far less than the importance of the subject would seem to warrant. In part, the increased attention to how wars end may be a function of a change in our time horizon. In an era of nuclear weapons, when enormous and indiscriminate destruction can take place in a very short span of time, the problem of war termination assumes much greater significance than it had in earlier eras when a delay of months, even years, in war's end might add only marginally to gratuitous suffering.

The analytical assumptions underlying most studies of war may have also contributed to a downplaying of war termination as an issue. Those assumptions, imbedded in the realist approach to international relations, emphasize rational choice based on calculations about state interests or intentions and relative capabilities. A war ends, according to this approach, when the costs of continuing the war outweigh the benefits to the contending states' interests. Critical to the calculus is the balance of power between the states involved. This way of thinking about war's end seems to deflect attention away from the problems of arranging a transition from war to peace. A war is supposed to end more or less automatically once the balance of power shifts or the cost-benefit ratio becomes unfavorable. Whether in recognition or in anticipation of stalemate or an adverse shift in the balance, one contender or the other will sue for peace. Alternatively, if prestige—or the reputation for power—is the critical interest at stake, both sides may be reluctant to take the initiative and seek a settlement.

The problem of war termination comes into clearer focus if the analysis starts from premises different from those shared by the orthodox and revisionist accounts. To that end I have employed two other approaches, both of which disaggregate the state into its constituent organizations and groups. The organizational-process approach underscores the routine behavior of government organizations and the resistance of routines to change. The internal-politics approach highlights the competing interests of bureaus within the government as well as conflicts among publics outside and suggests the difficulty of getting agreement within as well as between governments to end a war.

I have chosen to focus on a single case study in order to show how these approaches can shed light on the problem of war termination and to generate hypotheses for scholars to use in the future to examine other cases. This book, I hope, will not be the last word on the subject.

Nor is it the first. It is important to acknowledge Paul Kecskemeti, Fred Iklé, Herman Kahn, and especially Thomas Schelling for their pioneering work on war termination even as I propose an alternative to the ways they approached the subject. I have also benefited greatly from the scholarship and teaching of Richard Neustadt, Morton Halperin, and Graham Allison, whose work on the bureaucratic and domestic politics has helped inspire mine.

I owe much to other scholars as well. A few who went out of their way to be generous with their time and suggestions are I. M. Destler, Haruhiro Fukui, David Titus, Clement Vose, Lawrence Olson, Alexander George, McGeorge Bundy, and especially the editors of the Cornell Series in Security Affairs, Robert Jervis and Robert Art, whose detailed comments and criticisms went well beyond the call of duty. Many librarians were very helpful, in particular those at Wesleyan University, the Stimson Collection at Yale University, and the Library of Congress, but I owe special thanks to E. J. Reese and John Taylor at the National Archives for their indefatigable efforts to track down documents for me. Lee Messina typed earlier drafts of the manuscript. My students were quick to spot ambiguities in them. I am indebted, too, to the Brookings Institution, especially to John Steinbruner and Herbert Kaufman, for arranging accommodations for me there and to the Joint Committee on Japanese Studies of the American Council of Learned Societies and the Social Science Research Council under the chairmanship of Gary Saxonhouse, for their help in funding the completion of the work. And finally, I want to express my love and gratitude to my wife, Meg, without whose constant encouragement this work might never have reached its end.

LEON V. SIGAL

New York, New York

Abbreviations of
Frequently Cited Sources

FRUS   U.S. Department of State, *Foreign Relations of the United States* (Washington, D.C.: Government Printing Office).

IMTFE   International Military Tribunal for the Far East, *Record of Proceedings, 1946–1948* (Washington, D.C., Library of Congress, 1974, microfilm).

"Interrogations"   U.S. Army, Far East Command, Military History Section, "Interrogations of Japanese Officials on World War II" (typescript).

"Statements"   U.S. Army, Far East Command, Military History Section, "Statements of Japanese Officials on World War II" (typescript).

USSBS, *Interrogations*   U.S. Strategic Bombing Survey (Pacific), Naval Analysis Division, *Interrogations of Japanese Officials*, Report No. 72 (Washington, D.C.: Government Printing Office, 1946).

Fighting to a Finish

[1]

Pacific Endgame

This is the patent age of new inventions
For killing bodies, and for saving souls,
All propagated with the best intentions.
—Byron, *Don Juan*

On April 1, 1945, Allied forces invaded Okinawa. Four days later the Soviet Union formally notified Japan that it would not renew their treaty of neutrality; the treaty stipulated that such notice be given one year prior to its expiration date. That very day in Tokyo, the government of Prime Minister Kuniaki Koiso fell. A retired admiral and onetime Privy Council president, Kantarō Suzuki, received the imperial summons to form a new government. A week later, on April 12, Harry S Truman succeeded to the presidency of the United States upon the death of Franklin Delano Roosevelt. Within a month Germany surrendered.

The United States announced the capture of Okinawa on June 22 after three months of bitter fighting that claimed the lives of 12,281 Americans and 110,000 Japanese, the highest toll of any campaign in the entire war. Four days earlier, President Truman had met with the chiefs of staff to approve preparations for Operation Olympic, an invasion of the Japanese home islands, with November 1 as the planning date for an assault on Kyushu. That same day in Tokyo, Prime Minister Suzuki met with the war, navy, and foreign affairs ministers and the chiefs of staff and set in motion an attempt to open talks with the Soviet Union. Senior U.S. officials learned of the Japanese demarche shortly thereafter through the interception and decoding of Japan's diplomatic cable traffic.

On July 16 the Big Three convened at Potsdam. In the course of their deliberations, Joseph Stalin reaffirmed an agreement reached at Yalta in February that, assuming satisfactory completion of negotiations with China over territorial concessions, the Soviet Union would enter the war about three months after the surrender of Germany. On the opening day of the conference, the American delegation received preliminary reports of a successful test of the first atomic bomb at Alamogordo, New Mexico. On July 26, the last day of the conference, the United States, Great

Britain, and China issued the "Potsdam Declaration," setting forth their terms for ending the war and threatening Japan with "prompt and utter destruction" if it did not "proclaim now the unconditional surrender of all the Japanese armed forces." The declaration made no mention of the atomic bomb or of impending Soviet entry into the war. Nor did it spell out what would become of Emperor Hirohito after Japan's surrender. It noted only that occupation forces would be withdrawn after their objectives had been accomplished and a "peacefully inclined and responsible government" had been established "in accordance with the freely expressed will of the Japanese people."

On July 28 the United States monitored what officials took to be Japan's response to the declaration. It came in the form of a reply by Suzuki to a question posed at a press conference, broadcast by Radio Tokyo and translated in Washington: "I believe the Joint Proclamation by the three countries is nothing but a rehash of the Cairo Declaration. As for the government, it does not find any important value in it, and there is no other recourse but to ignore it entirely and resolutely fight for the successful conclusion of the war."[1]

On August 6 an American B-29 dropped an atomic bomb on Hiroshima without warning, devastating the city and killing as many as 80,000 people. On August 8 Soviet Foreign Minister Vyacheslav Molotov summoned Japan's ambassador to Moscow, Naotake Satō, and handed him a formal declaration of war. Within hours Soviet forces were crossing the frontier and attacking what remained of the Japanese army there. On August 9 the United States dropped a second atomic bomb on a Japanese city, this time Nagasaki, destroying much of it, killing about 38,000 people, and wounding an equal number.

The next day the Japanese government used Swiss and Swedish intermediaries to notify the Allies of its willingness to accept the terms of Potsdam, but on one condition: "with the understanding that the said declaration does not comprise any demand which prejudices the prerogative of His Majesty as a Sovereign Ruler."[2] The same day, after reports of Japan's suit for peace had reached Washington, planes of the U.S. army air forces and navy launched heavy conventional bombing raids against Tokyo and other Japanese population centers.

On August 11 the United States transmitted to the Swiss the Allied reply to Japan's suit for peace. It left the emperor's ultimate fate open to interpretation while suggesting a role for him to play in the days immediately ahead: "From the moment of surrender the authority of the

---

[1]U.S. Department of State, *Foreign Relations of the United States* (hereafter FRUS): *The Conference of Berlin (Potsdam), 1945* (Washington, D.C., 1960), II: 1293.

[2]Note from Swiss chargé to Secretary of State, August 10, 1945, in *FRUS, 1945, VI: The British Commonwealth; The Far East* (Washington, D.C., 1969), p. 627.

Emperor and the Japanese Government to rule the state shall be subject to the Supreme Commander of the Allied powers who will take such steps as he deems proper to effectuate the surrender terms."[3] The reply reached Tokyo on August 12. The next day, U.S. navy planes attacked Tokyo in one of the heaviest carrier-based raids of the war. Starting around midnight of August 14–15, the army air forces struck Japanese cities with a thousand-plane mission, their largest of the war.

In the course of that attack, Japan notified the Allies of its unconditional acceptance of the terms of Potsdam:

> His Majesty the Emperor is prepared to authorize and ensure the signature by his Government and the Imperial General Headquarters of the necessary terms for carrying out the provisions of the Potsdam declaration. His Majesty is also prepared to issue his commands to all the military, naval, and air authorities of Japan and all the forces under their control wherever located to cease active operations, to surrender arms and to issue such other orders as may be required by the Supreme Commander of the Allied Forces for the execution of the above-mentioned terms.[4]

Local military commanders in Tokyo put down a plot by junior army officers to prevent the broadcast of an announcement of Japan's surrender recorded by the emperor. With the dispatching of cease-fire orders to field commands, and with the suppression of further acts of insubordination by diehards, Japanese military resistance effectively ended. The war between the United States and Japan was over. On September 2, on board the battleship *Missouri* at anchor in Tokyo Bay, representatives of the Japanese government and military high command of Japan formally signed the instrument of surrender. A peace treaty would not be concluded until 1951.

Some Puzzles from the Accounts of the War's End

Hostilities had nevertheless continued for at least a year after most senior officials on both sides of the Pacific had conceded any prospect of a Japanese victory. The longer the war dragged on thereafter, the more Japan's military position deteriorated. Naval battles at Midway and Leyte Gulf all but eliminated Japan's fleet. With the fall of Saipan in June 1944, Japan's home islands came within range of American land-based bombers, which began reducing Japanese cities and industries to rubble. A

---

[3]Note from Secretary of State to Swiss chargé, August 11, 1945, in ibid., pp. 631–32.
[4]Note from Swiss chargé to Secretary of State, August 14, 1945 (Washington time) in ibid., pp. 662–63.

naval blockade gradually strangled Japan's sea-lanes of resupply and reinforcement and permitted American carrier-based aircraft to pound the home islands almost at will. Japan's armies fought on, but they could do little more than exact a toll in casualties for every Allied advance. Yet neither side moved decisively to end the war. "Within reach of the B-29s, subject to ever-tightening blockade and facing an early air offensive against the home islands, Japan could have thrown in the sponge without fear of forgoing any serious chances of victory," concluded the U.S. Strategic Bombing Survey in 1946:

> But while defeat is a military event, the recognition of the defeat is a political act. The timing of the political recognition of the military realities is only partly determined by the actual situation on the fronts. The international situation, the domestic balance of power, the interests and antagonisms of relevant political groups—they all weigh heavily when the grim realities of the armed contest have to be translated into the blunt language of capitulation.[5]

Seldom has the issue of war termination been framed more clearly.

The translation of military defeat into war termination took more than a year. Was the war needlessly prolonged? How much loss of life and destruction of property could have been avoided in the waning months of the war? How could the two sides have expedited the end of the war with a minimum of gratuitous suffering? Why did they not do so? These questions lie at the core of scholarly concern about the end of the war in the Pacific—and indeed, about war termination in general.

Why did Japan not seek an end to the war as soon as its military defeat appeared irreversible? Japan's bargaining leverage at war's end is the reason, concludes Paul Kecskemeti in his path-breaking book on war termination, *Strategic Surrender*. Japan might have calculated that the United States, at the point of invading the Japanese home islands, would assess the potential costs and prefer to settle for less than unconditional surrender in order to induce Japan to stop fighting. "The Japanese surrender," says Kecskemeti, "illustrates the use of a defeated power's residual strength, combined with an insular position and an extreme will to resist, for the purposes of obtaining political concessions in return for surrender."[6]

Yet Kecskemeti acknowledges that he cannot explain why Japan did not open negotiations with the United States sooner, instead of approaching only the Soviet Union. "It is difficult," he notes, "to under-

[5]U.S. Strategic Bombing Survey (Pacific), *Effects of Strategic Bombing on Japan's War Economy*, Report no. 53 (Washington, D.C., 1946), p. 57.
[6]Paul Kecskemeti, *Strategic Surrender* (New York, 1964), p. 210.

stand the obstinacy with which the Japanese government clung to the mirage of a *rapprochement* with Moscow, and later to that of mediation by Moscow, even when it became obvious that the Soviet Union did not have the slightest interest in helping Japan out of the war."[7] Kecskemeti's wording obscures three distinct and contradictory purposes that could have motivated Japan's demarche to Moscow: to secure continued Soviet neutrality in the Far East, to obtain increased Soviet aid or even a formal alliance, and to have the Soviet Union weigh in on Japan's side in mediating an end to the war. Had Japan's sole objective been to use Moscow's good offices to find a way out of the war, why were the government's instructions to its ambassador there so vague about his mission?

Moreover, if Japan did use its "residual strength" to obtain "political concessions," then why did it surrender when it did? Kecskemeti's answer is that Japan accepted the terms of Potsdam only after the United States had softened them: "The American readiness to spare the Emperor's position alone induced Japan to surrender."[8] Yet the Allied reply to Japan's suit for peace was vague and noncommittal on this very point. How did it satisfy Japan about preserving the throne in ways that the Potsdam Declaration had not?

If modifying the terms of settlement on the subject of the emperor could have induced Japan to surrender earlier, why had the United States refrained from making such an offer? Kecskemeti contends that the United States acted in "the belief that surrender could only result from military pressure. The possibility that surrender could be hastened by offering political incentives to the Japanese leaders received little attention."[9]

In direct contradiction to Kecskemeti, historian Herbert Feis, who served in the State Department during the war, attempts to document American efforts to end the war "by inducement"—by enumerating the benefits to Japan of surrendering. He depicts the Potsdam Declaration as the culmination of these efforts, even though it omits any specific commitment to preserving the throne or sparing its incumbent. Yet Feis himself is led to wonder "why the American government waited so long before offering the Japanese those various assurances which it did extend later."[10]

In relating why issuance of the Potsdam Declaration was postponed from May until late July, Truman writes as if the declaration were in-

[7]Ibid., p. 177.
[8]Ibid., p. 198.
[9]Ibid., p. 161.
[10]Herbert Feis, *The Atomic Bomb and the End of World War II*, 2d ed. rev. (Princeton, N.J., 1966), chap. 3, p. 188.

[5]

tended to compel, not induce, Japan to surrender. He stresses the need to have waited until all the military threats capable of causing Japan's "prompt and utter destruction" were at hand. Issuing the proclamation from Potsdam, Truman believed, "would clearly demonstrate to Japan and to the world that the Allies were united in their purpose."

> By that time, also, we might know more about two matters of significance for our future effort: the participation of the Soviet Union and the atomic bomb. We knew that the bomb would receive its first test in mid-July. If the test of the bomb was successful, I wanted to afford Japan a clear chance to end the fighting before we made use of this newly gained power. If the test should fail, then it would be even more important to us to bring about a surrender before we had to make a physical conquest of Japan.[11]

Yet if the Potsdam Declaration was supposed to flex Allied muscles, why was the Soviet Union not included as a signatory even it meant delaying the declaration two weeks until the Soviet declaration of war? And if the threat to use the atomic bomb was potentially that compelling, why did the Potsdam Declaration omit any mention of "this newly gained power"?

Furthermore, if the United States wanted "to afford Japan a clear chance" to surrender before dropping the atomic bomb, then why did it allow so little time to elapse between release of the Potsdam Declaration on July 26 and the bombing of Hiroshima on August 6? Secretary of War Henry Stimson cites Prime Minister Suzuki's press conference comments as evidence that further delay would have been pointless because Japan was not about to accept the terms of Potsdam.[12] By contrast, Kecskemeti regards Stimson's conclusion as confirmation that the United States was "not aware" of Japan's real intentions but that this "miscalculation" was "well-nigh unavoidable." In Kecskemeti's assessment, "the Japanese government gave the impression of rejecting the Potsdam Declaration, and the United States government could hardly guess that the failure of the Japanese to accede immediately to the Potsdam terms meant simply that they were maneuvering to surrender through a circuitous route."[13] Yet Secretary of State James F. Byrnes indicates in his memoirs that he had already seen evidence of Japan's maneuvering in intercepted messages between Japanese diplomats in Tokyo and Moscow and had dismissed it as inconclusive. The decoded cable traffic, by his reading, provided no basis for delaying the atomic bombings: "As late as July 21

[11]Harry S Truman, *Year of Decisions*, vol. 1 of *Memoirs* (Garden City, N.Y., 1955), p. 417.
[12]Henry Stimson, "The Decision to Use the Atomic Bomb," *Harper's* 194 (February 1947): 104–5.
[13]Kecskemeti, *Strategic Surrender*, p. 195.

the Japanese militarists caused their government to wire [Japan's] Ambassador [in Moscow], 'We cannot consent to unconditional surrender under any circumstances. Even if the war drags on, so long as the enemy demands unconditional surrender we will fight as one man against the enemy in accordance with the Emperor's command.' That cable, which we intercepted, depressed me terribly. It meant using the atomic bomb; it probably meant Russia's entry into the war."[14]

But if the American objective was unconditional surrender, why did the United States qualify its insistence on deposing the emperor after the atomic bombings, though not before? And why, if the United States knew what it did about Japan's unwillingness to surrender without assurances about the preservation of the throne, did it not couple an offer of such assurances with continued conventional bombing and blockade without resorting to the atomic bomb as soon as it became available? And why would a demonstration of the bomb's power on a less populated target not have sufficed to compel Japan's surrender?

These questions have engendered considerable controversy among historians. Enumerating American losses during the Okinawa campaign, Feis concludes that American officials correctly calculated atomic bombing would be the least-costly strategy for ending the war: "Their reckoning, I believe the record clearly indicates, was governed by one reason deemed paramount: that by using the bomb the agony of war might be ended most quickly and lives be saved. It was believed with deep apprehension that many thousands, probably tens of thousands, of lives of Allied combatants would have to be spent in the continuation of our air and sea bombardment and blockade, victims mainly of Japanese suicide planes."[15] Feis neglects to mention that kamikaze attacks could have taken a heavy toll only after American forces launched their invasion of Japan, and that was not scheduled to take place until November 1. Furthermore, ending the war as quickly as possible was one objective, and minimizing the cost in Allied lives was another—and there were trade-offs between them. "After all," Kecskemeti observes, "the vital question from the American point of view was not whether the Japanese government surrendered in August or September, but whether it could or could not be induced to surrender without offering last-ditch resistance."[16]

Feis and the so-called orthodox historians fall back on a second line of defense for dropping atomic bombs on Japanese cities without warning. Affecting Japan's calculations at the margin about the costs and benefits

[14]James F. Byrnes, *All in One Lifetime* (New York, 1958), p. 308.
[15]Feis, *Atomic Bomb*, p. 192.
[16]Kecskemeti, *Strategic Surrender*, p. 204.

of continuing the war would not yield the desired result. The United States would have to "shock" Japan into surrendering. Feis says of those who decided against demonstrating the bomb on a less-populated target: "No matter what the place and setting for the demonstration, they were sure it would not give an adequate impression of its appalling destructive power, would not register its full meaning in human lives. The desired impression on the Japanese, it was concluded, could be produced only by the actual awful experience."[17] As evidence for his contention, Feis cites the view of Stimson that "the atomic bomb was more than a weapon of terrible destruction; it was a psychological weapon."[18] Sheer terror would somehow bring Japan to its senses.

By this reasoning, even the atomic bombing of Hiroshima was apparently not deemed shocking enough to compel Japan to surrender. The United States immediately followed the bombing with some of its heaviest conventional bombing raids of the war. "During these three days," writes Truman, "we indicated that we meant business." Then came the atomic bombing of Nagasaki. "This second demonstration of the power of the atomic bomb apparently threw Tokyo into a panic," Truman concludes, "for the next morning brought the first indication that the Japanese Empire was ready to surrender."[19] Even then, conventional bombing by the United States continued with unabated ferocity until after Japan gave formal notice of its surrender on August 14, Washington time.

Why did Japan sue for peace when it did? Karl Compton, a member of the National Defense Research Committee, set the tone for postwar retrospectives by U.S. officials in December 1946 when he attributed Japan's surrender to the atomic bombing. "It was not one atomic bomb, or two, which brought surrender. It was the experience of what an atomic bomb will actually do to a community, *plus the dread of many more*, that was effective."[20] Compton's account won prompt endorsement from President Truman and subsequent citation by Stimson in his own firsthand account. These accounts not only state that, in retrospect, the bomb shocked Japan into surrender; they also imply that the decision to use the bomb had anticipated its shock effect. They provide no direct evidence that this anticipation had indeed motivated officials at the time.

[17]Feis, *Atomic Bomb*, p. 199.
[18]Henry L. Stimson and McGeorge Bundy, *On Active Service in Peace and War* (New York, 1948), p. 630.
[19]Truman, *Year of Decisions*, p. 426.
[20]Karl T. Compton, "If the Atomic Bomb Had Not Been Used," *Atlantic Monthly* 178 (December 1946): 56 (emphasis in the original). Cf. Truman letter to Compton, in P. M. S. Blackett, *Fear, War, and the Bomb* (New York, 1949), p. 129; and Stimson, "Decision," p. 106.

After the war, when other senior U.S. officials—including Air Force Chief of Staff Henry H. Arnold and General Curtis LeMay of the army air forces, and Admiral William Leahy, military adviser to President Truman, sought to downplay the bomb's impact on Japan, those involved in the weapon's development were quick to question their judgment. In his review of Admiral Leahy's memoirs, for instance, former under secretary of war Robert Patterson restated the case for dropping the bomb: "He could not have studied the messages that passed between the Tokyo Government and the Japanese Ambassador at Moscow for a month prior to Hiroshima. In those messages the idea of surrender was utterly rejected. The time sequence—the bomb on Hiroshima on August 6, the bomb on Nagasaki on August 9, announcement by Japan of willingness to surrender on August 10—should suffice to prove a relationship of cause and effect."[21]

Patterson's account omits an intervening event that could also have accounted for Japan's offer of surrender: Soviet entry into the war on August 8. That event finally prompted Japan to sue for peace, according to Kecskemeti: "The main factor that determined the timing of the surrender note was the Soviet declaration of war. It finally dispelled the illusions the Japanese leaders had entertained up to that time concerning Russian mediation. We may say in this sense that the Soviet declaration of war played a bigger role in triggering Japan's final move to make a direct offer of surrender than did the atomic bombs."[22]

On the basis of its interrogations of Japanese officials shortly after the war, the U.S. Strategic Bombing Survey contested claims that the "shock" of atomic bombings or Soviet entry, or even the threat of an American invasion, had been necessary. Continuation of conventional bombing and blockade would have ended the war without them: "Based on a detailed investigation of all the facts and supported by the testimony of the surviving Japanese leaders involved, it is the Survey's opinion that certainly prior to 31 December 1945, and in all probability prior to 1 November 1945, Japan would have surrendered even if the atomic bombs had not been dropped, even if Russia had not entered the war, and even if no invasion had been planned or contemplated."[23]

If the United States did not need the atomic bombs to compel Japan's surrender and could have postponed their use on cities, then why did it drop the bombs when it did? The so-called revisionists have sought an answer in U.S.-Soviet relations. Picking up where the Strategic Bombing

---

[21]Robert P. Patterson, "Leahy's Inside Story of the Business of Making War," *New York Times Book Review*, March 19, 1950, p. 3.

[22]Kecskemeti, *Strategic Surrender*, pp. 198–99.

[23]U.S. Strategic Bombing Survey (Pacific), *Japan's Struggle to End the War*, Report no. 2 (Washington, D.C., 1946), p. 13.

Survey leaves off, P. M. S. Blackett writes, "Since the next major United States move was not to be until November 1, clearly there was nothing in the Allied plan of campaign to make urgent the dropping of the first bomb on August 6 rather than at any time in the next two months." The atomic bombings, he asserts, were aimed at forcing Japan's surrender before Soviet entry into the war, in order to forestall any efforts by the Soviet Union to take credit for victory or to claim any more spoils of war: "If the bombs had not been dropped, America would have seen the Soviet armies engaging a major part of the Japanese land forces in battle, overrunning Manchuria and taking half a million prisoners. And all this would have occurred while American land forces would have been no nearer Japan than Iwo Jima and Okinawa. One can sympathize with the chagrin with which such an outcome would have been regarded." And even if the United States could not prevent Soviet seizure of part of Manchuria, it could at least avert Soviet participation in the postwar occupation of Japan proper. "The hurried dropping of the bombs on Hiroshima and Nagasaki was a brilliant success," Blackett writes, "in that all the political objectives were fully achieved. American control of Japan is complete, and there is no struggle for authority there with Russia."[24]

Perhaps a better way to secure Japan as a postwar U.S. bastion in the Far East was to have quietly explored a compromise peace, as the United States had attempted in Italy. This strategy would have run less of a risk of permanently alienating Japan. In Kecskemeti's words, "Another form of political action, backstage contacts with the enemy to determine whether there was a mutually acceptable basis for surrender, was never contemplated, since it ran counter to the fundamental American belief that anything smacking of negotiation would fatally detract from the completeness of victory and thereby jeopardize future peace."[25] Although Kecskemeti fails to note the several "backstage contacts" that did take place between the two sides, one question remains: If obtaining Japan's surrender prior to Soviet entry was that important an objective for the postwar Pacific balance of power, then why did the United States fail to pursue these contacts more seriously?

For other revisionists who regard U.S.-Soviet relations as the motive for the atomic bombings, the decision of the United States was too momentous to satisfy an objective as mundane as Blackett's. "It would be wrong to conclude that the atomic bomb was used simply to keep the Red Army out of Manchuria," argues Gar Alperovitz, because "Ameri-

---

[24]Blackett, *Fear, War, and the Bomb*, pp. 130, 135, 137. Cf. Norman Cousins and Thomas K. Finletter, "A Beginning for Sanity," *Saturday Review of Literature*, June 15, 1946, pp. 7–8, an earlier version of this argument, cited by Blackett.

[25]Kecskemeti, *Strategic Surrender*, p. 162.

can interests in Manchuria, although historically important to the State Department, were not of great significance." Nothing less than the global balance of power was up for grabs. In his view the atomic bombs were dropped "to convince the Russians to accept the American plan for a stable peace. And the crucial point of the effort was the need to force agreement on the main question in dispute: the American proposals for Central and Eastern Europe." At the same time, the United States was trying to forestall Soviet entry into the war in the Pacific by shoring up Chinese resistance to Soviet territorial demands in their negotiations. "No longer interested in preserving the possibility of an early declaration of war, Truman and Byrnes now hoped to use the negotiations only as a way to hold off the Red Army attack while the atomic bombs were brought into action," Alperovitz concludes.[26] But if Soviet participation was no longer desired, why were preparations proceeding for the invasion of Kyushu predicated upon timely Soviet attack on Japanese forces in Manchuria to prevent their redeployment home? And if the real target for the atomic bomb was the Soviet Union, why was it necessary to use it against Japanese cities without warning instead of staging a combat demonstration? And why was it necessary to strike a second Japanese city and follow that up with the heaviest conventional bombing raids of the war?

From a quite different political perspective, U.S. diplomacy at the wartime summit meetings also comes into question if Japan was on the verge of surrendering. In a preface to Toshikazu Kase's account of the waning months of the war, David Rowe disputes "the heavy price paid to Stalin at Yalta to bring the USSR into a war which, as this book shows, was already won by us and lost by the Japanese at the time of the Yalta meeting. The movement in Japan towards surrender had begun as early as 1944 when key personnel of the Japanese government concluded that the war was lost."[27] Yet, if "key" Japanese officials had already reached that conclusion by 1944, why did it take them so long to sue for peace?

With this question the review of various accounts of the end of the war in the Pacific comes full circle. Each account leaves important questions unanswered. Other accounts supply the answers, only to raise new questions of their own. Neither the latest wrinkle in historiographic fashion nor the discovery of new documentary evidence has succeeded in reconciling the contradictions within and among the various accounts. To some extent the disputes may just be due to the ultimate ambiguity of

---

[26]Gar Alperovitz, *Atomic Diplomacy: Hiroshima and Potsdam* (New York, 1967), pp. 239–40, 183.

[27]David N. Rowe in his preface to Toshikazu Kase, *Journey to the Missouri*, ed. David N. Rowe (New Haven, 1950), p. vii.

historical evidence, ambiguity that is sufficient to permit a variety of interpretations.

Yet the persistence of lacunae, internal inconsistencies, and mutual contradictions in the accounts of the ending of the war in the Pacific may have a deeper reason. In large part, they may be a logical consequence of the mode of inference that these accounts adopt implicitly, if not explicitly. That mode of inference is one of rational choice. Reasoning back from observable state behavior, these accounts all conclude that whatever a state said or did must have been the most efficient or rational means of achieving its goals, or national interests.

RATIONAL CHOICE AND WAR'S END

In following a rational choice approach to state behavior, accounts of war's end in the Pacific attribute the various statements and acts emanating from the United States and Japan to the national interests—or goals or intentions—that the two sides were pursuing. They differ in the particular interests or goals or intentions that they impute to the two sides, but they all accept the premise that national interests motivate state action.

This theoretical approach underlies not only most historical accounts of the end of World War II, but also most of the literature on war termination in general. It conceives of international relations as the strategic interaction among states, each consciously anticipating the reactions of other states to its own statements and actions and deliberately trying to influence its rivals' behavior by pursuing strategies designed to affect their calculations of the costs and benefits of alternative courses of action. It conceives of individual states as if they were persons, or unified actors, with a small set of more or less consistent goals or interests, calculating the costs and benefits of alternative means of achieving these goals and choosing the most cost-effective means. One major implication of such cost-benefit accounting is that momentous acts must serve commensurately large interests—no less so when the act is magnified through the lens of retrospection.

The validity of these assumptions is not at issue: all theoretical approaches make simplifying assumptions. Indeed, the rational-choice approach is the preferred way of thinking about international politics because of the very simplicity of its assumptions and the resulting parsimony and power of the explanations it generates. The criterion for choosing one approach over another is instead goodness of fit: how well it accounts for significant details of historical events.

Critical anomalies appear in all the rational-choice accounts of the end of the war between the United States and Japan, regardless of the specific interests they attribute to the warring sides. Is it possible to construct any internally consistent rational-choice explanation out of such seemingly inconsistent acts by the United States as omitting any commitment in the Potsdam Declaration to preserving the throne but retaining the emperor once Japan did surrender? Or avoiding any specific mention in that declaration of impending Soviet entry into the war and the existence of the atomic bomb when those threats might have compelled Japan's surrender, only to have both threats carried out within two weeks of its issuance? Or dropping a second atomic bomb on a Japanese city without warning so soon after dropping the first and intensifying the conventional bombing even after Japan sued for peace and then accepted the terms of Potsdam? What more or less constant and consistent set of national interests can be imputed to Japan for its delay in opening talks with the United States while approaching the Soviet Union, or its insistence on preserving the throne only to accept unconditional surrender without any firm guarantee on the emperor's future? While the possibility of deriving a complex preference function to fit all the key pieces of both states' behavior cannot be ruled out in principle, no analyst has succeeded in deriving one in practice.

Rational-choice approaches too have largely guided the study of war termination in general—to the extent that the subject has been studied at all. The voluminous literature in military history, strategic studies, and international relations has much to say about the outbreak of wars, their political, economic, and social causes and consequences, the military and diplomatic efforts to wage and limit them, and the peace settlement that follow. Yet that literature has surprisingly little to say about how wars end.

In place of analysis there is metaphor: wars wind down, war machines grind to a halt, war weariness sets in. The imagery characteristically identifies victory or defeat on the battlefield with war's end. Yet few wars in modern times have ended in outright conquest. And seemingly decisive military advantage or disadvantage has seldom produced a prompt and automatic end to the war, any more than stalemate has. To translate the results on the battlefield into war termination requires political intervention. Armies do not end wars; states do. A distinction must also be made between terminating a war and concluding a treaty of peace. Wars have often ended well in advance of any resolution of the political dispute that led to the war or the signing of any formal peace treaty.

To the extent that studies of war termination do exist, they have tended to adopt the same rational-choice approaches that accounts of the end of the war between the United States and Japan do. These studies see in the behavior of states at war's end evidence of their inten-

[13]

tions or national interests. They differ according to how much they attribute state action to conscious strategic calculation and how much they attribute it to irrationality, miscalculation, "moods," or "shocks."[28] Yet they share the premise that all states behave at war's end as if they were unitary purposive actors in pursuit of their own national interests—as if they were chess players engaged in endgame.

.Over the course of any war, the warring states have three broad policy alternatives, or generic strategies, for terminating it:

To negotiate with the enemy, either face-to-face or through a third party, and to do so overtly or in secret

To modify their war aims—or terms of settlement—unilaterally in order to facilitate accommodation with the other side

To escalate or de-escalate their use of military force by stepping up mobilization at home, deploying new weapons, expanding the war to new theaters, inducing allies to enter the fray, or refraining from taking these steps.

Rational-choice approaches help clarify the trade-offs among these alternatives in terms of a state's goals or national interests. In weighing whether to sue for peace or fight on, a state must estimate the rate at which its capabilities will decrease relative to its enemy's capabilities by comparing rates of attrition, and calculate the likelihood that by continuing the war it can improve the terms of settlement, compared with what it would presently obtain, by more than the additional costs of prolonging the war. And rational calculation sets a normative standard for the point at which wars should end, a point beyond which it is no longer rational or cost-effective for the combatants to continue fighting. This is what economists call the break-even or loss point, where marginal benefits fall below marginal costs with no expectation of improvement. In this sense, choosing when to end a war does not differ from deciding when to shut down a firm or a plant, even though the uncertainties and complexity of the calculation may be greater. Those decisions are supposed to ignore sunk costs and compare prospective costs and benefits of stopping or continuing.

Kecskemeti uses rational calculation to specify choice points and clar-

[28]On these distinctions, see Lewis F. Richardson, "War Moods," *Psychometrica* 13 (September 1948): 147–74, and ibid. (December 1948): 197–232; Anatol Rapoport, *Fights, Games and Debates* (Binghamton, N.Y., 1960), pp. 9–12, 47–59; Berenice A. Carroll, "War Termination and Conflict Theory: Values, Premises, Theories, and Policies," *How Wars End: Annals of the American Academy of Political and Social Science* 392 (November 1970): 18; and Janice G. Stein, "War Termination and Conflict Reduction, or How Wars Should End," *Jerusalem Journal of International Relations* 1 (Fall 1975): 5–14. Game theory picks up where economics leaves off in treating states as if they were individuals engaged in "fights" or "games" and firms calculating costs and benefits.

ify trade-offs among strategic options. He concerns himself with the terminal stage of a war, when the losing side still retains some residual capacity to impose considerable costs on the victor: "The critical point is reached when prolongation of the fighting would inevitably break up the structure of the besieged unit." At that point both sides would be better off with a settlement: "What the loser avoids by offering to surrender is a last chaotic round of fighting that would have the characteristics of a rout. Surrender is then the only rational decision for the loser since it means that the losses that would be involved in the last battle are not incurred. By the same token, *accepting* surrender is a rational decision for the winner: he can obtain his objective without paying the costs of the last battle." Kecskemeti uses the rational-choice approach to derive not only a normative standard for determining when a state should stop fighting, but also an explanation of why states in fact do stop fighting. For Kecskemeti and others, "surrender is a matter of choice; in fact, it is this choice character of surrender that makes this concept an interesting one in the theoretical analysis of warfare."[29]

In practice, however, it is difficult to make the necessary calculations. "Belligerents involved in an attrition situation, of course, will not always act strictly in accordance with military rationality," Kecskemeti acknowledges. "The information available to military leaders in the course of operations is in general too fragmentary to enable them to make optimal decisions." Besides the unknown and unknowable, the incommensurability of costs and benefits confounds calculation: "It is not suggested here that decision-makers, frustrated by the early military outcome, can make a neat comparison between two well-defined quantities: the political stake on the one hand and the additional cost of a possible better outcome on the other. No such comparisons can be made because war costs and political stakes cannot be measured in homogeneous units."[30]

Yet the difficulty with rational choice as an explanation of war termination may go deeper than the possibility of miscalculation or incalculability. War termination in practice raises two critical questions that rational-choice approaches have trouble answering. For one, why are wars so much easier to start than to end? As one student of the subject who departs from the prevailing intellectual tradition has noted, "If the decision to end a war were simply to spring from a rational calculation about gains and losses for the nation as a whole, it should be no harder to get out of a war than to get into one."[31] For another, why do wars

---

[29]Kecskemeti, *Strategic Surrender*, pp. 8–9 (emphasis in the original).
[30]Ibid., pp. 8, 19.
[31]Fred C. Iklé, *Every War Must End* (New York, 1971), p. 16. Cf. Graham T. Allison, "Conceptual Models and the Cuban Missile Crisis," *American Political Science Review* 63 (September 1969): 702–3.

tend to last far beyond their loss point? Allowing for miscalculation, states should be no less likely to terminate a war before the loss point than after it. Yet seldom, if ever, in the wars of the past century have states stopped fighting before marginal cost had far exceeded marginal benefit. They have continued to fight long past the point at which rational choice, in theory, predicts that they should have stopped fighting and long past the point when the states, in practice, recognized that the outcome was clear and irreversible.

One possibility is that one side believes it can still gain marginally better terms of settlement by prolonging the test of wills, and its rival feels compelled to resist. Another is that cognitive or emotional processes under the stress of a test of wills in the terminal stage of a war inhibit leaders from recognizing trade-offs between continued prosecution of the war and acceptance of a settlement, rigidifying the bargaining positions of the contending states. A third is that domestic politics on one side or the other reinforces intransigence. Yet these considerations should not always work to prolong rather than shorten the war. That war termination is a test of wills might suggest why the war tends to last somewhat beyond the loss point, but why should one side or another continue to prolong the war so far beyond that point, and if they did, why would the war ever end? Why would cognitive processes cause only leaders who favor continued prosecution of the war to ignore trade-offs, and not those who favor a settlement? Why would domestic politics not cause a collapse at the front sooner, as it did in Russia in 1917 or possibly in Germany two years later?

In war termination, as under other circumstances, treating states as if they were calculating individuals making rational choices among competing strategies is a preferable way for analysts to approach the subject of international relations, but exclusive reliance on any one approach may obscure as much as it reveals. An example is the literature on the end of the war in the Pacific. A critical reexamination of such studies shows that many of their assertions are simply untenable, while others are subject to alternative interpretations that are more logically consistent, if not always more parsimonious. Such a reexamination may also help to recast thinking about war termination in general with a view toward minimizing the gratuitous loss of life and destruction of property in ending future wars.

Toward a Reconsideration of War Termination: Hawks versus Doves

At war's end, when the goals and strategies that the state should pursue are likely to be at issue, and when the scope and intensity of political conflict within states may be as great as that between states, the assumption that states are unitary actors motivated by relatively consistent objectives may be open to question. To solve the puzzles posed by rational-choice accounts and to explain inconsistencies in the behavior of the warring states, it is useful to proceed from a different premise—that leaders within each state disagree with one another over how best to end the war. Instead of stressing common values and shared perceptions of the world, the starting point is to discover lines of cleavage within the leadership and to disaggregate the state along those lines.

One way to do this is to classify officials as "hawks" or "doves" struggling to influence their state to fight on or to end the war expeditiously. In this approach, war termination comes about when doves in one warring state in effect ally themselves with doves in the enemy camp and get their respective governments to agree to stop fighting, over the opposition of hawks on both sides.

The idea of factional rivalry between hawks and doves enters at least peripherally into some accounts of war termination in the Pacific. For instance, Secretary of War Stimson, in recounting the decision to drop the atomic bomb, mentions that "its use against the enemy might well be expected to produce exactly the kind of shock on the Japanese ruling oligarchy which we desired, strengthening the position of those who wished peace, and weakening that of the military party."[32] Similarly, in *Japan's Decision to Surrender*, the benchmark for many American accounts that followed, Robert Butow writes of a "fateful struggle between the contending groups—typified by the statesman and the soldier."[33] Even Kecskemeti refers occasionally to a "power struggle" in Tokyo "whereby the military leadership was toppled from its dominant position."[34] Based on the findings of the U.S. Strategic Bombing Survey and Butow's detailed study of Japan's struggle to end the war, Kecskemeti contests Stimson's conclusion that the atomic bombing had a decisive impact:

> After the dropping of the bombs the discussions show no manifest change in the attitudes held by either the end-the-war group or the military extremists. The deadlock in the Supreme War Council and the cabinet persisted after Hiroshima and Nagasaki, and even after the Soviet declaration of war. It was not a change in the attitude of the military leaders that enabled the Emperor to offer surrender, but the fact that the Emperor was the strongest factor in the political setup then existing. He was not obliged to defer to the military.[35]

[32]Stimson, "Decision," p. 105.
[33]Robert J. C. Butow, *Japan's Decision to Surrender* (Stanford: Stanford, Calif., 1954), p. 6.
[34]Kecskemeti, *Strategic Surrender*, p. 210.
[35]Ibid., pp. 199–200.

Yet if Emperor Hirohito was so strong that "he was not obliged to defer to the military," why had he waited that long before insisting on surrender?

Perhaps the fullest exposition of the hawk-versus-dove theory is Fred Iklé's *Every War Must End*. Iklé attributes the difficulty of war termination to the gross asymmetry in political power between hawks and doves in wartime. Hawks have a far easier time blocking any settlement through a tacit alliance with enemy hawks than do doves on both sides trying to achieve a settlement. Every time hawks get either side to pass up an opportunity for war termination, they reinforce the insistence of hawks on the other side to continue prosecuting the war. By contrast, doves need clear signals of enemy doves' willingness and ability to halt the fighting in order to further their own efforts toward a settlement, but overt manifestation of the doves' readiness to compromise with the enemy leaves them open to charges of appeasement—even treason—and hence to political if not physical evisceration at home. The problem, writes Iklé, is not a dearth of channels of communication between the warring sides. "The difficulty arises when the central leadership is divided, and when the 'doves' (who may be in control of the foreign office or one of the military services) must first establish that the enemy's terms can be lived with and then try to win support for their peacemaking effort. This has to be done unobtrusively, even furtively; and it can easily come close to a conspiracy where the line between treason and patriotism appears blurred." In the case of war termination in the Pacific in 1945, Iklé shows how hawks in Washington, by blocking any change in the formula of unconditional surrender, effectively disarmed doves in Tokyo, "who could not prevail without guarantees that the Emperor would be allowed to remain." Iklé concludes, "The 'hawks' in Washington, unwittingly teaming up with the 'hawks' in Tokyo, almost prevented Japan's surrender."[36]

Whatever the validity of Iklé's approach as a first approximation of how officials behave, to the extent that they conceive of the other side as divided between hawk and dove factions they may be motivated to act in ways consciously designed to appeal to one faction or the other and to strengthen it vis-à-vis its internal rival. Some officials did have such views and acted accordingly, most notably, Secretary of War Stimson, Under Secretary of State Joseph C. Grew, and Foreign Minister Shigenori Tōgō. Yet many more officials recognized divisions in the enemy camp at the start of the war than near its conclusion. The change in perception may simply be due to the disruption of diplomatic inter-

[36]Iklé, *Every War Must End*, pp. 93–94.

course and consequent lack of firsthand political reporting from enemy capitals, but it may also have psychological roots.[37]

Implicit in Iklé's hawk-dove dichotomy are two premises: first, that officials were divided by philosophical differences over the utility of force in achieving a satisfactory settlement or, alternatively, by disparities in the priority they attached to war and peace as values; and second, that adherents of both persuasions held more or less consistent beliefs, whether out of philosophical and moral conviction or psychological need, and acted on those beliefs. Yet few, if any, senior officials in Washington or Tokyo were so motivated. Most showed little consistency in their orientation toward international relations in general or toward war termination in particular. Neither hawks nor doves, they behaved like politicians and bureaucrats.

THE ORGANIZATION AND POLITICS OF WAR TERMINATION

As politicians and bureaucrats, officials who act on behalf of the state at war's end do so out of a mix of motives rooted in domestic and bureaucratic politics. Even in authoritarian political systems such as Japan's in World War II, politicians must mobilize popular support, maintain governing coalitions, anticipate the reactions of domestic groups, and fend off potential rivals at home. Similarly, bureaucrats do not operate in a societal vacuum. They have to muster and maintain political support in publics and parliaments. They have a clientele to serve and a constituency to mobilize.

In this approach the struggle over war termination may be subordinated to differences over internal politics and power. For example, divisions within the political elite and the armed forces led to France's collapse in 1940. Marshal Pétain and various rightist factions preferred collaboration with the German invaders, while army and navy units eventually coalescing under the leadership of Charles de Gaulle chose to continue the war. Later, various resistance groups within France took up arms to contest the settlement with Germany. The struggle for the soul of France thus coincided with a struggle over domestic and bureaucratic power. Similarly, the Allied invasion of Sicily in 1943 intensified internal political dissension in Italy, culminating in a coup d'état on July 25 that overthrew Benito Mussolini and led the king to invite Marshal Pietro Badoglio to form a new government. As the Badoglio government was secretly suing for peace in August, the Germans occupied Italy. A

---

[37]Robert Jervis, *Perception and Misperception* (Princeton, N.J., 1976), pp. 323–29.

surrender of Italian armed forces was eventually arranged on September 3, the day British forces landed on the southern tip of Italy, and announced five days later, just after the main Allied force hit the coast at Salerno. Supported by Italian partisans, the Allies battled their way north. In October the Badoglio government declared war on Germany and was embraced by the Allies as a co-belligerent.

From the perspective of internal politics, officials do not work for the state; they hold particular positions in one of its component organizations. The state has an internal division of labor. It consists of bureaus with their own distinctive tasks, or roles and missions, which they have the authority and responsibility to perform by law and custom. To carry out these responsibilities, to run their own programs effectively, bureaus must acquire their own capabilities, especially money, manpower, and morale. Preserving, sometimes expanding their roles and missions and acquiring the capabilities to perform them without outside help or interference become the goals, or interests, that motivate officials who work in government bureaus. And sometimes they are reluctant to carry out roles and missions that bureau careerists consider nonessential even if that means a smaller budget and fewer personnel. These organizational interests set their stakes and structure their stands in any controversy. Organizational position shapes perspective and shades information for officials, framing the face of the issue they perceive. Position defines responsibility, what officials seek to accomplish. In the words of Rufus Miles, "Where you stand depends on where you sit."[38] No one appreciated the importance of bureaucratic position more keenly than the chief cabinet secretary in Japan's last wartime government, Hisatsune Sakomizu: "A public servant must be a deliberate opportunist. Even if he should seem to have a certain ideology, this must be related, not to his personality, but to his position."[39]

Organizational interests give officials substantial stakes in decisions and actions leading to war termination. Even at such momentous times as war's end, and perhaps especially then, the national interest may not be easy to discern. Its ambiguity permits officials to identify the national interest with the interests of their own organizations.[40]

[38]This is the main proposition of the bureaucratic politics approach elaborated by Richard Neustadt and Morton H. Halperin and in Graham T. Allison, *Essence of Decision* (Boston, 1971), chap. 5.

[39]Quoted in Masao Maruyama, *Thought and Behavior in Modern Japanese Politics*, ed. Ivan Morris (London, 1963), p. 123.

[40]The concept of organizational interest is a simplifying assumption, permitting analysts of state behavior to aggregate large groups of individuals according to underlying commonalities of motive while necessarily understating the variety of idiosyncratic motives they have as individuals. At the same time, organizational interest is a complicating assumption, implying that disaggregating the state into its principal component organizations and imputing interests to them will permit construction of accounts that fit state

Some versions of the bureaucratic-politics approach differ from rational-choice approaches principally in the level of aggregation they consider appropriate. They disaggregate the nation into its component departments or bureaus and speak of organizational interests rather than of national interests, but they retain the key rational-choice assumption that actors can and do reconcile or trade off conflicting values or interests at that level. The version of bureaucratic politics used here starts from a different assumption: neither the states' acts nor the organizational interests that motivated them are the product of conscious calculation, making explicit trade-offs among competing values and reconciling internal inconsistencies. Instead, it postulates that individuals or organizations may ignore trade-offs.

Informed by work on cognitive processing and cybernetics, it assumes that the belief systems of bureaucrats are motivated not by inner needs or desires but by the need to adjust themselves to others in their immediate social environment—those inside their own organization and others within the government. These beliefs systematically bias their perceptions of the world.[41] In short, what they see depends on where they stand and sit. Motivated bias distorts individuals' selection and processing of information. While cognitive processing applies to the thinking of individuals, cybernetics addresses the behavior of organizations. Instead of optimizing, which requires choices among competing values, organizations "satisfice." They assume that the means they choose to attain their paramount value will also satisfy lesser values. When it does not, they pursue values, or organizational interests, sequentially one at a time, rather than trying to choose policies that reconcile an array of competing values or interests all at once.[42]

Government bureaus have organizational interests other than institutional maintenance or expansion, expressed in terms of the size of their budgets or the number of their personnel. Morton Halperin enumerates these interests:

---

behavior better than imputing national interests to the state as a whole. The interests themselves need not be the conclusion of conscious calculation, but may be habits of mind or routines of behavior, accustomed ways of thinking and acting within the organization. As evidence of organizational interests, it is necessary to show that members of the organization acted as if they shared a set of goals and did so with some consistency over time. Any number of interests can be inferred from the acts and statements of officials; what is critical is to infer from their behavior in time t, a small array of specific interests that the analyst then applies to the study of their behavior in time t + 1. This was done in the case that follows, although much of the analysis is omitted for ease of presentation.

[41]This conception of motivated bias is set out in M. Brewster Smith, Jerome S. Bruner, and Robert W. White, *Opinions and Personality* (New York, 1964), pp. 39–46.

[42]The concept of "satisficing" is developed in James G. March and Herbert Simon, *Organizations* (New York: 1968). John Steinbruner further elaborates the cognitive processing and cybernetic paradigms in his *Cybernetic Theory of Decision: New Dimensions of Political Analysis* (Princeton, N.J., 1974), chaps. 3–4.

[21]

Roles and missions—The particular responsibilities that any organization is charged with carrying out under law, custom, or administrative rule. Officials examine policy proposals with a view toward ensuring their organization's effectiveness in carrying out the roles and missions they want most to protect, acquiring those they desire, and ridding themselves of others they do not want to assume.

Organizational essence—The primary roles and missions that the dominant group of career officials in the organization believe it should perform in preference to all others for which it is responsible.

Capabilities—Some organizations have substantial and expensive capabilities that they deem necessary to carry out their roles and missions, especially those they consider part of the organization's essence. They will be concerned with maintaining and acquiring those capabilities.

Budgets—For organizations with expensive capabilities, concern about the absolute size of their budgets is most intense.

Budget shares—For all organizations, whether or not they have costly capabilities, the absolute size of their budgets may matter less than their relative share of the total state budget compared to rival organizations. So, for instance, one branch of the armed services may oppose an increase in the defense budget if it fears that other services may receive a disproportionate share of the increase.

Prestige—The concern about budget shares exemplifies a more general concern with the perceived influence, or prestige, of the organization in the eyes of others. Relative budgetary success is one measure of prestige. An interest in prestige may lead an organization to support proposals that increase the dependence of other organizations on it.

Morale—An organization's budget share is also one indicator of its perceived influence or standing in the eyes of its own members, or its morale, an important capability for all organizations. An organization's effectiveness depends on the motivation of its personnel, on their belief that what they do makes a difference, that others appreciate their efforts, and above all, that they have room for advancement within the organization.

Autonomy—Career members of an organization believe that they know best what capabilities the organization needs and how best to carry out its roles and missions. They seek to minimize interference from the outside, especially exogenous changes in the organization's standard operating procedures.[43]

The particular organizational interests that American and Japanese agencies pursued in 1945 are elaborated in the chapters that follow and are summarized in a chart in the Appendix.

[43]With minor modifications, this array of interests is drawn from Morton H. Halperin, "Why Bureaucrats Play Games," *Foreign Policy* 2 (Spring 1971): 70–90; Morton H. Halperin, *Bureaucratic Politics and Foreign Policy* (Washington, D.C., 1974), chap. 3; and Halperin, "War Termination as a Problem in Civil-Military Relations," *Annals of the American Academy of Political and Social Science* 392 (November 1970): 86–95.

Wars may end, but the work of government bureaus goes on. There are still programs to promote and roles to perform, budgets to parcel out, missions to conserve or expand, careers to advance. And how the war ends may affect the jobs of officials for years to come. Some organizations, some officials, and some programs may become identified with the success or failure of the war effort; others do not. As wars draw to a close, officials do battle on two fronts at once: on one, to bring the enemy state to terms, and on the other, to end the war in a way that best serves their organizational interests. The stands they take on the war abroad depend on the stakes they see in the battle at home.

Out of the welter of competing interests and conflicting stands, how do government decisions and actions emerge? Analysts often conceive of decision-making as a debate in which advocates of various policy options reason together before a prime minister or president, who sits in judgment and renders decisions based on the persuasiveness of the advocacy. The debate analogy is misleading, however. Seldom is every option put forth or every relevant argument voiced with equal cogency. And bureaucratic politics involves much more than persuasion—argumentation on the intellectual merits of alternative courses of action. It involves bargaining—threats and promises, deals and logrolling, tactics and maneuvers—to influence results. In this bargaining, what participants say pro or con may matter less than who favors which option and how hard they are prepared to fight for their preferences. In short, power may count more than persuasiveness. Organizations charged with implementing decisions thereby have influence far beyond the validity of their arguments. So do participants who can appeal to supporters outside the bureaucracy in parliament and publics. Organizational procedures sort out who must participate and who may, amplifying some voices and muting others.

Implementation does not follow automatically from decision. Decisions may only set off a new round of bargaining over the details of implementation. And action need not presuppose decision. Government agencies often act on their own in the absence of, even in defiance of, authoritative decisions to do otherwise. Some acts that foreigners may take as the deliberate decisions of the state, calculated to affect them, may just be maneuvers designed to influence decisions at home or the autonomous activity of one of the state's component organizations.

The mode of inference in the internal politics approach is that if a state did something that act was the result of a compromise decision among participants with conflicting interests and policy preferences, or a maneuver to influence a decision, or the autonomous behavior of one organization or faction in the state. The approach interprets the contents of

[23]

official statements, not as evidence of the state's intentions or even of their drafters' personal beliefs, but as arguments used tactically to advance their policy preferences. Because officials' arguments for a particular course of action are not necessarily identical to their reasons for taking the stands they did, and because their post hoc recollections of events may not correspond to either, it is essential not to uproot these arguments, reasons, and recollections from their political context in order to interpret them properly. Even though an observer can never know the motives of participants with any certainty, he can still impute interests to them and their organizations based on regularities in their past behavior and then construct accounts of the state's behavior as if officials acted in behalf of their organizations.

Still other acts of the state may simply be the manifestation of organizational routine, of bureaus doing today more or less what they did yesterday, again without much conscious deliberation or formal decisions at the top of the government. To coordinate the activity of large numbers of bureaucrats, organizations develop routines—standard operating procedures and programs—for taking action. They do things "by the book."

Organizational process as well as internal politics affects war termination. Much of the machinery of the warring states is geared to prosecuting the war, not to ending it. And states react to war as they might to an earthquake: autonomous organizations, each with its own responsibilities and programs for carrying them out, independently follow their own routines in dealing with the various effects of the war without necessarily getting at its causes. Wartime interaction takes the form of bullets and bombs, death and destruction, signals and slogans. Each form of interaction impinges on a different organization, which responds according to its own programs—programs not necessarily well adapted to the particular circumstances or coordinated with the programmed responses of other organizations in the government. So, air forces drop bombs while foreign offices exchange notes, each according to its own standard operating procedure. And it is difficult to get them to act in concert and to change what they are doing or stop it altogether.

In this theoretical perspective, the organizational process approach, the mode of inference is that if a state did something that act must have been the output of a preexisting program of one of the state's component organizations, not the purposive behavior of the state as a whole acting according to calculations of relative costs and benefits of alternative courses of action.[44]

Organizational process and internal politics approaches have implications for thinking about war termination that are radically different from

[44]The organizational-process approach, rooted in the work of Herbert Simon and others, is elaborated in Allison, *Essence of Decision*, chap. 3.

those of rational-choice approaches. First, states are not unitary actors, but congeries of separate organizations with different routines, or shifting coalitions of participants with conflicting interests. Inconsistency is the rule, not the exception, in state action. Second, the interaction among enemy states does not take the form of action-reaction. At a minimum, organizational routine and internal politics intervene. But more fundamental, to bureaucrats working at their desks in the nation's capital, even to military officers at field headquarters, the enemy state is far removed from their daily preoccupations. Few have visited it, and even fewer appreciate how their enemy counterparts behave. What has some concreteness lies closer at hand, in their own offices, in the corridors of power at home. The enemy is an abstraction, only dimly apprehended, onto which officials often project their own mundane concerns. Happenings in the enemy camp may pass unnoticed unless they impinge directly on organizational interests, stakes, and stands or evoke organizational routines. "Politics stops at the water's edge" may be an apt epigram, not at all in the intended sense that foreign policy is and should be "above politics," but in quite another sense: that the politics that matters is bureaucratic and domestic politics, not international politics. Third, even at such historic moments as the end of World War II, officials continue to transact business as usual, following time-worn routines, pursuing long-standing interests, seemingly oblivious of the extraordinary events outside their offices. Great events need not have great causes.

It is the central contention of this book that the approaches of internal politics and organizational process help clear up many of the anomalies in rational-choice accounts of the end of the war between the United States and Japan. These approaches may also prove to be of heuristic value in thinking about war termination in general and limited nuclear war in particular.

[2]

Talks without End:
Japan's Approach to Moscow

I came not to send peace, but a sword.
—Matthew 10:34

Of the three generic strategies for war termination—negotiation, unilateral modification of war aims, and escalation and deescalation of military force—only negotiation requires at least some conscious interaction among enemy states. Enemies cannot conduct negotiations with the same degree of self-absorption that they wage war. Each side must, to some extent, take its foe into account.

This unavoidable reciprocity, articulating verbal formulas that in turn elicit symbolically appropriate if not always acceptable responses from the enemy, has at once both advantages and disadvantages for war termination. Negotiating commits some officials within warring governments to participating in a shared process. It may also give participants a common stake in its successful conclusion. Within each government, moreover, the need to formulate a negotiating position generates action channels that engage these officials and force them to make decisions under pressure of deadlines—deadlines that are at times more compelling than the press of other business. As an action-forcing process, negotiating may make the difference between war termination and continued warfare. Sometimes too this process may lead officials to reconcile diplomatic moves with military ones, breaking down the compartmentation ordinarily imposed by wartime secrecy and bureaucratic specialization.

The need for reciprocity also has disadvantages, however. Officials who commit their states to take the diplomatic initiative may be at political risk at home if the enemy fails to respond or if talks break down once under way. The more visible the initiative at home and abroad, the greater the risk. For this reason, opening negotiations may not be the most politic way to begin terminating a war, even though most wars eventually end through negotiations.

Although it is commonly assumed that states at war have difficulty

[26]

finding a way to talk to each other because of the disruption of diplomatic discourse, inadequate channels of communication seldom pose an insurmountable barrier to talks in practice. Some channels are always available for exchanging messages with relatively high fidelity. Indeed, as a war nears its end, the proliferation of channels may become more of a problem than their unavailability, as self-styled intermediaries yearning to play a role in peacemaking interfere with the transmission of clear signals between governments. "The world was filled with candidates for the Nobel Peace Prize," Secretary of State Dean Rusk once lamented during the Vietnam War. "All sorts of people talked with North Vietnam in all parts of the world. They would come back seven months pregnant: peace was about to be delivered."[1] What makes the choice of diplomatic channels difficult is the need to avoid premature exposure to the domestic political risk of seizing the diplomatic initiative.

Whether to approach the enemy directly or to seek mediation, whether to use formal, official channels with the political commitment that they entail or to employ an extragovernmental emissary who can be disowned more readily, and how to arrange the approach can be important choices in any negotiating strategy. Yet a preoccupation with modalities can sometimes deflect attention from the primacy of substance. Governments often belabor the choice of channel as if to postpone struggling over what is to be negotiated.

Each side is also aware that negotiating can serve purposes other than war termination. Negotiations can be used to prolong the fighting by providing military assistance or denying it to the enemy, forging an alliance or forestalling one, and arranging a theater settlement or separate peace that permits forces to be redeployed. Even direct communication with the other side can afford states an opportunity to glean strategic intelligence, especially about political divisions within the enemy camp, and to wage psychological warfare aimed at exacerbating internal divisions and disrupting enemy alliances.

At best, diplomacy can complement military strategy; it can seldom substitute for it. Some generals and admirals in Japan hoped that diplomacy might succeed where strategy had failed: to strengthen Japan in preparation for a decisive battle against enemy invaders. Failing that, they still advocated waging that battle in anticipation that the threat to do so would strengthen Japan's bargaining position in negotiations to terminate the war. Japanese diplomats had grave doubts about this course of action. They intended to use negotiations for an altogether different purpose. Under cover of arranging for an accretion of military

---

[1] *San Francisco Chronicle*, July 4, 1971, p. A-1.

strength, they wanted to arrange for mediation and a negotiated settlement of the war. But even the diplomats were not prepared to accept the Allies' terms—unconditional surrender. When a state tries to open negotiations without first having resolved internal differences over the substance of those negotiations, it may obscure the purpose of its approach. This need not confuse the other side, which may simply assume the worst about its enemy's intentions.

PRIVATE HOPES FOR PEACE

States seldom start a war with precise plans for restoring peace other than through military victory. Japan was no exception. While great care went into planning the initial military operations of the war, Japan's leaders gave scant attention to how the war might end. This omission was perhaps all the more extraordinary under the circumstances because few of those involved in Japan's decision to fire the first shot against the United States had much confidence in their nation's chances of victory, especially in a prolonged war of attrition.

In November and December 1941 the United States was building up its already sizable fleet and air forces at Pearl Harbor in Hawaii and Clark Field in the Philippines and imposing an oil embargo on Japan. Although U.S. officials believed that they were deterring war by doing so, the American buildup and oil embargo only reinforced the conviction among Japanese leaders that war with the United States was inevitable and spurred them to war sooner rather than later, when they believed they would be relatively worse off militarily. Deterrence of premeditated war thus helped provoke preventive war. Japan's leaders took a leap of faith or, more precisely, of despair. Their fatalistic acceptance of war's inevitability, while amenable to psychological explanation, was not especially conducive to rational calculations about war termination. Insofar as any Japanese made such calculations, they rested on the hope that the war in Europe would so preoccupy the United States and so exhaust its resources that it would eventually accept a modus vivendi in the Far East, allowing Japan to retain some if not all of the territory it had seized and at least retain a foothold in China.[2]

---

[2]Army Chief of Staff Gen Sugiyama was a notable exception. He ventured the guess that the war would be over in three months, a claim that prompted skeptical questions from the emperor himself. More typical military assessments, such as the one included in reference materials for the imperial conference of September 6, 1941 were much more pessimistic. The Japanese navy went along with the decision for war at the critical Liaison Conferences with the army and the government even though it did not assess the military balance at the

Hopes of military victory thus dominated the thoughts of peace that Japanese officials did commit to paper at the start of the war. Yet with little prospect of winning such plans for peace turned into dreams, and dreams evanesced in the winds of war. A "Draft Proposal for Hastening the End of the War," adopted at the Liaison Conference of November 15, 1941, envisioned either a short war in which the navy somehow succeeded in luring the American fleet into Japanese-controlled waters and sinking it, convincing the United States to sue for peace; or else a longer war in which Japan along with Germany and Italy managed to defeat Great Britain and thereby undermine America's will to fight. Japan intended to do its "utmost to prevent the outbreak of war with the Soviet Union" by confining its expansionary thrust to the southwestern Pacific. The plan held out the possibility of "arranging a peace between Germany and the Soviet Union" and "bringing the Soviet Union into the Axis camp."[3]

Within two years, the tide of battle had made these prewar plans obsolete. But as the war dragged on, terminating it received little attention in Tokyo. Most Japanese officials were too busy planning how to prosecute the war to consider how to stop it. Others whose duties did include the conduct of diplomacy were reluctant to think about war termination lest they appear to undercut the war effort and leave themselves open to accusations of treason by those whose only conception of war's end was victory. The mere mention of peace in any official forum was risky, so Japanese officials who considered terminating the war had to scheme in private. Few did. The lack of official give-and-take contributed to the unreality of plans that were drawn up. It also ensured that nothing became of them.

Typical of the private hopes for peace was a scheme that Kōichi Kido, Lord Keeper of the Privy Seal, confided to his chief secretary on January 6, 1944. As intermediary between the emperor and the cabinet, the Lord Keeper of the Privy Seal was responsible for providing political advice to the throne.[4] His position necessarily involved him in gathering domes-

---

time as particularly favorable to Japan, only as less unfavorable than it would be later. War thus "made sense" only on the assumption, widely shared among the leaders, that it was inevitable. Nobutake Ike, ed., *Japan's Decision for War* (Stanford, Calif., 1967), pp. 130–31, 152, 236–38, 282–83; U.S. Strategic Bombing Survey (Pacific), Naval Analysis Division, *Interrogations of Japanese Officials*, Report No. 72 (hereafter, USSBS, *Interrogations*) (Washington, D.C., 1946), II: 324, 331; and the testimony of Lieutenant General Teiichi Suzuki before the International Military Tribunal for the Far East (IMTFE), in IMTFE, *Record of Proceedings*, 1946–1948 (Washington, D.C., Library of Congress, 1974, microfilm), p. 35206, contain evidence of the differing army and navy assessments of the military balance in late 1941. Hereafter the IMTFE *Record of Proceedings* will be referred to as *IMTFE*.

[3]Ike, *Japan's Decision for War*, pp. 248–49.

[4]Deposition of Count Nobuaki Makino, Kido's predecessor as Privy Seal, in *IMTFE*, Miscellaneous Documents, Defense Doc. No. 2247 (Tokyo, 1946–48), p. 3.

tic political intelligence and in bargaining with those in the cabinet who wanted to catch the emperor's ear. Kido's plan sought to take advantage of his pivotal position in political maneuvering during a change in government. The emperor's role on such occasions was analogous to that of a British monarch at the time: after taking informal soundings among political notables, he invited someone to form a new government. Precisely how consultation proceeded was one of the "mysteries of state," shrouded in court secrecy as if to establish the appropriateness and legitimacy of the emperor's choice by denying that any choice had been made, as well as to preserve the emperor's transcendence by denying his involvement in politics. Those consulted were the senior statesmen, or *jushin*, a group consisting of the Privy Council president and all former prime ministers who were no longer holding cabinet portfolios. Anticipating the fall of the Tōjō government, Kido envisioned having the senior statesmen venture beyond merely recommending a successor to outline "the diplomatic course" that the new cabinet should follow.

Kido foresaw the need for Japan to make "very considerable concessions" in order to obtain a settlement, though he was not yet prepared to concede what he defined as Japan's minimum objective in the war, breaking out of "encirclement by the ABCD" powers—the Americans, British, Chinese, and Dutch. The "concessions" he had in mind provided some measure of victory for Japan: neutralization of the areas it had occupied with the exception of Manchuria, and the administration of smaller territories by an international commission composed of Japan as well as the Soviet Union, China, Great Britain, and the United States.

Only when Kido discussed the timing of his initiative did he reveal much awareness of Japan's predicament. It "should not coincide with the collapse of Germany," but should occur "prior to the time that the United States, Great Britain, and the USSR unite in their hostility against Japan." He was particularly anxious to avoid a repetition of what had occurred a few months ago in Italy. After knocking Germany out of the war, he feared, the Allies would "intensify their political offensives," making it essential for the government "to devise counter-policies lest traitors like Badoglio make their appearance in large numbers" in Japan. Once the Soviet Union agreed to enter the war against Japan, it would no longer serve as a go-between, which Kido felt it might otherwise agree to do.[5]

Kido plotted an approach to Moscow through Berlin, a route to be followed by every other Japanese official who wanted to open negotia-

---

[5]Kido diary, January 6, 1944, quoted in *IMTFE*, Miscellaneous Documents, Doc. No. 1632W (105), pp. 1–2. Kase, *Journey to the Missouri*, pp. 130–31, quotes the same passage, omitting the reference to the Soviet Union.

tions with the Russians. Bureaucratic politics had much to do with the circuitousness of that route. Until the war in Europe was over, the Japanese army blocked all direct approaches to the enemy of Japan's ally. The army insisted upon living up to Japan's treaty obligations with Germany, which forbade either party from seeking a separate peace. That all but precluded peace talks. The army was willing to go along with several attempts at promoting a modus vivendi between the Germans and the Russians in hopes that Japan could then conclude an alliance with the Soviet Union and fight on. Germany's imminent surrender not only would leave Japan to take on the ABCD powers alone, but might also tempt the Russians to side with them against Japan in the expectation that victory in the Far East would yield rewards commensurate with those from victory in Europe. One Japanese army staff paper drafted in the spring of 1944 even went so far as to suggest that Germany's surrender would be an appropriate occasion to sue for peace.[6] Yet most army officers continued to hold out hope that Soviet entry into the war on the ABCD side could be forestalled. That left the way open for a diplomatic approach to Moscow, though not a suit for peace, if the Japanese army had anything to say about it.

General Hideki Tōjō's resignation in July 1944 after 33 months in power gave the senior statesmen the opportunity to follow the course that Kido had laid out, but they did not. Although some postwar accounts assert that, during the interregnum, court bureaucrats and politicians intervened behind the scenes to install a government that "could pave the way for ending the war," the burden of participants' testimony and official records does not support this interpretation.[7] Indeed, it lends weight to the inference that the senior statesmen tried to form a government that could wage the war more effectively and put Japan in a better position to negotiate a favorable settlement.

At the instigation of Prince Fumimaro Konoye, four of the seven senior statesmen had begun meeting intermittently in 1943 to assess Japan's war prospects and canvass alternatives for the future. After an abortive attempt to insert one of their number, Admiral Mitsumasa Yonai, into Tōjō's cabinet, some senior statesmen began lobbying for a change of gov-

[6]"Measures for the Termination of the Greater East Asia War" (prepared by the Twentieth Group under the chairmanship of Colonel Sei Matsutani, cited by Colonel Sako Tanemura, a member of the Group and later secretary to the army chief of staff), in U.S. Army, Far East Command, Military History Section, "Statements of Japanese Officials on World War II" (typescript) (hereafter "Statements"), IV, no. 61977, p. 211. Cf. Butow, *Japan's Decision to Surrender*, pp. 26–27; and Lieutenant General Masao Yoshizumi, (Chief of the Military Affairs Bureau, War Ministry), in "Statements," IV, no. 54484, p. 608.

[7]Kase, *Journey to the Missouri*, p. 86. Strategic Bombing Survey (Pacific), *Japan's Struggle to End the War*, p. 2, and Butow, *Japan's Decision to Surrender*, pp. 15–19, 23–29, also offer this interpretation.

[31]

ernment. Their campaign culminated one week after the fall of Saipan with adoption of a resolution calling for Tōjō's resignation on grounds of ineffective prosecution of the war: "New life must be injected into the minds and hearts of the people if the nation is to surmount the difficulties besetting it."[8] On July 18 Privy Seal Kido informed the emperor of the senior statesmen's resolution. Later that morning Tōjō resigned.

In response to an imperial summons, the senior statesmen convened that afternoon to recommend a successor to Tōjō. The discussion, as recorded by Kido, is rather elliptical, perhaps an indication that preliminary soundings had already been taken in private, or perhaps a reflection of the customary indirection of Japanese political culture, or just an instance of the propensity of politicians everywhere, accentuated by the political climate of wartime, to be circumspect about revealing their preferences at large meetings. If Kido's account is accurate, any discussion of war policy was ancillary to the main question on the agenda—who should become prime minister. Those present who were closely identified throughout their careers with a particular organization in the Japanese government—Admirals Yonai and Okada of the navy, General Abe of the army, and Privy Seal Kido of the court—each resisted efforts to name a career member of his organization to the premiership. After nearly five hours of discussion Abe relented, and the senior statesmen, running down the list of available army officers, submitted three names to the emperor. Heeding army objections to transferring a general from the fighting front, Hirohito nominated General Kuniaki Koiso, who was then serving as governor-general of Korea. The senior statesmen had given some thought to designating as many as five men to serve jointly in the cabinet, and Konoye, taking advantage of the delay to await General Koiso's return to Tokyo, made the rounds of his fellow senior statesmen with a proposal to name Admiral Yonai head of government along with Koiso.[9] The choice of Yonai was not without significance: he had the political stature to express the navy's qualms about continuing the war.

Koiso and Yonai were granted a joint audience with the Emperor, but they received little guidance on the future conduct of the war. Of those present, Koiso, for one, did not take the emperor's vague intimations as a mandate to seek a settlement. He recalls that Hirohito encouraged them to "put forth efforts to attain the objective of the Great East Asia War" and cautioned them "not to irritate the Soviet Union."[10] Soviet goodwill would be needed, whether Japan sought Soviet mediation or

[8]Butow, *Japan's Decision to Surrender*, p. 28.
[9]Kido diary, in *IMTFE* testimony, pp. 31084–103.
[10]Koiso, in "Statements," II, no, 55906, p. 267.

intervention against the Allies. The time for the palace to "pave the way for ending the war" was yet to come.

AN ELUSIVE QUEST FOR PEACE THROUGH MILITARY VICTORY

The Koiso government's attempts to open negotiations with China and, through Germany, with the Soviet Union must be understood in the light of Japan's military strategy. That strategy, determined largely by the Japanese army against the express wishes of the navy and the government, limited the menu of available diplomatic options. The government could take no initiative on talks unless the army approved or at least refrained from open opposition.

The loss of Saipan in July 1944 convinced Prime Minister Koiso, along with a number of high-ranking officers, especially in the navy, that Japan was losing the war and that the outcome was irreversible, but this did not prompt the government to sue for peace. Recalling the riots that followed the settlement of the Russo-Japanese War in 1905, Koiso explains: "If the government, being aware of the fact that we were fighting a losing war, had immediately ventured to sue for peace, it would have been compelled to surrender under merciless terms, and [that] would have given rise to internal disorder, because the people, who had been led only to believe that the war was being won, would probably have become indignant over such [a] surrender."[11] Irreconcilables in the army would have been quick to spearhead disorder.

Instead of immediately opening negotiations, Koiso first tried to change military strategy. Evoking memories of Tennozan, a decisive battle fought in 1582 that led to the unification of most of feudal Japan under the rule of Hideyoshi, Koiso called for throwing Japan's dwindling military resources into one all-out effort to win a battle before seeking an end to the war. "Let's make a peace overture only after such a victory," he reasoned, because the terms of settlement would certainly be somewhat less onerous "if we ride on the wave of victory" when suing for peace. If Japan were to lose that decisive battle and all but exhaust itself in the effort, it would have to sue for peace. Either way, Koiso's Tennozan strategy would end the war.

While defeat in a decisive battle prior to the invasion of Japan proper might have appealed to some Japanese leaders, it was not a gamble the army intended to take. A Tennozan strategy, though not known by that name, was the preferred strategy of many in the upper ranks of the

---

[11]Ibid., p. 272. For typical navy assessments, see Fleet Admiral Osami Nagano and Admiral Kichisaburo Nomura, in USSBS, *Interrogations*, II: 356, 393.

army general staff. An alternative strategy—fighting to the last man in order to demonstrate the moral, if not the material superiority of the Imperial Way—claimed some adherents among the more zealous of the junior officers, but it never became the strategic concept of the army. Unlike Koiso, however, army planners concluded that the best site for a decisive battle was Japan itself, where short lines of supply and communication, knowledge of the terrain, and full mobilization of the civilian population would give the army a comparative advantage it would not enjoy on either Leyte or Luzon.

The idea of a decisive battle was motivated by the army's interest in its morale. Those in the officer corps who were schooled in *bushidō* or otherwise imbued with a faith in the superiority of the spiritual over the material had always regarded morale as an important service interest. The impending end of the war under less than ideal conditions gave it even greater priority. Prospective defeat is more than the continuation of war by other means: it draws attention to organizational maintenance after the war. For some of the junior officers, the interest in morale dictated a fight to the finish; for most of their superiors, it required peace with honor.

For Japan, the minimum condition for peace with honor was preservation of the national polity (*kokutai*). To many in army ranks this was synonymous not only with preserving the throne and the person of the emperor, but also with maintaining "the right of supreme command," the constitutional prerogative of the armed services to enjoy direct access to the throne for ratification of their decisions on military strategy. That prerogative effectively gave the services autonomy from the cabinet and the service ministries in taking military action. Service morale and the right of supreme command were intimately related in the minds of army men. According to Masao Maruyama, "The sense of superiority that the military felt toward the 'provincials,' as they so pointedly described civilians, was unmistakably based on the concept of being an *Imperial* force."[12] To the army, unconditional surrender was the ultimate indignity. Preservation of the national polity, as the army interpreted it, was an essential condition for settling the war. And fighting and winning a final battle before negotiating a settlement might leave a lasting impression of having won peace with honor rather than having lost the war. Beyond that, the army had not considered what terms it was willing to accept, but it was reluctant to contemplate giving up the territory

[12]Maruyama, *Thought and Behavior in Modern Japanese Politics*, p. 14 (emphasis in the original).

so hard won during the war. That meant at the very least retaining a foothold in China, Manchuria, Formosa, and Korea.

Navy leaders saw things differently. A decisive battle for the homeland, win or lose, would leave the navy with only a minor role to play. Leyte and Luzon were more suitable sites for the fleet to demonstrate its usefulness. Even if the army refused to go all out for a victory there, the navy had little choice: American air superiority would render the fleet useless for homeland defense once islands within range of Japan fell into enemy hands. One senior army planner attributes the navy's stand in interservice struggles over strategy in 1944 to its interests in capabilities and in roles and missions: "Even if [navy] combat strength were held in reserve," the chief of the army's Operations Bureau told interrogators after the war, "it would have been wasted prior to the decisive battle for the homeland, and the possibility of annihilation would be great."[13] Once it had committed whatever remained of its fleet against the United States in Leyte Gulf and the loss of the Philippines had reduced its flow of oil to a trickle, the navy would retain little means of—or interest in— fighting a decisive battle for the homeland. Worse yet, what little it had left was likely to be used to support the army, leaving the navy with little capability and even less autonomy. That was a particular concern of naval aviators, an increasingly powerful subgroup within the service, once all their aircraft carriers were destroyed or demobilized and their planes were consigned to homeland defense.

For Yonai the war's turning point had come much earlier, at Midway, "because of the heavy fleet losses suffered there."[14] Yonai's private conviction had received institutional confirmation in a report prepared by a naval general staff officer on detail from the Navy Ministry. Commissioned to study the war's "lessons" as of September 1943, Rear Admiral Sōkichi Takagi concluded—based on projections of fleet, aviation, and merchant marine losses, shortages of wartime materials, and restiveness among the intelligentsia—that Japan was losing the war. His findings were very closely held, but he did present them orally to Yonai in March 1944, a year before the admiral was to join the Koiso government as navy minister. Ranging far beyond an assessment of naval capability, Takagi openly proposed negotiating a settlement of the war. Although approaching the Soviet Union was risky, he noted, a direct feeler to the United States or Great Britain would arouse intense opposition among junior officers, perhaps leading to internal unrest. For terms of settlement, Takagi hoped that Japanese withdrawal from China, Man-

---

[13]Lieutenant General Shuichi Miyazaki, in "Statements," II, no. 50574, p. 506.
[14]Yonai, in USSBS, *Interrogations*, II: 331.

churia, and northern Sakhalin would satisfy the Allies, but he cautioned that they might insist on concessions in Formosa, Korea, and the Kuriles, as well.[15] Both sets of territories had been included as part of the terms set forth in the Cairo Declaration the preceding December. China and Manchuria were the responsibility of the Japanese army, but loss of Formosa, Korea, and the Kuriles might be more difficult for Takagi's fellow officers to accept because it would jeopardize the defense of Japan's sea-lanes, a navy mission.

From the very outset the Japanese navy had been a reluctant combatant. Unlike their army compatriots, many naval officers had visited the United States and Great Britain before the war, or trained there, personally acquainting themselves with their American and British rivals and acquiring firsthand an appreciation of enemy strength. Their experiences instilled realism in their estimates of relative capabilities. As Admiral Isoroku Yamamoto, who planned the attack on Pearl Harbor, put it before the war, "Anyone who has seen the auto factories in Detroit and the oil fields in Texas knows that Japan lacks the national power for a naval race with America."[16] If war with the United States was inevitable, the only hope in the navy's view lay in striking first, then taking advantage of the war in Europe to arrange a quick settlement in the Pacific. Failing that, Japan was doomed to defeat. But once the war broke out the navy was reluctant to challenge the army over strategy. This was partly due to the relative weakness of its domestic political base: on the home front the navy was no match for the army with its network of backstop associations organized throughout Japan down to the prefectural level.[17] And it was due partly to the divisions in its own ranks: a faction of the naval general staff, some of them German-trained, had always sided with the army on questions of strategy, from the wisdom of concluding the Axis Pact and mobilizing for war to the conduct of the war once it began.[18] Yet the dominant view in the Japanese navy was that if Japan were to fight a decisive battle as a precursor to suing for peace, the sooner it did so, the better.

With tacit navy support, Koiso sought institutional rearrangements

[15]Butow, *Japan's Decision to Surrender*, pp. 20–22. Takagi was no ordinary navy officer. He had headed the Navy Ministry's Research Section before the war, which had functioned as a "brain trust" and political operating arm of the navy, and Takagi himself had developed personal ties to Kido and Konoye. See Asado Sadao, "The Japanese Navy and the United States," in Dorothy Borg and Shumpei Okamoto, eds., *Pearl Harbor as History* (New York, 1973), p. 232.

[16]Sadao, "The Japanese Navy and the United States," p. 237.

[17]Admiral Kishisaburo Nomura, in USSBS, *Interrogations*, II: 386.

[18]Sadao, "The Japanese Navy and the United States," pp. 228–29. For the views of a navy hawk, see Rear Admiral Gumpei Sekine, "America's Strategy against Japan," trans. A. J. Grajdanzev, *Pacific Affairs* 14 (1941): 215–21.

that would put him in a better position to impose his strategic preferences on the army. First, he moved to assume the War Ministry portfolio. Tōjō had concurrently held the posts of prime minister, war minister, and chief of staff from February to July 1944, but when Koiso tried to capitalize on the precedent the army balked. Then Koiso tried resurrecting the prewar Liaison Conference under a new name—the Supreme Council for the Direction of the War (SCDW)—as a forum for reconciling and coordinating diplomatic and military strategy with domestic policy. This time he succeeded. Included in the SCDW's membership were the prime minister, the ministers of war, navy, foreign affairs, finance, and home affairs, the director of the Cabinet Planning Board, and the chiefs of staff and vice-chiefs of staff of the army and the navy. Each principal could bring staff members to its meetings; armed service representatives did so regularly.[19] So large a gathering biased the results: word of any compromise would inevitably leak, and anticipation of that eventuality hardened the stands of the servicemen present while tempering the views of the others. It also allowed the services to exercise considerable control over the agenda through their representatives in the SCDW's secretariat.

Notwithstanding these impediments, on August 19 the SCDW approved Koiso's Tennozan strategy. Yet implementation did not flow from decision. In late October, at the time of the American landing on Leyte, Koiso sought and received assurances that the Japanese army would take the offensive and that the navy would allocate more ships to the island's defense. On the basis of these assurances, he referred to the battle for Leyte as a "Tennozan" in a radio broadcast to the nation. Much to his chagrin, he belatedly learned on December 20 that the army high command had "abandoned plans for a decisive battle on Leyte in favor of a decisive battle at Luzon."[20] The army's change of strategy turned a military defeat into a propaganda debacle for the government: withdrawal from Leyte, coming within weeks of Koiso's public pronouncement, gave the Japanese people their first firm basis for doubting the inevitability of victory.

Still, the chimera of peace through military victory drew Koiso on. The army again assured him that its next campaign would be an offensive

[19]For details of the SCDW's establishment and functioning, see Yale C. Maxon, *Control of Japanese Foreign Policy* (Berkeley, Calif., 1957), p. 192; Koiso, in "Statements," II, no. 55906, pp. 263–64; Shigenori Tōgō, *Cause of Japan* (New York, 1956), p. 108; Takeo Tanaka (chief cabinet secretary under Koiso), in *IMTFE* testimony, p. 32537; Admiral Koshiro Oikawa (chief of the naval general staff), in "Statements," III, no. 61341, p. 107; Yoshimasa Suezawa, in U.S. Army, Far East Command, Military History Section, "Interrogations of Japanese Officials on World War II" (typescript) (hereafter "Interrogations"), II, no. 62051, pp. 278, 280.

[20]Koiso, in "Statements," II, No. 55906, p. 273.

[37]

one. At Luzon, however, the army never did try to seize the initiative against the American invaders. Instead, it redefined its objective there as "a weakening operation" to "draw blood" from the enemy. When Koiso berated Army Chief of Staff Yoshijiro Umezu for the army's failure to launch an offensive and try for a decisive victory, Umezu said he could do "nothing" because the campaign was "in the hands of the operational command at the front." When Koiso proposed that he seek a command from the emperor to start an offensive, Umezu refused to override his commander in the field.[21]

Ultimately, if the army was to fight a Tennozan anywhere, it would be to repel an American invasion of Japan's home islands. On February 26, 1945, senior officers in the army general staff and the War Ministry convened and reached agreement on a strategy of decisive battle to repel the expected invasion of Japan.[22]

The devastating defeat suffered by the Japanese fleet at Leyte Gulf left the navy with few strategic options of its own. By the end of 1944 it had lost 7 of 12 battleships, 19 of 25 aircraft carriers, 103 of 160 submarines, 31 of 47 cruisers, and 118 of 158 destroyers and had begun decommissioning what remained of the fleet, reassigning the crews to aviation. It was reduced to conducting "bleeding" operations against the American fleet.[23] By spring only the "special attack," or kamikaze, forces of crash boats, midget submarines, human mines and torpedoes, and aircraft under the command of Admiral Takajirō Ōnishi had a role to play in the war—hardly an inspiring one to navy traditionalists. Once the war reached the home islands, the navy would have few battles left to fight and not much of a fleet left to fight them. Worse yet, with only a supporting role to play in a decisive battle for the homeland and with dwindling capabilities to carry out even that role, the navy anticipated coming under increased army pressure to unify the armed services. That would have put naval aviators under army command, which was not a promising precedent for peacetime. As the chief of the naval general staff, Admiral Soemu Toyoda, saw it near war's end, unification would mean partitioning the single service department into two sections, one for the army and one for the navy, and "with an Army man as minister, it would have been inevitable that the navy section would have become a relatively weak service."[24] Even a unified command for defense of the

[21]Ibid., p. 275.
[22]Tanemura, in "Statements," IV, no. 61977, p. 213.
[23]Masanori Ito, *The End of the Imperial Japanese Navy*, trans. Andrew Y. Kuroda and Roger Pineau (New York, 1956), appendix 2; Vice-Admiral Paul H. Weneker (German naval attaché in Tokyo) and Toyoda (chief of the naval general staff), in USSBS, *Interrogations*, I: 285, 298, 315.
[24]Toyoda, in USSBS, *Interrogations*, II: 321. Cf. Saburo Hayashi with Alvin D. Coox, *Kōgun: The Japanese Army in the Pacific War* (Quantico, Va., 1959), pp. 152–53.

homeland, an arrangement that both services had successfully resisted in the past, was unpalatable to the navy under the circumstances. Navy interests stood to gain little from a prolongation of the war.

As the fleet struck bottom, the Japanese navy moved openly to oppose the army strategy of holding forces in reserve in order to wage a decisive battle for the homeland. The navy, says Admiral Kishisaburo Nomura, "thought the war would be almost hopelessly gone if a landing were made, but the Army people always thought we should fight even after the landing."[25] The navy urged, instead, defense of the islands on the approach to Japan proper, a strategy that at least gave it significant roles and missions to perform, even in defeat.

HOPES OF A SEPARATE PEACE

Essential to the Japanese army's strategy of decisive battle was the continued neutrality, if not the active support, of the Soviet Union. At the least, even a token Soviet withdrawal from Manchuria might free some Japanese forces there for redeployment home.[26] At most, Soviet intervention on Japan's side might reverse the course of the war, allowing Japan to obtain a more favorable settlement. But the army's insistence that Japan live up to the Axis Pact, precluding any separate suit for peace, required that any approach to Moscow pass through Berlin. That left open one possible diplomatic initiative: brokering a peace settlement between Germany and the Soviet Union. A separate peace on the eastern front would facilitate a German redeployment westward to counter an Allied breakout from their beachhead in Normandy, which in turn might compel the United States to redeploy troops from the Pacific theater, relieving pressure on Japan's beleaguered forces. However farfetched a German-Soviet rapprochement may have been, it provided the only pretext for a diplomatic approach to Moscow that the Japanese army could not resist. But any attempt to exploit this approach to end the war would face strong opposition if army diehards were to learn of it.

The Foreign Ministry was in a poor political position to brook that opposition. Called the Kasumigaseki, or "Misty Barrier," for its location in Tokyo, the ministry was dominated by an elite corps of career diplo-

---

25Nomura, in USSBS, *Interrogations*, II: 392.

26See Vice-Admiral Weneker, in MAGIC Diplomatic Summary No. 1072, March 2, 1945, National Security Agency (NSA) Records, Box 13, SRS 1593–1607, Record Group (RG) 457, National Archives, pp. 6–7, and USSBS, *Interrogations*, I: 286; and Yoshizumi, in "Statements," IV, no. 54484, p. 608.

mats who dominated key ambassadorial postings. The foreign minister too was almost always chosen from its ranks. The most sensitive of Japan's relations abroad had been those with Moscow, Washington, and London, and diplomats in the European-American Bureau who had served in those capitals constituted an elite within an elite. Yet a corollary of foreign service elitism was aloofness from domestic politics. In the words of one Foreign Ministry careerist, "Owing to their preoccupation with external affairs and their extended absence from home, our diplomats were generally quite ignorant of the situation in Japan and often assumed an attitude of such indifference to the political and economic questions at home that they lost what little influence they once possessed." Gradually, it seemed to him, a "misty barrier" had developed between the Foreign Ministry and the public.[27] Aloofness took its toll in public support, leaving the ministry politically weak and its careerists hesitant to take on sensitive wartime negotiating missions that might end in failure even when they enjoyed army support.

Foreign Minister Mamoru Shigemitsu, a former ambassador to the Soviet Union, had tried an approach to Moscow during the Tōjō government. In the fall of 1943 he proposed dispatching a special envoy there, a move the Russians interpreted as an attempt to bring about a separate peace between Germany and the Soviet Union. The Russians rejected the approach.[28] General Hiroshi Ōshima, Japan's ambassador to Berlin, sounded out Chancellor Adolf Hitler and Foreign Minister Joachim von Ribbentrop on several occasions in 1943 and 1944 about seeking a settlement with Moscow. Neither thought much of the idea. While von Ribbentrop's response was diplomatic in tone, Hitler's was characteristically forceful: the only way to end the war on the Eastern Front, he insisted, was "to paralyze Russia by force of arms."[29] Failing to arrange a German-Soviet rapprochement, Shigemitsu turned his attention to improving Russo-Japanese relations. Urging "strenuous efforts" to that end, "taking maximum care, of course, that we do not give the impression that we are weak," he instructed Japan's ambassador to Moscow, Naotake Satō, to inquire in particular about "private arrangements" to extend the Neutrality Pact between the two states and about the possibility of reaching an understanding between the two over China.[30] Satō made little headway in Moscow.

[27]Kase, *Journey to the Missouri*, pp. 16–17. The U.S. State Department had not yet moved to Foggy Bottom.

[28]MAGIC Diplomatic Summary No. 756, April 20, 1944, NSA Records, Box 13, SRS 1271–85, RG 457, National Archives, p. 5.

[29]MAGIC Diplomatic Summary No. 675, January 30, 1944, NSA Records, Box 13, SRS 1191–1220, RG 457, National Archives, p. 4.

[30]MAGIC Diplomatic Summary No. 756, April 20, 1944, NSA Records, Box 13, SRS 1271–85, RG 457, National Archives, p. 5.

Undaunted, Shigemitsu renewed his overtures to Moscow when he retained the foreign affairs portfolio in the Koiso government. At the repeated urging of the prime minister, Shigemitsu authorized Foreign Ministry planning for another try. On September 12, 1944, the ministry completed a draft working paper for the approach. It listed three aims: "(1) maintenance of neutrality and improvement of diplomatic relations between Japan and the Soviet Union; (2) realization, as far as possible, of peace between Germany and the Soviet Union; and (3) improvement of Japan's situation through the assistance of the Soviet Union, in case Germany should fall out of the present war."[31] The working paper also raised the possibility of Soviet mediation of the war in China. German consent was a precondition to all the diplomatic options except one— Soviet mediation between Japan and the Allies—but that option was to be pursued only in the event of Germany's defeat. So long as the army had its way, Japan might determine the direction of its diplomatic demarches, but Germany would set the pace, either by its consent or by its capitulation.

Shigemitsu cabled instructions to Satō on November 24. Anticipating an eventual falling out among the Allies, he told Satō to foster Soviet "reconsideration" of its ties and to probe for any possibility of a Soviet settlement with Germany.[32] The ambassador broached the subject of extending the Neutrality Pact with Soviet Foreign Minister Molotov on February 22, but Molotov put him off.[33]

Instead of continuing to direct its attention to the Soviet Union, the Koiso Government then moved in another direction altogether, trying for a separate peace in China. But a theater settlement, while limiting the geographic scope of the war, could hardly be construed as unambiguous evidence of Japan's desire for peace: although a cease-fire on the mainland would have removed one major impediment to eventual accommodation with the United States, it also would have permitted the army to redeploy troops home to meet the expected American invasion. It was this very ambiguity that made a separate peace with China acceptable to some Japanese army officers, if appropriate terms could be arranged.[34]

[31]*IMTFE* testimony, Exhibit 3557, pp. 34552–53. The third objective was inserted at his own insistence, according to Shigemitsu, in "Statements," IV, unnumbered, September 9, 1949, p. 286. Cf. Mamoru Shigemitsu, *Japan and Her Destiny*, ed. F. S. G. Piggott (New York, 1958), p. 326; and Tanemura, in "Statements," IV, no. 61977, p. 210.

[32]Pacific Strategic Intelligence Section, "Japan as Mediator in the Russian-German Conflict," December 29, 1944, NSA Records, Box 4, SRH 067, RG 457, National Archives, p. 17.

[33]Pacific Strategic Intelligence Section, "Abrogation of the Soviet-Japanese Neutrality Pact," April 23, 1945, NSA Records, Box 4, SRH 071, RG 457, National Archives, p. 8.

[34]Hayashi, *Kōgun*, pp. 176–77; Tōgō, *The Cause of Japan*, p. 303; Lieutenant General Torashiro Kawabe (deputy chief of the army general staff), in "Statements," II, no. 52608, p. 93.

Having taken part in an attempt by the Tōjō government to arrange a cease-fire in China while serving as ambassador there, Foreign Minister Shigemitsu was content this time to let the army take the lead, but he stipulated that any approach to the Nationalist government in Chungking have the prior consent of Japan's puppet government in Nanking, lest it undermine that regime. With Koiso's active support, the effort at negotiating a theater settlement in China won the approval of the SCDW and the emperor. A vice-minister of war was dispatched to China to open talks.[35]

The Japanese army had maintained secret channels to Chungking and Yenan even after Japan granted formal recognition to the Nanking government. The army's Chinese contacts generally fell into one of two categories: those seeking special dispensation for themselves from China's occupiers, or Shanghai businessmen anxious to spare their city from becoming a battleground. As a professional diplomat, Shigemitsu was privately contemptuous of these self-styled and self-serving "peace brokers." Nevertheless, the army continued to make use of them, albeit more as intelligence sources than as diplomatic intermediaries.

Groping for a way out of China and not content to let the army try its hand, Koiso decided on his own to use one such peace broker, Miao Pin. Expelled from the Nationalist party as a collaborationist for his promotion of cultural and political reconciliation with Japan, Miao became vice-president of the Legislative Council in Nanking while maintaining contact with the chief of staff of the Nationalist army. Only the intercession of Japan's occupation forces, whom he provided with intelligence, had prevented the Nanking government from executing him for his contact with Chungking.[36] Somehow, despite his checkered past, Miao managed to attract Koiso's attention. With a favorable report from a longtime personal friend whom he had asked to investigate Miao in late fall, Koiso sought approval of his senior cabinet colleagues to invite Miao for exploratory talks in Tokyo. Japan's ambassador to Nanking, learning of the move, warned Shigemitsu against peace brokers who demand demonstrations of Japan's good faith—whether they take the form of "a unilateral withdrawal of Japanese troops, the dissolution of the Nanking Government, or the cessation of Japanese Army attacks on Chungking"—without giving any "guarantee about the results" that would follow

---

[35]Shigemitsu, *Japan and Her Destiny*, p. 326, and in "Statements," III, unnumbered, January 13, 1950, p. 292.

[36]Ibid., , p. 331; Wesley R. Fishel, "A Japanese Peace Maneuver in 1944," *Far Eastern Quarterly* 8 (August 1949): 390n; Koiso, in "Statements," II, no. 55906, p. 278; and Akira Iriye, *Power and Culture: The Japanese-American War, 1941–1945* (Cambridge, Eng., 1981), pp. 8–9. On this occasion Miao seems to have been acting as an agent of the Nationalist secret police.

from these acts. He was particularly chary of Miao Pin: "The government authorities must be very careful about his reception; otherwise we shall merely expose our weakness for nothing, without getting any intelligence about the other party."[37] Shigemitsu agreed, but in the end he and Yonai deferred to War Minister Gen Sugiyama and Koiso, who insisted on proceeding.

Upon his arrival, Miao tried to circumvent the cabinet and deal directly with the palace: on March 17 he met with Prince Higashikuni, who had played an active role in past negotiations with China, to request an audience with the emperor.[38] Four days later Koiso convened the SCDW to discuss his plans for Miao's mission. The stiff terms Miao was proposing for a China settlement aroused intense opposition. Miao demanded that Japan withdraw all its forces from China, that it "detain" the leaders of the Nanking government and install the Chungking government in its place, and that it "make peace with the United States and Great Britain."[39] The last condition, ostensibly requiring prior settlement with the Allies, would have reversed what Koiso says he had in mind in opening negotiations with the Chinese. "The immediate question," he told interrogators after the war, "was peace between Japan and China, but since the United States and Britain were backing China, we did anticipate that China might not be able to conclude a peace without the consent of the United States and Britain. That would have paved the way for peace between Japan and the United States and Britain."[40] It also would have permitted reinforcement of Japan proper, and that is why the Japanese army supported a separate peace in China.

Even without the last condition, Miao's terms were unacceptable in Tokyo. Shigemitsu was vehement in his disapproval, calling the proposed deal "a flagrant violation of the decision already taken" to avoid "intrigue behind the back of the Nanking Government." Sugiyama and Umezu both opposed opening talks; Umezu even hinted at a coup by army subordinates if the government went ahead.[41] On March 27 Koiso reported to the throne on his China scheme. While he seemed intent on pressing forward with it in the face of opposition, the emperor, already apprised of the mission by Prince Higashikuni, questioned the advisability of using Miao. He then held separate audiences with the foreign, war, and navy ministers, all of whom voiced opposition to the idea. Hirohito then summoned Koiso and, noting the absence of a consensus,

---

[37]MAGIC Diplomatic Summary No. 1093, March 23, 1945, NSA Records, Box 13, SRS 1608–22, RG 457, National Archives, pp. 2–4.
[38]Koiso, in "Statements," II, no. 55906, p. 279; Butow, *Japan's Decision to Surrender*, p. 53.
[39]Koiso, in *IMTFE* testimony, p. 32259.
[40]Koiso, in "Statements," II, no. 55906, p. 279.
[41]Shigemitsu, *Japan and Her Destiny*, p. 332.

suggested he drop efforts to achieve a separate peace with China. The Nationalist Chinese subsequently hanged Miao for treason.[42]

The emperor's expressed displeasure at the way Koiso had proceeded was tantamount to a vote of no confidence. As if the collapse of Koiso's China initiative were not trouble enough, American troops began landing on Okinawa on April 1, shortly after the Japanese army had withdrawn one division from the island, once again in defiance of Koiso's Tennozan strategy.[43] The Koiso government's other diplomatic initiative also came to naught. A renewed attempt by Ambassador Ōshima to arrange a political settlement between Germany and the Soviet Union, this time at the instigation of German Foreign Minister von Ribbentrop, was blocked by Hitler in late March.[44] Then on April 5 the Soviet Union gave Japan formal notification of its intention not to extend the Russo-Japanese Neutrality Pact beyond its April 25, 1946, expiration date.[45] The Koiso government had been unable to heed the emperor's injunction not to alienate the Soviet Union.

Within a week Koiso's diplomatic and military strategy had collapsed, and with it his government. He had failed to open talks with either the Soviet Union or China. The army had again refused to commit itself to executing his Tennozan strategy. Its withdrawal from a decisive battle for Okinawa gave Koiso a pretext for resigning. On April 3 Sugiyama notified Koiso of his intention to leave the government and to recommend General Korechika Anami as his successor. Koiso resolved to assume the War Ministry portfolio himself "in order to establish direct contact and a harmonious working relationship" with the armed services.[46] He threatened to resign if the army refused his request. As he well might have expected, it did, precipitating his resignation. On April 4 he informed Privy Seal Kido of his intention, laying the blame at his continued inability to resolve differences among the army, navy, and government over politico-military strategy. The following day the gov-

---

[42]Ibid., pp. 332–33, and in "Statements," III, unnumbered, September 9, 1949, p. 292; Koiso, in *IMTFE* testimony, pp. 32260–61, and in "Statements," II, no. 55906, p. 284.

[43]Koiso, in "Statements," II, no. 55906, p. 282.

[44]Ōshima's March 31 Report to Foreign Minister Shigemitsu on Recent Conversations with von Ribbentrop, MAGIC Diplomatic Summary No. 1104, Messages on Ōshima–von Ribbentrop Meetings, April 3, 1945, NSA Records, Box 13, SRS 1624–37, RG 457, National Archives, pp. A1–12.

[45]This came as no surprise to Shigemitsu, who was alerted to the possibility the previous November when Stalin in a speech marking the anniversary of the Russian Revolution had denounced Japan as an aggressor nation. See Shigemitsu, *Japan and Her Destiny*, pp. 337–38; Tōgō, *Cause of Japan*, p. 267; and Kase, *Journey to the Missouri*, p. 96. Kase (p. 154) incorrectly characterizes the Soviet action as "a bolt from the blue." To the contrary, in March Shigemitsu had predicted a Soviet attack on Japanese forces in Manchuria.

[46]Koiso, in "Statements," II, no. 55906, p. 282. Cf. Yoshizumi, in "Statements," IV, no. 54484, p. 600; Kido diary, April 4, 1945, in *IMTFE*, Miscellaneous Documents, No. 1632W (117); Shigemitsu, in "Statements," III, unnumbered, September 9, 1949, p. 291.

ernment formally resigned. In a brief statement the Board of Information announced Koiso's fall, explaining that it would permit "formation of a more powerful cabinet in view of the gravity of the situation."[47]

THE SUZUKI GOVERNMENT: A NAVY-PALACE ENTENTE

The senior statesmen convened on April 5 to recommend a successor to Koiso. It was another opportunity for Kido to put his peace plan into effect, committing the new government to negotiate an immediate end to the war. But contrary to some postwar claims, he did not seize the opportunity. The presence of General Tōjō, attending his first senior statesmen's conference as a former premier, may have suppressed frank talk about suing for peace, though Kido was the only person present who even hinted at the problems with all-out prosecution of the war.

Now that the war was about to be brought home to Japan, Kido noted, a number of conditions on the home front were becoming matters of "grave concern." One was popular morale: "The public does not always cooperate earnestly with the measures taken by the government. A large number tend to be indifferent." Coping with food shortages, boosting industrial productivity, and preserving domestic tranquillity required a government that inspired public confidence. Another condition that warranted "careful attention" in Kido's view was "antimilitarism," now "substantially" in evidence.[48] Statistics compiled by the Police Bureau of the Home Ministry showed that public unrest was on the rise—to 607 incidents during the year ending March 1945, up from 406 the previous year and 308 the year before that; antiwar and antimilitary acts shot up to 224 incidents, from 56 and 51 in the two preceding years. The military police (*Kempetei*) recorded comparable increases in antimilitary rumors.[49] Of particular concern to military professionals were the increasing reports of "disorderliness on the part of officers and men swarming in towns and villages." In the words of Colonel Saburo Hayashi, secretary to the war minister, "These actions, which incurred severe antipathy throughout the nation, were ascribable to the decline in the quality of personnel as a result of the great increase in forces mobilized." They were a source of consternation to generals preparing to defend Japan against invasion: "They felt that the solidarity of soldiers, officials, and citizens was absolutely necessary for the crucial campaign in the homeland."

[47]Yukichi Kuroki, "From War to Peace Cabinets," *Contemporary Japan* 14 (April–December, 1945): 183.

[48]Kido diary, in *IMTFE* testimony, p. 31132.

[49]Thomas R. H. Havens, *Valley of Darkness: The Japanese People and World War Two* (New York, 1978), p. 70.

[45]

Army leaders "seized every opportunity" to impress upon the troops the need for "self-discipline."[50] Still, to Kido, these conditions did not call for terminating the war, only for reorganizing the government so that "the people will follow us."

Kido also alluded to the problems of civil-military coordination raised in Koiso's letter of resignation. That prompted the senior statesmen to consider whether the new prime minister should be drawn from active service ranks in order to be eligible to attend meetings of the Supreme Command, where the army and the navy thrashed out issues of military strategy. Most conferees agreed that an army or navy man was still the best choice, though not necessarily someone still on active duty. Kido had been lobbying behind the scenes for Kantarō Suzuki, a retired admiral and Privy Council president. When his name first came up, Suzuki demurred. He proposed instead that the job go to Prince Fumimaro Konoye, who had headed three governments in the 1930s. He reasoned that Konoye was younger and therefore more able to "stand the strain," but Konoye, who had earlier argued that the nominee should be someone free from past involvement in cabinet politics, now successfully disqualified himself on those grounds. Admiral Okada remained noncommittal, but Kido and Privy Councillor Hiranuma warmly endorsed Suzuki.[51] Just as Suzuki seemed on the verge of nomination over his own strong protestations, General Tōjō began an impassioned appeal in favor of General Shunroku Hata. An army officer on the active list had to fill the post, he insisted, because repelling the invasion was the army's job. Then Tōjō issued a blunt warning: if an army officer were not named, the army might stand "aloof," refusing to supply a minister of war and thereby preventing formation of a new government. The veiled threat drew a rebuke from Okada.[52] After adjourning for dinner, Kido drew Suzuki aside and implored him to accept the imperial mandate to form a new government if it were offered. Later that evening Suzuki had an audience with the emperor, and after trying to beg off because of age, deafness, and political inexperience, he finally relented and began canvassing some of the senior statesmen for a list of possible cabinet appointees.

Suzuki was not just being unduly modest about his political acuity. As premier-designate, he initially asked Okada to become his navy minister without even bothering to clear the choice with the navy. Okada had

[50]Hayashi, *Kōgun*, p. 151.

[51]Kido diary, in *IMTFE* testimony, pp. 31134–38. Reijiro Wakatsuki was the first to propose Suzuki, "a certain person" who had been nominated but "not selected" on a "previous occasion," when the senior statesmen had recommended a successor to Tōjō. Kido mentions his prior consultations in "Statements," II, no. 62131, p. 182.

[52]Kido diary, in *IMTFE* testimony, pp. 31140–41; cf. p. 31121.

been retired from active duty for seven years. Worse yet, while serving as prime minister in 1936 he had barely escaped assassination at the hands of army extremists during the February 26 incident, which nearly claimed Suzuki's life as well. Okada himself was appalled at Suzuki's naiveté. He turned down the appointment to the cabinet, thinking it would only inflame the diehards. When he went to Suzuki's home to confer, he found the elderly man surrounded by people "who were not even accustomed to making phone calls." Okada immediately recommended the appointment of his son-in-law, Hisatsune Sakomizu, as Suzuki's chief cabinet secretary. Having served as private secretary to Okada during his premiership, Sakomizu had some experience in cabinet politics.[53]

Some accounts of Japan's decision to surrender have hailed the formation of the Suzuki government as a move toward peace privately arranged by the palace. They have depicted the elderly admiral as a dedicated dove who calculated that prolonging the war would not pay. They blame his slowness in moving toward a settlement with the Allies on the threat of a coup or assassination by the diehards, and they dismiss the absence of recorded expressions of Suzuki's intention to seek a prompt end to the war as evidence of *haragei*, the Japanese practice of communicating almost wordlessly by inference and indirection and getting a "sense of the meeting" by gut intuition and tacit understanding. This art, not foreign to backroom politics elsewhere, is considered a sign of astuteness rather than deviousness in Japanese political culture. Yet testimony from Sakomizu that Suzuki did not have any end clearly in mind casts doubt on this interpretation. "Admiral Suzuki grasps things synthetically and judges things intuitively," says Sakomizu. "I think, therefore, he would not judge [the] war situation in an analytical way, that such and such a fact would bring such and such a result."[54] Prime Minister Suzuki manifested less of a commitment to peace and consummate political skill in pursuing it than ambivalence about how best to negotiate the shoals of war termination and unsureness in his tacking, once he did set his course.[55] He was no dove, but a consensus politician, a navy/palace careerist who had risen to the rank of chief of staff in one service and grand chamberlain in the other. His government was no "peace cabinet," but an unstable coalition of bureaucratic functionaries

---

[53]Lester Brooks, *Behind Japan's Surrender* (New York, 1968), pp. 26–27.

[54]Sakomizu, in "Interrogations," II, no. 62004, p. 144.

[55]For the first view of Suzuki, see Strategic Bombing Survey (Pacific), *Japan's Struggle to End the War*, p. 6; Sakomizu, in "Interrogations," II, no. 62004, p. 142; John Toland, *The Rising Sun* (New York, 1970), p. 787; Brooks, *Behind Japan's Surrender*, p. 30; and Suzuki, in "Interrogations," II, no. 531, p. 306. For the second view, see Butow, *Japan's Decision to Surrender*, pp. 67–72, and Shigemitsu, *Japan and Her Destiny*, p. 353.

that shifted the political balance slightly away from the army, putting the navy and the palace into at least formal ascendancy for the first time since 1941.

The cross-pressures on Suzuki and the ways he responded to them in composing his cabinet exemplified his noncommittal stand on the war. Sounding like a hawk among hawks and a doves among doves, he managed to draw irreconcilable factions into his cabinet while straddling the issues that divided them. For the foreign affairs portfolio, Suzuki consulted senior statesman Kōki Hirota, who recommended Shigenori Tōgō. Tōgō, who was foreign minister at the time of Pearl Harbor, had never had much enthusiasm for the war, but perhaps more important to Hirota and Suzuki, he had served as ambassador to Moscow before the war and, while there, had arranged an amicable settlement of the Man-chukuo–Outer Mongolia border dispute. Tōgō was reluctant to enter the cabinet. He conferred with Suzuki on April 8 to ascertain whether the prime minister and he shared "not only the desire for prompt peace but also the estimate of the war situation." Suzuki's estimate that Japan had the capacity to fight two or three years longer if necessary only confirmed Tōgō's initial doubts: "Having heard him state his estimate of the war situation, which differed from mine, although I found him sincere and earnest for prompt peace, I felt that I could hardly accept the responsibility of directing diplomacy unless we had identical opinions on the prospect [for] the war, and left, telling him so."[56] Tōgō soon found himself overwhelmed by entreaties to reconsider. He agreed to meet with Suzuki once more, and this time won the premier's assent to have the SCDW conduct an assessment of Japan's capabilities and to draw up plans for ending the war if that assessment showed the nation less able to continue the struggle than Suzuki had contended. Based on this understanding, Tōgō agreed to serve as foreign minister.[57]

While continuing to coax Tōgō into the cabinet, Suzuki also had to propitiate the armed services. The navy posed no problem; Admiral Yonai agreed to stay on as navy minister. But the army could block Suzuki's efforts by "standing aloof" and refusing to nominate a war minister. Some senior officers in the Military Affairs Bureau viewed Suzuki's accession with equanimity: his brother, Takao Suzuki, had been a well-regarded general and the Admiral himself was not thought to harbor any desire for an immediate end to the war. Yet rumors quickly began circulating that Suzuki was "a Badoglio" ready to accept unconditional surrender. And Suzuki's naval background kindled resentment after

[56]Tōgō, in *IMTFE* testimony, p. 35779.

[57]See Tōgō, in "Statements," IV, no. 50304, pp. 245, 256; Tōgō, *Cause of Japan*, pp. 269–71; affidavit of Yasumasa Matsudaira (Kido's private secretary), in *IMTFE* testimony, p. 35596; and Suzuki, in ibid., p. 35591.

Yonai came out against an army proposal to unify the armed services in preparation for defending the homeland. As soon as Suzuki received the imperial command to form a new government, the outgoing war minister, the vice-minister, and the chiefs of the Military Affairs Bureau and its Military Affairs Section stipulated three conditions for army participation, which they presented to Suzuki in writing: "(1) Prosecution of the war to the bitter end; (2) Proper settlement of the problem of Army-Navy unification; and (3) Every possible effort for complete [mobilization] of the nation for the prosecution of the war."[58] The premier-designate accepted the army's terms "without hesitation," and the army nominated General Korechika Anami to be war minister. Later that day, the commander of the military police denounced the new government as a "Badoglio cabinet" and demanded that the army block its formation, but the outgoing war minister equivocated, leaving the question to his successor.

Like many a political leader at war's end, buffeted by rival bureaucrats pursuing incompatible objectives, Prime Minister Suzuki drifted first in one direction, then in another, desperately trying to keep his government from breaking apart on the shoals of war termination.

TIPTOEING TOWARD MOSCOW

Soviet notification of its intention not to renew the Neutrality Pact, followed a month later by German capitulation, renewed Japanese interest in a diplomatic approach to Moscow. The first event intensified interest in Soviet intentions; the second opened the way to direct talks by removing the army's precondition—prior German consent. If the army no longer posed an impediment to seeking talks, it still held out for an unattainable negotiating objective: to get as much Soviet assistance as possible in preparation for the decisive battle for the homeland.

Plans for the decisive battle were now taking shape. On April 15 the army reached agreement on its plan and shortly thereafter forwarded it to the navy for consideration. According to General Shuichi Miyazaki, chief of the Operations Bureau, which oversaw army planning, the army "hoped to concentrate its strength entirely in the area where American forces would make their first landing, and it hoped to strike a decisive blow, thereby forcing the enemy to abandon [its] intention of attempting a second landing or else seriously delay this move." Then, "taking ad-

---

[58] Yoshizumi, in "Statements," IV, no. 54484, p. 600. Cf. Major General Yatsugi Nagai (chief of the Military Affairs Section), in ibid., II, no. 61885, pp. 613–16; Colonel Masao Inaba (chief of the Budget Branch, Military Affairs Section), in ibid., I, no. 62083, p. 569; and Sakomizu, in "Interrogations," II, no. 62004, p. 143.

vantage of this success," the army "proposed to seize an opportunity for peace negotiations."[59]

Timing was critical to the plan's success. Once the invaders had established a beachhead, Japan would not have the firepower to dislodge them. The "most propitious" moment for the decisive battle would come as the enemy was assaulting the beaches. But that posed a problem for army strategists—where to pre-position enough manpower and firepower to beat back the invaders. There was disagreement at Imperial General Headquarters whether the enemy would strike first at Kanto, Kyushu, or Nagoya, not to mention where the precise landing site would be. Local commanders all resisted efforts by headquarters to deplete the forces at their disposal in order to reinforce another command. One solution was to mobilize civilians to man Japan's ramparts, but civilians were no substitute for the seasoned veterans scattered throughout other theaters of war.

The most obvious places from which to draw down forces were China and Manchuria. Yet the number of divisions that planners could redeploy without leaving the residual forces defenseless was limited, unless some political accommodation could be reached in those theaters. Moscow was the most likely place to try, in view of repeated diplomatic failures in China. Intelligence reports of a Soviet buildup on the Manchurian border lent urgency to the request that Imperial General Headquarters incorporated into its April 15 plan: "The Greater East Asiatic War has now reached such a critical point [that] it was definitely beyond the power of military strategy alone to save the situation. We demanded [that] diplomatic quarters make a determined move toward improving relations with the Soviets."[60]

The vice-chief of the general staff was the first to call on Foreign Minister Tōgō to present the army demand. He was followed in rapid succession by Army Chief of Staff Umezu and by the vice-chief of staff of the navy, which hoped to replenish depleted supplies by swapping some of its cruisers for Soviet oil and aircraft.[61] Tōgō had reservations about the more extravagant of the services' desires. An alliance with the Soviet Union was now out of the question, in his estimation, precluding

[59]Miyazaki, in "Statements," II, no. 54194, p. 530. Cf. Lieutenant General Torashiro Kawabe (Army vice-chief of staff), in ibid., no. 50820, p. 77; Tanemura, in ibid., IV, no. 61977, p. 207; Miyazaki, in ibid., II, 50770, p. 540, and unnumbered, July 1, 1949, p. 533; and Hayashi, *Kōgun*, pp. 158–61.

[60]U.S. Army, Far East Command, Military History Section, Japanese Research Division, *Imperial General Headquarters Army High Command Record*, Japanese Monograph No. 45 (mimeographed), p. 175; cf. p. 235; Tanemura, in "Statements," IV, no. 61977, p. 207; Major General Masakazu Amano (chief of the army's Operations Section, Imperial General Headquarters), in ibid., I, no. 54480, p. 35; and Hayashi, *Kōgun*, p. 170.

[61]Tōgō, *Cause of Japan*, p. 279. Cf. Kase, *Journey to the Missouri*, p. 153.

the admirals' hopes for resupply: "I explained how preposterous their idea was, pointing out that, since it would be a violation of neutrality to accept such commitments, Russia could not supply the materials unless she were prepared to go into the war on our side, which, in view of the existing military situation, could hardly be the case."[62] Continued Soviet neutrality was the most Japan could expect, Tōgō believed. That was a realistic object of negotiations. But Tōgō himself saw in the services' demands "a God-sent opportunity" to seek much more than that: "Now that the future prosecution of the war had become so awkward, the Russian problem had to be attacked from the point of view of ending the war rather than of merely [maintaining] the Soviet status of nonbelligerence. I was intending to move for an early peace, and I determined for that purpose to make use of the desires of the military services."[63] The service chiefs and the foreign minister could each content himself that talks with Moscow would serve his own interests so long as the purposes of those talks remained unspecified. That is the stuff of bureaucratic compromise—and diplomatic disaster.

Germany's capitulation brought little change in Japan's public stance. To buoy sinking morale, Prime Minister Suzuki issued a statement on May 3 reaffirming the government's intention to prosecute the war: "Although the present changing situation in Europe has in no respect been unexpected on our part, I want to take this opportunity to make known once again at home and abroad our faith in certain victory."[64] Behind the scenes, however, Japan's leaders began plotting an approach to Moscow.

The crucial meetings took place on May 11, 12, and 14 with only "the Big Six"—the prime minister, the foreign minister, and the army and navy ministers and chiefs of staff—in attendance. Staffs were barred at the suggestion of Tōgō, who wanted to avoid a repetition of his experiences at prewar Liaison Conferences, where "the secretaries would arrange the agenda" and "monopolize a substantial proportion of the discussion." Worse yet, "since the minor officials learned what went on at the meetings from the secretaries, it was essential for council members to speak firmly if they were not jeopardize their control over their underlings, and, as a result, extremely radical opinions were voiced by known conservatives" and issues "tended to be decided in favor of the strongest group present"—the army.[65] Moreover, once Big Six deliberations got underway, Navy Chief of Staff Koshiro Oikawa proposed that

---

[62]Tōgō, in "Statements," IV, no. 50304, p. 244.
[63]Tōgō, *Cause of Japan*, p. 280. Cf. Tanemura, in "Statements," IV, no. 61977, p. 209.
[64]Quoted in *Contemporary Japan* 14 (April–December 1945): 273–74.
[65]Tōgō, in "Statements," IV, no. 50304, p. 244. Cf. Oikawa, in ibid., III, no. 61341, p. 107; and Tanemura, in ibid., IV, no. 61977, p. 210.

all information about the substance of the discussions be withheld from subordinates, even from vice-chiefs of staff and vice-ministers. The others agreed. In accepting these procedures, Army Chief of Staff Umezu and War Minister Anami gave the first indication that, however opposed they might be to a negotiated settlement of the war, they would eschew obstructionist tactics to advance their aim. Yet the procedural dilemma was ultimately inescapable: even if they were prepared to be less intransigent with their Big Six colleagues in private, implementation of any Big Six decision would require compliance from the very subordinates they were now excluding from involvement in decision-making. Moreover, curiosity throughout the government was so intense that the existence of the sessions, as well as their agenda, soon became common knowledge in the upper reaches of the bureaucracy.[66]

From the start of Big Six meetings, disagreement between the service representatives and the foreign minister over the purpose of the demarche to Moscow became apparent. Umezu gave the army's military assessment: "The Soviet Union has recently been busy moving troops to the Far East. The Army is keeping a vigilant eye on this, but it cannot fully prepare for operations on both the Pacific and Manchurian fronts." He renewed the army's demand for "diplomatic measures to keep the Soviet Union from participating in the war against us." Discussion then turned to the extent to which Japan could expect Soviet help. "I maintained," recounts Tōgō, "that it was useless to expect any military or economic aid whatever."[67] That assertion immediately set off a "rancorous" dispute with Navy Minister Yonai, who insisted that "there was still time" to seek Soviet assistance. Tōgō stood his ground: "Of course, it was desirable that we prevent Russia from attacking us, and I was entirely agreed that we should try to do this." But seeking Soviet military aid would only "waste the precious time left" that could be put to better use trying to assure continued Soviet neutrality, or "at most" Soviet mediation on Japan's behalf to obtain a more favorable settlement of the war.[68] Suzuki, trying to keep the services on board, seconded Yonai: "We would lose nothing by sounding out the USSR casually" about the possibility of military aid. The Big Six then settled on a compromise—to seek negotiations with three objectives, in order of priority: "first, to keep the USSR out of the war, a necessity which was felt strongly by all; second, to induce her to adopt a friendly policy toward Japan; and third, to seek her mediation in the war."[69]

[66]Tōgō, *Cause of Japan*, p. 284; Captain Yoshimasa Suezawa (chief of the Naval Affairs Section and Navy Ministry representative on the SCDW secretariat), in "Interrogations," II, no. 62051, p. 275; Toyoda, in USSBS, *Interrogations*, II: 319; Yoshizumi, in "Statements," IV, no. 61338, p. 608.

[67]Tōgō, in "Statements," IV, no. 61672, p. 281, and no. 50304, p. 246.

[68]Tōgō, *Cause of Japan*, p. 285.

[69]Tōgō, in "Statements," IV, no. 50304, p. 246.

At that point discussion turned to the question of compensating the Soviet Union for satisfying Japan's objectives. Tōgō, noting that the Soviet Union "was bound to feel that more was to be derived from helping the Allies than from throwing in her lot with a nation tottering on the brink of defeat," argued that Japan would have to make substantial concessions in order to achieve any of its aims. The terms he proposed, virtually identical to those set forth in the Foreign Ministry working paper of September 1944, amounted to restoration of the status quo prior to the Russo-Japanese War, with two exceptions: that Korea remain in Japanese hands and that Southern Manchuria be neutralized. The Big Six reached tentative agreement on these terms.[70]

Tōgō then informed his colleagues of his intention to have senior statesman Kōki Hirota hold "unofficial conversations" with the Soviet ambassador in Tokyo, Jacob Malik. Hirota, a former ambassador to Moscow, enjoyed the confidence of Tōgō, whose appointment as foreign minister he had helped engineer. The choice of this informal channel sidestepped potential service objections to using Ambassador Satō in Moscow for the mission.[71] It also insulated the Foreign Ministry somewhat against political backlash at home if word of the approach should leak.

On May 14 the Big Six turned again to the third aim of the demarche— Soviet mediation of an end to the war. Consideration of possible terms of settlement, which necessarily implied a drastic curtailment of Japan's war aims, immediately provoked intense controversy. According to Tōgō, "War Minister Anami pointed out in forceful language that we should remember above all that Japan still retained a large chunk of enemy territory and had not lost the war." Tōgō retorted that "it was the forthcoming developments on the war front that would count, and that it was impossible to visualize peace conditions merely on the basis of captured or lost territory."[72] Chief of Staff Umezu immediately closed ranks behind his army colleague, while Yonai seconded Tōgō. By emphasizing "the forthcoming developments," Tōgō was implicitly questioning the army's ability to score a victory in the decisive battle for the homeland and thereby improve Japan's bargaining position in negotiations to terminate the war. That put Tōgō in the exposed position of directly challenging the army's ranking officers in their area of expertise. "As the atmosphere of the conference became tense," he recalls, Yonai intervened to suggest that they "leave this subject for a while." Suzuki seconded Yonai, point-

---

[70]Ibid., and Tōgō, *Cause of Japan*, p. 287. The terms are enumerated in Brooks, *Behind Japan's Surrender*, pp. 138–39. The gist of the decisions taken in the three meetings was put into writing and signed by all six men. The original was destroyed in a May 25 air raid and Tōgō prepared another from memory, which Brooks excerpts.

[71]Tōgō, *Cause of Japan*, pp. 280, 287.

[72]Tōgō, in "Statements," IV, no. 50304, p. 248.

ing out "that it would still be possible to proceed with exploring the Soviet attitude" without the specific aim of mediation. Sensing their concern that the results of the three meetings not be "nullified" by the controversy, Tōgō "withdrew" his proposal to seek Soviet mediation.[73]

Consequently, the critical issues raised by the third objective of the demarche—Japan's capacity to continue the war and the concessions required for peace—barely joined, were sidestepped because they threatened to disrupt any attempt at reaching consensus. The approach to Moscow remained wholly consistent with the army's strategy of fighting a decisive battle for the homeland.

BLOCKING OTHER CHANNELS

At the same time that the Big Six was deciding to activate diplomatic channels to Moscow, the Foreign Ministry was trying to close down other channels. Intermittently throughout the war, those in Tokyo who were trying to establish contact with the other side had looked to three neutral states besides the Soviet Union as possible channels: Switzerland, Sweden, and the Vatican. No one in authority inside the Japanese government ever gave formal sanction to these approaches. Japan's internal politics had made that too risky a course to try. But now that Japan's leaders had opted to approach Moscow, keeping any other channels open was all the more risky at home: it could alert the diehards and jeopardize Foreign Ministry efforts to get Moscow to mediate on Japan's behalf in order to arrange an acceptable negotiated settlement.

Switzerland had been the earliest target. On June 11, 1942, just days after Japan suffered its critical reverse at Midway, Shigeru Yoshida paid a call on Privy Seal Kido. Yoshida, a former ambassador to England with pronounced—and all too well-known—pro-British and pro-American sympathies, told him of a plan, presumably cleared with others in advance, to send Prince Konoye to Switzerland "without any definite mission." Once there, Konoye could informally sound out representatives of various governments about arranging an end to the war. Kido put Yoshida off, saying he would like to think over the "propriety" of such a move.[74] At the time, of course, Japan was in a good position to insist on favorable terms for a settlement.

Two years later, under far less propitious circumstances, Konoye himself broached the idea of seeking neutral mediation, again through an extra-governmental emissary, the managing director of the newspaper

---

[73]Ibid., no. 61672, p. 283, and Tōgō, *Cause of Japan*, pp. 287–88.
[74]Kido, in *IMTFE* testimony, p. 31065.

Asahi, Bunshiro Suzuki. This time, instead of approaching his own government, Konoye had Bunshiro Suzuki contact Sweden's ambassador to Japan, Widar Bagge. Konoye contemplated ceding not only all the territories seized in World War II but also Manchukuo, concessions far more extensive than any the government was willing to accept then or at any time prior to the final week of the war. Bagge recognized an unauthorized gambit when he saw one: "Mr. Suzuki told me that Prince Konoye and a group of men around him were responsible for this plan, which they wanted me to forward to the Swedish Government with the request that through Swedish channels a feeler should be made in London."[75] The Swede reported the September 1944 meeting both to Stockholm and to Washington. Everyone in the U.S. capital dismissed the contact except a handful of psychological warfare specialists in the Office of Naval Intelligence (ONI) who tried to exploit it to promote a rift between the army and the navy in Japan and thereby hasten the end of the war.[76] Koiso also learned of Konoye's action indirectly and became intrigued with the idea of sending the prince to Switzerland, but nothing ever came of it.[77] Konoye would not be the last Japanese to go into the peace business for himself, but these efforts, lacking any substantial political base or formal sanction at home, got nowhere. At times they may even have undermined bureaucratic support for more authoritative approaches.

The only senior official in Tokyo to initiate an approach to a neutral state other than the Soviet Union was Foreign Minister Shigemitsu. In late March 1945, as Bagge was about to return home after twenty years of service in Tokyo, Shigemitsu arranged to probe the Swede's willingness to use his good offices in Japan's behalf. The Japanese diplomat who made the contact, Tadashi Sakaya, had befriended Bagge while serving as Japan's ambassador to Finland. According to Sakaya, Bagge volunteered his services, suggesting that the Swedish government sound out U.S. intentions and asking whether Shigemitsu would agree to the move. If Bagge was acting on his own authority, he may have been exceeding instructions. A few days later, Shigemitsu called in Bagge for a "very frank" conversation, in which he acknowledged the gravity of Japan's military position and said it was now time "for the Japanese diplomats to try to get the country out of the war."[78] Now it was Shigemitsu's turn to exceed his authority: "I asked him to ascertain what peace terms the United States and Britain had in mind and to inform me through [Sue-

---

[75]Bagge, in ibid., p. 34560.
[76]Ellis M. Zacharias, "The A-Bomb Was Not Needed," *United Nations World* 3 (August 1949): 26–27.
[77]Koiso, in "Statements," II, no. 55906, p. 278.
[78]Bagge affidavit, in *IMTFE* testimony, p. 34561. Cf. Sakaya affidavit, in ibid., p. 35456.

masa] Okamoto, our Minister in Stockholm. I stipulated only that the terms be consonant with the honor of Japan."[79] Sakaya subsequently called on Bagge at Shigemitsu's request in order to emphasize the necessity of acting "as soon as possible."[80] Before Bagge could arrange his departure, however, the Koiso government fell.

On April 11, two days after Tōgō had replaced Shigemitsu as foreign minister, Sakaya briefed him on the contact with Ambassador Bagge. Sakaya, who had not been present at the Bagge-Shigemitsu meeting and learned of the details only afterward in conversations with both participants, left Tōgō with the impression that Shigemitsu had stopped short of a formal request for mediation, asking the Swedish government to sound out U.S. intentions at "its own instance."[81] Tōgō then instructed Sakaya to tell Bagge that "such services by [him] and his Government would be very much appreciated" and to invite the ambassador to meet with him, if possible, before departing.[82]

On April 12 Sakaya relayed Tōgō's message to Bagge, who left Japan the following day without calling on the foreign minister. Traveling by plane to Manchuria and then by train across Siberia, Bagge took about three weeks to arrive home. On May 10 he contacted Ambassador Okamoto, described his conversations in Tokyo, and inquired whether Okamoto "had received any confidential telegrams about efforts to negotiate peace."[83] Okamoto, completely in the dark, cabled home for instructions. By having Bagge assume responsibility for sounding out the United States, Tōgō had modified the mission Shigemitsu entrusted to the Swede. Now Bagge, unwilling to proceed on his own initiative, or perhaps hoping to solicit a formal request for mediation from Tokyo, neglected to mention his last-minute message from Tōgō in asking Okamoto to renew his government's instructions. "The telegram," recalls Tōgō, "stated that Mr. Bagge called on Okamoto and informed him that if formally requested by the Japanese Government, the Swedish Government would be glad to sound out the peace intentions of the American Government."[84]

[79]Shigemitsu, *Japan and Her Destiny*, p. 339.
[80]Bagge affidavit, in *IMTFE* testimony, p. 34562.
[81]Sakaya affidavit, in ibid., p. 35456.
[82]Tōgō, in ibid., p. 35780, and Tōgō, *Cause of Japan*, p. 277.
[83]Bagge affidavit, in *IMTFE* testimony, p. 34563.
[84]Tōgō, in "Statements," IV, no. 61672, p. 284. On this occasion Bagge may have been acting as more than a neutral emissary. Ellis M. Zacharias, deputy director of the ONI, says: "Concealed behind this cover name Dolphin was a top-ranking diplomat of a neutral European country who secretly worked for the Allied cause inside Japan. He was one of the three principal informants of the Allies." Switzerland, Sweden, and the Vatican were the only European neutrals that maintained missions in Tokyo at the time. Zacharias identifies another of the three informants as "a Scandinavian diplomat who enjoyed the confidence of the Dowager Empress, Hirohito's mother" ("The A-Bomb Was Not Needed," p. 27).

Okamoto's cable does not seem to have arrived in Tokyo until after May 14, the day the Big Six took up the question of seeking Soviet mediation. In the course of their discussion, the six considered who else's good offices Japan might use, but rejected the alternatives because of the unwillingness or inability of other states to weigh in on Japan's behalf to get more acceptable peace terms. In Tōgō's words, "The Vatican was the first to be mentioned, but in view of the Pope's negative attitude toward the war, it was deemed virtually impossible to hope for aid from that quarter. Chiang Kai-shek would not have been out of the question except that China had committed herself to Japan's unconditional surrender by the Cairo Proclamation. As for the neutral countries, there was little likelihood that either Switzerland or Sweden would make a serious effort to obtain a conditional peace for Japan."[85] Unconditional surrender was unacceptable in Tokyo. Moreover, Japan's leaders were reluctant to seize the initiative and ask for mediation, preferring instead to have another state take the lead. Their unwillingness either to contemplate unconditional surrender or to seek mediation stemmed from a single overriding consideration, which they seldom stated—fear of opposition at home. Kido put it this way in his diary after a conversation with Shigemitsu about seeking mediation: "Should the secret leak out, it would defeat the purpose. Not only that, the fighting services would stiffen in their attitude," casting the die of final resistance.[86]

Moscow had three potential advantages over other neutral states for Japan's leaders. First, inadvertent leaks were less of a possibility there. Second, as Tōgō had anticipated, he could conceal a request for mediation from army diehards amid other negotiating aims—securing Soviet aid, or at least continued neutrality, in preparation for the decisive battle for the homeland. "The Army's desire for peace," notes Tōgō, "had originated in the idea of acting through the USSR, a fact which would facilitate utilization of it as the intermediary." Third, only active mediation by a power willing to throw its weight behind Japan could possibly obtain the terms the Japanese leaders considered the minimum necessary for a settlement. Anticipating postwar rivalry between the United States and the Soviet Union, some Japanese leaders calculated that Japan's value as an ally in that struggle might induce the Russians to weigh in on its behalf, or at least to refrain from open alliance with the United States against it. The Soviet attitude toward Japan "need not be severe," reasoned War Minister Anami, because "the USSR would find itself in confrontation with the United States after the war and therefore would not desire to see Japan too much weakened."[87]

---

[85]Tōgō, in "Statements," IV, no. 50304, p. 254. For the date, see *IMTFE* testimony, p. 35782.
[86]Kido diary, June 26, 1944, in *IMTFE* testimony, p. 31074.
[87]Tōgō, *Cause of Japan*, pp. 286–87.

In the end the Big Six deferred seeking Soviet mediation, but not until they had ruled out alternative neutral channels. By the time Okamoto's cable had arrived from Stockholm, the question of a formal Japanese request for Swedish mediation was no longer moot.

As if the situation were not already delicate enough, a military attaché in Stockholm, Major-General Makoto Onodera, apparently acting without authorization from Tokyo, met with Prince Carl on May 7 to request that his uncle, King Gustaf, be prepared to mediate a settlement at some future date. The prince passed word to the Swedish Foreign Office. On May 16, noting that the Swedish foreign minister considered the new initiative an "obstacle," Bagge asked Okamoto to put a stop to it. Okamoto cabled Tōgō, who notified General Army Chief of Staff Umezu. Umezu agreed to curb Onodera.[88] To Tōgō the incident revealed "two more obstacles" to using Sweden's good offices. First, a "rumor was spreading in European diplomatic circles" about a Japanese request for Swedish mediation; and second, "full cooperation" between Ambassador Okamoto and his military attaché was "difficult," a diplomatic way of alluding to suspicions that Onodera may have deliberately sabotaged the Bagge mission.[89] Far from opening a way to peace, the Swedish channel was now threatening to interfere with the Soviet one.

Some observers have cited the Bagge contact as evidence that Japan was actively seeking an end to the war, while others have questioned Japan's choice of the Moscow channel over all others. Neither interpretation gives adequate recognition to the domestic political context of choosing a negotiating channel. In the light of Japan's internal politics at the time, it is less difficult than Kecskemeti suggests "to understand the obstinacy with which the Japanese government clung to the mirage of a *rapprochement* with Moscow."[90] Nor does the explanation for this "obstinacy" lie in Tōgō's consistent advocacy of "closer relations with Moscow," his "strong position in Moscow since the time he was Japanese ambassador there," his "personal acquaintanceship with Molotov and other Russian leaders," or any unspecified "habit of mind," as some participants have claimed.[91] The Japanese leadership was far from reaching

---

[88]Okamoto, "in Statements," III, no. 61477, p. 143. The Swedish Foreign Office alerted the American ambassador, who reported the contact to the State Department on May 11, 1945 (*FRUS, 1945,* VI: pp. 479–80). U.S. naval intelligence reported on the Onodera move in CINCUSFLT, Pacific Strategic Intelligence Section, "Russo-Japanese Relations," July 2, 1945, NSA Records, Box 4, SRH 079, RG 457, National Archives, pp. 16–17.

[89]Tōgō, in "Statements," IV, no. 61672, p. 284.

[90]Kecskemeti, *Strategic Surrender,* p. 177.

[91]The first interpretation is Shigemitsu's, in *Japan and Her Destiny,* p. 355; the second is Bagge's, in his affidavit, in *IMTFE* testimony, p. 34563; the third is Masuo Katō's, in *The Lost War: A Japanese Reporter's Inside Story* (New York, 1946), p. 132; and the fourth is Kase's, in *Journey to the Missouri,* p. 166. Tōgō's own summation appears in *Cause of Japan,* p. 278.

consensus on the terms and timing of a suit for peace. Unconditional surrender was out of the question in Tokyo because few were prepared to risk the diehards' wrath in proposing it, and even those who were believed it could well provoke a coup d'état. Only Moscow might have been willing and able to weigh in on Japan's behalf to obtain more acceptable conditions for a settlement. Moreover, the only diplomatic initiative acceptable to the Japanese army was an approach to Moscow, though not with the aim of seeking Soviet mediation to end the war. A request for Swedish mediation only risked premature exposure and turmoil at home without holding out much hope for pressuring the Allies to moderate their demand for unconditional surrender. From mid-May on, it was Moscow or nowhere for Japan's diplomats.

INDIVIDUAL INITIATIVES

Decisions reached at the highest level in Tokyo could not prevent Japanese officials in the field from engaging in diplomatic maneuvers of their own, especially when those decisions were very closely held. The farther these officials were from Tokyo, it seemed, the more they believed they understood Japan's interests, and the longer the war dragged on, the more they felt those interests called for a prompt suit for peace. However well intentioned their initiatives, they were doomed from the outset because the officials undertaking them were in no position to commit the Japanese government and could offer their interlocutors little assurance to the contrary. Far from regarding these maneuvers as opportunities for serious talks, the Allies either dismissed them or exploited them for intelligence or psychological warfare purposes.

Outside of Sweden, Switzerland provided common ground for these unofficial gambits. There, rival intelligence services kept a close watch on one another. Their presence made informal contact easy to arrange. The first such contact occurred at the instigation of Japan's naval attachés in Berlin. Their original plan was to transfer two assistant attachés to neutral capitals, where they could make contact with U.S. representatives in an effort to stimulate direct talks between the two governments. One attaché who was supposed to go to Sweden failed to leave Berlin in time to avoid internment by advancing Allied forces, but the other, Commander Yoshiro Fujimura, did make his way to Berne on March 21. There he got in touch with Dr. Friedrich Hack, one of those figures who emerge briefly from the shadows at war's end to play bit parts and then disappear. Hack, a German native who had hosted the talks that led to the Anti-Comintern Pact in 1936, was later imprisoned for anti-Nazi activity, only to be released to the custody of associates of his in the Japanese navy, who shipped him off to Japan and eventually found refuge for him in Switzerland. Acting as Fujimura's intermediary, or "cut-out," Hack met with three men who had ties to Allen Dulles, the station chief for the Office of Strategic Services (OSS) in Berne. Though initially confusing Allen with his brother, John Foster Dulles, Fujimura was aware that Dulles supervised American covert operations in Europe and was in the process of arranging the surrender of German forces in Italy. The OSS operatives insisted that Hack maintain strict secrecy: the Italian surrender was arousing Soviet suspicions that the United States might try to arrange a last-minute separate peace with Germany as well. On April 26, two days after the initial contact, the OSS requested a draft of Japan's terms of surrender and details on Fujimura's background. The written reply affirmed Fujimura's "desire to obtain the opinion of the United States concerning direct Japanese-American peace negotiations," but Fujimura instructed Hack to express orally his intention "to persuade the Navy Ministry" and "to urge" the Japanese government to accept "an immediate termination of the war."[92]

These arrangements were so tenuous that they gave Dulles every reason not to take the approach as an authoritative one. Circumstantial evidence suggests that he viewed it in an altogether different light. Subsequently questioned by the president's military adviser, Admiral William D. Leahy, about reports that "some of his agents were endeavoring to arrange for conversations with Japanese officials regarding peace terms with Japan," Dulles denied "knowledge of any such activity" and told Leahy he did not "believe" any of "his group" was involved.[93] The OSS did notify the State Department of the contact, but not until June 4. The notification took the form of an intelligence report rather than a request for action: "Fujimura indicated to source [Hack] that the Navy circles who now control the Japanese Government would be willing to surrender but wish, if possible, to save some face from the present wreckage. These navy circles, he declares, particularly stress the necessity of preserving the Emperor in order to avoid Communism and chaos."[94]

On May 3 Hack received word that the State Department had authorized direct contact between the United States and Japan to commence through the Dulles-Fujimura channel. Five days later Fujimura addressed a cable to the navy minister and the navy chief of staff, classifying it as an "urgent operational dispatch" in an effort to circumvent routine chan-

---

[92]Fujimura, in "Statements," I, no. 64118, pp. 141–42.
[93]Leahy diary, June 14, 1945, Library of Congress.
[94]Memorandum from OSS Acting Director G. Edward Buxton to Secretary of State, June 4, 1945, in *FRUS*, 1945, VI: 486.

nels, and transmitting it in navy code to ensure secrecy. In it he reported the May 3 proposal without mentioning any previous contact, implying that the initiative had come from Dulles. He identified Dulles as "a leading political figure of America," a description that fit John Foster Dulles more aptly than Allen Dulles. Fujimura ventured a personal endorsement—"that the only course for Japan to pursue at present when the fall of Berlin is imminent is to plan for immediate peace with the United States"—and closed with a request for immediate instructions.[95]

Fujimura was accustomed to receiving replies within eight to ten days, but this time Tokyo took longer to respond. His cable caught the navy in the midst of a high-level shake-up that may have disrupted internal routine: on May 15 Vice-Admiral Zenshiro Hoshina became chief of the Naval Affairs Bureau, and on May 29 Admiral Soemu Toyoda took over as chief of staff and Vice-Admiral Takajirō Ōnishi became vice-chief.[96] A reply finally reached Berne on May 21 or 22, warning Fujimura "to be very cautious" because "certain points" were "indicative of an enemy plot." Fujimura dismissed the message as routine stalling, "a makeshift reply" by subordinates, "the same old game the junior staff members played, licking the pencil" for higher-ups.[97] Fujimura was correct. Captain Yoshimasa Suezawa, chief of the Naval Affairs Section, who received the action request, had read it with some misgivings. Perhaps justifiably chary of Dulles, about whom Fujimura's cable had little to say, and skeptical that the United States had made a proposal on so "vital" a matter as peace negotiations "to a mere Navy commander," Suezawa suspected a covert psychological warfare operation to exacerbate army-navy rivalry in Japan: "We became suspicious that the United States, taking note of the fact that the Japanese navy, even before the war, had been reluctant to go into the war against the United States, was attempting to sound out the attitude of the Japanese Navy rather than resorting to a proper diplomatic approach."[98]

Impatient at the inordinate delay, Fujimura had sent six more telegrams in the intervening two weeks in an effort to rouse the navy to support his initiative. Now he responded immediately, citing evidence to "corroborate" his claim that he was not falling victim to an "enemy plot." His reply was reassuring enough for Suezawa to forward the cable to his superior, Naval Affairs Bureau Chief Hoshina, and to circulate copies to ranking officers on the naval general staff. Hoshina concluded that Fu-

[95]Fujimura, in "Statements," I, no. 64118, pp. 142–43.
[96]Ibid., p. 145; Toyoda, in ibid., IV, no. 57670, p. 377, and no. 57669, p. 400. Cf. Tōgō, *Cause of Japan*, p. 345.
[97]Fujimura, in "Statements," I, no. 64118, p. 146.
[98]Suezawa, in "Interrogations," II, no. 62051, p. 274. Cf. Toyoda, in "Statements," IV, no. 57670, p. 280.

jimura could proceed after taking "precautions against being duped."[99] Similarly, the chief of the Operations Bureau of the naval general staff, Rear Admiral Sadatoshi Tomioka, decided that "even if this was a trick, it would at least give us a clue to the outline of American terms for terminating the war." Sensitive to the hawkish sentiments of Ōnishi, his new immediate superior, Tomioka circumnavigated the chain of command and took the proposal directly to the navy's new chief of staff, Toyoda, for his concurrence. But Toyoda favored arming Japan for a decisive battle in hopes of bluffing the Allies into opening negotiations before beginning their invasion. He ordered Tomioka not to concern himself with peace talks: "All you have to do is to devote yourself heart and soul exclusively to military operations."[100]

While Fujimura's initial messages were still making the rounds, he continued to bombard Tokyo with more, reporting the redeployment of U.S. and Soviet forces to the Far East, predicting that Japan's approach to Moscow would fail and that the Soviet Union would enter the war on the Allied side, and stressing the urgency of direct talks with the United States. He also had Hack take soundings of what the negotiating position of the United States would be on three issues of utmost concern to the navy: preservation of Japanese sovereignty, in particular, the future role of the emperor; "retention of the merchant marine in its present state"; and continued Japanese control of Formosa and Korea. With the sinking of the battleship *Yamato* at Okinawa, "it became apparent" to Fujimura "that the Japanese Navy had finally been destroyed." Now he threw caution to the winds, trying to keep the OSS interested by offering to Tokyo to lobby in person for the opening of talks. His U.S. contacts suggested, instead, inviting a high-ranking Japanese representative to come to Switzerland. On June 15 Fujimura sent a cable, his twenty-first since May 8, to Navy Minister Yonai, relaying the American proposal. It closed with bluntness verging on impertinence: "Only through achievement of peace with America by sacrificing the remaining war potential and national strength can you serve your country."[101]

Had the OSS deliberately set out to inspire army-navy rivalry in Japan it could not have found a more enthusiastic, if unwitting, agent for attaining that end. Fujimura increasingly became a source of contention within the navy itself. When Vice-Chief of Staff Ōnishi learned of the

[99]Hoshina, in "Statements," I, no. 61883, p. 471. Cf. Fujimura, in ibid., no. 64118, pp. 146–47. There is nothing in the postwar interrogation reports to support the claim that the navy shakeup was the result of the Fujimura initiative, although some circumstantial evidence is consistent with that claim, which is made in David Bergamini, *Japan's Imperial Conspiracy* (New York, 1971), pp. 72–73.

[100]Tomioka, in "Statements," IV, no. 60957, pp. 336–37. Cf. Toyoda, in ibid., no. 57670, p. 378.

[101]Fujimura, in ibid., I, no. 60957, pp. 147–48.

initiative, he denounced it as "an American scheme for pitting the Japanese Army and Navy against each other." Navy Minister Yonai was more receptive, even though he was aware of interservice tensions as well as the psychological warfare broadcasts that the ONI was beaming at Japan to exacerbate these tensions. But Ōnishi's strong stand carried the day, according to Naval Affairs Bureau Chief Hoshina: "The domestic atmosphere surrounding us demanded that we restrain any strong arguments for peace."[102] Yonai informed Tōgō of Fujimura's activities and cabled the attaché on June 20, reining him in: "Your point is fully understood. As the papers relating to the affair have been referred to the Foreign Minister, you are requested to take proper measures in close cooperation with the Minister and other persons concerned at your place."[103] The next day Ambassador Shunichi Kase asked Fujimura for details of his contacts with Dulles' operatives. At this point, not unwitting that the United States had long since broken Japan's naval and diplomatic codes and that the contact with Japan might become an open secret in Washington and source of renewed suspicion in Moscow, Dulles closed down the Fujimura channel.[104]

Kase was himself engaged in a similar maneuver, but in this instance, the roles of Japan and the United States may have been reversed. Early in May, Lieutenant General Seigo Okamoto, who oversaw Japanese intelligence operations in Europe from his post as military attaché in Switzerland, arranged for two of his countrymen at the Bank for International Settlements in Basel to approach a Swedish adviser to the bank, Per Jacobsson, with a request that he serve as intermediary between them and Dulles. The pair, Kojiro Kitamura and Ken Yoshimura, conferred with Jacobsson several times between July 10 and 13 and won his assent. They said that Kase knew of their approach and that General Okamoto was in direct communications with Army Chief of Staff Umezu. Dulles harbored doubts about the "seriousness of the approach," based on assessments by OSS sources that it was "initiated locally" rather than on "instructions from Tokyo," but he arranged to have Jacobsson driven to Wiesbaden for an interview on July 15.[105] Jacobsson

---

[102]Hoshina, in ibid., no. 61883, p. 471. Tōgō refers to the ONI's broadcasts in Telegram 944 to Ambassador Satō in Moscow, July 25, 1945, in *FRUS: Conference of Berlin*, II: 1261, as does Kase, *Journey to the Missouri*, p. 199.

[103]Fujimura, in "Statements," I, no. 64118, p. 149. Tōgō confirms being approached by Yonai around this time, but he confuses this initiative with another in *Cause of Japan*, p. 300. He claims he tried to get the navy to instruct its attaché in Berne, Kitamura, to try to sound out Dulles about America's peace terms. Cf. Tōgō, in "Statements," IV, no. 50304, p. 254.

[104]Brooks, *Behind Japan's Surrender*, pp. 133–34.

[105]Memorandum from OSS Acting Director Charles S. Cheston to Secretary of State, July 13, 1945, in *FRUS, 1945*, VI: p. 489.

told Dulles that throughout his conversations with the two Japanese, they had dwelt on the importance of preserving the emperor and that Kitamura had instructed him to probe the Americans on this vital point. In reply, Dulles made no commitments on "dynastic and constitutional questions," but he did hint at flexibility on the part of the United States: "If competent Japanese authorities accepted unconditional surrender, appropriate Allied authorities would determine how such a surrender should be effected." The OSS report of the meeting makes clear that Dulles did not regard his two contacts as competent Japanese authorities: "Jacobsson is personally convinced that these approaches are serious and that the Japanese group in Switzerland is in constant cable contact with Tokyo. This conviction appears to be based on impressions only, since his two Japanese contacts never stated precisely that they had received instructions from any authorized agency in Tokyo."[106] Yet the position of Okamoto and his personal ties to Umezu, under whom he had served in Manchuria in the 1930s, are indications that this approach, while not aimed at starting negotiations, could well have been designed to gather political intelligence for Umezu about the negotiating position of the United States. If so, it succeeded.

Describing Japan's contacts with the OSS as "peace feelers" obscures their significance. Backstage contacts between the United States and Japan did take place, but they fulfilled objectives other than opening negotiations on terminating the war. They were used for psychological warfare to divide the enemy camp or for intelligence-gathering about enemy negotiating positions without incurring the political obligations of formal mediation or negotiation.[107] For negotiations, whether mediated or direct, to lead to a settlement, there must be authoritative decisions that commit the governments involved. In the absence of authoritative decisions, most officials in Japan and the United States were reluctant to assume responsibility for initiating contacts out of fear of stirring internal opposition. Lacking political commitment, the individual initiatives that did occur were condemned to diplomatic impotence.

Preparing for the Decisive Battle for the Homeland

Japan's diplomatic efforts now focused exclusively on the Soviet Union. As the Hirota-Malik talks got under way in Tokyo, Japanese

---

[106]Memorandum from OSS Director William J. Donovan to the Secretary of State, July 16, 1945, in ibid. p. 490.

[107]The OSS official history makes the point this way: "The existence of an undercover agency provided a logical channel for secret negotiations. Wavering enemy or satellite leaders and groups could thereby make known their desires to appropriate Allied authori-

army strategists were completing plans for a decisive battle for the homeland. Before they could begin preparations in earnest, however, they had to satisfy two requirements. First, they needed new statutory authority to mobilize the nation for homeland defense. While grants of emergency powers by imperial ordinance would suffice, the legislative route offered greater likelihood of unifying the armed services over navy opposition. [108] Second, popular morale had now deteriorated to the point that absenteeism in war plants was cutting into productivity. As evidence of its concern, the government established an advisory body in early June "to investigate public opinion." [109] If the army was to conscript substantial numbers of civilians for homeland defense, as well as fill out reserve units, the public would need inspiration from above. Convening the Diet was the army's solution to both problems. But orchestration of the Diet session indicates just how far the Japanese government was from coalescing behind a suit for peace.

Navy members of the cabinet were reluctant to call the Diet into session. When Chief Cabinet Secretary Sakomizu tried to persuade Prime Minister Suzuki of the need to do so, Suzuki put him off. Sakomizu took this as a sign of the elderly man's uneasiness about making speeches and answering interpellations. At a late May cabinet meeting on the question, Navy Minister Yonai was more forthright about his objections, warning colleagues that "only confusion would prevail." One onlooker understood him to mean that "only jingoism would be advocated if the Diet were convened because the situation was such that no one dared talk in public about terminating the war, and there was the danger that the Government would find itself compelled to make a fatal promise." [110] Worse yet from the navy's standpoint, the Diet might also mandate service unification. To improve working relations with the army and head off pressure for unification, Yonai had taken the precaution of having Toyoda installed as navy chief of staff. [111] In the end, though, Suzuki and Yonai acceded to the army's demand for an extraordinary

---

ties without incurring the prohibitive risk of public exposure. Such authorities, in turn, could probe vulnerable points in enemy morale without the possibility of official embarrassment." See U.S. War Department, Strategic Services Unit History Project, *War Report of the OSS*, II: *The Overseas Targets* (New York, 1976), p. 321.

[108] Sakomizu, in "Interrogations," II, no. 62003, pp. 137–38.

[109] Vice-Admiral Teiji Nishimura (chief secretary to Prime Minister Suzuki), in ibid., no. 531, pp. 309–10.

[110] Admiral Seizō Sakonji (minister of state), in "Statements," III, no. 58226, p. 205. Cf. Sakomizu, in "Interrogations," II, no. 62003, pp. 137–38; and Tōgō, *Cause of Japan*, pp. 290–91.

[111] Oikawa, in "Statements," III, no. 61341, p. 109, suggests that he was replaced because Yonai believed Toyoda "would be suitable for broaching such a delicate subject" as war termination with Umezu, who hailed from the same district in Japan.

[65]

two-day session of the Diet to reinvigorate popular morale. The cabinet scheduled it for June 9.

In anticipation of the convening of the Diet, the army began pressing for adoption of its strategy of decisive battle. Its April 15 plan, to which the navy had yet to respond, could serve as a platform to whip up parliamentary enthusiasm and in turn rally public support. It could also provide a pretext for unification. The immediate stimulus for army pressure to adopt its strategy, however, was an unauthorized act by a well-placed junior officer who had gotten wind of the Big Six deliberations and decided to take countermeasures "without conferring with anyone." During the third week in May, before the cabinet had decided to convene the Diet, Colonel Sako Tanemura, who concurrently served as chief of the Military Affairs Section of the War Ministry, assistant secretary to the chief of staff, and a member of the SCDW secretariat, submitted the army plan, "The Fundamental Policy for the Future Conduct of the War," to Sakomizu and requested an imperial conference to endorse the strategic concept of a decisive battle for the homeland.[112] To justify that endorsement, the Military Affairs Bureau, political arm of the War Ministry, concocted an "Estimate of the Situation for Spring 1946." The army's Operations Bureau had already prepared its own assessment as part of planning for the expected invasion of Kyushu in fall 1945, but the new estimate, completed on June 1, had a different purpose and was accordingly more optimistic: it postponed the start of the decisive battle until spring on the premise that the United States would first land in China, then at Shikoku Island, east of Kyushu, before getting around to assaulting the heart of Japan, the Kanto Plain. This delay would give the army time to complete defense preparations, enhancing its prospects of repelling the invaders.[113] In the internal battle over military strategy, estimates are weapons, often forged for that very purpose.

The Army's estimates were not the only ones at hand. Suzuki had commissioned an independent assessment of Japan's capabilities, the price Tōgō had exacted for joining the cabinet. While preparing a military estimate was outside the cabinet's province, a survey of supplies of critical matériel was a matter of domestic policy. Normally that task would have been the responsibility of the Planning Board, which tended to follow the army's lead, but it was instead assigned to the cabinet secretariat under the direction of Sakomizu. Sakomizu, himself a former

---

[112]Tanemura, in "Statements," IV, no. 61977, p. 207. Cf. Sakomizu, in "Interrogations," II, no. 62003, pp. 137, 139; Kido, in "Statements," II, no. 61476, p. 190.

[113]For a brief discussion of the origins of the two estimates and the discrepancies between them, see Lieutenant General Shuichi Miyazaki (chief of the Operations Bureau), in "Statements," II, no. 50568, pp. 513–14. Cf. Hayashi, *Kōgun*, pp. 170–74; Tanemura, in "Statements," IV, no. 61977, p. 213; and Amano, in ibid., I, no. 50511, p. 27.

Planning Board official, used a variety of informal sources to gather the information he needed—indiscretions from army representatives on the cabinet secretariat, personal contacts at Imperial General Headquarters, even leads from newspaper reporters upon whom Sakomizu had bestowed expense accounts for wining and dining army officers.[114] The cabinet secretariat's assessment of "The Present Condition of Our National Power" cast doubt on Japan's ability to carry on the fight: "The ominous turn of the war, coupled with the increasing tempo of air raids, is bringing about great disruption of land and sea communications and essential war production. The food situation has worsened. It has become increasingly difficult to meet the requirements of total war." Perhaps most critical of all, Allied control of the sea had virtually dammed the flow of oil: "With oil reserves on the verge of exhaustion and the delay in plans for increased output of oil, we are faced with an extreme shortage of aviation fuel. This, of course, will have a serious effect on the planning of future operations, especially after the mid-year." Continued popular support for the war effort was also in doubt: "Morale is high, but there is dissatisfaction with the present regime. Criticisms of the government and the military are increasing. The people are losing confidence in their leaders, and the gloomy omen of deterioration of public morale is present. The spirit of public sacrifice is lagging and among leading intellectuals there are some who advocate peace negotiations as a way out."[115] The findings convinced Sakomizu that a campaign to boost popular morale was imperative: he became the "number one advocate" for convening the Diet.[116]

The SCDW secretariat, faced with trying to reconcile the cabinet's pessimistic report with the army's newfound optimism, simply papered over the inconsistency by drafting a new—and discrepant—conclusion and appending the two reports to it for submittal to the SCDW. Backed by secretaries from some of the ministries, Sakomizu then attempted to tone down the army's report. General Yoshizumi and Admiral Hoshina did not attend the key meeting on May 29, but sent their assistants instead. In Sakomizu's estimation, these junior officers "did not seem to represent accurately" the views of their superiors. They balked at any softening of the army's draft, accepting just one change, even that over the outspoken opposition of the army's representative and drafter of the army estimate, Colonel Sako Tanemura: they reaffirmed the policy se-

[114]Sakomizu, in "Interrogations," II, unnumbered, April 21, 1949, pp. 121–22. Cf. Yonai, in USSBS, *Interrogations*, II, p. 332; and Kase, *Journey to the Missouri*, p. 148.

[115]"Survey of National Resources as of 1–10 June 1945," Strategic Bombing Survey (Pacific), *Japan's Struggle to End the War*, pp. 16–17.

[116]Sakomizu, in "Interrogations," II, no. 62003, pp. 139–40. For a different account of the report's origins, see Suezawa, in ibid., p. 62051, p. 278. Cf. Tōgō, *Cause of Japan*, p. 291.

cretly agreed to by the Big Six by substituting the sentence, "Diplomatic measures toward the Soviet Union and China will be vigorously taken," for a more hawkish formulation in the original Army draft, "Thorough-going diplomatic steps toward the Soviet Union will be promptly taken in order to facilitate the prosecution of the war."[117] Had the Diet debate made the original formulation public it would have doomed the approach to Moscow.

Otherwise, the resulting "Fundamental Policy for the Future Conduct of the War" appealed to the most ardent hawk. The inspiration of Tanemura and his fellow junior officers exceeded the army's own strategic objective. While army plans called for the winning the decisive battle for the homeland as a prelude to suing for peace, the "Fundamental Policy" proclaimed: "We shall—through the unity of our nation and the advantages of our terrain—prosecute the war to the bitter end in order to uphold the national polity, protect the imperial land, and assure a basis for future development of the nation."[118] It was an inherently unlimited call for more war, a suicide pact to fight to the last man, the abandonment of military strategy. Later it would provide a rallying cry for diehards opposed to complying with orders to surrender.

Those higher up accepted their subordinates' draft with equanimity. It suited the purpose of whipping up enthusiasm among hawkish Diet members while not, at least in their minds, overriding the agreement reached earlier in the privacy of the Big Six meetings. Army Chief of Staff Umezu affixed his seal to the draft on May 30 before departing on a trip to Manchuria. Just before a June 5 meeting of senior Navy Ministry and general staff officers to consider the draft, Hoshina showed it to Navy Minister Yonai, who treated it as a mere formality. "Leave it as it is," he told Hoshina, who understood him to mean that while the Big Six was considering ways to end the war, it was important to maintain a public posture of firm resolve in support of the war effort.[119] Suzuki did not look at the documents until the morning of June 6, the day of the SCDW meeting. His look of dissatisfaction prompted Sakomizu to relate a parable about a monkey trainer who, when his monkey objected to compensation of three acorns in the morning and four in the evening, proposed instead four in the morning and three in the evening, which the monkey accepted. So long as Suzuki remained determined not to change policy, Sakomizu elaborated, he "might as well" not offend the army "for the time being."[120] Alone among the Big Six, Foreign Minister

[117]Tanemura, in "Statements," IV, no. 61977, pp. 206, 209.

[118]Butow, *Japan's Decision to Surrender*, p. 99, n. 69. Cf. Suezawa, in "Interrogations," II, no. 62051, p. 279; and Sakomizu, in ibid., no. 62006, p. 147.

[119]Hoshina, in "Statements," I, no. 61978, pp. 475–76; and Tanemura, in ibid., IV, no. 61977, p. 209.

[120]Sakomizu, in "Interrogations," II, no. 62003, p. 140.

Tōgō objected when notified of the SCDW meeting. He claims to have had no "previous intimation" of it and was "astounded" at its agenda, even though his cabinet colleagues, Suzuki and Yonai, were not surprised. Yet even Tōgō's pique was directed more at Sakomizu's effrontery in infringing on Foreign Ministry prerogatives by undertaking "a review of international conditions" than at the substance of the "Fundamental Policy."[121]

At a full-dress meeting on June 6, with subordinates in attendance, the SCDW formally ratified the army proposal with little dissent. Firsthand accounts differ in attributing the lack of contention to a fear of hawkish reprisal or to acceptance of the secretariat's premise that the tough-sounding posture would evoke a favorable reaction from the Diet and bolster sagging morale. Only Tōgō struck an occasional discordant note during the proceedings. At one point he contested the army's claim that fighting on the home islands would give a tactical advantage to the defense by calling attention to enemy air superiority. At another point he parried Sakomizu's contention that diplomacy might yet retrieve the initiative lost on the battlefield by stating the converse, that only a military success could lead to a diplomatic one. Otherwise, the reciting of set speeches and the reading of reports absorbed hours and emitted an air of unreality. For example, Toyoda, presenting the navy's estimate of enemy shipping losses, "about 20 per cent if the landing occurs around July and 25 per cent if it comes in September," penciled in projections of 30 to 40 per cent on his own carbon copy and then raised the figure to 50 per cent in his oral presentation to the SCDW.[122] Suzuki blandly accepted the projections of the Munitions Ministry's that enemy bombing would have no effect on Japanese production of 1,700 aircraft a month: he pleaded unfamiliarity with the subject on the grounds that it was "a bit too technical." He believed that "by going underground we could prevent bombing from having very much effect," but the planned construction on which his belief was premised never broke ground.[123] When the formalities were over, the SCDW approved the "Fundamental Policy," and a day later the cabinet added its endorsement. On June 8 most of the participants reassembled in Hirohito's presence for a repeat performance—albeit somewhat abbreviated and even more formal. Toyoda's capsule eyewitness account is telling: the imperial conference was "a dull one," but "the Emperor sat throughout the meeting silently and with a grave look on his face," an expression which Toyoda took as evidence that Hirohito "was dissatisfied with the decision."[124]

---

[121]Tōgō, *Cause of Japan*, p. 291.

[122]Toyoda, in "Statements," IV, no. 57669, p. 399, accounts for the first change by saying that the original estimate had neglected the effect of army suicide planes.

[123]Suzuki, in "Interrogations," II, no. 531, p. 309. Cf. Tōgō, *Cause of Japan*, p. 292.

[124]Toyoda, in "Statements," IV, no. 57670, p. 377.

The June 9 opening of the Diet heard a rousing call to arms from Prime Minister Suzuki: "The war must go forward, even if it is over my dead body." He ruled out any settlement on the terms then offered by the Allies: "The people of Japan are dedicated servants of the Imperial Throne. The Japanese will lose the meaning of their existence if the national polity is impaired. An unconditional surrender as proposed by the enemy, therefore, is tantamount to the death of all 100 million people of Japan. We have no alternative but to fight." Suzuki said he took courage from the national unity and shortened lines of supply that an invasion would bring, and he urged "stepped-up efforts" to overcome food shortages and transportation bottlenecks. But his allusion to a 1918 visit of his to San Francisco, where he prophesied that the United States and Japan would "incur the wrath of the gods" if they ever fought each other, infuriated the more hawkish of the Diet men, who berated him through much of the ensuing debate. They also directed their scorn at the other navy man in the cabinet, Navy Minister Yonai. When the hawks then introduced a bill promoting service unification, it convinced many observers that some army officers were unofficially encouraging the attack on the navy.[125] The ensuing uproar forced a two-day extension of the Diet session. When the cabinet informally convened to consider yet another day's extension in order to enact a watered-down version of the unification bill, Yonai threatened to resign, bringing down the government, unless his colleagues moved for immediate adjournment. Learning of the threat, War Minister Anami pleaded with Yonai not to carry it out. Kido joined the appeal. The government then introduced compromise legislation that passed, and the Diet adjourned on June 13.[126]

The navy had successfully staved off service unification, which might have strengthened the army's position in the waning days of the war. What effect the Diet session had on popular morale cannot be determined, but the government's effort to inspire the Diet could have encouraged military operations that were far less limited than those envisioned in the army's strategy of a decisive battle for the homeland. Tōgō, for one, confesses surprise at how little was made of the commitment to the "Fundamental Policy": "Curiously, never thereafter did the Army make a point of continu[ing] the war on the ground of this decision."[127]

---

[125]For excerpts of Suzuki's speech, see Brooks, *Behind Japan's Surrender*, p. 31. On service unification, see Tōgō, *Cause of Japan*, p. 293; and Sakonji, in "Statements," III, no. 58226, p. 205. Yoshizumi, in ibid., IV, no. 54484, p. 602, and one of his subordinates in the Military Affairs Bureau, Lieutenant Colonel Masatoshi Shirai, in ibid., III, no. 54472, p. 279, deny army complicity in the attacks on the navy.

[126]Sakonji, in "Statements," III, no. 58226, pp. 206–7.

[127]Tōgō, *Cause of Japan*, p. 294.

Yet if those in command of the army still adhered to the strategy of decisive battle, other more literal-minded officers just below them took the "Fundamental Policy" as their marching orders.

INVOLVING THE EMPEROR

Emperor Hirohito's troubled countenance at the imperial conference of June 8 may have manifested no more than a concern that the barely concealed discrepancies among the "Fundamental Policy" and its accompanying estimates meant a lack of consensus in the SCDW, but Privy Seal Kido and Foreign Minister Tōgō were determined to capitalize on the emperor's apparent dissatisfaction in order to involve him in their own efforts to terminate the war. He alone could break the impasse among lesser officials, or transcend it.

Kido, abreast of political currents, "was unable to discern as yet any trend leading to the termination of the war" in the Suzuki cabinet. Ruling out direct talks with the United States and Great Britain because the military services were "absolutely opposed," Kido did discover some officers in the Japanese army "who were attempting to bring about peace by utilizing the good offices of the Soviet Union." If this course were pursued, Kido hoped, "it might be possible to induce the Army to join in our plan for peace." His hope was similar to the one that had animated Tōgō at the Big Six meetings in May, though Kido himself was not yet aware of what had transpired then.[128] Reading over the documents in preparation for the June 8 imperial conference—in particular, the estimate of "The Present Condition of Our National Power"—Kido was galvanized into drafting his own "Tentative Plan to Cope with the Situation." As set forth in his diary entry of June 8, the plan called for "Imperial intervention" to arrange a negotiated settlement of the war. While the "orthodox way of opening peace negotiations" would be to have the armed services recommend ending the war and then have the government frame a negotiating position and invite talks, Kido judged it "almost impossible to do so at this juncture." By the time the services got around to proposing a settlement, it might be "too late" for Japan to avoid "Germany's fate." That delay might also jeopardize a critical interest of the palace: in Kido's words, the "security of the Imperial family and vindication of the national polity, Japan's minimum demands, may not be guaranteed." To avoid that result, Kido proposed that Japan send an emissary to Moscow with a "personal message" from the emperor requesting Soviet mediation and indicating Japanese readiness to with-

---

[128]Kido, in "Statements," II, no. 61541, p. 174. Cf. Tōgō, in ibid., IV, no. 50304, p. 257.

draw from territories it had occupied during the war and to disarm to a "minimum" level "required for her national defense." He intended to spell out other terms after "seeking the views of experts in various quarters." On June 9, after showing his idea to his chief secretary, Yasumasa Matsudaira, and asking him to take soundings among his associates in the army, the navy, and the Foreign Ministry who had been secretly discussing possibilities for ending the war, Kido obtained Hirohito's permission to consult with the prime minister and the ministers of war, navy, and foreign affairs.[129]

Kido could not arrange an appointment with any of the ministers until the Diet adjourned on June 13. First he spoke to Navy Minister Yonai, who reacted cautiously. After perusing the sketchy details and asking "if that was all there was to the plan," Yonai inquired about the prime minister's reaction. Yonai's caution is understandable: Kido had hardly been known for his dovishness in the past, and his plan fell short of what the Big Six had already been secretly considering. Prime Minister Suzuki, the next to call on Kido, was even more circumspect. Kido recalls that his appeal to do the best to end the war "for the sake of the imperial family's security" and the preservation of the national polity "struck a sympathetic chord in the Prime Minister, who emphatically pledged to do his bit." But Suzuki did not endorse Kido's plan: "He remarked that it was all very well but that he would like to think it over." Feigning ignorance of Yonai's stand, Suzuki excused his inclination to defer judgment on the grounds that "it seemed the Navy Minister was strongly in favor of continuing the war."[130]

Without Kido's knowledge, Tōgō had renewed efforts to get the Big Six "to implement Point Three" of its initial agreement—that is, to seek Soviet mediation to end the war. Immediately after the Diet adjourned, Tōgō had approached Yonai, who promised to take up the matter with the prime minister and the war minister. After a June 15 cabinet meeting, Yonai reported to Tōgō that Suzuki had raised no objection "but thought it best that the Foreign Minister himself should go to Moscow to conduct the negotiations." Tōgō shied away from doing so on the pretext that he "had to remain in Tokyo to work on preparations at home for peace." No doubt Tōgō's presence at the Big Six meetings was necessary to keep pressure on his reluctant colleagues, but he also thought it

[129]Kido diary, June 8, 1945, in *IMTFE* testimony, pp. 31149–51; Kido, in "Statements," II, no. 61476, pp. 190–91. Kido's chief secretary had been meeting in secret with Colonel Makoto Matsutani of the army general staff, Rear Admiral Sōkichi Takagi of the navy, and Toshikazu Kase of the Foreign Ministry, all of them reputed to be outspoken doves. Cf. Kase, *Journey to the Missouri*, pp. 176–77.

[130]Kido, in *IMTFE* testimony, p. 31154, and in "Statements," II, no. 61476, pp. 191–92. On June 15 Kido again spoke to Yonai, and the two exchanged their impressions of Suzuki's views.

impolitic for the Foreign Ministry to take the lead in approaching Moscow.

Later that day Tōgō called on Privy Seal Kido. In the course of their conversation, Tōgō, realizing that Kido was in the dark about the Big Six deliberations in mid-May, brought him up to date. While Tōgō expressed no opposition "in principle" to Kido's plan, he was primarily interested in committing the emperor to intervene in the policy process. "It would be extremely gratifying to me," he told Kido, "if the Emperor should say now that we were to work to end the war without delay, for there could be no greater aid to the attainment of my purpose than such words from the Throne." At the same time, Tōgō underscored his concern that diplomatic channels not be used to approach Moscow out of fear that "the Foreign Ministry would be in a very difficult position." He raised just one question about Kido's plan: how could it be reconciled with the adoption of the "Fundamental Policy" of June 8, but Kido dismissed his concern: "Oh, that. It's all right."[131]

The last of the four ministers to see Kido was War Minister Anami on June 18. Before Kido could broach his plan, however, Anami preempted the discussion, citing rumors circulating that Kido was about to resign and warning that if the home front were left untended "the peace movement would become strong and cause trouble." The veiled threats were an inauspicious start, but Kido plunged ahead and presented his plan anyway. Anami's rejoinder reaffirmed his commitment to the army's strategy: "In your position," he said, "it is only natural that you take the stand [that] you do. We military men, however, strongly desire to carry out a decisive battle on the homeland. Wouldn't it be to our advantage if peace were established after we had given the enemy a terrible beating in the decisive battle on the homeland?"[132]

Palace involvement showed some effect when the Big Six convened later that day. Suzuki reported on his conversation with Kido, and then Tōgō, citing the lack of progress in the Malik-Hirota talks, won approval to expedite negotiations. Anami, doubtful about keeping the Russians out of the war, was willing to have a study commissioned to determine whom to approach for mediation, but the meeting broke up without agreement on a formal request for Soviet mediation. Instead, the Big Six decided to sound out the Soviet willingness to mediate and to weigh in on Japan's behalf to obtain better terms than unconditional surrender:

Although we have no choice to continue the war so long as the enemy insists on unconditional surrender, we deem it advisable, while we still

---

[131]Tōgō, *Cause of Japan*, pp. 293–95 and in "Statements," IV, no. 50304, pp. 257–58; Kido, in *IMTFE* testimony, pp. 31155–56.
[132]Kido, in "Statements," II, no. 61476, pp. 192–93.

possess considerable power of resistance, to propose peace through neutral powers, especially the Soviet Union, and to obtain terms which will at least ensure the preservation of our monarchy. With that in mind, we entrust it to the foreign minister to ascertain the Soviet attitude by the beginning of July with a view to terminating the war if possible by September.[133]

The Big Six left open the question of what terms Japan was prepared to accept beyond stipulating that the throne be preserved.

On June 20 Suzuki reported the results of the meeting to Kido, who relayed them to the emperor along with a recommendation that he hold an audience for the Big Six. Later that afternoon Tōgō had an audience with Hirohito. Ascertaining that the emperor was not yet fully apprised of the Big Six deliberations in May, Tōgō took the opportunity to relate the substance of those discussions, as well as the latest details of the Malik-Hirota talks. "The Emperor approved the steps taken as entirely satisfactory," says Tōgō. "He also said that from recent reports of the Army and Navy Chiefs of Staff it had come to light that operational preparations in China and even in Japan were deficient, which made it imperative that the war stop as soon as possible, and that he desired that, difficult though it may be to end it, every effort be devoted to that purpose."[134]

The imperial conference of June 8, and Kido's subsequent round of conversations with key ministers, convinced him "that an indirect indication of the Emperor's opinions from me was not enough and that it was necessary for us to arrange for a meeting at which the Emperor could announce his opinions to them directly."[135] In the trifurcated policy process of wartime Tokyo, policy integration and coordination was difficult without palace involvement. As one naval aviator described it, "The whole organization was split into three—that is, the Navy, the Army, and what is known as the government—and the only one [who] could coordinate the three was the Emperor."[136] But the court bureaucracy had shied away from involving the emperor personally in policymaking, lest it risk his position of neutrality and transcendence and expose them to retaliation. Because the emperor's seal was necessary to confer authority on decisions made elsewhere, the palace had always been an action channel—a forum for debate and a locus of bargaining.

---

[133]Kase, *Journey to the Missouri*, p. 184. Kido, who was not present, testifies that the Big Six agreed to seek mediation, but Tōgō stops short of that claim, saying that the Six decided only that the Soviet Union "be sounded out" about mediation (Kido, in "Statements," II, no. 61476, p. 193; Tōgō, *Cause of Japan*, p. 296).

[134]Tōgō, *Cause of Japan*, p. 297, and in "Statements," IV, no. 50304, p. 257.

[135]Kido, in "Statements," II, no. 61541, p. 175, and no. 61476, p. 193, and in *IMTFE* testimony, pp. 31160–61.

[136]Minoru Genda, who served as a staff officer at Imperial General Headquarters from November 1942 until January 1945, in USSBS, *Interrogations*, II: 497.

By controlling access to the throne and invoking the emperor's prestige, officials inside the palace could exert subtle influence outside its walls. Yet their leeway was limited and their involvement was inobtrusive. As honest brokers they were willing to help crystallize consensus, or block action when consensus was lacking, but they stopped short of overtly involving the emperor himself to recommend a course of action. Yet his direct, personal intervention was essential to try to breach the walls of Japan's policy process and resolve contradictions among the cabinet and the armed services at war's end. That meant joining the political fray and taking sides.

The Big Six went to the palace on June 22. Hirohito's manner of speaking was somewhat oblique, as befit his customary stance transcending politics. "The basic policy for directing the war had been decided on at a previous council in the presence of the Emperor," he told them. "For the measures of bringing the war to a close, it is also desired that we should, without being hampered by traditional ideas, study concrete means and strive for their prompt realization."[137] Somehow the Big Six got the message. After Suzuki agreed to take the steps that the emperor desired, Yonai declared that "the time was now pressing" for prompt "realization" of Point Three of the Big Six agreement of May 11–14, to seek Soviet mediation to end the war. Tōgō seconded him, stressing the need to make it worthwhile for the Russians to do more than merely act as a go-between. Finally, the emperor asked Army Chief of Staff Umezu for his views. Although "he had no objection to the plan," Umezu urged "great caution" in carrying it out. Acknowledging the need for caution, Hirohito nevertheless wondered "if, being too cautious, we might miss the chance." Umezu conceded the need for prompt action. But an imperial audience was not a forum for reaching decisions, and neither the SCDW nor the cabinet pursued the matter further in the days to come.[138]

Nonetheless, armed with his sense of the meeting, Tōgō called on Kōki Hirota the following day to review his conversations with Soviet Ambassador Malik. On June 4 and 5 Hirota had met with Malik to explore Soviet attitudes in general, but the Russians, about to join the Americans and the British at Potsdam, were in no hurry to discuss the benefits of benevolent neutrality with the Japanese. Hirota gave Tōgō an upbeat report, noting that "the atmosphere of the talks was friendly, that the Russian side responded satisfactorily and the conversations looked hopeful." But Malik had been noncommittal on specifics: he

[137]Note appended to Kido diary, dated June 22, 1945, in *IMTFE* testimony, pp. 31162–63. Cf. Tōgō, *Cause of Japan*, p. 297.
[138]Kido, in *IMTFE* testimony, pp. 31163–64; Tōgō, in "Statements," IV, no. 50304, p. 258.

"showed great interest in the improvement of Russo-Japanese relations, promised to report the conversation to Moscow, and expressed a desire to begin concrete talks as soon as he received instructions to do so." The two had met twice since, on June 14, but "the talks did not show much progress." When Tōgō prodded Hirota "to speed things up" after the June 18 Big Six meeting, Hirota cautioned against giving Malik the impression that Japan was "in a great hurry," but Tōgō, while conceding that Hirota's negotiating tactics might be appropriate under normal circumstances, insisted that "haste was absolutely vital" in this instance.[139] Yet Malik continued to put off Hirota. Now Tōgō informed his emissary of the emperor's wishes expressed to the Big Six the previous day and urged him to see Malik again.

Hirota arranged a meeting for June 24, but in the absence of any authoritative decision to request Soviet mediation, he could only elaborate the list of Japanese concessions in return for Soviet benevolent neutrality, and the talks remained stalled. On June 29 Hirota submitted his only written proposal: if the Soviet Union would conclude a non-aggression treaty with Japan, his government would free Manchuria, give up fishing rights in Soviet waters that it had won in the Russo-Japanese War, in exchange for Soviet oil, and consider any other matters Malik cared to raise. It made no mention of mediation. Malik promised to report the proposal to his government, but Tōgō discovered that he was sending his dispatches home the leisurely way—by diplomatic pouch instead of cable.[140] It turned out to be the last meeting between Hirota and Malik; pleading diplomatic illness, Malik managed to evade further contact.

Japan's reaction to the slow pace of the talks was no less leisurely. Frustrated at his lack of progress, Tōgō eventually began lining up Suzuki and Yonai behind a new approach. Instead of clarifying the purpose of the talks, he proposed just a change of venue. He proposed that "the only feasible move was to send a man to the USSR." They agreed. On July 2 he had an audience with Prince Takamatsu, the emperor's younger brother. Arguing that Japan "had no alternative to seeking Soviet mediation," Tōgō recommended sending an emissary to Moscow. Takamatsu, noting that he had heard the same suggestion from Yonai, asked whom Tōgō had in mind for the job. Prince Konoye, Tōgō replied. Later Tōgō raised the possibility of Konoye with Suzuki. The name apparently drew favorable reactions, because on July 8 Tōgō sounded out Konoye

---

[139]Tōgō, in "Statements," IV, no. 50304, p. 259; Tōgō, *Cause of Japan*, p. 289. A U.S. intelligence report of the contact from an intercepted cable of July 28 from Tōgō to Satō in Moscow is in CINCUSFLT, Pacific Strategic Intelligence Section, "Russo-Japanese Relations," July 14, 1945, NSA Records, Box 4, SRH 084, RG 457, National Archives.
[140]Tōgō, in "Statements," IV, no. 50304, p. 261, and Tōgō, *Cause of Japan*, p. 298.

himself. The prince quickly got to the point: what terms would Japan propose? Tōgō deemed it advisable to defer the specifics: "I said that I thought the only course open to us was to try for anything at all short of unconditional surrender." Konoye "was of the same opinion and asked to be given carte blanche as to terms if he went to Russia." Tōgō "agreed that it might be best not to make any decisions in advance."[141] A premature decision might lock Japan into nonnegotiable demands. Tōgō would try for agreement in Moscow before seeking it in Tokyo. But the consequence was that Konoye would not have a negotiating position to take to Moscow and could not be sure of getting acceptance in Tokyo of any agreement he reached.

Meanwhile the subject of an imperial emissary to Moscow had come up in an audience that Suzuki had with the emperor. Whether or not Hirohito had already been briefed by his brother is not clear from the written record, but Tōgō's message seems to have gotten through. "It will not do to miss the opportunity" of sounding out the Soviet Union's "real intentions," the emperor told Suzuki. "How about frankly asking the Soviet Union for her mediation? How about dispatching a special envoy there with my personal message?"[142] Suzuki and Tōgō both reported their conversations to the Big Six on July 10. Two days later Hirohito held a fifteen-minute private audience with Prince Konoye. The unusual procedure permitted him to issue personal instructions without fear of disclosure. Konoye's account is that he was to report directly to the emperor on the progress of the talks. The emperor placed no restrictions on the terms he was willing to accept.[143] What others might find acceptable was a different matter.

The choice of Konoye was fraught with political significance. The prince had served as prime minister on no fewer than three separate occasions before the war and his name had figured prominently among the candidates to replace Koiso. His prominence may have owed less to his personal stature than to his seemingly unique qualifications as a compromise candidate between the army, which respected him, and its opponents, who hoped he could control it.[144] In audiences with the emperor in February, Konoye had been particularly outspoken in his opposition to continuing the war. "What we have to fear," he argued

---

[141]Tōgō, in "Statements," IV, no. 50304, pp. 261–62.

[142]Note appended to Kido diary entry of July 7, 1945, in *IMTFE* testimony, p. 31165. Kido debriefed Suzuki as he emerged from the emperor's chambers. Hirohito's request came earlier, according to Toyoda, in USSBS, *Interrogations*, II: 319, and Yasumasa Matsudaira, in "Statements," II, no. 60745, p. 429.

[143]Tōgō, in "Statements," IV, no. 50304, p. 262. He later denied this account in his *Cause of Japan*, p. 305.

[144]In July 1940 the army supported Konoye "unanimously" according to then Vice-Minister of War Anami, Kido diary, July 8, 1940, in *IMTFE*, Exhibit 532.

then, "is not so much defeat as a Communist revolution which might take place in the event of defeat."[145] His anticommunism, it has been suggested, may have been stimulated by public disclosure around that time that an associate of his, Richard Sorge, had been arrested as a Soviet spy. Nonetheless, the Sorge connection perhaps made him more acceptable to Moscow. These considerations may have influenced Koiso to consider sending him on a similar mission to Switzerland several months earlier, but two others made him a prime candidate now. Unlike Tōgō or Hirota, he was willing to go to Moscow, even at the risk of assassination by the diehards.[146] And Konoye's loyalty to the throne was unassailable; he would not lightly sacrifice the national polity for the sake of peace, unless it was the emperor's wish.

Prime Minister Suzuki reported Konoye's audience with the emperor to the Big Six on July 14. They agreed to have a general, an admiral, and a vice-minister of foreign affairs accompany Konoye on his mission—a deputation representing all the agencies responsible for war and peace. When they turned to the question of peace terms, however, consensus broke down, just as it had in May. War Minister Anami did not budge from his previous stand that because Japan was still holding most of the territory it had conquered it had not lost the war, and that peace terms had to reflect that fact. Tōgō and Navy Minister Yonai also repeated what they had said in May about the need to minimize Japan's demands. "The debate became so heated," says Tōgō, that after a while Yonai whispered to him "that the conference would break up" if they continued to press the point and "suggested that we talk about it some other time."[147] Once again, Japan's leaders, deadlocked over irreconcilable differences, had to defer a decision on surrender terms, establishing no concrete basis on which mediation might proceed.

SATŌ TRIES HIS HAND—AND TŌGŌ'S PATIENCE

Konoye's departure for Moscow was contingent upon Soviet willingness to receive him. To secure an invitation, Tōgō opened yet a third channel to Moscow. On July 11 he cabled instructions to Japan's ambassador there, Naotake Satō, no longer limiting him "solely to the objec-

---

[145]Konoye, Memorandum of conversation with the Emperor, February 1945, Strategic Bombing Survey (Pacific), *Japan's Struggle to Surrender*, p. 21. Cf. Richard Storry, "Konoye Fumimaro: 'The Last of the Fujiwara,'" *Far Eastern Affairs* 2 (1960) (St. Antony's Papers no. 7): 20.

[146]On Hirota's reluctance, see Tōgō, in "Statements," IV, no. 50304, p. 260. On the risk of assassination, see Yasumasa Matsudaira, in ibid., II, no. 60475, p. 429.

[147]Tōgō, in ibid., IV, no. 50304, p. 263.

tive of closer relations." Now Satō's mandate was to include "sounding out the extent to which we might employ the USSR in connection with the termination of the war." Again it stopped short of a formal request for mediation: "Please bear in mind not to give them the impression that we wish to use the Soviet Union to terminate the war." Tōgō sought to convey the sensitive state of deliberations in Tokyo: "The foreign and domestic situation for the Empire is very serious, and even the termination of the war is now being considered privately."[148]

Four hours later he sent a cable hinting at possible Japanese concessions in return for continued Soviet neutrality: "We consider the maintenance of peace in Asia as one aspect of maintaining world peace. We have no intention of annexing or taking possession of the areas which we have been occupying as a result of the war."[149] Tōgō also told Satō to ask whether T. V. Soong, China's foreign minister, was presently in the Soviet Union. Rumors of Soong's presence there had led to conjecture at the palace of a Soviet rapprochement with Chiang in preparation for Soviet entry into the war.

The next day Tōgō cabled another request—that Satō arrange for Soviet authorities to receive the Konoye mission as soon as they returned from Potsdam. He put the emperor's prestige behind the approach: noting that Konoye would be "bearing his personal letter," he added, "It is His Majesty's heart's desire to see the swift termination of the war." Yet Tōgō had nothing new to say about the minimum conditions Japan would find acceptable, except to state in no uncertain terms its unwillingness to accept unconditional surrender.[150]

Shortly thereafter Satō's reply to the first of Tōgō's cables arrived in Tokyo. It was exceedingly undiplomatic in tone: "I believe it is no exaggeration to say that the possibility of getting the Soviet Union to join our side and go along with our reasoning is next to nothing. That would run directly counter to the foreign policy of this country as explained in my frequent telegrams to you." He dismissed Tōgō's rationale—"We consider the maintenance of peace in Asia is one aspect of maintaining world peace"—as "nothing but academic theory" because "England and America are planning to take the right of maintaining peace in East Asia away from Japan, and the actual situation is now such that the mainland of Japan itself is in peril." Satō insisted on more concreteness: "As you already know, the thinking of the Soviet authorities is realistic. It is difficult to move them with abstractions, to say nothing about the futility of trying to get them to consent to persuasion with phrases

---

[148]Telegram 890 from Tōgō to Satō, July 11, 1945, in *FRUS: Conference of Berlin*, I: 874–75.
[149]Telegram 891 from Tōgō to Satō, July 11, 1945, in ibid., p. 875.
[150]Telegram 893 from Tōgō to Satō, July 12, 1945, in ibid., p. 876.

beautiful but somewhat remote from the facts and empty in content." It was imperative, Satō concluded, that Japan "first of all firmly resolve to terminate the war," especially "if worse comes to worst" and the war "turns extremely disadvantageous to our side." Then the Soviet Union "might be moved" to mediate, but even so the result "will very closely approximate unconditional surrender." He asked Tōgō to forgive his frankness, but added, "In international relations there is no mercy, and facing reality is unavoidable."[151]

However clear international reality may have seemed to Satō in Moscow, his lecture did not clarify domestic reality confronting Tōgō in Tokyo. The foreign minister was as aware as his ambassador that trying to get the Soviet Union to intercede on Japan's behalf with the United States in order to improve the terms of surrender was a desperate and losing gamble, but he had little choice. Moscow was the only place he could turn to pursue a diplomatic end to the war. While Satō was insisting that Japan must first resolve to end the war before turning to Moscow, Tōgō had tried that and failed. Now he was hoping to use the approach to Moscow in order to forge that resolve at home. Unconditional surrender was politically unacceptable, but terms very close to that—surrender on the sole condition that the throne be spared—might prove acceptable once mediation got under way and his colleagues became convinced that Japan lacked bargaining leverage to obtain better terms. Tōgō had pushed to the very limits of his authority in asking Satō to sound out Moscow on mediation. Now he found himself coping with insubordination from an ambassador who, in his realism about the war and zeal for peace, was willing to accept the unacceptable—unconditional surrender. Tōgō's resentment of Satō's reply still shows through in his comments to interrogators four years later: "What it contained was not the opinion of the Soviet Government; the Russians had not said any such thing. It was Satō's own opinion. I told Satō that we could surrender unconditionally without Russian assistance, but that we were not prepared to do so; I recommended that he spend more time in working with the USSR and less in sending me such telegrams."[152]

On July 13 Ambassador Satō tried to see Soviet Foreign Minister Molotov, but he was told to convey his messages to the deputy foreign minister instead. He did so, presenting a written request that the Soviets receive Konoye and emphasizing the emperor's personal involvement. His Russian interlocutor expressed "doubts" about obtaining a reply before Molotov's imminent departure for Potsdam. Satō cabled home a report of the contact, along with another cable restating his personal

---

[151]Telegram 1392 from Satō to Tōgō, July 13, 1945, in ibid., pp. 875–76.
[152]Tōgō, in "Statements," IV, no. 50304, p. 263.

view that the Russians would "simply not consider" helping Japan "in terminating the war" and that "nothing other than a proposal for peace and termination of hostilities" would do if Konoye's mission were to succeed. Tōgō's way of negotiating, he warned, far from preserving the throne, would only be "provoking trouble" for the emperor.[153] Adding injury to insult, Satō allowed word of the negotiations to get into Japanese news dispatches from Moscow the next day. Tōgō chided him about the indiscretion: "If word should ever leak out, the results would be most dire." Knowledge of the negotiations was confined to the Big Six, he told Satō, and urged him, on his side, to keep it to himself "so that we may have nothing to regret."[154]

The cable traffic back and forth across the Sea of Japan continued unabated over the next week, with both diplomats reiterating their previous stands. Then on July 19 Satō transmitted the Soviet reply. Literally noncommittal, it declined to receive Konoye for the present time, on the grounds that the purpose of his mission was "not clear" and that the emperor's views, as set forth in the note, were "general in form and contain no concrete proposal." Satō accompanied the Soviet reply with yet another personal plea for peace at any price.[155] Tōgō's reply made clear not only his appreciation of Satō's argument, but also the reason for his own opposition to it: "It is impossible at this time to ask the Soviet Union unconditionally for assistance in obtaining peace; at the same time, it is also impossible and to our disadvantage to indicate the concrete conditions immediately at this time on account of internal and external relations. Under such delicate circumstances, we hope to have Prince Konoye transmit to the Soviet Union our concrete intentions based on the Emperor's wishes" and "to have the Soviets deal with the United States and Great Britain" in return for Japanese consideration of "Soviet demands in Asia."[156]

The United States, for its part, was only too well aware of where Japan was turning in its quest for peace. Having broken Japan's diplomatic and naval codes, U.S. naval intelligence units were decoding and translating Japanese cable traffic to and from Moscow, as well as Berlin and other capitals. Although the texts were very closely held, Secretary of War Henry Stimson and Navy Secretary James Forrestal read periodic summaries of the Tōgō-Satō exchanges and President Truman and Secretary of State James F. Byrnes were familiar with their contents.[157] The

---

[153]Telegrams 1385 and 1386 from Satō to Tōgō, July 13, 1945, in *FRUS: Conference of Berlin*, I: 879–81.

[154]Telegram 910 from Tōgō to Satō, July 17, 1945, in ibid., II: 1248.

[155]Telegram 1417 from Satō to Tōgō, July 19, 1945, in ibid., p. 1251.

[156]Telegram 932 from Tōgō to Satō, July 21, 1945, in ibid., p. 1258.

[157]Forrestal entered a detailed summary of Tōgō's cables to Satō on July 11 and 12 and

OSS had also been sending back reports of its contacts with the Japanese, and Allen Dulles even traveled from Berne to Potsdam to brief Stimson in person on them.[158] Stalin mentioned Soviet receipt of "peace feelers" from Japan to Presidential Assistant Harry Hopkins in Moscow on May 28 and to Churchill in Potsdam on July 17, and gave Truman copies of the notes that Satō had handed over in Moscow four days earlier.[159] Despite the intelligence gleaned from reading Japan's "mail," the United States never gave formal consideration to opening diplomatic negotiations with Japan.

THE JAPANESE 'PEACE FEELERS'

By 1945 Japan had lost the war, but its leaders were not yet prepared to sue for peace. The army continued to hold out for a decisive battle for the homeland, hoping that it could stave off the initial Allied assault and in so doing secure for itself and the nation some measure of honor in defeat. Still others in army ranks were girding for a fight to the death. No leader, civilian or military, had expressed readiness to accept surrender without at least firm Allied assurances about preserving the throne. Under these circumstances the Big Six, even under prodding from the palace, was unable to define acceptable terms for ending the war or opening negotiations. Japanese internal politics was proving intractable when it came to translating a military result into a diplomatic and political one.

Not until the last week of the war did Japan make a direct and official approach to the United States. Once the war had turned irreversibly

---

Satō's replies into his diary on July 13, 15, and 24 (Walter Millis ed., *The Forrestal Diaries* [New York, 1951], pp. 74–76). Stimson notes his receipt of the exchanges in a diary entry for July 16. Forrestal's special assistant for atomic energy, Rear Admiral Lewis L. Strauss, saw the July 12 message from Tōgō and Satō's reply of July 14. He claims they were transmitted to Admiral Leahy, who took them with him to Potsdam, but Leahy had left Washington on July 6. Truman and Byrnes received oral summaries of the cables on July 17, but Byrnes did not learn of the details until July 28, when Forrestal filled him in (according to Strauss, in his *Men and Decisions* [New York, 1962], pp. 188–89, and Byrnes, in his *All in One Lifetime*, pp. 292, 297). It is not clear whether senior officials were also briefed on the Onodera initiative.

[158]Stimson diary, July 20, 1945, Henry L. Stimson Papers, Yale University Library. I am grateful to the Yale University Library for permission to quote passages from the diary.

[159]Hopkins reported Stalin's comment in a cable to the president from Moscow, May 30, 1945, in *FRUS: Conference of Berlin*, I, p. 160. Ambassador Charles E. Bohlen recorded it more fully in a May 28 memorandum of conversation, in ibid., pp. 44–45. Stalin's conversation with Churchill is recorded in John Ehrman, ed. *Grand Strategy*, Vol. 6 of *History of the Second World War* (London, 1956), p. 302. His July 17 meeting with Truman was noted in shorthand by Bohlen, who reconstructed the conversation from his notes on March 28, 1960, in *FRUS: Conference of Berlin*, I: 87, II: 1587. Stalin also read the texts of the Japanese notes to the tenth plenary session (see ibid., II, p. 460; Truman, *Year of Decisions*, p. 396).

against it, Japan did make several authoritative attempts to negotiate with China and the Soviet Union, but all these attempts failed. The purposes of these diplomatic approaches was no more evident to participants at the time than it has been to historians since. None had the primary object of negotiating an end to the war in the Pacific. By refusing to commit themselves to negotiations at all, and then by trying to open talks without reaching internal agreement on what they were negotiating about, Japan's leaders not only produced puzzlement but also ensured failure.

The so-called Japanese "peace feelers" served a variety of purposes for their initiators. The demarches to China were designed to reach a separate peace in that theater in order to facilitate the army's strategy of decisive battle for the homeland. The individual initiatives of General Okamoto in Switzerland and Ambassador Satō in Moscow were essentially aimed at gathering political intelligence, probing the enemy's negotiating position without making the political commitment of formally opening negotiations or requesting mediation. Foreign Minister Shigemitsu's abortive move through Sweden's ambassador to Tokyo, Widar Bagge, served a similar purpose until Bagge tried without success to wring a formal request for mediation out of Japan. Commander Fujimura's unauthorized initiative, which sought to commit his own government to direct negotiations with the United States, readily lent itself to OSS exploitation for the purposes of intelligence-gathering and psychological warfare.

Only the Hirota-Malik talks and the Konoye mission had the full authority of the Japanese government behind them, but even their purposes were obscured by internal politics. The Hirota-Malik talks were the product of a compromise that satisfied the divergent, indeed antithetical, interests of various members of the Big Six. For army leaders, as well as for some navy officers, these talks were aimed at securing Soviet benevolent neutrality, to preclude the Russians from allying with the United States and Great Britain against Japan, and to gain Soviet assistance, if not active intervention, for the decisive battle for the homeland. For Foreign Minister Tōgō and Navy Minister Yonai, the talks opened a way to Soviet mediation of a negotiated settlement of the war once they failed to attain the army's objectives.

The proposed Konoye mission to Moscow was designed by some to request Soviet mediation to end the war. Yet it sought more than Soviet good offices to act as a neutral go-between in arranging Japan's surrender; it hoped to bring Soviet bargaining leverage to bear on Japan's behalf to improve the terms of settlement. As Tōgō put it, "The procedure for unconditional surrender was simple; it would not have entailed sending Konoye. No one in Tokyo at the time agreed to unconditional surrender."[160] The private channel between the palace and prince Konoye might have allowed the special envoy's instructions to be modified in secret, but the Japanese government had yet to authorize a formal request for Soviet mediation—not to mention reaching agreement on attainable peace terms. Tōgō and his allies were hoping to exploit the opening of talks in Moscow as an action-forcing device to crystallize Big Six agreement on peace terms, but even such well-positioned doves as Tōgō were unsure of success. When all else fails, negotiating may be a way to forge political agreement at home to terminate a war, but it is no substitute for that agreement.

The army, meanwhile, was trying to use diplomacy as a substitute for military success. A separate peace with China, and continued Soviet neutrality in the Pacific, would permit Japan to concentrate its forces on the home islands to meet the expected invasion. Efforts to reduce the geographic scope of the war only to increase its intensity is not what is usually meant by de-escalation. Nor would the army's strategy necessarily lead to an end to the fighting. More likely, it would have prolonged the war. Even if the army did succeed in throwing back the initial invasion attempt, thereby improving Japan's bargaining position, there was no guarantee that it would then agree to open talks. And if the army counterattack failed, the strategy of decisive battle virtually assured continued fighting because the casualties suffered by the invaders would have stiffened their resistance to concessions for Japan and put them in a position to force capitulation. Only if the strategy of decisive battle was intended to be a bluff—and worked—would it have succeeded in reducing death and destruction during war termination, but that does not seem to have been the Japanese army's intent. Rational choice can account for Japan's adoption of this strategy. It has more trouble accounting for the refusal of Japan's leaders to consider a strategy of military de-escalation. The only open challenge to the army's strategy of decisive battle came from with the army itself—from the diehards prepared to fight to the last man.

Neither of Japan's authoritative approaches to Moscow ever made it clear what Japan wanted. The tentativeness and ambivalence with which Japan made those approaches are incomprehensible within a rational choice framework of analysis. They are symptomatic of the delicacy of political relations within the governing coalition in Tokyo. Diplomatic failure had brought down many a government in Tokyo before and during the war; by war's end even diplomatic success could cause political collapse. Any Japanese diplomatic initiative required at least the acquiescence, if not the active support, of the highest-ranking officers in

---

[160]Tōgō, in "Statements," IV, no. 50304, p. 264.

the army and the navy, who had to be willing to withhold word of it from the more ardent of their subordinates. To gain army and navy acquiescence, any diplomatic move had to have among its avowed purposes some accretion of military power—either by forging a new alliance or by neutralizing an avowed or potential enemy—regardless of the doubtful prospects for achieving that aim. After the war some Japanese officials sought to characterize as "peace feelers" initiatives that at least in part tried to enhance Japan's ability to fight on. The diplomats went along with the soldiers and sailors because they saw the opening of talks as the only way to arrange a settlement of the war. Japan's willingness to enter into negotiations without first agreeing on a negotiating position meant that it would engage in talks without end.

For its part, the United States did not attempt to initiate negotiations with Japan. American officials who did make informal contact with the enemy exploited these openings to gather intelligence and engage in psychological warfare rather than to seek a diplomatic settlement of the war. What the United States "knew" about Japan's readiness to end the war was hardly unambiguous. Like most raw intelligence, especially political intelligence, the intercepts lent themselves to partisan analysis. By emphasizing one point over another, it was possible for officials to put on them any construction they wanted. The critical uncertainty was whether or not Tōgō and his allies were likely to win their internal struggle to sue for peace—and no American had any basis for accurately assessing that, other than their own predispositions or their predilections for aiding Japan's doves by American initiatives. As Allen Dulles recalls about reporting the Swiss contact with the Japanese to Stimson: "I told him the whole story. He asked me a number of questions: my attitude about the Emperor; did I think these people were sincere; did they have authority? On the last I said, "I can't tell you. I don't think anybody knows what's going on in Tokyo well enough to say. But I think they're sincere."[161]

At the time the U.S. government had no action channel for preparing agreed intelligence estimates and, even within the OSS, analysts were unable to agree to the likely outcome of Japan's internal struggle to surrender. On September 8, 1944, for instance, the Research and Analysis Branch of the OSS produced an estimate that had all the earmarks of internal disagreement over the emperor's role in Japan's policy process. After noting the influence of "extremist groups" that "advocate the return of the Emperor to active participation in political affairs," it concluded on a very different note: "Accordingly the war will continue until

[161]Dulles, quoted in Len Giovannitti and Fred Freed, *The Decision to Drop the Bomb* (New York, 1965), pp. 215–16.

the Emperor says, "'Cease!' "[162] If Hirohito was a captive of the extremists, how would he stop the war? Similarly, on April 20, 1945, the OSS reported on the formation of the Suzuki government and concluded, "In no sense did the Cabinet change imply a weakening of Japan's support for the war." Yet other statements in the estimate qualified, even nullified, that conclusion: "The composition of Japan's third wartime Cabinet . . . demonstrates the submergence of the extremist military clique which committed the nation to an all-out war policy in 1941. Nevertheless, the new Cabinet does not appear to have the strong political leadership required to abandon that policy and take Japan out of the war." This was followed by: "Suzuki can scarcely be expected to offer unconditional Japanese surrender to the Allies, but he may launch peace feelers immediately following the end of the war in Europe in an attempt to salvage the Home Empire from imminent ruin."[163] Intelligence data available in Washington gave hawks and doves alike ammunition for their fight over American politico-military strategy, and each interpreted the data and the estimates in the light of his own policy stands.

Yet one point was clear to senior U.S. officials regardless of where they stood on war termination. Perhaps as early as July 9, when the United States monitored Japanese news broadcasts reporting Suzuki's speech to the Diet, very likely by July 16, when Stimson read translations of the Tōgō-Satō exchanges of July 11–13 and briefed Truman and Byrnes on them, and almost certainly by July 20, when Allen Dulles informed Stimson of OSS contacts with Japan, U.S. senior officials knew that the critical condition for Japan's surrender was the assurance that the throne would be preserved. To understand why the United States refused to make that concession, it is necessary to turn to the domestic and bureaucratic politics of war aims in the United States.

[162]U.S. Office of Strategic Services, Research and Analysis Branch, "The Japanese Emperor and the War," no. 2261S, September 8, 1944, pp. 1, 3.

[163]U.S. Office of Strategic Services, Research and Analysis Branch, "Crisis in Japan," no. 3061S, April 20, 1945, pp. 1–2.

[3]

The Fight to
Modify War Aims

When lenity and cruelty play for a kingdom,
the gentle gamester is the soonest winner.
—William Shakespeare, *Henry V*

In war, unlimited aims call for unlimited means. The Roman legions at Carthage were not the last victors to make a desert and call it peace, nor were the ruling few of Melos, under siege by Athens, the last leaders to sacrifice all for goals they could not hope to attain.

Conversely, war termination calls for self-limitation with regard to ends, some narrowing in the disparity of war aims between the contenders. Defining war aims is one way to exercise self-restraint—to define is to limit. The more narrowly the warring parties construe their aims, the closer they come to mutual accommodation and the less exertion they justify on the home front. That is the major premise of Karl von Clausewitz's classic treatise *On War*. In theory, if not always in practice, he reasons, because war "is controlled by its political object, the value of this object must determine the sacrifices to be made for it in *magnitude* and also in *duration*."[1]

Having clear-cut war aims can make mutual adjustment possible, whether unilaterally or by negotiation, as a way of ending a war. In the absence of well-defined aims, war may be more difficult to terminate. Again, to quote Clausewitz, "The political object—the original motive for the war—will thus determine both the military objective to be reached and the amount of effort it requires."[2] But as a war intensifies the reverse may be the case. As Clausewitz understood only too well from the Napoleonic wars, even when the contending states begin with a definite set of aims, these aims may expand as the war escalates, if for no other reason than to enable leaders to justify wartime privation to

[1]Karl von Clausewitz, *On War*, ed. Michael Howard and Peter Paret (Princeton, N.J., 1976), p. 92 (emphasis in the original).
[2]Ibid., p. 81.

their people. In the words of Gordon Craig and Alexander George, "sacrifice creates value."[3] That was so in America's war with Japan, and its war aims expanded accordingly. In 1945 unconditional surrender was an object worthy of all-out war that commanded an ever-greater expenditure of lives and resources.

Toward the end of the war in the Pacific, U.S. officials considered whether to offer Japan more acceptable terms than unconditional surrender. Strategic calculation would have suggested one of three courses for the United States: a forthright public commitment to spare the emperor in order to induce Japan's surrender; firm insistence on unconditional surrender accompanied by threats of Soviet intervention and atomic bombing; or a pledge to preserve the throne along with threats of further escalation. The United States adopted none of the three.

Statements of war aims often emerge from governments as the result of internal compromise—compromise that has more to do with the bureaucratic and domestic politics of those who draft the statements than of those in the enemy camp to whom they are addressed. The Potsdam Declaration is an example. Officials of the United States responsible for obtaining Japan's surrender and running the postwar occupation sought to preserve the throne as an instrument for accomplishing those tasks. Yet the American public, by a lopsided majority, favored unconditional surrender and arraignment of Emperor Hirohito as a war criminal— judging from comments in Congress and on editorial pages and the findings of public opinion polls. So while organizational interests inclined some officials to moderate American war aims, domestic politics precluded them from saying so in public.

What was to become the Potsdam Declaration passed through three stages of drafting, each dominated by a different senior official with his own stake in its formulation and his own conception of its purpose. Initially conceived as an inducement to Japan's surrender, it was turned into an ultimatum and eventually emerged as neither. The proposal for a public proclamation of war aims originated with Acting Secretary of State Joseph C. Grew in May 1944. Grew, the ambassador in Tokyo at the start of the war, was intent on offering Japan more conciliatory terms as a way of hastening the end of the war and eventually fostering a rapprochement between the United States and Japan. But Grew's proposal soon became entangled in an interservice struggle over military strategy. Each armed service took its stand on war aims predicated on its own organizational interest in a preferred strategy for terminating the war. The navy favored a shift away from unconditional surrender be-

[3]Gordon Craig and Alexander George, *Force and Statecraft: Diplomatic Problems of Our Time* (New York, 1983), p. 124.

cause it was a war aim too demanding to be attained by its strategy—naval blockade and air bombardment. The army, in contrast, wanted to win the war by invading Japan's home islands and initially resisted any modification of war aims. Only after the army had secured presidential approval in June 1945 to proceed with its plans for invasion did Secretary of War Stimson move to satisfy a secondary interest of the army—use of the throne to arrange the cessation of hostilities and postwar occupation. He did so by supporting Grew's efforts to spare the emperor, until the army drew back from a public commitment to that end. At the same time he redrafted Grew's proclamation to play up the new military threats facing Japan, turning inducement into ultimatum. During final consideration of the proclamation in late July, Secretary of State James F. Byrnes largely excluded Grew and Stimson. Under the influence of Soviet specialists in the American delegation at the Potsdam Conference, whose principal preoccupation was postwar relations with the Soviet Union, not the end of the war with Japan, Byrnes presided over the elimination of all references to impending Soviet involvement in the war and use of the atomic bomb. Apprehensive about adverse public reaction to any retreat from unconditional surrender, he embraced the army's stand that nothing be done to jeopardize future retention of the emperor while eschewing any public pledge to that end. Thus, stripped of all specific threats and inducements not previously disclosed, the Potsdam Declaration was reduced to mere propaganda, which could be used to justify whatever military escalation followed.

UNCONDITIONAL SURRENDER:
ORIGINS OF A DOMESTIC IMPERATIVE

In April 1945 the stated policy of the United States on the terms of settlement with Japan was still the expansive one that President Roosevelt had first promulgated after conferring with Prime Minister Churchill at Casablanca on January 23, 1943—that of unconditional surrender. These words were peculiarly American, a formula derived from the chemistry of American politics. First uttered by General Ulysses S. Grant at Fort Donelson, unconditional surrender was an apt slogan for a civil war in which Grant was to accept the surrender of the rebel army, not of the Confederacy itself, because its very existence as a state was the issue in contention. Unconditional surrender was known to Franklin Roosevelt's generation as the rallying cry of Theodore Roosevelt, General John J. Pershing, and their fellow hawks against President Wilson's plea for armistice and "peace without victory" in World War I. "The ghost of Woodrow Wilson was again at his shoulder," Robert Sherwood writes

[89]

of Franklin Roosevelt at Casablanca.[4] While Roosevelt's commitment to unconditional surrender at the time was not as casual as he himself would later make it seem, it had received only cursory review—and by an irregular procedure at that. A commission composed of State Department officials, members of Congress, and a handful of notables from outside the government, the Subcommittee on Security of the Advisory Committee on Postwar American Foreign Policy, used the phrase when it proposed that "nothing short of unconditional surrender by the principal enemies, Germany and Japan, could be accepted."[5] The role of the Subcommittee on Security and the status of its chairman—it was an advisory commission, and the chairman was the president of the Council on Foreign Relations—are two indications that unconditional surrender did not emerge from official action channels as a formal statement of policy. The recommendation had been passed along to the White House, apparently without prior clearance from Secretary of State Cordell Hull, just before the conference at Casablanca. There the Joint Chiefs of Staff gave it only perfunctory consideration.

The origins of unconditional surrender suggest too that it was intended more as propaganda than as a war aim or a peace term. Churchill sought to portray it that way to Clement Attlee, his Labourite deputy prime minister in Great Britain's wartime coalition government, in soliciting the cabinet's views about referring to unconditional surrender in the conference communiqué. Calling the term "a declaration of the firm intention of the United States and the British Empire to continue the war relentlessly until we have brought about the unconditional surrender of Germany and Japan," Churchill contended that it "would stimulate our friends in every country."[6] Two such countries of particular concern were Italy and the Soviet Union. Italy was deliberately left off the list of Axis powers that would have to surrender unconditionally. "The omission of Italy," Churchill cabled Attlee, was designed to "encourage a break-up there," a conclusion that the cabinet unanimously rejected. Urging, instead, that Italy be included, Attlee and Anthony Eden replied, "Knowledge of rough stuff coming to them is surely more likely to have the desired effect on Italian morale." The Soviet Union was fore-

---

[4]Robert E. Sherwood, *Roosevelt and Hopkins* (New York, 1950), p. 697. On its use in World War I, see Harry R. Rudin, *Armistice 1918* (New Haven, 1944), pp. 102–4, 123–24, 137–38, 173–78; and Earl S. Pomeroy, "Sentiment for a Strong Peace, 1917–1919," *South Atlantic Quarterly* 43 (October 1944): 325–37.

[5]Harley A. Notter, *Post-War Foreign Policy Preparation, 1939–1945* (Washington, D.C., 1949), p. 127. Cf. Herbert Feis, "Some Notes on Historical Record-Keeping, the Role of Historians, and the Influence of Historical Memories during the Era of the Second World War," in *The Historian and the Diplomat*, ed. Francis Loewenheim (New York, 1967), pp. 102–3.

[6]Sherwood, *Roosevelt and Hopkins*, p. 973n.

most in the Roosevelt's mind, according to his son, Elliott. The president saw unconditional surrender as a sop to Stalin, whose suspicions were likely to be aroused by the agreement at Casablanca to postpone opening a second front in Europe. "Of course, it's just the thing for the Russians," he told Churchill at the time. "They couldn't want anything better. Unconditional surrender. Uncle Joe might have made it up himself."[7] So unlimited a war aim would be difficult to achieve without help from the Soviet Union, offering Stalin some reassurance against any separate peace. But the omission of Italy might have proven less reassuring in Moscow.

In the end the joint communiqué from Casablanca made no mention of unconditional surrender. Instead, President Roosevelt used the words at a background briefing for the press following distribution of the communiqué. By speaking under rules prohibiting direct quotation or attribution of his remarks, Roosevelt may have sought to minimize his commitment to that objective, but he succeeded only in obscuring its meaning:

> Some of you Britishers know the old story—we had a general called U. S. Grant. His name was Ulysses Simpson Grant, but in my, and the Prime Minister's, early days he was called "Unconditional Surrender" Grant. The elimination of Germany, Japanese, and Italian war power means the unconditional surrender by Germany, Italy, and Japan. That means a reasonable assurance of future world peace. It does not mean the destruction of the population of Germany, Italy, or Japan, but it does mean the destruction of the philosophies in those countries which are based on conquest and the subjugation of other people.[8]

Back in Washington a week later, Roosevelt restated the point at another press conference, offering even fewer specifics and pretending he had merely been promulgating long-standing policy at Casablanca: "We formally reemphasized what we had been talking about before, and that is we don't think there should be any kind of negotiated armistice, for obvious reasons. There ought to be an unconditional surrender."[9] Reporters never asked what those "obvious reasons" were and Roosevelt did not elaborate.

---

[7]Elliott Roosevelt, *As He Saw It* (New York, 1956), p. 117, cf. p. 109. The younger Roosevelt assumes, however, that the phrase was a casual inspiration of the moment. On the president's discussion with the Joint Chiefs of Staff (JCS), Dwight D. Eisenhower, *Crusade in Europe* (Garden City, N.Y., 1948), p. 138; and Minutes, JCS Meeting, January 7, 1943, OPD, Exec. 10, item 45, National Archives. The president brought up the subject in the context of "giving impetus to the Russian morale."

[8]Roosevelt Presidential Press Conferences, no. 875, January 24, 1943 (Hyde Park, N.Y., Roosevelt Library, microfilm, 1957). His remarks were an interpolation of previously prepared notes, which he consulted during the briefing. Cf. Sherwood, *Roosevelt and Hopkins*, pp. 696–97; Samuel I. Rosenman, *Working with Roosevelt* (New York, 1952), pp. 370–71.

[9]Roosevelt Presidential Press Conferences, no. 876, February 2, 1945.

Ten days after his return from North Africa, the president hinted at factors closer to home that inhibited him from getting very specific about American war aims. In a dictated note sketching out ideas for an upcoming speech, Roosevelt referred to "a great many people" who were "demanding that I come back and tell them what the boundaries of France, or the Netherlands or China or Russia or any other place in the world are going to be after the war is won." He worried about divisive public discussion of this "iffy" question: "It is all right to think about it, but to rush into print and have an argument about it now" would only lead to "useless running up and down the field" and "getting people all excited about something that is not yet ripe."[10] Among the people most likely to get "all excited" about boundary settlements were many of the president's own partisans—Eastern European ethnic groups concentrated in the industrial North and Midwest, hitherto preponderantly Democratic but now growing restive, if not yet disaffected, over the prospect of Soviet domination of their former homelands.[11]

Roosevelt's desire to delay discussion of the postwar settlement cut against the grain of public sentiment: 59 percent of a nationwide sample polled in 1943 wanted the Allies to "start talking and preparing *now* for the kind of peace we want after the war," in preference to concentrating on "winning the war, letting peace plans wait."[12] Poll results notwithstanding, the issue was one on which the public could usually be prevailed upon to follow the president's lead. The opposition party, rather than challenge the president or risk alienating potential votes, took its cue from Roosevelt and adopted a posture of wait-and-see cloaked in militancy. The Republican National Committee's resolution on war aims declared, "We will recognize no peace with those enemies except peace with victory and we will never entertain any proposals of peace until such victory be won. There shall be no appeasement or compromise."[13]

---

[10]Rosenman, *Working with Roosevelt*, p. 373. For the speech, to the White House Correspondents' Association on February 12, see Samuel I. Rosenman, ed., *The Public Papers and Addresses of Franklin D. Roosevelt, 1943: The Tide Turns* (New York, 1950), pp. 71–81. Cf. Sumner Welles, *Where Are We Heading?* (New York, 1946), pp. 18–19; and James L. Chase, "Unconditional Surrender Reconsidered," *Political Science Quarterly* 70 (June 1955): 272–74.

[11]These partisan concerns occasionally found their way into diplomatic exchanges. When the British were about to grant recognition to three Baltic republics under Soviet control, for instance, State Department officials, anticipating public outcry, sought to head the British off (*FRUS*, 1942, III: *Europe*, pp. 538, 540). Cf. the exchange between Roosevelt and Stalin at Teheran, in *FRUS: The Conferences at Cairo and Teheran* (Washington, D.C., 1961), pp. 594–95.

[12]National Opinion Research Center poll of May 2, 1943, *Public Opinion Quarterly* 7 (Summer 1943): 334. An August 12 poll using a slightly different question got nearly the same response (ibid. [Winter 1943]: 760).

[13]Louise Holborn, ed., *War and Peace Aims of the United Nations* (Boston, 1943), I: 649; cf. November 16, 1942, speech by Wendell Willkie, p. 655. Cf. also the January 10, 1945, speech by Senator Arthur Vandenberg, whose Michigan constituency included many

The unconditional surrender formula could have served a more immediate domestic political purpose as well. Two months before the Casablanca Conference, during the invasion of North Africa, the United States had permitted Admiral Jean Darlan to assume command of Free French forces there—much to the dismay of American liberals who looked upon Darlan as a collaborator, if not an out-and-out fascist. According to Robert Sherwood, Roosevelt's invocation of unconditional surrender had to be seen in that context: "Undoubtedly his timing of the statement at Casablanca was attributed to the uproar over Darlan and Peyrouton and the liberal fears that this might indicate a willingness to make similar deals with a Goering in Germany or a Matsuoka in Japan."[14]

From its informal origins in the hyperbole of U.S. politics, unconditional surrender gradually became more than a propaganda slogan. Through frequent repetition, it became policy. And insofar as it became a rallying cry for the American people, that policy resisted change. Yet unconditional surrender remained open to a variety of interpretations. It could mean complete disarmament of enemy armed forces or transfer of control over those forces from the vanquished to the victors, dismantling of its war-making and industrial capacity or seizure of enemy war matériel as reparations, fundamental transformation of its political and social structure or modest changes in its political system after a purge of those leaders judged responsible for the war. Repeating the vague formula without spelling out its meaning may have postponed bickering over the spoils of war or the arrangements of peace, but it left Japan in the dark about the consequences of defeat. Imprecision could reinforce enemy intransigence and confound those in Tokyo trying to sue for peace.

No sooner had unconditional surrender been made public than the British and the Russians began questioning its propaganda value. At various times too, geopolitical rivalry moved them to press the Americans for a clearer statement of war aims.[15] Yet Roosevelt continued to resist any public disavowal of unconditional surrender.

The only other policy pronouncements to discuss Allied war aims did little to clarify the terms of a possible settlement with Japan. In the Atlantic Charter, issued before the United States was even at war, the Americans and the British forswore "aggrandizement, territorial or other," and pledged to "respect the right of all peoples to choose the form

---

Eastern European immigrants, in Arthur H. Vandenberg, Jr., and Joe Alex Morris, eds., *The Private Papers of Arthur Vandenberg* (Boston, 1952), pp. 132–38.

[14]Sherwood, *Roosevelt and Hopkins*, p. 697.

[15]Charles E. Bohlen, *Witness to History, 1929–1969* (New York, 1973), pp. 157–58; *FRUS*, 1942, III: 499–526, 530–33, 536–42, 558–62; *FRUS*, 1944, I: *General*, pp. 493–94, 501–2, 592; Cordell Hull, *The Memoirs of Cordell Hull* (New York, 1948), II: 1572–81.

of Government under which they will live."[16] Yet within the U.S. government doubts remained about whether this pledge extended to the Axis powers. In the Cairo Declaration the United States, Great Britain, and China spelled out the postwar disposition of territory in the Far East. Japan was to be "stripped" of all the islands in the Pacific it had seized or occupied since the beginning of World War I; all the territories "stolen from the Chinese, such as Manchuria, Formosa, and the Pescadores," would be restored to China; Korea would become independent "in due course"; and Japan would be "expelled from all other territories which she has taken by violence and greed."[17] The last phrase, which opened the way to Soviet claims dating back to the Russo-Japanese War, was somewhat in conflict with the implication of "no territorial aggrandizement" that the Japanese home islands would remain intact after the war. After the 1944 presidential election, the Allies agreed at Yalta to a more detailed postwar settlement, but the agreement was kept secret, in part to avoid arousing Americans of Eastern European descent. After Yalta, when Roosevelt might have considered backing away from unconditional surrender, he was in no condition to do so. Two months later he died.

Harry Truman's stand on unconditional surrender was resoundingly reinforced four days after he assumed the presidency, when he delivered his first address to Congress. "I was applauded frequently," he recalls, "and when I reaffirmed the policy of unconditional surrender, the chamber rose to its feet."[18] The reaction of Congress echoed public sentiment on the issue. Public opinion polls consistently registered the appeal of unconditional surrender. And whether it was due to resentment over Pearl Harbor or to racism, Americans bore much more of an animus toward Japan than toward Germany. Asked "Which country do you think we can get along better with after the war—Germany or Japan?" 67 percent said Germany and 8 percent said Japan.[19] Americans also regarded the Japanese as more likely to make war than the Germans.[20] American attitudes toward postwar treatment of the Japanese were correspondingly harsher too. Asked an open-ended question—"If you had your say, how would we treat the people who live in Germany

[16]U.S. Department of State, *Bulletin*, August 16, 1941, p. 125.

[17]Ibid., December 4, 1943, p. 393.

[18]Truman, *Year of Decisions*, p. 42.

[19]Gallup poll, June 10, 1943, *Public Opinion Quarterly* 7 (Fall 1943): 501. Indirect evidence that racism was a factor in Americans' attitudes comes from breaking down the sample along racial lines: for whites the responses were Germany 70 percent and Japan 7 percent; for blacks the responses were 30 percent and 22 percent, respectively.

[20]National Opinion Research Center (NORC) polls, ibid. (Winter 1943): 755–56; 8 (Fall 1944): 448; 9 (Spring 1945): 93; Harry H. Field and Louise M. Van Patten, "If the American People Made the Peace," ibid., 8 (Winter 1944–45): 509–12.

[or Japan] after the war?"—65 percent advocated leniency toward the German people, though not their leaders; 42 percent, wanted strict supervision of their economic and political life, including isolation, policing, and disarmament; and 8 percent preferred more punitive measures, including torture and even extermination. Toward the Japanese the replies were 40, 49, and 20 percent, respectively.[21] Most Americans felt that the emperor, in particular, should be punished: 33 percent of a national sample favored executing him; 17 percent wanted him put on trial; 11 percent preferred imprisonment; and 9 percent favored exile. By comparison, 4 percent wanted nothing done to the emperor, on grounds he was merely a figurehead, and only 3 percent wanted to use him as a puppet to run Japan after the war.[22]

Survey results suggest also that Americans were willing to bear the costs of an uncompromising stance on war aims. A June 1, 1945, poll posed the alternatives: "Japan may offer to surrender and call her soldiers home provided we agree not to send an army of occupation to her home islands. Do you think we should accept such a peace offer if we get the chance, or fight on until we have completely beaten her on the Japanese homeland?" Those favoring continued prosecution of the war outnumbered those preferring to accept the peace offer by a nine-to-one margin.[23]

In this political climate, anyone who tried to change America's war aims unilaterally had to undo an oft-stated policy that had overwhelming domestic political support, leaving himself open to attack from right and left. Even bringing the issue up for discussion inside the government was risky: opponents might leak word of it, arousing public antipathy and congressional consternation. But a slogan was not much of a policy. The closer the United States drew to victory, the less guidance unconditional surrender gave to officials who were planning for war's end. And insisting on such uncompromising terms might only delay that end.

---

[21]The percentages total more than 100 percent because some respondents offered more than one suggestion. On the treatment of the Germans, see NORC July 29, 1944, survey, ibid., 8 (Fall 1944): 449. On the treatment of the Japanese, see NORC December 10, 1944, poll, ibid., 9 (Spring 1945): 94. For comparable Gallup poll results on January 10, 1944, December 20, 1944, and August 22, 1945, see ibid., 8 (Spring 1944): 152; 8 (Winter 1944–45): 588; 9 (Fall 1945): 386.

[22]June 29, 1945, Gallup poll, ibid., 9 (Summer 1945): 246. Hadley Cantril, ed., *Public Opinion 1935–1946* (Princeton, N.J., 1951), p. 392, dates this survey May 29.

[23]To be precise, 84.1 percent to 9.5 percent, with 6.4 percent in in the "don't know" camp. *Fortune* poll, *Public Opinion Quarterly* 9 (Summer 1945): 249. A May 10, 1945 poll, commissioned by the *New York Herald Tribune* found 77 percent in favor of occupation by a United Nations force "for several years" and 10 percent opposed (Cantril, *Public Opinion,* p. 457).

GREW: USING THE EMPEROR TO CONTROL JAPAN

The official who took the lead in trying to moderate American war aims in hopes of arranging a settlement with Japan was Joseph C. Grew. In the late 1930s, as ambassador to Tokyo, he had tried in vain to bring about rapprochement between Japan and the United States. The attempt pitted Grew against Stanley Hornbeck and his fellow "China hands" in the State Department's Office of Far Eastern Affairs, who wanted the United States to denounce Japanese aggression in Manchuria and impose an oil embargo on Japan.[24]

For the State Department, an organization whose input and output consists largely of the spoken or written word, it was axiomatic that "policy is made in the cables." The routes that cable traffic took around the department demarcated its division of labor. Except for a few functional divisions to deal with congressional and public relations, the department was structured along geographic lines with country desks and regional offices. Cleavages formed along those geographic lines. Carrying out the department's missions abroad predisposed foreign service officers in embassies in the field and at country desks back in Washington to view the world from the perspective of the foreign government they dealt with. After all, effective representation of the United States abroad to some degree required them to represent their client states back home in the United States. Countering this tendency to "go native" was a traditional foreign service resistance to specialization. Rotation—short tours of duty and diversification of assignments—was designed to produce generalists imbued with a "broader view." A partial exception to that tradition was the Office of Far Eastern Affairs, the oldest of the State Department's geographic bureaus. Language barriers encouraged specialization among those posted to Japan, China, and the Soviet Union. With specialization inevitably came parochialism, arraying China specialists against Japan specialists.[25] Pearl Harbor put the "Japan-firsters" at a considerable disadvantage, both for having appeared "soft" on Japan before the war and because they had to report on their specialty at a distance after the break in diplomatic ties.

Geographic responsibilities defined interests and shaped perceptions of State Department officials. But the relatively circumscribed roles and missions that foreign service officers have defined as the department's organizational essence—representing American interests in foreign cap-

[24]Joseph C. Grew, *Turbulent Era: A Diplomatic Record of Forty Years, 1904–1945*, ed. Walter Johnson (Boston, 1952), II: 953–55; James C. Thomson, Jr., "The Role of the Department of State," in Borg and Okamoto, *Pearl Harbor as History*, pp. 81–106.
[25]Martin Weil, *A Pretty Good Club* (New York, 1978), pp. 213–17; "A New Far Eastern Policy?" (editorial), *Amerasia*, June 9, 1944, pp. 179–80.

itals, reporting, negotiating, and protecting American lives and property abroad—and the small claims that these activities made on the budget may have meant that organizational interests played somewhat less of a role in motivating officials at the State Department than they did, say, in the armed services. More generalized systems of belief or ideologies may have complemented organizational interests in motivating some American diplomats.

Joseph Grew was no dove in a flight of hawks, but he may have been more than a "Japan-firster." In some respects he was a forerunner of a generation of postwar policy-makers who conceived of the role of the United States in the world in global terms as the keeper of the balance of power or guarantor of a pax Americana. Like them, he envisioned the Soviet Union as America's arch-rival after the war. A memorandum Grew wrote on May 19, 1945, and circulated privately to the ambassador to Moscow, W. Averell Harriman, and Soviet specialist Charles E. Bohlen sets forth his vision of the postwar order. As "a war to end wars," Grew feared, World War II "will have been futile, for the result will be merely the transfer of totalitarian dictatorship and power from Germany and Japan to Soviet Russia, which will constitute in future as grave a danger to us as did the Axis." To Grew, Eastern Europe and the Far East formed a tapestry woven with but a single thread. That thread was Soviet hegemonic ambition: "Already Russia is showing us—in Poland, Rumania, Bulgaria, Hungary, Austria, Czechoslovakia, and Yugoslavia—the future world pattern that she envisions and will aim to create." With a "stranglehold" on these countries, the Soviet Union would "in the not too distant future be in a favorable position to expand her control, step by step, through Europe." The same pattern would recur in the Far East: "Once Russia is in the war against Japan, then Mongolia, Manchuria, and Korea will gradually slip into Russia's orbit, to be followed in due course by China and eventually Japan." In a yet inchoate way, however, Grew believed that Japan rather than China might serve as an anti-Soviet bastion in the Far East. In Grew's mind, "A future war with Soviet Russia is as certain as anything in this world can be certain. It may come within a very few years." It was therefore essential to maintain the fighting strength of the United States and to shore up relations with "the free world." As soon as the San Francisco conference completed drafting the United Nations charter, he urged, "our policy toward Soviet Russia should immediately stiffen, all along the line."[26] The stark vision was that of a model Cold Warrior. Precisely where the Japan specialist's preoccupations ended and ideology took over is difficult to discern, but both shaped Grew's stand on war termination in the Pacific.

[26]Grew, *Turbulent Era*, II: 1445–46.

If Japan was to fulfill Grew's hopes after the war, the occupation of its home islands would be of critical importance. A year earlier, just before he took charge of the Office of Far Eastern Affairs, Grew had set out his thoughts on the occupation in a memorandum to Secretary of State Hull. "Two fundamental desiderata" informed his vision: "(1) to render Japan incapable of ever in future threatening the peace" and "(2) to establish order in Japan with the least possible delay and with the least possible foreign personnel." In attaining these ends, he argued, "The enlistment of the cooperation of Japanese civil leadership will be of prime importance if we are to avoid the necessity of maintaining for a long period a vast military and civil army of occupation." Using Japanese functionaries would also avoid any need for America's allies to contribute forces to the occupying army. His conclusion, Grew knew, was controversial, and he backed into it gingerly: "In considering the question of available Japanese civil leadership, the potential use of the institution of the Throne immediately presents itself." He urged that no irreversible decision be made about the emperor's future. He rested his case on the principle of self-determination and the need for order: "Unless the Japanese themselves wish to abolish the institution of the Throne on the ground that it has failed to achieve victory and has therefore let them down—an unlikely contingency, I think—it would seem to be common sense on our part to preserve and support any nucleus in Japan which may serve as a rallying point for the preservation and maintenance of order as opposed to the preservation and maintenance of the military cult." Having tried to distinguish between eradicating militarism and abolishing the throne, Grew did not insist that Hirohito himself remain in power: "It is the institution rather than the individual that is important."[27]

Aware that his proposal would attract few votes, Grew could only appeal for statesmanship: "In our democracy, Government must constantly listen to public opinion, but sometimes it is wise, in the best interests of our country, to lead rather than follow public opinion when that opinion is uninformed as to facts." Yet Grew himself was not yet prepared to breast the public tide. His views soon leaked, and by December 1944, under questioning at his confirmation hearing to be Under Secretary of State, he trimmed them ever so slightly: "I have never held and have never stated that the Japanese Emperor should be retained after the war, nor have I ever held or stated that the Japanese Emperor should be eliminated after the war." All he wanted, he testified, was to leave the matter "fluid" until "we get to Tokyo" and "can size up the situation." In the event that "the Emperor remains as the sole stabilizing force," he added, "I would not wish to have ourselves committed to a course which

[27]Ibid., pp. 1413–14.

[98]

might conceivably fix on us the burden of maintaining and controlling for an indefinite period a disintegrating community of 70,000,000 people."[28]

Grew's stand, linked as it was to his ideological distrust of the Soviet Union, inclined him to concede Japan's right to retain the emperor if that would obviate the need for Soviet entry into the war and Soviet involvement in the occupation. It also predisposed him to propose terms that were more conciliatory than unconditional surrender if that would settle the war without invasion of Japan's home islands and foster postwar rapprochement between the United States and Japan.

Retaining the emperor could serve various purposes: a bargaining chip to concede in inducing Japan to end the war, a source of traditional authority to invoke in getting Japan's compliance with orders to surrender, or an administrative convenience for managing the occupation. So too a commitment to the emperor could take various forms. It might entail a public pledge to maintain the imperial institution, the current line of succession, or Hirohito personally, or to leave the choice of their own form of government up to the Japanese people, consistent with the oft-proclaimed right of self-determination. Alternatively, it might entail an internal decision not to say anything that would preclude retention of the emperor: at a minimum it meant not condemning Hirohito as a war criminal before the war was over; beyond that, it could mean having the emperor authorize the instrument of surrender and remain on the throne to legitimate the occupation. Grew's intent, which can be inferred from his actions and statements, was to delay any irreversible decision to eliminate the emperor, at least for the moment. Over time, in the expectation that priorities within the government would shift toward bringing the war to a close and arranging the surrender and occupation of Japan, he hoped to use the emperor as a means toward those ends, using a public commitment to preserve the throne as a concession to achieve a settlement of the war, then using the throne to arrange the surrender and occupation and ultimately to promote Japan's reconciliation with the United States.

About the time that Grew was first sketching his picture of postwar relations in the Pacific, planning was beginning on arrangements for a cease-fire and occupation. His protégés' membership on the Interdivisional Area Committee for the Far East (IDACFE), the State Department planning team, and his own accession to the directorship of the Office of Far Eastern Affairs, replacing Stanley Hornbeck, ensured that Grew would guide postwar planning within the State Department. The committee, in response to questions put to it by the War and Navy departments, prepared a set of memoranda elaborating, in greater detail than

[28]Ibid., pp. 1417, 1419.

Grew had, the political and economic policies to be applied to Japan. Of critical concern to military planners was the duration of the occupation. In a May 4, 1944, memorandum, the committee underscored its principal recommendation that *"a prolonged occupation of Japan should be avoided."*[29] If American policy were premised on a short occupation, then Grew's preference for using the emperor as an administrative convenience followed.

In a subsequent memorandum, the committee ventured the prediction that "an attempt from the outside to abolish the institution of the Emperor" would "probably be ineffective" so long as the Japanese people persisted in their "almost fanatical devotion to their sovereign." It went on to warn that preventing a "revival" of that institution might require "indefinite occupation of Japan." Without the emperor, moreover, Japan would be harder to control. "Japanese functionaries," the committee argued, "consider the throne as the source of authority to hold office. Therefore, if the emperor is deprived of his rights of sovereignty, it might be well that a substantial group of Japanese officials would feel that their country had lost its independence and that it would be impossible for them to serve under foreign masters."[30]

The committee sought to portray itself as steering a middle course between extremes of eliminating the emperor altogether and restoring him to full sovereignty. It proposed keeping the emperor in protective custody and allowing him to conduct only those functions "which relate to the delegation of administrative duties to subordinate officials," with the proviso that if this did not "facilitate the use of Japanese personnel" the commander of the occupation forces might then "suspend" all the emperor's functions. At the same time the committee insisted on desanctifying the throne by having the occupation forces "refrain from any action which would imply recognition of or support for the Japanese concept that the Japanese emperor is different from and superior to other temporal rulers, that he is of divine origin and capacities, that he is sacrosanct or that he is indispensable."

The State Department replies were couched in terms that would appeal to the army planners posing the questions. Those planners were anticipating the day the army would take charge of the occupation. That

[29]IDACFE, "Japan: Occupation: Duration," Memorandum to the War and Navy departments, May 4, 1944, in *FRUS*, 1944, V: *The Near East, South Africa, The Far East*, p. 1218 (emphasis in the original).

[30]IDACFE, "Japan: Relation of Emperor to Military Government," Memorandum to the Navy and War departments, May 9, 1944, in *FRUS*, 1944, V: 1250–51. Other studies in the government supported this conclusion, such as one done in the Foreign Morale Analysis Division of the OWI: Alexander H. Leighton and Morris E. Opler, "Psychiatry and Applied Anthropology in Psychological Warfare against Japan," *American Journal of Psychoanalysis*, 6 (1946): 22, 25.

was not a responsibility that it was eager to assume. A prolonged occupation would divert resources from its essential mission—ground combat with firepower and mobility. Carrying out that mission required maintaining peacetime strength adequate to fight a war on the ground in Europe. Already the armed services were anticipating pressure for reconversion to peaceful pursuits. By V-E Day, a member of the Joint Chiefs of Staff recalls, "We recognized that the big cry would now be, 'Bring the boys home! The war is over!'"[31] That cry would grow ever more insistent as V-J Day neared. Of the three armed services, the army, with substantial manpower requirements, was most vulnerable to this insistence.

Yet supplementing American occupation forces with Allied troops was not an acceptable alternative. If the army had to run the occupation, it intended to do so on its own. It resisted any infringements on its autonomy, whether they came from London or Moscow or Foggy Bottom. This organizational interest in autonomy inspired its reaction to a State Department position paper on the Allies' role in the occupation in March 1944 well before it had had any experience with joint occupation in Germany. Consistent with Article 2 of the Moscow Declaration stipulating that the Four Powers "will act together in all matters relating to the surrender and disarmament of the enemy," State Department planners argued that the command and composition of the occupation forces "would call for joint rather than unilateral decision, thus underscoring the possibility of occupation by combined forces." Citing the advantages of sharing the burdens of occupying Japan—in particular, of including "Asiatic units" in the occupying force—the State Department called for Allied "representation," though not a representation so large that it would "prejudice the dominantly American character" of that force. It also proposed establishment of a military council to advise the American commander of the force. The council's role was likened to that of "staff officers to a commanding officer," with neither the authority to overrule him nor the responsibility for executing his commands.[32] The army rebuffed the proposal as an encroachment on its autonomy. A Joint Staff counterproposal for a Far Eastern Advisory Commission to serve as a forum for U.S. "consultation" with its Allies and to be based in Washington, far removed from Japan, eventually became the position of the United States.[33]

---

[31] Henry H. Arnold, *Global Mission* (New York, 1949), p. 560.

[32] IDACFE, "Japan: The Composition of Forces to Occupy the Far East," Memorandum to the Navy and War departments, March 13, 1944, in *FRUS, 1944*, V: 1203.

[33] *FRUS, Conference of Berlin*, I: 394. For a succinct characterization of the commission in action, see Edwin O. Reischauer, *The United States and Japan* (Cambridge, Mass., 1950), pp. 47–49.

The State Department proposal to use the emperor as an instrument for the surrender and occupation of Japan appealed to army interests. Sparing the emperor held out the possibility of eliciting Japanese compliance, permitting the army to run the occupation on its own without substantial manpower or Allied interference. Yet, to judge from the level at which this issue was being handled in the army, the occupation remained of secondary importance throughout the spring of 1945. Of paramount concern was its fight with the navy and the air force over the choice of strategy for ending the war.

Grew, however, had much more in mind than just using the emperor to facilitate Japanese compliance with surrender and occupation. He wanted to concede the continued existence of the emperor as a means of expediting war termination without having to invade the home islands. That put him in direct conflict with the army, which was stalling any proposal to spare the emperor.

MILITARY PLANS AND THE EMPEROR

Unconditional surrender may have been just political hyperbole to some civilians in the U.S. government, but it constituted marching orders for the armed services. At successive Anglo-American conferences since Casablanca, whenever the Combined Chiefs of Staff laid out their "Overall Strategic Concept for the Prosecution of the War" they had always stipulated as an objective "Upon the defeat of the Axis in Europe, in cooperation with other Pacific Powers and, if possible with Russia, to direct the full resources of the United States and Great Britain to bring about at the earliest possible date the unconditional surrender of Japan."[34] This strategic objective had priority over all others whenever the armed services sought to justify their strategies, programs and plans.

The army, the army air forces, and the navy each had its own strategy for ending the war. The army preferred to invade Japan's home islands. For that invasion to succeed, it deemed Soviet intervention against Japan essential in order to tie down Japanese forces in Manchuria and prevent them from reinforcing garrisons in Japan proper. The navy, in contrast, believed the optimum strategy was a naval blockade of Japan, along with aerial bombardment. The army air forces favored strategic bombing of Japan's cities with conventional ordnance. Unlike the army's strategy, neither the air force's strategy nor the navy's required Soviet entry into the war, but neither could hold out much promise for achiev-

[34]Ehrman, *Grand Strategy*, p. 279.

ing "at the earliest possible date the unconditional surrender of Japan." The atomic bomb did not play a major role in any of the services' strategies. Few military men knew of its impending development, and those who had learned of it informally could not discuss it in official forums, so planning for final operations against Japan proceeded as if the Manhattan Project did not exist.

In preparation for the Big Three summit meeting at Yalta, the Joint Chiefs of Staff (JCS) had reached agreement in January 1945 on a plan for terminating the war. It was a masterpiece of interservice logrolling:

a. Following the Okinawa operation to seize additional positions in order to intensify the blockade and air bombardment of Japan in order to create a situation favorable to:
b. An assault on Kyushu for the purpose of . . . further intensifying the blockade and air bombardment in order to establish a tactical condition favorable to:
c. The decisive invasion of the industrial heart of Japan through the Tokyo Plain. [35]

The navy and the air force could accept the plan's characterization of the invasion of the industrial heart of Japan because it would be "decisive" only if their own strategies had not brought about Japan's surrender in the meantime. The agreed paper also left open two other navy-backed options. "Planning," it said, "will be continued for an operation to seize a position in the Chusan-Ningpo area," which would postpone the army's invasion of Kyushu. An "examination" was also "being conducted of the necessity for and cost of operations to maintain and defend a sea route to the Sea of Okhotsk" by securing bases in the Kuriles for the Navy, though these operations were regarded as a "remote" possibility because they would drain away resources from more essential missions. By not foreclosing any of the services' preferred strategies, the agreement permitted proceeding with preparation and implementation of all of them— at least until the president made his preference known.

Yet if the army's invasion was to remain a viable option, its prerequisite, Soviet entry into the war, had to be secured at Yalta. Joint Staff planners addressed this need in the days before the summit. At issue was not Soviet entry per se, but its timing. "Russia's interests in the Far East and in postwar world politics will undoubtedly force her entry into the war against Japan," the planners reasoned, but not until American advances in the Pacific had brought the United States to the verge of

---

[35]"Operations for the Defeat of Japan," Memorandum by the U.S. Chiefs of Staff, CCS 417/11, January 22, 1945, in FRUS, The Conferences at Malta and Yalta, 1945, (Washington, D.C., 1955), p. 395.

"speedy and conclusive defeat of Japan," or "Soviet strength in Siberia is sufficient to offer prospects of success in operations against the Kwantung army." If the Russians could be induced to launch an offensive in Manchuria "at least three months prior to our invasion of Kyushu," it might prove "decisive." In the planners' judgment, American logistical and operational support would constitute a "significant" inducement to the Russians. "We desire Russian entry at the earliest possible date consistent with her ability to engage in offensive operations," the planners concluded, "and are prepared to offer the maximum support possible without prejudice to our main effort against Japan." Consistent with the army's interest in autonomy, the role assigned to the Soviet Union was a supporting one, precluding its direct participation in the invasion of the home islands and hence in the postwar occupation of Japan: "We consider the mission of Soviet Far Western Forces should be to conduct an all-out offensive against Manchuria to contain Japanese forces in North China and Manchuria that might otherwise be employed in the defense of Japan; to conduct, in conjunction with U.S. strategic air forces based in Siberia, intensive air operations against Japan proper; and to interdict lines of communication between Japan and the mainland of Asia."[36] In so specifying the purposes of Soviet involvement, the planners tried to satisfy the army's requirements for invasion without prejudice to the preferred strategies of the navy and the army air forces.

If the objective of bringing about the unconditional surrender of Japan at the earliest possible date seemed unattainable without invading Japan's home islands, and if Soviet intervention was a prerequisite for that invasion, then those who preferred a different military strategy for ending the war would have to propose a less demanding objective and question the need for that ally. They were not long in doing so. One who made the link between softening war aims and the navy's preferred strategy was the military adviser to the president, Admiral William D. Leahy, who was "unable to see any justification" for invading "an already thoroughly defeated Japan." He recalls, "I feared that the cost would be enormous in both lives and treasure. It was my opinion at the time that a surrender could be arranged with terms acceptable to Japan that would make fully satisfactory provisions for America's defense against any future trans-Pacific aggression."[37]

[36]"Russian Participation in the War against Japan," January 18, 1945, JCS 1176/6, in ibid., p. 392, and JCS 1176, November 23, 1944, in U.S. Department of Defense, *The Entry of the Soviet Union into the War against Japan: Military Plans, 1941–1945* (Washington, D.C., September 1955, mimeographed), pp. 39–41. Rephrasing the Soviet role in the January revision was a concession to the army's rivals. Cf. Forrestal's note on a February 28, 1945, conversation with General MacArthur, in Millis, *Forrestal Diaries*, p. 31.

[37]William D. Leahy, *I Was There: The Personal Story of the Chief of Staff to Presidents Roosevelt and Truman Based on His Notes and Diaries Made at the Time* (New York, 1950), pp. 384–85.

In continuing to oppose the army's strategy, the navy came to regard surrender on terms as a desirable alternative to unconditional surrender and ultimately to see a pledge to spare the emperor as an appropriate concession for arranging a settlement of the war. Among the first to reach that conclusion was Ellis M. Zacharias, a captain in the Office of Naval Intelligence and a protégé of Chief of Naval Operations Admiral Ernest J. King. Zacharias had served in Tokyo before the war and was later assigned to an ONI section engaged in psychological warfare operations that bore the cover name "OP-16-W." On March 19 Zacharias briefed Navy Secretary James Forrestal on "a strategic plan to effect the occupation of Japan," which essentially combined the navy's strategy of blockade and bombardment with a psychological warfare campaign designed to divide and discredit the Japanese high command and induce Japan to surrender before the army could invade. The plan was premised on intelligence reports dating back to December 1944 that the ONI interpreted as indicating the coalescence of a peace party within the Japanese government around disgruntled navy leaders. Zacharias conceived of a series of broadcasts introducing himself as "an official spokesman of the United States Government" and addressing Japan's leaders by name in an intimate and factual manner. An accompanying briefing paper detailing these tactics made Zacharias' purpose clear in its opening sentence: "To make unnecessary an opposed landing in the Japanese main islands, by weakening the will of the High Command, by effecting cessation of hostilities, and by bringing about unconditional surrender with the least possible loss of life to us consistent with early termination of the war." Yet unconditional surrender took on new meaning as Zacharias intended to redefine it over the course of his broadcasts. It meant nothing more than the "complete cessation of hostilities and yielding of arms." At the same time, he intended to reconstrue American war aims in an accommodative direction. Citing the treatment meted out to territories already occupied, he would "emphasize with authority what we will *not* do, but avoid any specific commitments as to what we *will* do, in order to combat present Japanese atrocity predictions."[38] Zacharias won approval from Forrestal and King. When the army's assent was not forthcoming, Zacharias succeeded in circumventing the Joint Chiefs of Staff and getting a go-ahead directly from the White House. His first broadcast was aired on May 8.

The other weak link in the army's strategy of invasion was its reliance on timely Soviet intervention. Just as prospects for that intervention

---

[38]Ellis M. Zacharias, *Secret Missions: The Story of an Intelligence Officer* (New York, 1946), pp. 335–36, 342–48, 360 (emphasis in the original). Cf. Zacharias, "The A-Bomb Was Not Needed," p. 26.

were improving, some U.S. officials began questioning its value. On April 8 the Soviet Union formally announced its intention not to renew its nonaggression pact with Japan. On April 16 Major General John R. Deane, chief of the American military mission in Moscow, cast doubt on the need for Siberian airfields to conduct bombing raids on Japan. Back in Washington for consultations, Deane presented a study prepared by his planning staff showing that the bombing could be done more cost-effectively from bases on the islands recently captured in the Pacific.[39] Without the Siberian bases, the air force no longer had any organizational interest in Soviet entry.

A more imminent threat to the army's strategy was the increasingly vocal disaffection with the Soviet Union around Washington. It reached a crescendo over an issue that had potentially serious repercussions in American domestic politics—Soviet insistence on seating its client, the Lublin government, as the Polish delegation to the San Francisco conference to charter the United Nations. On the afternoon of April 23 President Truman hastily convened a group of advisers to consider what he should tell Soviet Foreign Minister Molotov at a scheduled meeting that evening. In attendance were the service secretaries, Stimson and Forrestal; Leahy, King, Marshall, and Deane from the armed services; and Stettinius, Dunn, Harriman, and Bohlen from the State Department. It was a group predisposed to take a harder line, and it did. The consensus, according to Leahy, was "that the time had arrived to take a strong American attitude toward the Soviet Union and that no particular harm could be done to our war prospects if Russia should slow down or even stop its war effort in Europe and Asia."[40]

That was understandably a navy conviction, but two officials present did not share it, the two with the greatest organizational interest in assuring Soviet intervention—Secretary of War Stimson and Army Chief of Staff George C. Marshall. Both counseled caution. In President Truman's recollection, Stimson thought it "important to find out what the Russians were driving at." They may have caused "a good deal of trouble on minor military matters," in some cases making it necessary "to teach them manners," but on matters of major military concern "the Soviet government had kept its word and the military authorities of the United States had come to count on it." Gauging Truman's reaction,

---

[39]"Revision of Policy with Relation to Russia," April 16, 1945, JCS 1313/1, in U.S. Department of Defense, *Entry of the Soviet Union*, pp. 60–61. Cf. John R. Deane, *The Strange Alliance* (New York, 1947), pp. 262–63.

[40]Leahy, *I Was There*, p. 351. The group was perhaps reinforced in its toughness by its impression that Truman had already made up his mind to stand firm (Leahy diary, April 23, 1945); Martin J. Sherwin, *A World Destroyed: The Atomic Bomb and the Grand Alliance* (New York, 1975), p. 157.

Stimson recorded in his diary: "He was evidently disappointed at my caution and advice and passed along the circle coming to Forrestal." Much to Stimson's dismay, Navy Secretary Forrestal "became a yes-man." Insisting that "this difficulty over Poland could not be treated as an isolated incident," Forrestal argued, "If the Russians were to be rigid in their attitude we had better have a showdown with them now rather than later." Stimson notes that "nobody backed me up until it came round to Marshall," who shared his concern that a falling out with the Soviet Union might put the army's invasion plans in jeopardy:

> General Marshall said he was not familiar with the political aspects of the Polish issues. He said that from the military point of view the situation in Europe was secure but that we hoped for Soviet participation in the war against Japan at a time when it would be useful to us. The Russians had it within their power to delay their entry into the Far Eastern war until we had done all the dirty work. He was inclined to agree with Mr. Stimson that the possibility of a break with Russia was very serious. [41]

Navy and State Department officials nevertheless carried the day. While no ultimatum, the note that Truman handed Molotov did state bluntly the American reading of the Yalta agreement provisions on Poland. The effect that a harder line would have on army strategy did not go unappreciated in the navy. On May 11 Admiral King's chief of staff told Forrestal that "the necessity for Russia's early participation was very much lessened as a result of recent events, although the Army he didn't think shared that view." He was seconded by the deputy chief of naval operations, who went on to hint at the need for a change in war aims in the Pacific: "The best thing for us would be if the Japanese would agree to a basis of unconditional surrender which still left them in their own minds some face and honor." [42]

Support for invasion by the army was predicated on the belief that it alone could compel unconditional surrender. Now that the prerequisite for that strategy—Soviet intervention—had come under open challenge, it was time for opponents of the invasion to question the meaning if not the value of unconditional surrender as well. It had to be done delicately and obliquely, lest it leak and set off a public backlash—and just how delicately and obliquely was previewed in lower-level planning in preparation for a presidential decision on military strategy. An April 25 Joint Staff report, ostensibly proposing invasion, presented more clearly than ever the rationale for blockade and bombing, leaving invasion as a last

---

[41]Truman, *Year of Decisions*, pp. 77–79; Stimson diary, April 23, 1945.
[42]Vice-Admirals Charles M. Cooke, Jr., and Richard S. Edwards, paraphrased in Millis, *Forrestal Diaries*, p. 55.

resort. The report traced the development of Allied strategy from the Cairo Conference in December 1943, when the Combined Chiefs of Staff (CCS) had agreed "to invade Japan proper if this should prove to be necessary," to the second Quebec Conference ten months later, which endorsed "invading and seizing objectives in the industrial heart of Japan" to be preceded by efforts at "establishing a sea and air blockade, conducting intensive air bombardment, and destroying Japanese air and naval strength." The shift toward a strategy of invasion, the planners noted, reflected a "conviction" reinforced by military doctrine then prevalent that "invasion is a prerequisite to forcing the unconditional surrender of Japan." The political requirement to achieve that objective at the earliest possible date further strengthened the grounds for invasion: "While it may be possible to defeat Japan by sustained aerial bombardment and the destruction of her sea and air forces, this would probably involve an unacceptable delay." The planners then turned from the past to the present: "Discussion has continued as to whether or not a strategy of blockade and bombardment will not by itself bring about unconditional surrender." It was a curious way to introduce a report reaffirming the need for invasion, but the very next sentence made it clear that the authors' purpose was not quite that. The "phases" in the strategy endorsed at Quebec, they argued, "constitute one continuous campaign of a series of operations and should be considered as such."[43] In other words, the strategy of blockade and bombardment would be tried before the strategy of invasion. Rather than casting the navy and the air force in a supporting role to the army, the phased campaign could be interpreted as pursuing their alternative strategy for winning the war, blurring differences among the services.

The report then questioned whether unconditional surrender was attainable "by any means" whatsoever: "What can be accomplished is decisive military defeat *and the results equivalent to unconditional surrender*, similar to the present situation in Germany." Before taking the ultimate step of invading Japan, the planners proposed issuing "at the governmental level" a "declaration of intentions" to tell the Japanese "what their future holds." Without ever saying it in so many words, the planners hinted at a settlement on terms: "The concept of 'unconditional surrender' is foreign to the Japanese nature. Therefore, 'unconditional surrender' should be defined in terms understandable to the Japanese, who must be convinced that destruction or national suicide is not implied." Again, to define is to limit.

Having stated the case for blockade and bombardment, the report

---

[43]"Pacific Strategy," Report by the Joint Staff Planners, April 24, 1945, JCS 924/15, in U.S. Department of Defense, *Entry of the Soviet Union*, pp. 62–67 (emphasis added).

then reaffirmed the strategy of invasion as "the most suitable" to accomplish unconditional surrender. It did so on the grounds that the alternative—blockade and bombardment—"is a strategy of limited aim and may bring about a negotiated peace falling short of complete fulfillment of our war aims." And it noted an incompatibility between the two strategies when it came to ending the war as quickly as possible: "Should encirclement fail to bring about capitulation, it would then be difficult, costly, and time-consuming to disengage forces to mount [an] invasion."

In yet another shift the planners concluded that Soviet intervention was no longer a prerequisite for invasion: "Because of our estimated ability to interdict Japanese movement between the Asiatic mainland and Japan proper, early Russian entry into the war against Japan and attendant containing of the Kwantung army is no longer necessary to make the invasion feasible." Indeed, it could prove to be a diversion from the primary task: inasmuch as the Soviet Union had not as yet subscribed to the principles of the Cairo Declaration eschewing territorial aggrandizement, an attack by Soviet forces on Manchuria would "raise the question of introducing at least token U.S. forces into China."

Upon reviewing the report, the navy dissented on just one point, but perhaps the most vulnerable point in the army strategy from the president's political perspective—the casualty estimate. When the chief of naval operations, Admiral King, eventually did sign on, he insisted on formally registering his objection in a footnote to the report. It was the opening shot in the battle over U.S. military strategy in the Pacific. On May 10 the Joint Chiefs of Staff officially noted the report, making it the basis for future planning. [44]

A final decision on Pacific strategy had to await presidential consideration. In the meantime, opposition to invasion focused on the price of Soviet participation. The next occasion at which the question arose at senior levels was a May 1 meeting of the Committee of Three, the secretaries of state, war, and navy. During that meeting Forrestal suggested a need to reexamine political objectives in the Far East. He raised four questions that indicated he was thinking along the same lines as Grew about the possibility of a negotiated settlement that would obviate the need for invasion:

1. How far and how thoroughly do we want to beat Japan? In other words, do we want to morgenthau those islands—do we want to destroy the whole industrial potential?
2. Do we want to contemplate their readmission to the society of nations after demilitarization?

[44]Memorandum for Joint Chiefs of Staff by Chief of Naval Operations, May 2, 1945, JCS 924/15, Secretaries' Note, May 10, 1945.

3. What is our policy on Russian influence in the Far East? Do we desire a counterweight to that influence? And should it be China or should it be Japan?

4. Have we given careful thought to the question of how far this country will go toward the complete defeat of Japan—the quick, costly assault versus a long drawn-out siege? I said that it was conceivable to me that the people [who] desired a quick victory might turn out to be the appeasers in the case of Japan.[45]

Picking up where Forrestal left off, Grew addressed three questions to the service secretaries in a May 12 memorandum, formally reopening the issue of Soviet participation in the war against Japan:

1. Is the entry of the Soviet Union into the Pacific war at the earliest possible moment of such vital interest to the United States as to preclude any attempt by the United States Government to obtain Soviet agreement to certain desirable political objectives in the Far East prior to such entry?

2. Should the Yalta decision in regard to Soviet political desires in the Far East be reconsidered or carried into effect in whole or in part?

3. Should a Soviet demand, if made, for participation in the military occupation of the Japanese home islands be granted or would such occupation adversely affect our long term policy for the future treatment of Japan?[46]

"These questions cut very deep," Secretary of War Stimson noted in his diary on May 13, and were "powerfully connected with our success on S-1," code name for the atomic bomb. Stimson's reaction suggests that he already entertained private doubts of his own about the wisdom of invasion and the price of Soviet involvement. If the atomic bomb worked, it might avert both. Yet the next day he confided to Assistant Secretary of War John McCloy that it was premature to address Grew's questions. Now was not the time "to get into unnecessary quarrels" with the Soviet Union or "to indicate any weakness by talking too much"; it was time to "let our actions speak for themselves." The United States "really held all the cards"—a "royal flush" Stimson called it—because the Soviet Union could not "get along without our help and industries and we have coming into action a weapon which will be unique."[47] Organizational

[45]Millis, *Forrestal Diaries*, p. 52.

[46]Memorandum for Secretaries of War and Navy from Acting Secretary of State Joseph C. Grew, May 12, 1945, in U.S. Department of Defense,*Entry of the Soviet Union*, p. 69. Cf. Grew, *Turbulent Era*, II: 1456.

[47]Stimson diary, May 13–14, 1945. Cf. Richard C. Hewlett and Oscar E. Anderson, Jr., *The New World, 1939–1945*, vol. 1 of *A History of the United States Atomic Energy Commission* (University Park, Pa., 1962), p. 350. Stimson's remarks to Forrestal and Grew the next day, recorded in his diary, make clear his preoccupation with Manchuria and North China, not

interests cautioned against overplaying that hand for the moment. Soviet control of Manchuria and North China might have seemed an exorbitant price to pay for Soviet assistance against Japan, but that result might come about regardless of what the United States calculated or did, short of intervening militarily itself. Moreover, the army's invasion plans, yet to be approved by the president, were still contingent on timely Soviet assistance, and Stimson did not want to jeopardize that approval by calling into question the Soviet role. The next day Stimson called in McCloy and Army Chief of Staff Marshall to discuss Navy opposition to the army's strategy—"a slight difference of opinion" he called it. Marshall felt "we must go ahead" with the invasion, Stimson recorded in his diary, "and I think he is right." Yet time could ease Stimson's predicament: "Fortunately the actual invasion will not take place until after my secret is out." To Stimson, "the Japanese campaign involves therefore two great uncertainties: first, whether Russia will come in, though we think that will be all right; and second, when and how the S-1 will resolve itself."[48] Marshall remained convinced that, with or without the atomic bomb, the army would have to invade Japan in order to compel unconditional surrender at the earliest possible date. Stimson may have had higher hopes for the bomb, but should those hopes fail to materialize—and the bomb was still months away from a test—he thought it prudent to back Marshall in seeking the president's approval to prepare for the army's invasion. That meant doing nothing to discourage timely Soviet entry, while consoling himself with the thought that the atomic bomb might end the war before the Russians penetrated very far into Manchuria.

In reply to Grew's questions, the War Department tried to downplay the costs of Soviet involvement. The Soviet Union would go to war with Japan of its own accord anyway, without the need for further concessions: "Political inducements will not in fact affect the Russian decision as to when, if ever, she will enter the war." Nor had the United States paid any price for Soviet entry, since any concessions in the Far East made at Yalta were "within the military power of Russia to obtain regardless of U.S. action short of war." An exception was the Kuriles, sought by the navy as a base, but forestalling Soviet advances there would require a diversion of U.S. forces from the campaign against Japan proper. The department sidestepped the issue of a Soviet role in

Eastern Europe, in discussing the price to be paid for Soviet intervention. That is why he worried out loud to them about the timing of the Potsdam Conference. The visit of Chiang Kai-shek's foreign minister to Washington to urge the president to order an attack on Japan's forces in China may have evoked this concern.

[48]Stimson diary, May 15, 1945.

the occupation of Japan: "The discussion of this subject does not appear necessary at this time."[49]

As the war in Europe was drawing to a close, the fight over strategy in Asia was heating up. Grew's proposal to modify war aims in order to reach an accommodation with Japan before invasion and Soviet intervention became necessary had gained adherents in the navy, whose strategy for ending the war seemed inadequate to achieve unconditional surrender very soon. Yet America's war aim remained what it was seventeen months earlier. On May 8 the White House issued a statement marking Germany's surrender and reasserting that aim without much qualification: "Our blows will not cease until the Japanese military and naval forces lay down their arms in *unconditional surrender*." Amplifying what by now had become formulaic, the statement continued: "It means the termination of the influence of the military leaders who have brought Japan to the present brink of disaster."[50]

Mr. Grew Goes to the White House

Having mustered support in the navy for moderating war aims, Acting Secretary of State Grew now had to contend with the open opposition within his own department. While fighting rearguard skirmishes there, he maneuvered for direct entrée to the Oval Office. Taking advantage of his position as acting secretary of state while the secretary, Edward Stettinius, was tied up at the San Francisco conference, and assisted by White House Special Counsel Samuel Rosenman, he got an appointment with the president on May 28.

At the State Department's daily staff meeting that morning, Grew tried to leave his colleagues with the impression that the initiative for spelling out American war aims had come from the armed services, protesting that he "was not proposing any modification of the unconditional surrender terms," but he did acknowledge that he favored retaining the emperor. At that point the two department officials most concerned with domestic politics objected. Archibald MacLeish, a poet and liberal who was serving as assistant secretary of state for public and cultural affairs, warned of "a very unfavorable public reaction" to any reinterpretation of unconditional surrender. Dean Acheson, assistant secretary for congressional relations, seconded MacLeish, warning of "a

[49]Memorandum to Grew from the War Department, May 21, 1945, in U.S. Department of Defense, *Entry of the Soviet Union*, p. 71. Cf. Grew, *Turbulent Era*, II: 1458–59.

[50]White House press release, U.S. Department of State, *Bulletin*, May 13, 1945, p. 886 (emphasis in the original).

strong public and congressional reaction against any proposal for retaining the Emperor."[51]

Grew saw Truman later that day. In discussions with military planners he had couched his argument for preserving the throne in terms of coping with the postwar occupation; now he recast his brief to emphasize the need to overcome Japanese reluctance to end the war by sparing both the throne and its present occupant:

> The greatest obstacle to unconditional surrender by the Japanese is their belief that this would entail the destruction or permanent removal of the Emperor and the institution of the Throne. If some indication can now be given the Japanese that they themselves, when once thoroughly defeated and rendered impotent to wage war in the future, will be permitted to determine their own future political structure, they will be afforded a method of saving face without which surrender will be highly unlikely.[52]

He evoked the firebombing of Tokyo two days earlier in an effort to impart a sense of urgency about a public pledge on the future of the emperor: "The psychological impact of such a statement at this particular moment would be very great." Issuing the statement in the immediate aftermath of the Tokyo raid might also reduce the political fallout at home. Anticipating objections, Grew pointed out that the emperor was not the source of militarism in Japanese society, but a potential antidote against its postwar recrudescence: "Once the military extremists have been discredited through defeat, the Emperor, purely a symbol, can and possibly will be used by new leaders who will be expected to emerge once the Japanese people are convinced that their military leaders have let them down."

Grew then handed Truman a rough draft of a statement to be inserted into his Memorial Day message to Congress. Prepared at Grew's instruction by Eugene H. Dooman, a foreign service officer who had served in Tokyo under Grew and now chaired the subcommittee on Japan of the State-War-Navy Coordinating Committee (SWNCC), the statement was the first attempt to formulate what would eventually become the Potsdam Declaration. Its tone was peremptory: "The full application of our military power backed by our resolve *will* mean the inevitable and com-

---

[51]Minutes of the Secretary's Staff Committee, 100th meeting, May 28, 1945, in State Department Staff Committee Files, Records of the Intra- and Inter-Departmental Committees, RG 353, National Archives. Acheson and MacLeish pursued their opposition when Grew read the draft statement to the group. Grew tried to meet their objections by producing a memorandum from the Office of Far Eastern Affairs purporting to detect a "marked let-down in public sentiment for prosecution of the war as indicated by correspondence received."

[52]Grew, Memorandum of Conversation, May 28, 1945, in *FRUS*, 1945, VI: 545–46.

plete destruction of the Japanese armed forces and just as inevitably the utter devastation of the Japanese homeland." An enumeration of the terms of surrender followed. As previously stated in the Cairo Declaration, Japan's sovereignty would be confined to Honshu, Hokkaido, Kyushu, Shikoku, and such minor islands as the Allies determined. Japan would not be "morgenthaued," as Forrestal had put it, but would be "permitted to maintain such industries as are determined to offer no potential for war but which can produce a sustaining economy." The statement demanded elimination of "the authority and influence of those who have deceived and misled the people of Japan into embarking on world conquest," but it carefully refrained from including Emperor Hirohito among them. Instead it called for establishment of "a peacefully inclined, responsible government of a character representative of the Japanese people" and specifically added: "This may include a constitutional monarchy under the present dynasty if the peace-loving nations can be convinced of the genuine determination of such a government to follow policies of peace which will render impossible the future development of aggressive militarism in Japan." Japanese territory would be occupied "to the extent necessary to secure the achievement of the basic objectives" set forth in the statement. Calling upon Japan "to proclaim the unconditional surrender of all the Japanese armed forces," it concluded: "The alternative for Japan is prompt and utter destruction."[53] Into a formal demand for unconditional surrender, Dooman had managed to weave terms that Japan might find acceptable, in particular, an explicit commitment to spare the emperor.

"The President," reports Grew, "said that he was interested in what I said because his own thoughts had been following the same line." Yet Truman also recognized a bureaucratic end-run when he saw one and was not about to act without hearing from other senior officials concerned. He asked Grew to arrange a meeting of the service secretaries and the chiefs of staff to discuss the statement and report back to him.[54]

Grew wasted no time scheduling a meeting of the Committee of Three for the next day. Unlike SWNCC, use of this ad hoc forum permitted Grew to circumvent formal action channels within the State Department, where opposition to his proposal might resurface. Grew opened the session by reading the draft statement. Stimson endorsed it in principle, but questioned the timing of its release. Marshall seconded him. The statement tended to undermine the army case for invasion, though Stim-

[53]Grew, *Turbulent Era*, II: 1432–34. Dooman provides details of the statement's origin in Giovannitti and Freed, *Decision to Drop the Bomb*, pp. 92–93.

[54]Grew, Memorandum of Conversation, May 28, 1945, in *FRUS*, 1945, VI: 547. Cf. Grew, *Turbulent Era*, II: 1434.

son says he had another reason for delay: "It was an awkward meeting because there were people present," Grew among them, that kept him from discussing "the real feature which would govern the situation, namely S-1."[55] Conciliatory gestures to Japan, if needed, might prove more acceptable both in Tokyo and in Washington against a backdrop of threats of atomic bombing. Various accounts of the meeting make it clear that other participants were even more reluctant to compromise on the future of the throne. Elmer Davis, director of the Office of War Information (OWI) and hence responsible for maintaining morale on the home front, objected strenuously to any redefinition of war aims that might be construed as the basis for a negotiated settlement. Forrestal, while supporting Stimson's request for a delay, asked whether it would suffice to reassure the Japanese that unconditional surrender applied only to Japan's military forces and "that we do not propose to destroy Japan as a nation." No, replied Dooman, "if the Japanese become imbued with the idea that the United States was set on the destruction of their philosophy of government and of their religion we would be faced with a truly national suicidal defense."[56]

Grew reported the discussion to Truman that afternoon. He had failed. The president's Memorial Day message contained no hint of a compromise on war aims. It threatened Japan with "the kind of ruin which they have seen come to Germany" if it did not surrender promptly and unconditionally.[57]

That same day evidence arrived from Moscow that Japan was attempting to open talks. Harry Hopkins, in the Soviet Union to lay the groundwork for the Potsdam Conference, sent home two cables that provided some inkling of Stalin's thoughts about ending the war. The first reported that "the Soviet Army will be properly deployed on the Manchuria positions by August 8th"—the firmest indication yet of Soviet preparedness for timely intervention. Soviet willingness, however, "depended on the willingness of China to agree to the Yalta proposals" recognizing Soviet claims in Manchuria. The second cable described Stalin as "very anxious" to have Japan on the agenda at Potsdam. His anxiety, he seemed to suggest, stemmed from suspicions of a separate peace. "Certain elements in Japan," he told Hopkins, "are putting out peace feelers." That made it imperative for the Allies to "act in concert about the surrender of Japan." Stalin then came to the point: his desire

[55]Stimson diary, May 29, 1945. Later, writes Grew, he thought the military consideration alluded to was a reference to the battle on Okinawa then raging. It was not. See Grew, *Turbulent Era*, II: 1424.

[56]Millis, *Forrestal Diaries*, p. 66; Grew, Memorandum of Conversation, in *FRUS*, 1945, VI: 548.

[57]U.S. Department of State, *Bulletin*, June 3, 1945, p. 1006.

for a Soviet zone of occupation in Japan. "The Marshal," reported Hopkins, "expects that Russia will share in the actual occupation of Japan and wants an agreement with the British and us as to occupational zones." Stalin's statement of war aims was designed to increase Soviet chances of occupying Japan. He expressed a preference for unconditional surrender, even though he felt Japan would not capitulate. And should the Allies "be prepared to accept a modified surrender, Stalin visualized imposing our will through our occupying forces and thereby gaining substantially the same results" as unconditional surrender.[58] That would require an occupation force much larger than the army envisioned and prepared to remain in Japan far longer than it believed the American public would tolerate. Had any U.S. officials still not been cognizant of the relationships among military strategy, Soviet intervention, postwar control of Japan, and American war aims, Stalin was making the connections for them.

A Soviet share in the occupation was just what Grew wanted to avoid. On June 16 he tried again to get Truman to alter American war aims before the Big Three met at Potsdam. In so doing he may have exceeded his authority. A position paper from the Joint Chiefs of Staff suggesting that Japan might try to sue for peace on terms prompted Secretary of State Stettinius to ask Grew to explore the possibility of coupling a demand for unconditional surrender "with some assurances to Japan regarding [its] future." He was quite explicit about timing: "I think we should give careful thought to placing the matter on the agenda of the Big Three meeting."[59] Yet Grew had no intention of postponing the matter that long; he wanted to include a softening of terms in the statement marking American capture of Okinawa. Aware of Stalin's expressed preference for a fight to the finish with Japan, and anticipating an impending presidential decision on military strategy, Grew tried to turn these circumstances to his tactical advantage. Through White House Special Counsel Rosenman he forwarded a draft statement to the president for release as soon as Okinawa fell. He offered two reasons for his timing. First, he wanted to avoid associating the Soviet Union in any way with the victory over Japan: "As we are bearing the brunt of the war in the Pacific, I am not convinced that there is any good reason to defer such action until the meeting of the Big Three" at Potsdam. Second, mindful of the heavy toll that the battle for Okinawa had taken, Grew asserted that "the very large casualties which we are likely to suffer during assault operations in Japan might create a state of mind in the United States

---

[58]Hopkins cables to the president, May 29 and 30, 1945, in U.S. Department of Defense, *Entry of the Soviet Union*, pp. 72–74. Cf. Assistant Secretary of State Charles E. Bohlen, Memorandum of Conversation, May 28, 1945, in *FRUS: Conference of Berlin*, I: 41–45.

[59]Cable from Secretary of State to Acting Secretary, June 15, 1945, in *FRUS: Conference of Berlin*, I: 173.

which would be wholly unreceptive to a public statement of the character now proposed."[60] It was an argument calculated to appeal to a president uneasy about going ahead with the army's invasion.

Yet Truman remained unmoved. Grew arranged for an appointment on the morning of June 18 in hopes of having his draft statement tabled at the president's meeting with the Joint Chiefs of Staff that afternoon to resolve the question of military strategy. He proposed a commitment on the part of the United States not "to deprive the Japanese of a reasonable peacetime economy" and restated the pledge to preserve the throne in a way that made it seem implicit in the Atlantic Charter principle of self-determination: "Once we have rendered the Japanese incapable of again building up a military machine and once they have convinced us of their intention to fulfill their international obligations and to cooperate for the furthering of common peace and security, the Japanese will then be permitted to determine for themselves the nature of their future political structure."[61] The new formulation may have sought to still Truman's unease about the potential domestic reaction, but it did so at some sacrifice of clarity on the emperor's future status.

"While he liked the idea," Truman told Grew, "he had decided to hold this up until it could be discussed at the Big Three meeting." Grew made one last appeal: "I wanted to see every appropriate step taken which might encourage a peace movement in Japan and while it was all guess-work as to whether such a statement would have that effect I neverthe-less felt very strongly that something might be gained and nothing could be lost by such a step and in my opinion the sooner it was taken the better."[62] It was all to no avail. Truman asked Grew to have the subject placed on the Big Three agenda at Potsdam. It never made it to that agenda.

Stimson Drafts an Ultimatum

Four variants of a diplomatic approach were gradually crystallizing in the American policy process. Each had quite a different message for a putative peace faction inside Japan. Grew's approach was one of concili-ation: unilaterally modifying American war aims to accommodate Japan in an attempt to arrange a compromise peace. Essential to his approach was an explicit commitment to preserve the throne. Grew conceived of

---

[60]Grew memorandum to Rosenman, June 16, 1945, in Grew, *Turbulent Era*, II: 1435.

[61]Ibid. In making the case for the acceptability of this wording, Grew compared it to that of a New Year's Day message by Chiang Kai-shek, which is excerpted in Holborn, *War and Peace Aims*, II: 333–35.

[62]Grew, Memorandum of Conversation, June 18, 1945, in *FRUS: Conference of Berlin*, I: 177–78.

his approach as an alternative to applying increased military pressure in order to force Japan's capitulation. A different approach, slowly forming in Secretary of War Stimson's mind, was an ultimatum, offering some assurances to Japan, perhaps including an explicit commitment on the emperor, issued in hopes of compelling Japan to surrender by enumerating the threats it faced, in advance of carrying out those threats. The other two were propaganda ploys, one aimed at the Japanese people with the intent of undermining their morale by warning them in general terms of impending death and destruction but without any specifics, and another aimed at world opinion to show the good faith of the United States by offering Japan a chance to quit before clobbering it.

At his June 18 meeting with the Joint Chiefs of Staff, Truman gave his approval to army plans to invade Kyushu, westernmost of Japan's home islands, and to prepare for a subsequent invasion of Honshu and the Tokyo Plain. Only after the president's decision did Stimson feel free to consider alternative options for ending the war. As the Potsdam Conference approached, he picked up Grew's strategy of inducement and turned it into an ultimatum.

Preparations for the showdown on strategy had preoccupied the service secretaries and the chiefs of staff since late May. After the May 29 meeting with Grew that reopened the question of unconditional surrender, Stimson asked Marshall to have the Operations Planning Division (OPD) look into the prospects for a Japanese suit for peace and the possible effect on those prospects of publicly spelling out American terms. The OPD's two reports were designed to fend off attacks on the army's case for invasion. The first assessed the timing of Japan's acceptance of America's terms as "unpredictable." It papered over the distinction Grew had tried to draw between Japanese and German determination to prosecute the war: "Like the Germans, their protracted resistance is based upon the hope of achieving conditional surrender." It then cast doubt on chances of ending the war without applying the army's strategy: "Probably it will take Russian entry into the war, coupled with a landing, or imminent threat of landing, on Japan proper by us to convince them of the hopelessness of their position." The second report saw "definite merit" in a public statement "giving definition to 'unconditional surrender,'" but more for preinvasion psychological warfare than as a serious impetus to a preinvasion settlement: "We must make certain our military operations and preparations continue with undiminished pressure, even though we bring increasing political and psychological pressure on the Japanese to persuade them to capitulate."[63]

[63]U.S. Department of War, OPD, Draft Memoranda for Secretary of War, June 4 and 15, 1945, in Ray S. Cline, *Washington Command Post: The Operations Division*, vol. 2 of U.S. Department of the Army, Office of the Chief of Military History, *U.S. Army in World War II*, Series I: The War Department (Washington, D.C., 1951), pp. 344–45.

Soviet participation and potentially high casualties remained the weak points of the army's strategy. To bolster the first, Army Chief of Staff Marshall had taken the precaution of soliciting the views of his field commander, General Douglas MacArthur. Just in case MacArthur missed the point of his inquiry, Marshall jotted a note in the margin: "Russia's entry into the war would be a prerequisite to a landing in the Japanese homeland in December."[64] MacArthur hardly needed the reminder. He had already made his views abundantly clear to OPD planners in February in time for the Yalta Conference. Now he revised his earlier assessment for the sake of form: "The hazard and loss will be greatly lessened if an attack is launched from Siberia sufficiently ahead of our target date to commit the enemy to major combat."[65]

Okinawa, not quite secure after eleven weeks of intense combat that claimed over 12,000 American lives and inflicted a 35 percent casualty rate on the invading forces, had brought home to Truman the second weak point in the army's strategy. He aired his concern to Admiral Leahy on June 14. "It is his intention," Leahy alerted the chiefs of staff, "to make his decisions on the campaign with the purpose of economizing to the maximum extent possible the loss of American lives." This new expression of presidential concern prompted another message from Marshall to MacArthur inquiring whether MacArthur still held to his projection of 50,800 casualties in the first thirty days of a landing on Kyushu. Casualty estimates can serve a variety of purposes for anyone in MacArthur's position. High estimates justify an increase in reserves or a call for a change of strategy, while low estimates reassure political authorities to proceed as planned. Again, MacArthur did not disappoint his chief. He replied that the casualty estimate was "purely academic and routine," made for planning purposes, and had not come to his attention until now. He did "not anticipate such a high rate of loss." He then offered a terse defense of the army's strategy in terms of Truman's criterion: "I believe that the operation presents less hazards of excessive loss than any other that has been suggested and that its decisive effect will eventually save lives by eliminating wasteful operations of a nondecisive character."[66] Marshall passed along MacArthur's brief in his opening argument to Truman on June 18.

The Joint Chiefs of Staff presented just one option for presidential consideration. After two days of internal deliberations, June 14–15, they

---

[64]Feis, *Atomic Bomb*, p. 13.

[65]MacArthur to Marshall, Enclosure 2, Meeting of June 18, 1945, CCS 334, JCS 2-2-45, Records of the JCS, RG 218, National Archives.

[66]Ibid. In his June 18 presentation to the president, Marshall omitted the first part of MacArthur's message, which traced the origins of the 50,800 estimate. Cf. Memorandum from Leahy to JCS, June 14, 1945, in U.S. Department of Defense, *Entry of the Soviet Union*, p. 76; and Informal Memorandum from Marshall to General George A. Lincoln, May 8, 1945, in ibid., p. 51.

had managed to iron out a compromise on strategy in a way that did not foreclose winning the war either by blockade and bombardment or by invasion. They did so by dropping one phase of the navy's strategy, a landing on the China coast, and agreeing to the first step of the army's strategy, a landing on Kyushu, but they scrupulously avoided prejudging its ultimate step, invading Honshu and the Tokyo Plain. Because Kyushu could serve as a platform for continuing to blockade and bomb the rest of Japan, if Japan were to surrender well after the seizure of Kyushu but before a landing on Honshu, the navy and the army air forces could still claim that they had administered the coup de grace.

In their presentations to Truman, the chiefs of staff all stressed Kyushu's compatibility with either strategy: "The Kyushu operation," Marshall told the president, "is essential to a strategy of strangulation," not just the first phase of the Army's strategy of invasion. Admiral King agreed. So did General Ira C. Eaker, sitting in for Air Force Chief of Staff H. H. Arnold. The army made one other concession to navy sensibilities: it dropped its opposition to command arrangements made in April that avoided having navy forces serve under General MacArthur while acting in a supporting role during the invasion. Instead of a unified command, Admiral Chester Nimitz would command the American forces at sea, and MacArthur would command those on land. As King later described the deal, he "did not like the idea" of invading Kyushu at all, "but as unanimous decisions were necessary in the Joint Chiefs' meetings," he "reluctantly acquiesced, feeling that in the end sea power would accomplish the defeat of Japan, as proved to be the case."[67] Unanimity among the chiefs of staff was protection against civilian interference with service autonomy.

The Joint Chiefs maintained a united front throughout the June 18 proceedings with only momentary lapses. When the military adviser to the president, Admiral Leahy, raised the sore point of casualties, Chief of Naval Operations King was quick to side with the army, distinguishing Okinawa, a frontal assault against a highly fortified position, from Kyushu, where "landings would be made on three fronts simultaneously and there would be much more room for maneuver." Near the close of the meeting, however, when Truman asserted that one of his objectives at Potsdam "would be to get from Russia all the assistance in the war that was possible," King could no longer contain himself. "Regardless of the desirability of the Russians' entering the war," he wanted

[67]Minutes of the JCS Meeting with the President, June 18, 1945, CCS 334, JCS 2-2-45, Records of the JCS, RG 218, National Archives, excerpted in *FRUS: The Conference of Berlin,* I: 903–11; Ernest J. King and Walter Muir Whitehead, *Fleet Admiral King* (New York, 1952), p. 598. Cf. Leahy, *I Was There,* p. 383. Arnold sent a cable on the need for airfields on Kyushu (Arnold, *Global Mission,* pp. 566–67).

to emphasize that "they were not indispensable and that he did not think we should go so far as to beg them to come in. While the cost of defeating Japan would be greater, there was no question in his mind but that we could handle it alone," a point he felt "should greatly strengthen the President's hand" at Potsdam. What King did not bother to say was that having to go it alone would strengthen the navy's hand in realizing its own preferred strategy.

Faced with ostensible unanimity among his military advisers, Truman approved the services' plan to invade Kyushu and withheld any commitment to invading Honshu beyond going ahead with preparations: "We could do this operation and then make [a] decision as to the final action later," he said. Then he expressed hopes of "preventing an Okinawa from one end of Japan to the other."

Also on hand at the meeting were Forrestal, Stimson, and McCloy—a break with Roosevelt's practice of excluding civilians from his strategy sessions with the chiefs of staff. As the minutes of the meeting record, the presence of civilians significantly altered the agenda, if not the outcome. Stimson sounded one of the few discordant notes. While he saw "no other choice" but to approve the operations agreed to by the armed services, Stimson "still hoped for some fruitful accomplishment through other means to bring about surrender." He was thinking of a mass uprising in Japan rather than striking a deal or dropping the atomic bomb: he spoke of trying to "arouse" what he referred to as a "large submerged class in Japan who do not favor the present war and whose full opinion and influence had never yet been felt," but who would "fight tenaciously" in the event of an invasion by the United States. Admiral Leahy took advantage of the opening to question American war aims: "He feared no menace from Japan in the foreseeable future, even if we were unsuccessful in forcing unconditional surrender. What he did fear was that our insistence on unconditional surrender would result only in making the Japanese desperate and thereby increase our casualty lists." Truman, making clear his own reluctance to take so politically exposed a position, demurred: "It was with that thought in mind that he had left the door open for Congress to take appropriate action with reference to unconditional surrender. However, he did not feel that he could take any action at this time to change public opinion on this matter."[68]

As the meeting was about to break up, Truman asked for McCloy's opinion. McCloy responded that before the United States made a final

[68]Minutes of the JCS Meeting with the President, June 18, 1945, CCS 334, JCS 2–2–45, Records of the JCS, RG 218, National Archives. An entry for the date in Leahy's diary (Library of Congress) shows that he, unlike Stimson, did have a negotiated settlement in mind.

decision to invade or to drop the atomic bomb, it should undertake a political offensive. His reference to the bomb startled listeners, who had never before heard that subject broached at that large a gathering. McCloy recommended telling the Japanese "that they would be permitted to retain the Emperor and a form of government of their own choosing" but "that we had another and terrifyingly destructive weapon which we would have to use if they did not surrender."[69]

With Stimson's and McCloy's interventions, Grew's diplomatic initiative took on a new aspect. What had been, in Grew's mind, a proclamation restating American war aims in hopes of inducing a negotiated settlement of the war now became in Stimson's and Truman's minds a preinvasion ultimatum. On June 19, the day after the president had deferred a decision on Grew's proposal and approved a landing on Kyushu, the Committee of Three reopened its consideration of a public proclamation of war aims. It was Grew's impression that Truman was opposed to any change in war aims, but Stimson disagreed. The president, he insisted, was just opposed to Grew's timing. Yet Stimson's idea of appropriate timing indicates that his own differences with Grew ran deeper. "My only fixed date," he confided in his diary on June 19, "is the last chance warning, which must be given before an actual landing of the ground forces on Japan, and fortunately the plans provide for enough time to bring in the sanctions to our warning in the shape of heavy ordinary bombing and an attack of S-1."[70] In a conversation just after the meeting, Marshall reminded Stimson of another sanction to be added to his warning—Soviet entry into the war. That afternoon Stimson began drafting a memorandum to Truman on the warning.

When the Committee of Three reconvened a week later, Stimson read the memorandum to his colleagues. They agreed that such a warning should precede the invasion. Someone suggested Potsdam as an appropriate place to issue the statement. McCloy's minutes put the case for a warning cautiously, noting "general agreement" that even though it "might not achieve the capitulation desired, it might do so, and it was thought no harm would result from trying." In any event, doing so would have some propaganda value: "It might very well consolidate opinion for an out-and-out struggle if the Japanese did not respond and it might check in the U.S. a deterioration of will to complete the defeat of

---

[69]Forrestal recorded McCloy's recollection in a diary entry for May 8, 1947 (Millis, *Forrestal Diaries*, pp. 70–71). Cf. John J. McCloy, *The Challenge to American Foreign Policy* (Cambridge, Mass., 1953), p. 42; Strauss, *Men and Decisions*, p. 193; and Hewlett and Anderson, *The New World*, p. 364. McCloy's recollection is the sole source for his remark. That the minutes would have omitted McCloy's remarks is understandable in view of their wide circulation, but Forrestal's inability to recall his and Stimson's presence seems difficult to explain, unless McCloy spoke as they were leaving the room at meeting's end.

[70]Stimson diary, June 19, 1945.

Japan, as it would make clear the necessity for fullest efforts if the Japanese did not accede."[71] Grew had not carried his colleagues. Far from endorsing his program for a negotiated settlement, the minutes reflect agreement on an ultimatum that coupled a restatement of terms with an enumeration of impending threats against Japan. The job of drafting was left to a subcommittee of subordinates.

That the proclamation now emerging resembled an ultimatum can be seen from another point of reference. On June 27 Under Secretary of the Navy Ralph Bard, who represented his department on the Interim Committee, proposed negotiating directly with the enemy—something even Grew had been loath to mention. A peace move, Bard argued, consistent with navy strategy, could be made before using the atomic bomb or invading. After the Potsdam Conference "emissaries from this country could contact representatives from Japan somewhere on the China coast and make representations with regard to Russia's position and at the same time give them some information regarding the proposed use of atomic power, together with whatever assurances the President might care to make with regard to the Emperor of Japan and the treatment of the Japanese nation following unconditional surrender." In the belief that "the Japanese Government may be searching for some opportunity which they could use as a medium of surrender," Bard argued, his plan "presents the opportunity which the Japanese are looking for."[72]

Having secured the army's interest in invasion, at least for the moment, the War Department was now freer to consider a change in war aims. And as army planners increasingly turned their attention to the modalities of surrender and occupation, their stake in preserving the emperor correspondingly gained in priority. That stake was reflected in the briefing book that the OPD prepared for Potsdam. How could the army maintain its autonomy in the face of Soviet demands for a share in the occupation and mounting public pressure to bring the boys home? The response of War Department planners was to spell out "as completely as possible the detailed U.S. war aims" in hopes of getting Japan to surrender. That would not only permit an "enormous reduction in the cost of the war," but would also "give us a better chance to settle the affairs of the Western Pacific before too many of our allies are committed there and have made substantial contributions toward the defeat of Japan." Having acknowledged that Soviet assistance had a price, the planners were now prepared

---

[71]Committee of Three, Minutes of June 26, 1945 Meeting, in *FRUS: Conference of Berlin*, I: 888; Stimson diary, June 26, 1945; Millis, *Forrestal Diaries*, pp. 71–72; Memorandum from Colonel Charles H. Bonesteel of OPD to General George A. Lincoln, June 27, 1945, ABC 387, Japan 15–2–45, Section 1B, RG 165, National Archives.

[72]Memorandum on the Use of S-1 Bomb, June 27, 1945, in Strauss, *Men and Decisions*, p. 192.

to avoid paying it, if possible—and by scrapping unconditional surrender if necessary: "The present stand of the War Department is that Japanese surrender is just possible and attractive enough to the U.S. to justify us in making any concession which might be attractive to the Japanese, so long as our realistic aims for peace in the Pacific are not adversely affected."[73] In keeping with the department's change of heart, its representatives on the drafting subcommittee insisted on including a specific reference to sparing the emperor over the objections of State Department representatives, who voiced concern about criticism on the home front.[74]

On July 2 Stimson sent his "Proposed Program to Japan" to the White House on July 2, four days before Truman was scheduled to leave for Potsdam. Although it incorporated many of the features in Grew's program, it had quite a different thrust overall. A landing on Japan's home islands, Stimson argued, would "cast the die of last ditch resistance" and involve the United States in a struggle "more bitter" than the one against Germany. What the country needed was an "alternative to such forceful occupation of Japan which will secure us the equivalent of an unconditional surrender of her forces." His solution was an ultimatum, "a warning of what is to come and definite opportunity to capitulate." The warning would spell out "the varied and overwhelming character of the force we are about to bring to bear on the islands." Again and again he adverted to this point: "Success of course will depend on the potency of the warning we will give her." The memorandum itself was silent on the atomic bomb, but Stimson's letter of transmittal noted that the proclamation "would have to be revamped to conform to the efficacy of such a weapon if the warning were to be delivered, as would almost certainly be the case, in conjunction with its use." Properly timing its release was also critical. The warning had to precede the invasion by a long enough interval "to permit a national reaction to set in," yet come at a point when "the impending destruction, though clear beyond peradventure, had not yet reduced her to fanatical despair." Soviet entry was a key factor in the timing: "If Russia is part of the threat, the Russian attack, if actual, must not have progressed too far."[75]

The draft proclamation contained most of the inducements first enumerated by Grew. It also borrowed from Grew's earlier formulation explicitly permitting retention of the throne: "The occupying forces of

[73]U.S. Department of War, OPD, "Compilation of Subjects for Possible Discussion at Terminal," Tabs 39 and 62, Item 21, Exec. 5, RG 165, National Archives, excerpted in Cline, *Washington Command Post*, pp. 345–46.

[74]McCloy memorandum to Stimson accompanying his revision of the OPD's draft proclamation, June 29, 1945, ABC 387, Japan 15-2-45, RG 165, National Archives. Cf. Lincoln memorandum to Hull, "Demand for Japanese Surrender," June 29, 1945, which exaggerates Dooman's opposition.

[75]Stimson letter of transmittal and enclosure 1, Memorandum to the President, "Proposed Program for Japan," July 2, 1945, in FRUS: *The Conference of Berlin*, I: 890, 892.

the Allies shall be withdrawn from Japan as soon as our objectives are accomplished and there has been established beyond doubt a peacefully inclined, responsible government of a character representative of the Japanese people. This may include a constitutional monarchy under the present dynasty if it be shown to the complete satisfaction of the world that such a government will never again aspire to aggression." Yet the tough tone that the proclamation maintained throughout was better suited to selling its terms to Americans than to the Japanese. Threatening Japan with "utter devastation," it presented its offer as a nonnegotiable demand: "Following are our terms. We will not deviate from them. They may be accepted or not. There are no alternatives."[76] That Stimson intended the proclamation to be an ultimatum is further indicated by the June 26 entry in his diary, in which he contemplates warning Japan "after she has been sufficiently pounded, possibly with S-1."[77] But even as a take-it-or-leave-it proposition, Stimson's proclamation included the throne for the taking.

By transmitting the draft directly to the Oval Office, Stimson was able to circumvent the State Department, where those opposed to sparing the emperor might have a chance to air their dissent and delay transmittal— or worse yet, make the dispute public by leaking it. As he notes in his accompanying letter, Stimson had discussed the draft with "representatives of the State Department and the Navy Department, as well as with officers of the General Staff," but it had not been "placed in final form or in any sense approved as a final document by the Secretary of State or the Secretary of the Navy or the Joint Chiefs of Staff." In short, it lacked formal clearance. That especially applied to its most sensitive point, which he made on his own authority: "I personally think that if in saying this we should add that we do not exclude a constitutional monarchy under her present dynasty, it would add substantially to the chances of acceptance." Yet shortcutting clearance procedures to place the draft in Truman's hands before he left for Potsdam gave Stimson only a temporary advantage. Ultimately he and Grew were left in a poor tactical position to advance their cause, back home in Washington, as Truman sailed for Potsdam in the company of his new secretary of state, James F. Byrnes.

FEELING THE PINCH OF DOMESTIC POLITICS

As U.S. officials turned their attention from mapping military strategy to drawing up arrangements for surrender and occupation, the utility of

---

[76]Enclosure 2, "Proclamation by the Heads of State," in ibid., p. 894.
[77]Stimson diary, June 26, 1945.

the emperor loomed larger in their thoughts, just as Grew had anticipated. Yet expectations of a domestic political reaction loomed even larger, reinforcing the resistance of those who opposed any public commitment to preserving the throne.

Public antagonism to the emperor was a blend of hawkishness and liberalism. To hawks, "remember Pearl Harbor" was more than a rallying cry; it was a policy. To liberals, "all kings is rapscallions" was not just the folk wisdom of Huck Finn; it was an article of faith. To officials responsible for gauging popular and congressional sentiment from the mail, the polls, and their own sampling of press and Capitol Hill sentiment, a public restatement of war aims may have been a possible way out of the war, but it was certain trouble at home. The clearer the pledge to preserve the throne, the more convincing it might be to Japan, but the more certain it was to generate heat at home. It was a predicament sure to make the boldest of politicians hesitate.

Within the State Department the two assistant secretaries whose responsibilities impinged most directly on domestic politics, Dean Acheson and Archibald MacLeish, took the lead in opposing any reinterpretation of unconditional surrender. They put up daily resistance to Grew in the secretary's staff meeting.[78] Acheson would later characterize his role as congressional liaison as that of "an oracle who prophesied what Congress would or would not tolerate." The department had to heed him, "particularly if the oracle could do anything to effectuate his prophecies." Acheson's prophecy in this instance was that the draft declaration "would lead us into a trap both at home and in Japan."[79] He and his allies could also do something to effectuate it: disclosing the draft would arouse intense opposition from at least a substantial minority in Congress, both in the president's party and out, well placed to assure a public hearing.

MacLeish, assistant secretary for public and cultural affairs, had a prophecy of his own. A majority of the American people, he asserted, would resent any inconsistency between eradicating "the dominant and characteristic institutions of German life" and leaving the Japanese throne in place. On July 6, alerted that a new draft declaration was being prepared, MacLeish took his case to Secretary of State Byrnes. He questioned the attempt to depict the draft as a "clarification" of war aims. "Surrender *on terms*, even irreducible terms, is not unconditional surrender," he insisted. Framing the issue in a way most appropriate to his

[78]E.g., discussion of "Post-Defeat Policy Relating to Japan," Minutes of Secretary's Staff Committee, 124th meeting, June 26, 1945, State Department Staff Committee's Files, Records of the Inter- and Intra-Departmental Committees, RG 363, National Archives.
[79]Dean Acheson, *Present at the Creation: My Years in the State Department* (New York, 1969), pp. 89, 113.

own jurisdiction—public and cultural affairs—MacLeish denied "raising the question whether we should accept the irreducible Japanese terms" and said he was only asking "whether, if we do, we should not state explicitly what we are doing." If the previously announced policy of unconditional surrender was being changed, "the American people have a right to know it." By his own reading of public opinion, that would preclude any change. Then he came to the crux of the army's concern—"that only the emperor can surrender." While that was "a powerful argument for the immediate future," he conceded, it had to be "balanced against the longer-range consideration that however useful the emperor may be to us now, he may be a source of the greatest danger a generation from now." To liberals who believed that Japan's aggressiveness was rooted in its national character and tradition, it followed that extirpating that aggressiveness required no less than a fundamental transformation of Japanese social and political institutions. He urged that any decision be deferred, but that if there were to be changes in war aims "we should say so in words which no one in the United States will misunderstand."[80] Timing his initiative artfully, MacLeish got the memorandum to Byrnes on the day of the secretary's departure for Potsdam.

With his senior aides so bitterly at odds that no unified departmental stand seemed conceivable, Byrnes was relatively unconstrained by organizational interests. That was not so for domestic politics. This was impressed upon him when he tapped sources of advice outside routine channels. Just prior to leaving for Potsdam, he telephoned a fellow Southern politician who had preceded him as secretary of state, Cordell Hull. After reading Stimson's draft statement over the telephone, Byrnes asked Hull what he thought of it, particularly the passage about the emperor. To Hull, who had personally received Japan's declaration of war shortly after the attack on Pearl Harbor, it seemed "too much like appeasement." Its wording "seemed to guarantee continuance not only of the Emperor but also of the feudal privileges of a ruling caste under the Emperor." He recalls telling Byrnes that "the Emperor and the ruling class must be stripped of all extraordinary privileges and placed on a level before the law with everybody else."[81]

On July 16 Hull expanded on his views in a telegram to Byrnes. "The central point calculated to create serious difference," he said, was "a

---

[80]Memorandum from Assistant Secretary of State MacLeish to Secretary of State Byrnes, "Interpretation of Japanese Unconditional Surrender," July 6, 1945, in *FRUS: Conference of Berlin*, I: 895–96 (emphasis in the original). Grew had informed the Secretary's Staff Committee of the existence of the new draft on July 4, according to minutes of the 131st meeting.

[81]Cordell Hull, *The Memoirs of Cordell Hull* (New York, 1948), II: 1594.

proposed declaration by the allies *now* that the Emperor and his monarchy will be preserved in event of allied victory." The prospects for Japanese acceptance were uncertain inasmuch as "the militarists would try to interfere." Hull warned that "should it fail the Japs would be encouraged while terrible political repercussions would follow in the U.S." He counseled delay: "Would it be well first to await the climax of allied bombing and Russia's entry into the war?"[82] This was an argument that would appeal to a politician with Byrnes' presidential ambitions. It persuaded Byrnes that "terrible political repercussions" were too great to risk. He agreed with Hull that the declaration "should be delayed and, when made, should not contain the commitment to which you refer."[83] Byrnes' mind was made up. He would oppose inclusion of any specific pledge to retain the throne in any public proclamation of war aims.

Byrnes set sail for Potsdam, leaving State Department officials quarreling in his wake. On July 7 Grew presided over a meeting of the secretary's Staff Committee at which MacLeish and Acheson first learned the precise contents of the draft declaration. The draft, Grew explained, "was one which he had been charged by the President to work out with the Secretaries of War and the Navy"—by implication not something he needed to clear with his State Department subordinates. He then listed a formidable array of officials who had approved the draft—"Secretaries Stimson and Forrestal, Admiral King, and probably General Marshall." His opponents were not overwhelmed: notably absent from the list was Secretary of State Byrnes.

After MacLeish and Acheson had taken turns attacking the premises of the proposed proclamation, the shape of a potential compromise became discernible. The department's legal adviser, Green Hackworth, suggested it, asking "why the statement could not merely say (1) that we propose to get rid of the military control of Japan, and (2) we will give the Japanese people the opportunity to develop a government of their own choosing."[84] It omitted any explicit commitment to preserve the throne. Grew asked Hackworth to put his formulation on paper for consideration at their next meeting and instructed Assistant Secretary of State James C. Dunn, about to join Byrnes in Potsdam, to bear in mind the morning's discussion. For Grew this meant a retreat to his stand of a year ago, but even that did not go far enough for his opponents. Acheson "hoped there was nothing in the record of this Committee to indi-

[82] *FRUS: Conference of Berlin*, II: 1267 (emphasis in the original).
[83] Ibid., p. 1268. Cf. Margaret Truman, *Harry S Truman* (New York, 1973), p. 275.
[84] Minutes of the Secretary's Staff Committee, 133rd meeting, July 7, 1945, in *FRUS: Conference of Berlin*, I: 900–901.

cate that the Committee had approved of the proposed statement." Grew assured him that was so.

BYRNES FINESSES GREW AND STIMSON AT POTSDAM

In politics, issues can have many faces. What faces an official sees depends on his perspective, or the position from which he is looking. Sometimes too it depends on the policy context in which an issue arises, or the other issues that press on him at the same time. Process can thereby structure issues. The wording of the declaration to Japan was no exception. While the face of the issue back in the State Department was how to end the war with Japan and how to reconstruct Japanese society afterward, what seemed most pertinent to American delegates at Potsdam was how to deal with their conferees, the Russians. In focusing on the Soviet Union, the delegation lost sight of Japan, and consequently what to say to the Japanese was treated as a by-product of what to tell the Russians.

On June 18 Grew, acting on Truman's instructions, had inserted an item on the agenda for Potsdam proposing "a joint statement outlining the program for the treatment of Japan in the hope that Japan will be more inclined to accept unconditional surrender if the Japanese know what their future is to be." Sometime after June 30, however, this item was dropped from the agenda that the United States subsequently tabled.[85] At Potsdam, Truman did not raise any Far East questions in his formal discussions with Stalin and Churchill. The only Soviet-American exchanges on these issues took place in talks on joint planning between the two sides' military authorities on the last day of the conference. The official United States explanation is that the Soviet Union was not yet a party to the war against Japan and that because the other interested party, Chiang Kai-shek's government, was not among the conferees, no purpose would have been served by raising Far East subjects. A more plausible reason is that even if some U.S. officials still wanted Soviet intervention against Japan, none wanted to give the Soviet Union an opening to table new demands, particularly for a share of the occupation.

As befit Potsdam's agenda, the American delegation was heavily weighted with Soviet specialists. Indeed, the only member of the official

---

[85]Compare Dunn's copy of the proposed agenda, which had this item deleted in pencil, in ibid., pp. 199n and 201n, to "Agenda for the Meeting of the Three Chiefs of State," June 22, 1945, Secretary's Staff Committee, p. 188, and Memorandum from the Acting Secretary of State to the President, June 30, 1945, p. 201.

delegation with any expertise on Japan was Charles E. Bohlen, who had served briefly in Tokyo and had been interned there with Grew at the start of the war, but Bohlen's specialty was Soviet, not Japanese, affairs. The composition of the delegation troubled Grew, who fretted back in Washington that the draft declaration might be "ditched" en route "by people who accompany the President—Bohlen among others—who reflect the view that we cannot afford to hold out any clarification of terms to Japan which could be construed as a desire to get the Japanese war over with before Russia has an opportunity to enter."[86]

Grew's distress was a bit premature. At least two senior U.S. officials who favored a change of war aims managed to make their way to Potsdam. Stimson solicited last-minute invitations for McCloy and himself in a private meeting with Truman on July 3. Later, Forrestal joined the conferees on his own initiative. Grew, for one, considers Stimson's presence to have been decisive in getting Truman to issue the declaration by persuading Churchill to press the matter with the president.[87]

In the end, though, it was Byrnes, not Stimson, who put the Potsdam Declaration in final form, with some editorial assistance from Truman and Churchill. It was Byrnes who eliminated all references to the emperor from the document. Imprecision on this point was well suited to coalition-building within the American policy process: it fended off potential domestic opposition while satisfying bureaucrats who wanted nothing done to preclude Hirohito's continued reign. In failing to mention the emperor by name, however, the declaration was ill-suited to coalition-building within Japan, where those maneuvering to end the war needed explicit assurances on the throne as inducement to surrender. It was Byrnes too who saw to it that any allusion to Soviet intervention or the atomic bomb were excised. He did this in hopes of giving Japan a chance to surrender without encouraging premature entry of the Soviet Union into the war. Yet by omitting the two most compelling threats that Japan would face, he defused the ultimatum. And finally, it was Byrnes who set the timing of the declaration's release. By persuading Truman to issue it once the date of the first atomic bombing of Japan had been fixed, he hoped to forestall Soviet intervention, but all he succeeded in doing was shortening the time Tokyo had to consider the declaration and for Washington to ponder Japan's reply. When Byrnes had finished with it, the Potsdam Declaration no longer contained much new of substance. Neither a gesture of conciliation nor an ultimatum, it was reduced to mere propaganda.

A bureaucratic compromise on the emperor began taking shape in

---

[86]Millis, *Forrestal Diaries*, pp. 73–74.
[87]Grew, *Turbulent Era*, II: 1424–25.

strategy sessions of the Combined Chiefs of Staff on July 16–17. A joint estimate produced by the Combined Intelligence Committee heavily discounted prospects for unconditional surrender by means short of invasion. The necessary condition for war termination according to the estimate was to get the Japanese army to acknowledge defeat "with a sufficient degree of unanimity." Making concessions on the future of the emperor would not be convincing: "For a surrender to be acceptable to the Japanese Army it would be necessary for the military leaders to believe that it would not entail discrediting the warrior tradition and that it would permit the ultimate resurgence of a military Japan."[88] These terms, it went without saying, were out of the question. It followed that no change in terms would suffice to bring about war termination: the only way to end the war was to compel unconditional surrender by inflicting a crushing defeat on Japan's armed forces.

Nevertheless, when the Combined Chiefs took up the estimate, the British raised the possibility of reinterpreting unconditional surrender. "From the military point of view," Sir Alan Brooke said, "it seemed to the British Chiefs of Staff that there might be some advantage in trying to explain this term to the Japanese in a manner which would ensure that the war was not unduly prolonged in outlying areas." In those areas lay former Crown Colonies that the British wanted to reoccupy without delay. One way Brooke mentioned to expedite surrender was to preserve the throne. Pleased to find allies wherever he could, Admiral Leahy suggested that since the matter was "a political one" it would "very useful" if the prime minister were to raise it with the president.[89]

Overnight, word reached Potsdam of the successful atomic test at Alamogordo. The next day the American chiefs of staff renewed discussion of how to get the Japanese armed forces to comply with orders to surrender. Army Chief of Staff Marshall framed a compromise that, while not precluding the use of the emperor to facilitate compliance, would muffle dissatisfaction at home: "From a purely military point of view," he said, "the attitude of the Joint Chiefs of Staff should be that nothing should be done prior to the termination of hostilities that would indicate the removal of the Emperor of Japan, since his continuation in office might influence the cessation of hostilities in areas outside of Japan proper."[90] Marshall carried the day. The chiefs agreed on a mem-

---

[88]"Estimate of the Enemy Situation," July 8, 1945, CCS 643/3, in U.S. Department of Defense, *Entry of the Soviet Union*, p. 88; *FRUS: Conference of Berlin*, II: 36n.

[89]Minutes of the 193rd meeting, Combined Chiefs of Staff, July 16, 1945, in *FRUS: Conference of Berlin*, II: 36–37. For Leahy the need to gain compliance was less of a motive than the hope of arranging a preinvasion settlement (*I Was There*, p. 419).

[90]Minutes of the 196th meeting, Joint Chiefs of Staff, July 17, 1945, in *FRUS: Conference of Berlin*, II: 40.

orandum to the president recommending the necessary changes in the declaration. It argued that the phrase "This may include a constitutional monarchy under the present dynasty" was ambiguous. It could be "misconstrued as a commitment by the United Nations to depose or execute the present Emperor and install some other member of the Imperial family," or "radical elements in Japan" could take it "as a commitment to continue the institution of the Emperor and Emperor worship." The Joint Chiefs proposed redrafting the sentence along the lines of the principle of self-determination in the Atlantic Charter: "Subject to suitable guarantees against further acts of aggression, the Japanese people will be free to choose their own form of government."[91] Like the State Department, the armed services were prepared to forgo an explicit commitment on the throne for the moment so that nothing would interfere with its eventual retention.

Back in Washington, those who still held out hope of accommodating Japan on war aims were moving to realize that hope. Navy Captain Zacharias, who had begun his broadcasts to Japan in May by repeating Truman's words on the occasion of Germany's surrender, was now edging beyond stated American policy. In a July 7 broadcast Zacharias spoke of unconditional surrender as "a technical term which refers to *the form in which hostilities are terminated*," while noting that "the exact conditions of *peace* are something to be settled in the future."[92] He also pointed to the "attendant benefits as laid down by the Atlantic Charter." The charter had proclaimed "the right of all peoples to choose the form of government under which they will live."

Zacharias followed up his broadcast in another medium, an anonymous letter to the editor prominently displayed in the *Washington Post* of July 17. After stating that unconditional surrender applied to "the manner in which the war is terminated," and alluding to provisions of American military law, the letter noted that "the people of an occupied country owe temporary obedience to the authorities in whom military control is vested, but they continue to owe allegiance to the accredited authorities of their own sovereignty." It then invited Japan to initiate negotiations: "If the Japanese desire to clarify whether or not unconditional surrender goes beyond the conditions" already spelled out by the president, "they have at their disposal the regular diplomatic channels, the secrecy of which precludes any public admission of weakness." In particular, "If, as Admiral Suzuki revealed in the Diet, their chief concern is over Japan's future national structure [*Kokutai*], including the emperor's status after surrender, the way to find out is to ask. Contrary to a widespread belief,

---

[91]JCS, Memorandum to the President, July 18, 1945, in ibid., p. 1269.
[92]Zacharias, *Secret Missions*, p. 417 (emphasis in the original).

such a question can be answered quickly and satisfactorily to all who are concerned over the future peace of the Orient and the world."[93] Zacharias' broadcast and letter attracted considerable press play around the United States.

Acting Secretary of State Grew sought to turn the ensuing rumors and press inquiries about a change in American war aims into a commitment to that change. On July 10 he had a statement released to the press discounting rumors of Japanese peace feelers and reaffirming the policy of unconditional surrender. In a cable to Secretary of State Byrnes, Grew insisted that the move was necessary to "put a stop to growing speculation" at home and to foster "in Japan a situation where anything that the President may say as to unconditional surrender will mean and what it will not mean will have maximum effect." A close reading of Grew's text, however, could construe the announcement as fueling speculation and tacitly encouraging Japan to contact the United States, which is how well-informed Washington commentators were inspired to construe it. [94]

On July 19 Grew tried another gambit. He told Byrnes it would be necessary to frame a reply to the question put to the State Department by wire-service correspondents, "Is it true that plans for handling of Japan's unconditional surrender have been fully formulated and that President Truman has taken them to Potsdam?" Grew sought Byrnes' approval for a reply that implicitly drew back from unconditional surrender:

Papers on this subject as well as on a number of other matters of present importance have been supplied to the President, but no plan altering the policy already announced has been formulated by this Government. The implementation of the announced policy will depend, of course, on the situation as it develops. The treatment to be accorded the Japanese under the unconditional surrender terms as defined by the President will depend upon the circumstances under which the surrender occurs. If the Japanese surrender now, before we can invade their main islands on our inevitable march to Tokyo, it is logical that the situation thus created should call for treatment which would be different in nature from the treatment that would be required if the Japanese delay surrender or if they fail to surrender. [95]

[93]"A Constant Reader," letter to the editor, *Washington Post*, July 17, 1945, p. 4. Cf. Zacharias, *Secret Missions*, p. 317.

[94]Statement by Grew, "Concerning Japanese Peace Feelers," in U.S. Department of State, *Bulletin*, July 15, 1945, p. 84; cable from Grew to Secretary of State, July 13, 1945, in *FRUS: Conference of Berlin*, I: 902. At the same time, Grew was trying to fuel speculation within the government about Japanese peace feelers. A cable from the U.S. ambassador in Stockholm arrived in Washington on July 6 telling of the unauthorized and abortive approach to Sweden's Prince Carl by a Japanese military attaché in May. Whether he himself had solicited the cable or not, Grew was quick to relay it to Byrnes, who was at sea en route to Potsdam (ibid., II: 1589–90).

[95]Cable from Secretary of State to Acting Secretary, July 21, 1945, in *FRUS: Conference of Berlin*, II: 1272.

Grew warned of "steadily mounting public clamor for a statement of our proposed terms for Japan" if no reply were provided to reporters, a reaction he said "will be harmful to the Administration and will create in Japan the impression that we are weakening in our determination to see the war through to unconditional surrender and final victory." Byrnes saw through Grew's ploy. He dispatched a two-sentence reply to reporters' inquiries: "The policy of this Government on unconditional surrender by Japan has been repeatedly stated. Elucidations of this policy were issued by the President on May 8 and June 1." Grew had the last word nonetheless. He used the OWI's release of the transcript of Zacharias' July 7 broadcast and the press attention that it generated as a pretext to avoid releasing the reply authorized by Byrnes.[96]

If Grew's maneuvering betrayed his frustration at having been left back in Washington, Secretary of War Stimson felt no better off in Potsdam. Stimson chafed at knowing so little of what was transpiring, and he held Byrnes responsible for cutting him out of the action: "He gives me the impression that he is hugging matters in this Conference pretty close to his bosom, and that my assistance, while generally welcome, was strictly limited in the matters to which it should be given."[97] One matter from which he felt excluded was the wording of the declaration. Byrnes' strategy, like Grew's and Stimson's earlier, was to get the president on board first before seeking the assent of others. Byrnes' central role also gave State Department Soviet specialists the inside track. Stimson was able to gain access to the president, but usually on the pretext of bringing him up-to-the-minute reports on the atomic bomb.

The opportunity to do so was not long in coming. On July 16, the day after Stimson's arrival at the conference, word reached him of the successful test at Alamogordo. "From that date on," Leahy writes, "it was no longer a theory. We had the bombs."[98] The advent of the bomb strengthened Stimson's impulse to put out the ultimatum as soon as possible, in hopes of ending the war with Japan before the Soviet Union came in. It also weakened Stimson's resolve to include one key element in the ultimatum: the threat of Soviet intervention. Earlier in the day, before getting news of the test, he read cables reporting the Russo-Japanese talks that naval intelligence had intercepted and decoded. With these in mind, Stimson drafted a memorandum for the president which he forwarded to Byrnes along with a request that the secretary and the

---

[96]Cable from Acting Secretary of State to Secretary, July 22, 1945, in ibid., pp. 1273–74. Cf. Minutes of Secretary's Staff Committee, 146th meeting, July 23, 1945, State Department Committee Files, Records of the Inter- and Intra-Departmental Committees, RG 363, National Archives.

[97]Stimson diary, July 19, 1945.

[98]Leahy, *I Was There*, pp. 430–31.

president discuss the ultimatum with him. Instead of one warning, he now wrote of "warnings," a first "along the lines of the draft prepared by the War Department" to be released immediately, and another to follow the atomic attack and Soviet intervention. Prompted by "the recent news of attempted approaches on the part of Japan to Russia," he stressed the urgency of issuing the first warning "during the course of this Conference, and rather earlier than later"—without advance notice to the Soviet Union unless "an agreement satisfactory to us had been reached with the Russians on the terms of their entry into the Japanese war." At Yalta the Big Three had agreed to a set of conditions for Soviet assistance in the Far East: recognizing the status quo in Outer Mongolia, a Mongolian People's Republic; internationalizing the port of Dairen while safeguarding "the preeminent interests of the Soviet Union" there; leasing Port Arthur to the Russians for use as a warm-water port; joint Sino-Soviet operation of rail lines linking Dairen; return of the southern part of Sakhalin and adjacent islands to Soviet sovereignty; and Soviet annexation of the Kuriles.[99] The first four concessions required Chinese acquiescence, which could be rather slow in coming. At the same time, Stimson urged President Truman to resist any new Soviet demands, arguing that the Yalta agreements, "so long as they are interpreted consistently with our traditional policy toward China, should not cause us any concern from a security point of view." By "our traditional policy toward China," Stimson was referring to "the Open Door and the recognition of Chinese sovereignty over Manchuria," difficult to square with the Yalta arrangements. Even Soviet leasing of a naval base at Port Arthur was, for Stimson, "a trend in the wrong direction."[100]

Why the haste in issuing the ultimatum and the delay in notifying the Russians? Secretary of War Stimson was expressly concerned about Soviet participation in the occupation: "If the Russians seek joint occupation after a creditable participation in the conquest of Japan, I do not see how we could refuse them at least a token occupation." The "token occupation" Stimson envisioned, however, was unlikely to satisfy Stalin. While prepared to accept occupation or even "cession" of the Kuriles, a navy interest, Stimson did "not relish Russian occupation farther south," which would infringe on the army's autonomy. "If there is to be occupation of the main islands," Stimson made clear, "the conditions and terms must certainly be determined by us." The best way to assure that was to compel Japan to surrender before the Russians got very far into the war.

---

[99] *Agreement Regarding Entry of the Soviet Union into the War Against Japan,* in *FRUS: Malta and Yalta,* p. 984.

[100] Memorandum from Secretary of War to the President, July 16, 1945, in *FRUS: Conference of Berlin,* II: 1266–67, 1322–23.

Secretary of State Byrnes, who no longer shared the army's belief in the necessity of invasion, was prepared to go further than Stimson in trying to forestall Soviet intervention. The Sino-Soviet talks, having opened in Moscow on the last day of June, were dragging on. Byrnes took steps to prolong them. As recently as the first week of July, he had been reluctant to discourage Soviet entry, but once he received word of the success at Alamogordo, he worried that China's foreign minister, T. V. Soong, would give away more than necessary. "We received a report that Soong had told his government the Soviet Union was making claims extending beyond the Yalta agreement," Byrnes writes. "I was afraid Soong would find it difficult to resist Soviet pressure and would make additional concessions if he were in doubt about our attitude."[101] Soong needed little prompting: he had already broken off the talks on the pretext of having to return to Chungking for new instructions. Yet breaking off the talks was too abrupt a gesture for Byrnes. On July 23 he sent Chiang a message over Truman's signature: "If you and Generalissimo Stalin differ as to the correct interpretation of the Yalta agreement, I hope you will arrange for Soong to return to Moscow and continue your efforts to reach complete understanding." In urging resumption of the talks, Byrnes later says, he did not have any desire to see them reach any conclusion. Instead, he was afraid that if they did not resume "Stalin might immediately enter the war, knowing full well that he could take not only what Roosevelt and Churchill, and subsequently Chiang, had agreed to at Yalta," but also "whatever else he wanted" in the Far East. "If Stalin and Chiang were still negotiating," however, "it might delay Soviet entrance and the Japanese might surrender. The President was in accord with that view."[102] Should Japan surrender before the Red Army attacked, perhaps the Soviet Union would refrain from seizing what Byrnes thought it could—but if not, American complicity might be diminished.

Even Army Chief of Staff Marshall was having second thoughts about

---

[101]James F. Byrnes, *Speaking Frankly* (New York, 1947), p. 205. The most likely source of the report is Ambassador Hurley in Chungking, who sent two cables to Potsdam on July 19 and 20. Ambassador Harriman, in Moscow, had conveyed substantially the same message in a July 12 cable. (*FRUS: Conference of Berlin*, II: 1224–27; *FRUS*, 1945, VI: 923–33, 948–49). In stiffening China's back, Byrnes may even have been prepared to go a step further and renege on the concessions made at Yalta. He writes later in *All in One Lifetime* (p. 291), "The President and I felt that, without appearing to encourage Chiang to disregard any pledges made by Roosevelt at Yalta, we should let him know that the United States did not want him to make additional concessions to the Soviets," though this account, written during the Cold War, may have to be discounted somewhat.

[102]Byrnes, *All in One Lifetime*, p. 291. Further corroboration of Byrnes' objective comes from a memorandum of conversation written by Churchill after talking to Byrnes on July 23, in Ehrman, *Grand Strategy*, p. 292; from Millis, *Forrestal Diaries*, pp. 78–79; and from the notes of Byrnes' aide, Walter Brown, July 16, 20, 22, and 24, 1945, in Lisle A. Rose, *After Yalta* (New York, 1973), pp. 80, 318–19.

the priority he had attached to Soviet intervention. At the president's request, Stimson solicited Marshall's views on July 23. The general had to be circumspect lest he weaken the case for the army's invasion. He began by noting that the original purpose for which Soviet assistance had been sought—to tie down Japan's Kwantung army—was now being accomplished by the massing of Soviet forces on the Manchurian border. Still, he went on, there was little advantage in trying to proceed without the Russians. Even if the United States on its own "compelled the Japanese to surrender to our terms, that would not prevent the Russians from marching into Manchuria anyhow" and seizing "what they wanted in the surrender terms." From Marshall's display of impatience at the inability to conclude joint staff planning with the Russians, Stimson inferred that he thought, "as I felt sure he would, that now with our new weapon we would not need the assistance of the Russians to conquer Japan."[103] Yet Stimson may have projected his own enthusiasm for the atomic bomb onto Marshall. General Marshall remained unconvinced that the bomb alone could compel the unconditional surrender of Japan: dictating terms to the enemy without first entering its homeland was unprecedented in the annals of warfare among great powers. Atomic bombing might soften Japan up, but invasion would still be necessary. While he was willing to try the bomb and the ultimatum on Japan just in case they worked, Marshall was not prepared to jeopardize Soviet help in the event they did not. What had changed was his assessment of the costs, not the benefits, to the army of Soviet participation in the war—and the potential domestic repercussions. That participation now seemed almost a foregone conclusion, but even if it were not, any substantial interference with the army's autonomy over the occupation and subsequent recriminations at home seemed too step a price to pay for assuring it.

The waning urgency with which the army regarded Soviet intervention and the shift in the relative priority assigned to securing the invasion and running the occupation that motivated it were both reflected in a report on strategy approved by the Combined Chiefs of Staff at Potsdam. In conducting operations against Japan, the Americans insisted on autonomy, agreeing to "consult" with their British counterparts but stipulating that "in the event of disagreement the final decision on the action to be taken will lie with the United States Chiefs of Staff." While the invasion of Japan remained "the supreme operations of the war," the report downgraded the importance of Soviet intervention, listing it as one of the "additional tasks" along with aid to China and to forces in liberated areas. Gone were the imperatives of Yalta; in their place was a rather perfunctory request: "Encourage Russian entry into the war against Japan; pro-

---

[103]Stimson diary, July 23, 1945.

vide such aid to her war-making capacity as may be necessary and practicable in connection therewith."[104] The army's increasing preoccupation with autonomy over the occupation did not predispose it to play up the impending threat of Soviet entry in an ultimatum to Japan.

From Yalta on, and as recently as Stimson's memorandum of July 2, the assumption had been that the Soviet Union would be a signatory of any ultimatum against Japan, but the Russians were never asked to sign. According to Truman, "Stalin could not, of course, be a party to the proclamation itself since he was still at peace with Japan, but I considered it desirable to advise him of the move we intended to make. I spoke to him privately about this in the course of the conference meeting."[105] Truman's account seems confusing in two respects. First, there is no record of any notification of the Russians until Byrnes transmitted the declaration to Foreign Minister Molotov the day of its release. Far from it, on the several occasions when the Japanese peace feelers came up in conversation, Truman did not take the opportunity to inform Stalin. Second, the haste with which the declaration was issued—as soon as the first atomic bombing was scheduled—and attempts to stall the Sino-Soviet talks suggest an intent to delay the very event that the army had long, though less and less ardently, sought to expedite—timely Soviet intervention. As a consequence, the declaration made no mention at all of that impending event.

Similar considerations led Byrnes to contemplate telling the Russians as little as possible about the atomic bomb in advance of its use, lest they be spurred to intervene sooner. That meant omitting any word of it in the declaration, despite Stimson's recommendation that it would give added force to an ultimatum. The result was that the declaration would say nothing specific about the two most potent new threats facing Japan—the Red Army and the Bomb.

Conferring with Byrnes on the morning of July 17, Stimson found him now "opposed to a prompt and early warning which I had first suggested. He outlined a timetable on the subject . . . which apparently had been agreed to by the President, so I pressed it no further." But instead of dropping the matter altogether, Stimson took it up with British Prime Minister Churchill later that day. First he passed along the preliminary report on the atomic test. "He [Churchill] was intensely interested and greatly cheered up," reports Stimson, "but was strongly inclined against

---

[104]CCS report, approved by the Heads of Government of the United States and the United Kingdom, July 24, 1945, in *FRUS: Conference of Berlin*, II: pp. 1463–64. Cf. JCS memorandum, July 18, 1945, in ibid., pp. 1336–37; Leahy, *I Was There*, pp. 409–10; and, for a British view, Ehrman, *Grand Strategy*, pp. 263–69.

[105]Truman, *Year of Decisions*, p. 387.

any disclosure. I argued against this to some length."[106] The next day Churchill raised the idea of a public restatement of war aims with Truman. He recalls dwelling "upon the tremendous cost in American and to a smaller extent in British life" of coercing Japan into unconditional surrender. "It was for him to consider whether this might be expressed in some other way, so that we got all the essentials for future peace and security and yet left them some show of saving their military honor and some assurance of their national existence," but Truman "replied bluntly that he did not think the Japanese had any military honor after Pearl Harbor." Churchill tried one parting shot: "I contented myself with saying that at any rate they had something for which they were ready to face certain death in very large numbers, and this might not be so important to us as it was to them."[107]

Learning of Truman's cool reception to Churchill's appeal, Stimson gave up trying to wring a public commitment on the throne. In a July 20 memorandum to Truman he concurred with the formulation used by the Joint Chiefs of Staff two days earlier, with one minor emendation: in place of the phrase "until her unconditional capitulation" he substituted "until she ceases to resist," on the grounds that it "avoids repeating in other words the term 'unconditional surrender' where it is not necessary to do so."[108]

The next day a lengthy memorandum on the test explosion arrived by special courier from General Leslie Groves, in command of the Manhattan Project. "It gave a pretty full and eloquent report of the tremendous success of the test," Stimson exulted in his diary, "and revealed far greater destructive power than we expected in S-1." After showing the report to Marshall, Stimson read it aloud to Truman and Byrnes. Immediately Byrnes went to work putting the finishing touches on the declaration. It was done by the morning of July 23, when Stimson met with Truman. "He told me," Stimson records, "that he had the warning message which we had prepared on his desk, and had accepted our most recent proposed change in it, and that he proposed to shoot it out as soon as he heard the definite day of the operation"—once the date of the first atomic bombing was set.[109]

Stimson made one last try at getting the president to agree to a concession on the emperor, this time through less public channels after the

---

[106]Stimson diary, July 17, 1945. There seems to be no record of the conversation in which Truman and Byrnes set the timetable, but it would have taken place the previous evening.

[107]Winston Churchill, *Triumph and Tragedy* (Boston, 1953), p. 642.

[108]Memorandum from Stimson to Truman, July 20, 1945, in *FRUS: Conference of Berlin*, II: 1271–72.

[109]Stimson diary, July 23, 1945. Cf. Byrnes, *Speaking Frankly*, p. 206; and Byrnes, *All in One Lifetime*, p. 298.

declaration was issued. The two conferred alone on the morning of July 24. Stimson represented Army Chief of Staff Marshall as "feeling that the Russians were not needed." Then he showed Truman a cable that had arrived the previous evening from Washington providing the dates that atomic bombs would be available. According to Stimson, Truman said "that was just what he wanted, that he was highly delighted, and that it gave him his cue for the warning." The president also told Stimson that he had just sent the draft to Chungking for Chiang Kai-shek to co-sign it and that he would make it public as soon as he got a reply. With changes in the declaration all but precluded now that it was en route to Chiang, Stimson could only underscore the importance he attached to reassuring Japan on the continuation of the present dynasty and try to hold open that option for the future: "I hoped that the President would watch carefully so that the Japanese might be reassured verbally through diplomatic channels if it was found they were hanging fire on that one point. He said that he had that in mind and that he would take care of it."[110]

The effort to modify unconditional surrender by a public restatement of war aims was over. Grew had lost, as had Stimson, who summed up his defeat this way: "Unfortunately during the war years high American officials had made some fairly blunt and unpleasant remarks about the Emperor, and it did not seem wise to Mr. Truman and Secretary of State Byrnes that the Government should reverse its field too sharply; too many people were likely to cry shame."[111] Domestic politics had overwhelmed diplomatic initiative.

All that remained was to clear the declaration with the other signatories. The British delegation contented itself with five minor changes in wording, all of which Truman and Byrnes agreed to without debate. Churchill returned his own copy with a one-word emendation, which was also accepted. Chiang's assent was slower in coming, ostensibly delayed in transmission. Anticipating some reluctance on the generalissimo's part, Truman showed his impatience. On July 25 he fired off a blunt cable to Ambassador Patrick Hurley in Chungking, "If an answer is not received within twenty-four hours, the proclamation will be released by the President and the Prime Minister." Chiang's concurrence arrived the next day, with two reservations: first, that his name be listed ahead of Churchill's; second, that he be invited to all future Allied conferences dealing with the Far East.[112]

---

[110]Stimson diary, July 24, 1945.
[111]Stimson and Bundy, *On Active Service in Peace and War*, p. 626.
[112]Cable from the White House Map Room to Hurley, July 25, 1945, in *FRUS: Conference of Berlin*, II: 1281; Hurley to Byrnes, July 26, 1945, pp. 1282–83. Cf. Truman, *Year of Decisions*, p. 390.

On July 26, just as the declaration was being made public, a copy was dispatched by courier to Molotov. Later that evening Molotov's interpreter telephoned Byrnes to request that its release be postponed two or three days. Byrnes demurred, noting that it had already been released. [113] At a meeting the next day, Byrnes told Molotov that his request for postponement had reached him only that morning. Molotov insisted he had sent word the previous evening. Byrnes then dismissed Molotov's objections with the excuse that the Russians had not been consulted because they were "not at war with Japan and we did not want to embarrass them." The president, he added, had thought it important to issue the declaration immediately "for political reasons." The minutes of their conversation do not elaborate on those reasons. [114]

The final version of the Potsdam Declaration, as issued July 26, 1945, reads:

(1) We the President of the United States, the President of the National Government of the Republic of China and the Prime Minister of Great Britain, representing the hundreds of millions of our countrymen, have conferred and agree that Japan shall be given an opportunity to end this war.

(2) The prodigious land, sea, and air forces of the United States, the British Empire and of China, many times reinforced by their armies and air fleets from the west, are poised to strike their final blows upon Japan. This military power is sustained by the determination of all the Allied nations to prosecute the war against Japan until she ceases to resist.

(3) The result of the futile and senseless German resistance to the might of the aroused free peoples of the world stands forth in awful clarity as an example to the people of Japan. The might that now converges on Japan is immeasurably greater than that which, when applied to the resisting Nazis, necessarily laid waste to the lands, the industry and the method of life of the whole German people. The full application of our military power, backed by our resolve, *will* mean the inevitable and complete destruction of the Japanese armed forces and just as inevitably the utter devastation of the Japanese homeland.

(4) The time has come for Japan to decide whether she will continue to be controlled by those self-willed militaristic advisers whose unintelligent calculations have brought the Empire of Japan to the threshold of annihilation, or whether she will follow the path of reason.

(5) Following are our terms. We will not deviate from them. There are no alternatives. We shall brook no delay.

(6) There must be eliminated for all time the authority and influence of those who have deceived and misled the people of Japan into embarking on

---

[113]Byrnes, *All in One Lifetime*, pp. 296–97.
[114]Charles Bohlen's minutes of the Byrnes-Molotov meeting, July 27, 1945, in *FRUS: Conference of Berlin*, II: 449–50.

world conquest, for we insist that a new order of peace, security and justice will be impossible until irresponsible militarism is driven from the world.

(7) Until such a new order is established *and* until there is convincing proof that Japan's war-making power is destroyed, points in Japanese territory to be designated by the Allies shall be occupied to secure the achievement of the basic objectives we are here setting forth.

(8) The terms of the Cairo Declaration shall be carried out and Japanese sovereignty shall be limited to the islands of Honshu, Hokkaido, Kyushu, Shikoku and such minor islands as we determine.

(9) The Japanese military forces, after being completely disarmed, shall be permitted to return to their homes with the opportunity to lead peaceful and productive lives.

(10) We do not intend that the Japanese shall be enslaved as a race or destroyed as a nation, but stern justice shall be meted out to all war criminals, including those who have visited cruelties upon our prisoners. The Japanese government shall remove all obstacles to the revival and strengthening of democratic tendencies among the Japanese people. Freedom of speech, of religion, and of thought, as well as respect for the fundamental human rights, shall be established.

(11) Japan shall be permitted to maintain such industries as will sustain her economy and permit the exaction of just reparations in kind, but not those industries which would enable her to re-arm for war. To this end, access to, as distinguished from control of raw materials shall be permitted.

(12) The occupying forces of the Allies shall be withdrawn from Japan as soon as these objectives have been accomplished and there has been established in accordance with the freely expressed will of the Japanese people a peacefully inclined and responsible government.

(13) We call upon the Government of Japan to proclaim now the unconditional surrender of all the Japanese armed forces, and to provide proper and adequate assurances of their good faith in such action. The alternative for Japan is prompt and utter destruction.[115]

The declaration has all the calculated ambiguity of a statement aimed at reassuring such diverse audiences as hawkish Americans bent on vengeance and war-weary Japanese fearful of a Carthaginian peace. It retains much of the rhetorical flavor of an ultimatum, full of generalities about the potency and immediacy of Allied threats, arrayed against a set of nonnegotiable demands that in diplomatic practice have often turned out to be negotiable: occupation, cession of territory, disarmament, elimination of the industrial capacity to rearm, and reparations. It also repeats some conciliatory gestures made elsewhere: a promise of no reprisals against the populace and soldiery except for war criminals, respect for fundamental liberties, and assurance of continued economic sustenance. Yet the generality of the provisions betrays their propagandistic intent.

Even more telling than its contents are its omissions. Gone from the

[115]"Proclamation Calling for the Surrender of Japan," in ibid., pp. 1474–76.

declaration is any mention of the emperor's fate, leaving in doubt whether he was to be considered one of "those who deceived and misled the people of Japan" whose "authority and influence" were to be "eliminated for all time," or a war criminal destined to face "stern justice," or part of a "peacefully inclined and responsible government" to be established "in accordance with the freely expressed will of the Japanese people" once the victors had accomplished the objectives of their occupation.

How much softer were terms of Potsdam? Hardly softer at all, according to the State Department's Office of Far Eastern Affairs, which did an internal assessment of the declaration's departures from previously stated American policy. The assessors were reduced to legalistic nitpicking. The State Department had hitherto interpreted unconditional surrender to cover not only "all Japanese armed forces," but also the emperor, the government, and the people of Japan. Whereas the department had previously envisioned "a unilateral surrender with no contractual elements whatever," the declaration, by addressing itself to the "Japanese government," implied an international agreement, or contract. Instead of imposing surrender on Japan, Allied forces would rely initially on the "good faith" of the government of Japan: the terms of surrender would be implemented by that government with the occupation forces to act as guarantor, rather than by the occupation authorities themselves. This interpretation seemed to be in conflict with the twelfth paragraph, which "could be interpreted to mean that the government which accepts the terms shall immediately retire and leave the occupying force to govern Japan until the objectives stated here have been achieved and a 'peacefully inclined and responsible government' had been established by an election." The assessment also detected some ambiguity in the category of "all war criminals" inasmuch as singling out "those who have visited cruelties upon our prisoners" implied that its reach extended only to those who had violated the laws of war, while the department had previously assumed a broader definition "to include those responsible for the initiation of aggression." Finally, the declaration did not make clear whether the intention was to terminate Japanese sovereignty over the Kuriles and the Ryukyus as "minor islands" while holding out that fate for southern Sakhalin, a peninsula; department policy, the report noted, had never favored denying Japan sovereignty over "any of these three areas," thereby posing an oblique objection to the as-yet-secret terms of Yalta. [116] Taken as a whole, the Potsdam Decla-

---

[116]"Comparison of the Proclamation of July 26, 1945, with the Policy of the Department of State," in ibid., pp. 1285–87. The extent to which the Office of Far Eastern Affairs had tried to obscure the differences from unconditional surrender can be measured by comparing its assessment with that of others at the time, e.g., David N. Rowe, "Ultimatum for Japan," *Far Eastern Survey*, August 15, 1945, pp. 217–19.

ration's departures from unconditional surrender were hardly the stuff of a negotiated settlement.

Gone too from the proclamation is any specific reference to the new forces about to be unleashed on Japan—namely, the Red Army and the atomic bomb. Some intimation of the latter threat did reach Japan, albeit through unorthodox channels likely to make it seem more intriguing than compelling. A German spy ring operating in the United States that had come under the control of U.S. military intelligence was used to transmit disinformation to the Germans, who passed along much of it verbatim to their Japanese ally. The network remained in place after Germany surrendered and continued to be run by a special section of the Joint Chiefs of Staff. The week of July 23, after all reference to the atomic bomb had been stricken from the Potsdam Declaration, this channel was reactivated and used to transmit a vague hint about the newest threat to Japan: "A group of fourteen American scientists and mechanical engineers have gone on a special mission to work with British scientists on a new weapon that is said to be capable of shortening the war by many months."[117] How this hint came to be sent is still a mystery.

Adding little to the threats and promises that might alter Japan's calculations to continue the war, the declaration was also released in a way that denied time for rational choice. Eugene Dooman, for one, is convinced that the absence of explicit assurances about the throne and the implied transfer of sovereignty from the emperor to the people of Japan "raised an issue of supreme importance to the Japanese requiring a reasonable length of time for decision."[118] Yet the release of the declaration, less than a week before the first atomic bomb would be available for use on Japan and less than two weeks before the Soviet Union had pledged to enter the war, left little time for Japan to consider its reply and almost no time at all for the United States to respond in turn.

No longer was the Potsdam Declaration the opening move in Grew's strategy of conciliation aimed at inducing Japan to negotiate a settlement of the war. Nor was it Stimson's ultimatum, seeking to compel Japan to come to terms by threatening Soviet intervention and atomic bombing. The conclusion of the United States Army's official history of the OPD during World War II seems to be close to the mark: "The Potsdam Ultimatum was issued on 26 July 1945 as a calculated effort to lower Japanese will to resist while military pressures were building up."[119]

---

[117]Material prepared by the Special Section, Joint Security Control, of the Joint Chiefs of Staff, for transmission to Berlin via Hamburg the week of July 23, 1945, code-named Broadaxe, Records of the National Security Agency, Box 10, SRH-021, RG 457, National Archives.

[118]Giovannitti and Freed, *Decision to Drop the Bomb*, p. 227.

[119]Cline, *Washington Command Post*, p. 346.

Neither conciliation nor ultimatum, the Potsdam Declaration was no more than propaganda. And as such, it was better suited to public dissemination than to private transmittal through diplomatic channels to Japan.

JAPAN STILL AWAITS MOSCOW'S REPLY

The Japanese had little way of ascertaining what internal disagreements had shaped the wording of the Potsdam Declaration. What information they had did not point to any particular reading. Some officials were alert to signs of controversy emanating from Washington over the terms of surrender, and rumors did reach Tokyo of an impending statement to be issued jointly by the Allies at Potsdam. Foreign Ministry officials had been monitoring American broadcasts and press accounts for any clarification of unconditional surrender and had prepared daily summaries for senior Japanese officials, including the emperor. They paid particularly close attention to the broadcasts by psychological warfare specialists in the ONI. One dovish diplomat has gone so far as to credit these broadcasts with arming "the peace party in Japan with highly useful arguments for convincing vacillating minds that the sooner we abandoned futile resistance the better it would be for our nation."[120] Other, more highly placed Japanese officials took a less charitable view of broadcasts that could have alerted the diehards to maneuvers for a settlement.

Recipients of any message from abroad tend to concentrate on framing a reply without necessarily reaching prior agreement on what the other side meant, and in so doing they may be more concerned with their own internal politics than with those in the enemy camp. Reading messages by the light of their own official responsibilities, they each embrace interpretations best suited to advance the reply they prefer to make.

In late July, Japan's leaders were looking toward Moscow for a way out of the war. The Potsdam Declaration offered no reason to redirect their attention, insisting as it did on terms they all believed to be unacceptable—unconditional surrender. Now that those seeking an end to the war had achieved a hard-won but precarious agreement in the Big Six to approach the Soviet Union, they did not want to jeopardize it and thereby forgo any prospect, however remote, of Soviet assistance in

---

[120]Kase, *Journey to the Missouri*, p. 199. For details of Japanese monitoring of American public sources, see ibid., pp. 198–203, and Telegram 1476 from Satō in Moscow to Tōgō, in *FRUS: Conference of Berlin*, II: 1294–95.

bringing about a settlement on terms more favorable to Japan. Anything more forthcoming than a noncommittal reply threatened to arouse the diehards and to undo the Big Six agreement.

On July 25, Tokyo time, two days before Japan's receipt of the Potsdam Declaration, Japanese Foreign Minister Tōgō cabled Ambassador Satō urging him to take advantage of an anticipated recess in the Potsdam Conference to try to arrange a meeting with Soviet Foreign Minister Molotov. Tōgō called Satō's attention to the public debate on peace terms under way in Allied capitals, citing two recent formulations of unconditional surrender—one by Allen Dulles of the OSS in his meeting with Per Jacobsson in Berne, the other by Ellis Zacharias of the ONI in his broadcasts to Tokyo. Tōgō identified Dulles only as "a United States spokesman" and quoted him as saying, "As a rule, for the sake of formality, the Allies will hold fast to unconditional surrender until the end. However, should the Imperial Japanese Government surrender immediately, the Allies are actually prepared to modify the terms." Tōgō also took the Zacharias broadcasts to be authoritative: "Although a member of the United States Office of War Information," Zacharias' cover, "he broadcasts to Japan as a spokesman of the United States Government." Tōgō dismissed both formulations as "simple propaganda strategy" designed to hasten Japan's internal collapse. He instructed Satō "to communicate to the other party through appropriate channels that we have no objection to a peace based on the Atlantic Charter" but that unconditional surrender was out of the question: "The difficult point is the attitude of the enemy, who continues to insist on unconditional surrender. Should the United States and Great Britain remain insistent on formality, there is no solution other than for us to hold out until complete collapse because of this one point alone." He also told Satō to emphasize that the proposed Konoye mission was "not a mere 'peace feeler' but [was] in obedience to the Imperial command."[121]

That day Satō paid a call on Acting Soviet Foreign Minister Solomon Lozovsky. Asked to clarify the purpose of the Konoye mission, Satō said it was "to ask the Government of the USSR to assist in the termination of the war," specifically to "mediate in a friendly manner," not merely to act as a neutral go-between, and "at the same time to negotiate on matters which will solidify and improve relations between Japan and the USSR, which should become the basis of our diplomacy for the period during and after the war."[122] Lozovsky questioned Satō closely about any "concrete proposals" Konoye would be bringing with him—in particular, whether they would include terms for ending the war as well as

[121]Telegram 944 from Tōgō to Satō, July 25, 1945, in *FRUS: Conference of Berlin*, II: 1261.
[122]Telegram 1450 from Satō to Tōgō, July 25, 1945, in ibid., p. 1262.

for improving Soviet-Japanese relations. Satō replied in the affirmative. Then, trying to be as responsive as he could, Satō ventured further on his own authority: "It is outside the instructions which I have received to prepare a written text of the proposal which I made today. However, I shall prepare such a text for your reference on my own initiative and present it to you later" as a further gesture of Japan's seriousness of intent. [123]

Two days later, with the Potsdam Declaration in hand, Satō cabled Tōgō to warn that the Russians would not be responsive to "such a noncommittal attitude on our part" and that nothing less than a "concrete proposal" would satisfy them. He saw a link between Japan's initiative and the Potsdam Declaration, calling it a "scare-bomb directed against us" and a "counteroffensive, with our trial venture to terminate the war as its target." The declaration made Soviet willingness to mediate on Japan's behalf "very doubtful." As corroboration for this assessment, Tōgō cited a BBC broadcast saying that at Potsdam "Stalin [had] for the first time participated in a discussion of the war in the Far East." [124]

Tōgō had suspicions of his own that there was "some connection between the new joint declaration and our request" for Soviet mediation. In a message to Satō sent before the ambassador's cable reached Tokyo, he raised several questions about the possible connection and renewed his instructions that Satō meet with Molotov "without delay." "Countermeasures" to the Potsdam Declaration could wait "for the time being" until "after we receive and study the Soviet reply to our request." [125]

MOKUSATSU

American shortwave transmitters in San Francisco began beaming the declaration to Japan in English at 5 A.M. July 27, Tokyo time. Highlights were sent in Japanese five minutes later, and the full text was sent in Japanese at 7 A.M. Regular OWI programming for the Far East was canceled in order to permit full and repeated broadcasts of the proclamation in twenty languages, and overseas psychological warfare posts were ordered to read the full text without comment. [126]

[123]Telegram 1449 from Satō to Tōgō, July 25, 1945, in ibid., pp. 1263–64. Satō took the added precaution of sending the second message separately.
[124]Telegram 1458 from Satō to Tōgō, July 27, 1945, in ibid., pp. 1291–92.
[125]Telegram 952 from Tōgō to Satō, July 28, 1945, in ibid., pp. 1292–93.
[126]The OWI informed the president's delegation of its efforts by cable: White House Information Officer (Ayers) to Presidential Press Secretary (Ross), July 27, 1945, in ibid., p. 1290. State Department files have no record that Japan was sent a copy through diplomatic channels (ibid., p. 1290n).

Japan's Foreign Ministry, which picked up the text in routine monitoring of American broadcasts, was able to transcribe it by early morning. Upon reading a copy, Tōgō's "first reaction" was that "in view of the language, 'Following are our terms,' it was evidently not a dictate of unconditional surrender." He had the "impression that the Emperor's wishes had reached the United States and Great Britain," prompting a "moderation of their attitude." He felt "special relief," he recalls, at its economic provisions "at a time when such draconian retribution upon Germany as the 'Morgenthau Plan' for her reduction to a 'pastoral state' was being proposed." Yet he had serious reservations about its other provisions. He did not judge the territorial arrangements "fitting" with the terms of the Atlantic Charter. The wording on occupation sites and "the eventual form of the Japanese Government" contained "some ambiguities," and he foresaw "complications" that "might result from the language relating to disarmament and war criminals." He deemed it "desirable to enter into negotiations with the Allied Powers to obtain some clarification and revision—even if it should be slight—of disadvantageous points in the declaration."[127] Whatever Tōgō's private relief or reservations and however well-intentioned his personal desire to seek clarification or revision of the Allied terms, he did not make his sentiments known to his colleagues in the Big Six or the cabinet. Instead, he commissioned a legal analysis of the declaration by Foreign Ministry officials and proposed withholding any public response until Moscow replied to Japan's request to receive Prince Konoye.

If the foreign minister sought to postpone a divisive fight over the response, not all his Big Six colleagues were in a position to countenance so noncommittal a stance: the Potsdam Declaration posed a propaganda challenge that required a prompt reaction if it were not to impede them in the conduct of their official duties. Allied broadcasts were disseminating the peace terms far and wide, reaching Japan's people and troops at home and overseas. Under the press of American bombing, the populace was showing signs of restiveness, requiring reassurance by civil authorities. If Japan were to retain bargaining leverage for a more favorable settlement, senior military officers had to sustain the morale among subordinates at war's end. It was difficult, even for troops as dedicated as Japan's, to be the last to die for a lost cause; yet even a hint of surrender might be enough to galvanize the diehards into staging a coup d'état, overthrowing the government, suspending efforts to reach a settlement, and prosecuting the war to the death. Either way, indiscipline threatened an orderly termination of the war.

Later in the morning of July 27, Foreign Minister Tōgō reported to the

[127]Tōgō, *Cause of Japan*, pp. 311–12; cf. "Statements," IV, no. 50304, p. 264.

throne on the Potsdam Declaration and the Moscow talks: "I stressed that the declaration must be treated with the utmost circumspection, both domestically and internationally; in particular, I feared the consequences if Japan should manifest an intention to reject it." Yet he preferred to remain noncommittal rather than pursue any immediate clarification through diplomatic channels: "I pointed out further that the efforts to obtain Soviet mediation to bring about the ending of the war had not yet borne fruit, and that our attitude toward the declaration should be decided in accordance with their outcome."[128]

Tōgō took the same stand at a Big Six meeting that afternoon. Navy Chief of Staff Toyoda, Tōgō recalls, warned that word of the Allied declaration would soon get around and impair morale. Toyoda proposed putting out a statement "that the government regarded the declaration as absurd and could not consider it." Prime Minister Suzuki joined Tōgō in objecting. The Big Six then accepted Tōgō's suggestion "that for the time being we should wait to see what the response of the USSR would be to our approach to her."[129] Yet withholding all comment might only lend credence to the rumors sweeping the country that Japan was preparing to settle on terms approximating those set forth at Potsdam. According to Toyoda, even Navy Minister Yonai became convinced of the need to issue immediate instructions intended "to check the effects of the proclamation on front-line morale."[130]

Later that afternoon the cabinet held its regular weekly meeting. After reviewing the Moscow talks and the Potsdam Declaration, Tōgō repeated his recommendation to await a Soviet reply before acting on the Allied declaration. "No dissent from this treatment of the declaration was expressed," he recalls, "though there was considerable discussion of the way and the extent of making it public."[131] The prevailing sentiment, according to Chief Cabinet Secretary Sakomizu, was that "it would be necessary to avoid giving [a] shock to the people until the fundamental government policy had been finally decided." Yet keeping the declaration a secret was not an option; around-the-clock American broadcasts and leafleting by American planes saw to that. Tōgō then proposed its prompt release, but in expurgated form and "without comment." Through informal press guidance, the Board of Information could "lead the press to minimize publicity." Over the objections of the War Minister Anami, Tōgō's stand carried the cabinet. The rationale for the decision, Sakomizu

---

[128]Tōgō, *Cause of Japan*, p. 312.
[129]Ibid., p. 312; cf. "Statements," IV, no. 50304, p. 264. Toyoda's own recollection, (in ibid., no. 57670, p. 378), is at variance with Tōgō's, but he seems to have confused this occasion with a Big Six meeting to consider the Byrnes reply two weeks later.
[130]Toyoda, in "Statements," IV, no. 57670, p. 378.
[131]Tōgō, *Cause of Japan*, p. 313.

says, was that the government by its "reticence would convince the public that it was accepting the Three-Power Proclamation" at the same time that "the military would see in the official silence firm rejection of it." Of course, just the opposite could happen—and did. "The official reticence," admits Sakomizu, "became construed by the people that the government was ignoring the proclamation, whereas military circles interpreted the reticence as a sign that the government was acquiescing in it."[132]

Pressure from the armed services began to build for a public rejection of the terms of Potsdam. Theater commanders sent messages to the War Ministry demanding rejection.[133] Following the cabinet meeting, General Yoshizumi, chief of the Military Affairs Bureau of the War Ministry, pressed Sakomizu to overturn the cabinet decision: "If the government issues no announcement of rebuttal, the officers and men at the battle fronts will certainly become perturbed, judging that the government is going to accept the declaration. Accordingly, the government must issue such an announcement in a strong tone." A similar appeal came from the navy general staff. The protests had the desired effect. "I found it impossible," says Sakomizu, "to ignore the requests from the Army and the Navy."[134]

Next morning's newspapers in Japan carried the text of the Potsdam Declaration, deleting two sentences—one on the disarming of Japan's military forces and the other denying any intent to enslave or destroy Japan as a nation.[135] Eliminating the reference to disarmament may have had the effect of making the terms somewhat less intolerable to the armed services. Yet press treatment of the declaration was much harsher than Tōgō had desired. *Mainichi* headlined the text, "Laughable Matter," and *Asahi Shinbun* commented, "Since the joint declaration of America, Britain, and Chungking is a thing of no great value, it will only serve to re-enhance the government's resolve to carry the war forward unfalteringly to a successful conclusion!" Several newspapers characterized the

---

[132]Sakomizu, in "Interrogations," II, unnumbered, April 21, 1949, p. 123.

[133]Colonel Okikatsu Arao (chief of the Military Affairs Section of the War Ministry), in "Statements," I, no. 54226, p. 47. Amano, in ibid., no. 59617, p. 34, flatly contradicts Arao's assertion that messages came in from the front lines. Because all but one were said to be delivered by messenger, there would scarcely have been time for many to arrive from overseas.

[134]Sakomizu, in "Interrogations," II, no. 62016, p. 155. Toyoda, in "Statements," IV, no. 57670, p. 378, says that his diehard vice-chief of staff, Admiral Ōnishi, a friend of Sakomizu's, was the source of the navy protest. Cf. Tōgō, in ibid., no. 54562, p. 288.

[135]Pacific War Research Society, *Japan's Longest Day* (Tokyo, 1968), p. 329n. Kazuo Kawai, "*Mokusatsu*, Japan's Response to the Potsdam Declaration," *Pacific Historical Review* 19 (November 1950): 411, says that the phrases about the "utter destruction" of Japan and meting out "stern justice" to "all war criminals" and the reference to "self-willed militaristic advisers" were all toned down.

government's policy with a word that Prime Minister Suzuki had himself applied to the Potsdam Declaration in the course of cabinet deliberations—*mokusatsu*, literally translated "to take no notice of" but having a somewhat pejorative connotation: to "treat with silent contempt."[136] From participants' accounts, it is not clear whether Sakomizu, in conveying details of the cabinet meeting to the Board of Information, was doing so at the prime minister's behest or responding on his own to service pleas.

Whatever the source of the July 28 newspaper stories, cabinet reconsideration was not long in coming. At a regularly scheduled meeting between the government and the Supreme Command later that morning, the prime minister, his chief cabinet secretary, the chiefs of staff, and the service ministers had a half-hour discussion of the Allied proclamation. Tōgō, thinking this was "a routine weekly meeting without any special significance," did not bother to attend "because of more important business."[137] Yonai defended the government's decision, arguing for continued "silence," but when the other service representatives insisted on express rejection of the declaration, he relented. "Nobody at this meeting," says Toyoda, "even so much as hinted that he wanted to have the Allied proclamation considered seriously. However, they were unanimously in accord with the necessity of clarifying the government's attitude because of the shock this proclamation might bring the military personnel and the people."[138] The decision, Sakomizu recalls, was that "the government will make the attitude publicly known, in some form or another, that it has [no] intention of accepting the Potsdam Declaration."[139] The word *mokusatsu* accurately conveyed the sense of the meeting, satisfying service concerns while avoiding formal rejection of the terms of Potsdam.

A previously scheduled afternoon press conference by Suzuki provided a suitable forum for making the government's position public. Based on "a rough gist of the text" framed at the morning session, Chief Cabinet Secretary Sakomizu composed a draft that Suzuki read in response to a planted question: "I believe the Joint Proclamation by the three countries is nothing but a rehash of the Cairo Declaration. As for the government, it does not find any important value in it, and there is

---

[136]Butow, *Japan's Decision to Surrender*, pp. 145–46.
[137]Tōgō, *Cause of Japan*, p. 313. Tōgō's versions of the meeting here and in "Statements," IV, no. 54562, p. 288, are secondhand reconstructions. Both Sakomizu, in "Interrogations," II, no. 62016, p. 155, and Toyoda, in "Statements," IV, no. 57670, p. 378, imply that the expression *mokusatsu* did not appear in press accounts until after the July 28 meeting.
[138]Toyoda, in "Statements," IV, no. 57670, p. 378.
[139]Sakomizu, in "Interrogations," II, no. 62016, p. 155.

no other recourse but to ignore [*mokusatsu*] it entirely and resolutely fight for the successful conclusion of this war."[140]

Tōgō says he reacted with "amazement" to resulting news reports and "protested without delay to the cabinet when it met," but if he had read the newspapers the previous morning, it does not seem to have prompted him to attend the meeting of the prime minister and the high command. Tōgō's subsequent testimony nevertheless shows his clear appreciation of the significance of overturning the cabinet decision, even if he had done nothing to prevent it. As he told interrogators after the war, "Ignoring the declaration was vastly different from withholding comment for the time being, which had been the decision reached by the cabinet and the [Big Six]."[141]

Promulgation of the Potsdam Declaration was of no help to Tōgō and his allies. After considerable exertion they had managed to forge a fragile agreement in the Big Six to approach Moscow. High-ranking officers in the armed services and their hawkish allies in the country, antagonistic to any settlement on terms resembling those of Potsdam and suspicious of the talks in Moscow, constantly threatened to undo the Big Six agreement and bring down the government. In the absence of a definitive word from the Soviet Union about its willingness to receive the Konoye mission, Tōgō was hardly prepared to promote cabinet consideration of a proposal to seek clarification of the Potsdam Declaration, lest he arouse the hawks. As Tōgō himself put it, "The point is we had already asked the USSR for mediation and she had not yet explicitly declined our request. We on our part had instructed our ambassador to meet directly with Molotov. It was not that we were studying the situation, but that we wanted to wait and see how things would develop, at least until we received a reply from the Russians."[142] Wait-and-see was the posture of a politician in trouble at home hoping for rescue from abroad.

Some analysts have claimed that the United States misinterpreted Japan's reply,[143] but no senior official in Japan had any intention of considering the terms of Potsdam unless and until the Moscow talks

[140]Domei broadcast, carried by Radio Tokyo's Greater East Asia service and monitored by the U.S. Foreign Broadcast Intelligence Service at 3 A.M. July 28, 1945, Washington time. Translation in "Daily Report, Foreign Radio Broadcasts, July 30, 1945" (Washington, D.C., Federal Communications Commission, Washington, D.C. mimeographed), excerpted in *FRUS: Conference of Berlin*, II: 1293. Stimson, "Decision," p. 105, refers to an announcement calling the declaration "unworthy of public notice," which suggests that he may have seen a different translation.

[141]Tōgō, *Cause of Japan*, p. 313; "Statements," IV, no. 50304, pp. 264–65.

[142]Tōgō, in "Statements," IV, no. 50304, p. 266.

[143]Giovannitti and Freed, *Decision to Drop the Bomb*, p. 231, who base their conclusion largely on Sakomizu's interrogation, and Kawai, "*Mokusatsu*, Japan's Response," p. 413, among others, assert this.

broke down irreparably. While Tōgō wanted to keep open the possibility of seeking clarification of the Potsdam Declaration and did not want Japan to appear hostile to a negotiated settlement of the war, most Japanese officials were concerned less about reactions in Washington than about reactions at home.

Even though the terms of Potsdam were unacceptable to all of Japan's leaders, the way the Allies communicated these terms to Japan inclined even those Japanese seeking a settlement to dismiss them as propaganda instead of inviting clarification. The mass media may be the quickest way to send a message to the other side in wartime, but after being used for disseminating propaganda throughout the war they may no longer seem like high-fidelity channels. Using them to promulgate war aims without also using diplomatic channels may only stimulate incredulity and rejection in the enemy camp unless those war aims represent an attempt at accommodation. Then public announcement may be even more convincing to the enemy than diplomatic channels because it involves political commitment and runs political risks at home by alerting hard-liners and arousing opposition. That was exactly the risk neither side was prepared to run.

MODERATING WAR AIMS: POLITICS AS USUAL

Raymond Aron has remarked on the tendency of war aims to become hyperbolic in what he calls "the century of total war." Now, he says, "it was no longer a question of shifting frontier posts a few miles. Only sublime—and vague—principles such as the right of peoples to self-determination or 'the war to end war' seemed commensurate with such violence, sacrifice, and heroism. It was technical excess that gradually introduced ideologies in place of war aims. Both sides claimed to know what they were fighting *about*, but neither said what it was fighting *for*."[144] The need to motivate conscripts and publics in an age of mass mobilization and technologically enhanced destructiveness gave rise to limitless ambition in warfare. It underlay the reluctance of American leaders to moderate their demand for unconditional surrender.

Once war is under way, states have two paths for taking the initiative to limit the conflict unilaterally—that is, without enemy reciprocity. One is to alter the means by which the war is waged. The other is to limit the ends for which the state fights, making them more acceptable to the enemy and thereby improving prospects for mutual accommodation. These two paths may converge: states may try to end a war by induce-

---

[144]Raymond Aron, *The Century of Total War* (Garden City, N.Y., 1954), p. 26.

ment, softening the terms of settlement; by ultimatum, listing the threats it intends to carry out if the enemy fights on; or by a combination of promises and threats.

The Potsdam Declaration began as an attempt to induce the enemy to stop fighting, but it fell victim to domestic politics. Those promoting a unilateral change in war aims—Grew, Stimson, and the U.S. Navy— had to overturn an oft-stated policy that had amassed overwhelming popular and congressional support. They tried to avoid full-dress debate within the government because it could not have remained confined there but would have quickly leaked outside, where they assumed their views would have much less chance of acceptance. Rather than risk pillory, they took a more private path to policy innovation, trying to win the president over by sheer force of argumentation. Failing that, they resorted to subtle maneuvers on their own initiative addressed to Japan and intended to elicit a response which they could exploit back home. When these unauthorized efforts came to naught, so did any chance of getting a settlement of the war on terms.

The declaration released on July 26 omitted any explicit commitment to retain the emperor. Its formulation was a compromise between those who wanted to commit the United States to preserving the throne and those who did not, a lowest common denominator that satisfied the concern of the U.S. Army that nothing be done to preclude the emperor's continuation in office during the postwar occupation. It bowed in the direction of American public opinion without kowtowing to it. The compromise did little to meet the needs of those in Japan looking for a way out of the war, though it did leave some room for maneuver once Japan sued for peace.

Throughout the struggle to modify the terms of surrender, U.S. officials took their cues for action and their readings of events overseas by the light of stakes closer to home. The national interest, as understood by most participants, dictated inducing Japan to surrender without the need for further bloodshed and Soviet intervention and using the emperor to facilitate surrender, occupation, and postwar reconciliation. Yet officials did not act in accordance with that interest in wording the Potsdam Declaration. Nor did they behave like hawks or doves, adhering to a consistent set of attitudes about waging and terminating war. Instead, for all but one or two, bureaucratic and domestic politics may best account for how they acted. The antimonarchist impulse of liberalism may have partly inspired MacLeish and Acheson to take their stands, but their bureaucratic responsibilities for public and congressional relations are enough to account for their opposition to any public pledge to spare the throne. Even for Grew and Forrestal, suspicion of the Soviet Union and conceptions of the postwar balance of power in accounting for behavior complemented organizational interests. The marked inconsistency in Stimson's behavior reflects the political cross-pressures on his bureaucratic position. For Truman and Byrnes, new to their jobs and potential rivals for the presidency, domestic politics overrode bureaucratic politics. Anti-Soviet sentiment among European ethnic groups and, above all, opposition to any concessions on the emperor led them to conclude that neither threats nor concessions to Japan should be spelled out in the Potsdam Declaration. In the end, domestic politics triumphed over bureaucratic and international politics in shaping the Potsdam Declaration.

The stakes, constituencies, and routines that build up around declaratory policies of states inure them to change. Resistance to change is reinforced when stated policy is the aim for which a state has been waging war. Yet not all government organizations have the same stake in perpetuating war aims. The task facing those who would change war aims is to harness those organizations whose interests are served by that change. Excluding them would only make implementation of any change more difficult and postwar politics more divisive. For any strategy of war termination to succeed, there must be a stable coalition of permanent officials within the government who are prepared to support it and carry it out.

Even then, changing war aims while the fighting still rages becomes all the more difficult when officials anticipate public and parliamentary opposition. The more bitter the division outside the government, the harder it is to form a coalition for change inside. Some officials will be tempted to capitalize on external opposition by internal resistance to change. Yet attempts at mobilizing public support run the risk of dividing the nation and lowering morale in wartime. Perhaps even more important, they run the risk of damaging officials' political standing in the nation, of being branded appeasers, even traitors. Those risks may dictate the expedient of turning on tiptoe—maneuvering artfully to get the enemy to make the first move, encouraging allies at home to take public stands for softer terms, inspiring supporters in parliament to take the lead, or floating trial balloons in the press. Japan specialists in the U.S. State Department and navy men who favored unilateral modification of American war aims in order to induce Japan to sue for peace were reluctant to go public. Theirs was an insider strategy, as Arthur Krock, columnist for the *New York Times* disclosed in early July: "Those in office who would preserve Hirohito see no point in the national debate on the subject which is sought by those who differ with them, arguing that the average American has not the information to decide which policy will best serve our present and future interest."[145] Yet dismissals of popular

[145]*New York Times*, July 5, 1945, p. 12.

views as uninformed and appeals to statesmanship are no substitute for an effort to move public opinion on the issue.

War aims need not be changed in public. Sometimes a less challenging route, at least at the start, is to change peace terms through negotiations with the enemy. If these talks are conducted in quasi-public—and keeping them a complete secret is seldom easy—public leeway is still essential, at least for talking, if not for every change in peace terms. The failure of the United States to initiate talks with Japan has been attributed to a widely shared value in and out of the U.S. government. "Backstage contacts with the enemy to determine whether there was a mutually acceptable basis for surrender," writes Paul Kecskemeti, were "never contemplated, since [they] ran counter to the fundamental American belief that anything smacking of negotiation would fatally detract from the completeness of victory and thereby jeopardize future peace."[146] This assertion needs qualification, because it is difficult to find any senior American official who shared that "fundamental American belief" and because several actually did conduct such "backstage contacts" while many others contemplated them. The reason that direct negotiations were never initiated had less to do with official beliefs about war and peace than with their anticipation of a public and parliamentary backlash.

Officials' reactions to a public pronouncement on the other side may vary somewhat according to the positions they occupy. Unless the message impinges directly upon their official duties, they may pay little attention to it. Military officers, responsible for maintaining the nation's fighting capacity, may tend to perceive any public declaration by the enemy in terms of its impact on the morale of the troops under their command, and to a lesser extent on the enemy's will to fight. Officials in charge of war production and domestic propaganda may view an enemy statement primarily in terms of its impact on civilian morale. Cabinet ministers may think of how the statement affects their ability to maintain legislative and popular support for their programs. Only diplomats, by virtue of their jobs, may be disposed to view publicly promulgated war aims from a more distant perspective, to consider what differences the terms make for the negotiating positions of the two sides and for relations with third parties, perhaps assessing what political intelligence they may yield about the enemy coalition—about the other side's domestic and alliance politics. The diversity of perspectives hardly guarantees agreement on favorable reception for enemy pronouncements.

A unilateral modification of war aims, if it is designed to get the enemy to take it seriously, is perhaps better communicated privately. Publicity

[146]Kecskemeti, *Strategic Surrender*, p. 162.

can facilitate war termination to the extent that it provides evidence of the initiator's willingness to suffer the domestic consequences of accommodating the enemy. While softer terms may appeal to enemy doves, however, they also antagonize domestic hawks. The need to satisfy both audiences simultaneously often makes publication or clarity more of a risk than officials may want to bear. That is why states opt for privacy or obfuscation in communicating war aims to the other side.

Although to Americans looking for a way out of the war Japan's reply left little room for maneuver, it did leave some—had they been in position to take advantage of it. They could have taken time to explore Japanese attitudes further through diplomatic or intelligence channels, either directly or through neutral intermediaries or intelligence channels. But without a clearer signal of Japanese willingness to sue for peace than Japan's doves could provide, they were in no such position. For the rest of Washington, Tokyo's response was reason enough to proceed with planned military operations.

So unconditional surrender remained in the way of any settlement of the war. And unlimited ends called for unlimited means.

[4]

The Politics of Military Force

And let me speak to th' yet unknowing world
How these things came about. So shall you hear
Of carnal, bloody, and unnatural acts,
Of accidental judgments, casual slaughters,
Of deaths put on by cunning and forc'd cause,
And, in this upshot, purposes mistook
Fall'n on th' inventors' heads: all this can I
Truly deliver.

— Shakespeare, *Hamlet*
(passage underlined in copy of play
in Harry S Truman's private library)

Except in the rare cases of outright conquest, contending states in the final stage of a war, even after they have fought their way to victory, defeat, or stalemate on the battlefield, still face the problem of war termination. Simply stated, that problem is to reach agreement, tacit or explicit, to stop fighting. Reaching agreement may require giving aid and comfort to those in the enemy camp who want to end the fighting and who can maneuver their own government into doing so. Even if no formal negotiations, direct or mediated, are in progress, and even if no unilateral modification of war aims seems politically practicable to bring those aims more into line with the enemy's, one strategic option left to the warring states is tacit bargaining through the deployment or withdrawal of military forces, and the threat to use them or the promise to withhold their use. Such bargaining is intrinsic to the dialectic of war—no less near its end than at its outbreak. Even then the bargaining is not completely one-sided: if the losing side cannot step up the level of violence, it may still have the residual strength to continue resisting, thereby prolonging the war.

In using force to bargain with the enemy, states can escalate as well as de-escalate, or do both at once—by stepping up mobilization at home, deploying new weapons, expanding the theater of war, recruiting other allies, or refraining from taking these steps. But to communicate intent in the bargaining between states, escalation or deescalation must be clearly perceptible to both sides. The graduated stepping up or down of force implied in the metaphor of a ladder of escalation may not be discrete enough to be perceptible. A difference in kind, not of degree, may be necessary. Morton Halperin's distinction between "expansion" and "explosion" captures this difference, but only in the direction of intensified, perhaps uncontrolled, violence.[1] Following in the path of Thomas Schelling, who stresses the importance of clear and distinct focal points in tacit bargaining, Richard Smoke defines escalation in a way that applies also to de-escalation: "a step of any size that crosses a saliency" or perceived threshold, one that is "in some fashion discrete or discontinuous" and "hence noticeable by all parties."[2] In practice, however, one side's saliency may be another's blur. This conception of escalation—indeed the very idea of tacit bargaining itself—assumes that states are attentive to and observant of the force thresholds perceived by their foes, an assumption not always borne out in the interaction between the United States and Japan at the end of World War II.

As this calculus of war implies, the threat of force can compel an agreement to stop fighting as readily as its actual use. In bargaining during war termination, leaders trying to encourage enemy doves while disarming enemy hawks may sometimes find that force kept in abeyance can accomplish more than force applied. Escalation, by conveying a threat to do worse, exploits potential asymmetries in capabilities to coerce the other side into settling. De-escalation, by conveying a promise to do better, exploits normal conventions that limit warfare to induce the other side to cease hostilities altogether. In either case, force has to be withheld. Yet to judge from the actions of the United States and Japan, states tend to behave as if applying force were the only path to war termination.

For states to observe some conventions in the waging of war is not unusual: it is the very prevalence of conventions—for example, proper treatment of prisoners of war and rescue of survivors of hostile sinkings at sea—that differentiates war from slaughter, the killing from murder. That the exercise of restraint proved at all tenable in the relatively unbridled combat of World War II does suggest at least the possibility of tacit cooperation between hostile states that is the sine qua non of bargaining during war termination. Yet, in rational-choice approaches, for

---

[1]Morton H. Halperin, *Limited War in the Nuclear Age* (New York, 1963), p. 3.

[2]Richard Smoke, *War: Controlling Escalation* (Cambridge, Mass., 1977), p. 32. Cf. Thomas C. Schelling, *The Strategy of Conflict* (New York, 1963), chap. 3. The need for symbolically clear focal points in war termination is elaborated in Lewis A. Coser, "The Termination of Conflict," *Journal of Conflict Resolution*, 5 (December 1961): 347–53.

the observance of conventions to facilitate the termination of war, not just its limitation, the contending states must be willing and able to exert consciously reciprocal self-control. American and Japanese restraint in the war in the Pacific did not always have that character.

Dropping atomic bombs on two Japanese cities without warning was perhaps the most abrupt escalation of force in history. It was by no means the only escalatory move against Japan that the United States was contemplating by late 1944. Also under active consideration were blockade and invasion, incendiary bombing, and chemical and biological warfare (CBW), specifically the use of toxic gas. Only in some of these instances can decisions of the United States to escalate or not to escalate be understood as the product of strategic calculation, of rational choice, that consciously took the enemy into account. In all but a few instances, consideration of the impact that escalation would have on Japan's internal struggle to surrender was perfunctory at best. Insofar as internal politics mattered at all to U.S. officials, it was mostly the politics of Washington, not of Tokyo.

LIMITING CHEMICAL AND BIOLOGICAL WARFARE

Nearly all wars to date have been limited wars in the sense that one or both of the contending states acted with some self-restraint in their use of available force. As all-out as World War II was by the standards of previous wars, states did observe some conventions that limited the scope of violence. The restraint shown by nearly all combatants in their use of toxic gas is particularly noteworthy. For the first time in modern warfare, a major weapon introduced in one war was almost wholly withheld in the next.

Yet the warring states did not always exert the scrupulous and consciously reciprocal self-control over chemical weapons that balance-of-power calculations might suggest. In short, mutual deterrence did not always operate as a restraint on unilateral action, nor did it preclude the use of toxic gas altogether. Japan employed gas on at least one occasion against American troops, when in desperation a beleaguered local commander on Guadalcanal ordered the use of hydrogen cyanide grenades in January 1943, and on numerous occasions against China at the instigation of the army general staff, which wanted to test the effectiveness of toxic gas both as a tactical weapon on the battlefield and as an instrument of strategic intimidation against civilian populations. Evaluations of the tests in China left senior Japanese army officers so unenthusiastic about the advantages of chemical weapons that they declined to procure the stocks needed for full-scale introduction, and they did not train troops extensively in their use and in defensive precautions.[3] Similar assessments of the effectiveness of chemical agents, as well as the strenuous logistical requirements they imposed, inhibited the U.S. armed services from insisting on their use.

International law does not appear to have been a prominent consideration for either state. Like Japan, the United States had initialed but not ratified the 1925 Geneva Protocol outlawing chemical and biological warfare. It had also announced that it would abide by some but not all of the protocol's provisions.

The calculus of deterrence was initially a consideration in the self-restraint of the United States. At first the U.S. government even refrained from lending public credence to charges by China that Japan had used chemical weapons in numerous incidents—perhaps out of concern that to do so would generate public pressure for American counteraction. Then, on June 5, 1942, one month after the British had threatened to retaliate against any "unprovoked" introduction of toxic gas by Germany on the Eastern Front, President Roosevelt, at the request of China and after consultations with British Prime Minister Churchill, issued a comparable threat for the Far East at a White House press conference. Invoking still unsubstantiated Chinese accusations of Japanese use of "poisonous or noxious gases," Roosevelt read a statement prepared by the State Department: "I desire to make it unmistakably clear that, if Japan persists in this inhuman form of warfare against China or against any other of the United Nations, such action will be regarded by the Government as though it were taken against the United States, and retaliation in kind and in full measure will be meted out."[4] Although President Roosevelt described the statement as having the

---

[3]The Chinese reported 886 incidents of chemical warfare by Japanese troops prior to 1939, but the United States uncovered no incontrovertible proof of the use of lethal agents until October 1941, when the Japanese army employed mustard gas against the Chinese at Ichang, the first of several reports subsequently confirmed by U.S. intelligence. Paradoxically, these intelligence reports contributed to a gross overestimation by the United States of Japan's capacity for waging chemical warfare. See Frederic J. Brown, *Chemical Warfare: A Study in Restraints* (Princeton, N.J., 1968), p. 247; Stockholm International Peace Research Institute (SIPRI), *The Rise of CB Weapons*, vol. 1 of *The Problems of Chemical and Biological Warfare*, by Julian Perry Robinson with Milton Leitenberg (Stockholm, 1981), pp. 147–53, 328n. The Japanese army also field-tested biological warfare agents against both battlefield and civilian targets in China and conducted numerous experiments on prisoners of war, possibly including a few Americans captured in the China theater. Reports of these tests remained unsubstantiated by U.S. intelligence until after the war. See John W. Powell, "A Hidden Chapter in History," *Bulletin of the Atomic Scientists* 37 (October 1981): 44–52; P. Y. Chen, "Japan Confirms Germ War Testing in World War II," *Washington Post*, April 8, 1982, p. A-19; and Tracy Dahlby, "Japan's Germ Warriors," *Washington Post*, May 26, 1983, p. A-1.

[4]Roosevelt Presidential Press Conferences, no. 830, June 5, 1942. Sparring with reporters, Roosevelt said there had been several instances of Japanese use of toxic gas, but he refused to provide any details.

concurrence of "the various departments concerned," Secretary of War Stimson, for one, is not likely to have given his, because he considered the United States unprepared either "to enforce complete retribution" or to protect itself against retaliation.

Later someone in the army's Chemical Warfare Services seems to have changed Roosevelt's reference to "poisonous or noxious *gases*" to "poisonous or noxious *agents*."[5] The emendation had the effect of extending the reach of the statement to biological as well as chemical weapons. China's charges of Japanese germ warfare, made earlier that week, seem to have had no bearing on the timing of Roosevelt's statement, and the president himself made no allusion to them. The Chemical Warfare Services used his threat of "retaliation in kind" as justification for trying to develop and stockpile both chemical and biological weapons, as well as protective gear, in the event that words alone did not deter Japan.

A year later, on June 8, 1943, President Roosevelt formally reaffirmed a policy of no first use of CBW: "I state categorically that we shall under no circumstances resort to the use of such weapons unless they are first used by our enemies."[6] He warned that even tactical use by the enemy might result in strategic retaliation, but in spelling out the precise form that retribution might take, he confined himself to gas alone: "Any use of gas by any Axis power, therefore, will immediately be followed by the fullest possible retaliation upon munitions centers, seaports, and other military objectives throughout the whole extent of the territory of such Axis country."

The United States did not then have the chemical munitions stocks to make that threat credible, and it moved only slowly to procure them. Moreover, the reason Roosevelt gave for issuing the statement—"reports that one or more of the Axis powers were seriously contemplating use of poisonous or noxious gases and other inhumane devices of warfare"—tacitly denied what Japan had reason to believe the president knew, that it had already used such devices in China. That may have further detracted from the credibility of the American threat to retaliate. Only in 1944, as German resistance was collapsing and U.S. advances in the Pacific brought its bombers within range of Japan's cities, did Japanese CBW tests fall off sharply.

Early in 1944 the Japanese government issued its first clear statement of intent concerning chemical warfare. In messages relayed through the Swiss government and the apostolic delegate, Japan denied using gas during "the present conflict" and declared the intention "not to make

---

[5]Brown, *Chemical Warfare*, pp. 200–201, quotes the version in the files of the Chemical Warfare Services.

[6]Statement by the President, "Use of Poison Gas," June 8, 1943, in U.S. Department of State, *Bulletin*, June 12, 1943, p. 507.

use of it in the future on [the] supposition that the troops of [the] United Nations also abstain from using it."[7] The statement may have been prompted by a January 30, 1944, article by the *New York Times* military correspondent Hanson Baldwin noting that recent Anglo-American revelations of Japanese mistreatment of Allied prisoners of war might help ease "the compunctions of public opinion" against use of gas by the United States.[8] Only late in the war did deterrence seem to exert a restraining effect on Japanese CBW policy.

Allied vulnerability to retaliatory attack, upon which the American no-first-use policy was predicated, continued to deter initiation of gas warfare in the Pacific by the United States until the spring of 1945. "We were all ready to use it on some of the islands," Army Chief of Staff Marshall told David Lilienthal in 1947. "The reason it was not used was chiefly the strong opposition of Churchill and the British. They were afraid that this would be the signal for the Germans to use gas against England."[9] By agreement of the Combined Chiefs of Staff in 1942, the United States was free to retaliate unilaterally but was pledged not to initiate the use of gas without prior British consent. In 1944 that agreement was extended to cover retaliatory use as well, which required the approval of the British and all Commonwealth governments concerned.[10] The same logic of mutual deterrence presumably still applied, though perhaps less compellingly, to possible Japanese retaliation against other Allied troops and territory in the Far East — French and Dutch colonies, China, or, once it entered the war, the Soviet Union. The logic was certainly compelling enough for Chiang Kai-shek to make an arrangement with the commander of U.S. forces in China, Major General Albert Wedemeyer, stipulating that retaliation for Japan's use of gas, even against China's cities, not be taken against strategic targets and be undertaken only "upon a joint declaration" by the United States and China. The arrangement was concluded without the prior knowledge or consent of the War Department or the chiefs of staff.[11] Whether formal agreements were operative or not, the United States was under some obligation to notify its allies of its intent to initiate chemical warfare, in order to give them time to take defensive measures of their own, and it was under some restraint not to initiate it at all because of the threat of Axis retaliation against the Allies.

[7]Brown, *Chemical Warfare*, pp. 249–50.
[8]Hanson Baldwin, "A War without Quarter Forecast in the Pacific," *New York Times*, January 30, 1944, p. E-3.
[9]David Lilienthal, *The Journals of David Lilienthal*, II: *The Atomic Energy Years* (New York, 1964), p. 199. Cf. Fletcher Knebel and Charles W. Bailey, "Secret: The Fight over the A-Bomb," *Look*, August 13, 1963, p. 23.
[10]John Moon, "Chemical Weapons and Deterrence: The World War II Experience," *International Security* 8 (Spring 1984): 15–16.
[11]Brown, *Chemical Warfare*, pp. 279–80.

In 1944, as Germany's surrender seemed more and more of a foregone conclusion and as American island-hopping across the Pacific began to exact an appalling toll on American troops, the inhibiting effect of deterrence seemed to weaken. Proposals to employ toxic chemicals against the Japanese made their way up the chain of command in the United States with greater frequency, but they were temporarily held in check by the anticipated opposition of President Roosevelt.[12] Yet the more enduring check was the resistance of the armed services themselves. Professional and moral revulsion may have inspired part of that resistance: some military men personally recoiled at the thought of indiscriminate killing and inhumane weapons. Admiral William Leahy, military adviser to the president, was one officer so moved. During an informal conversation in July 1944, as Roosevelt and his military aides were sailing to Honolulu to confer on strategy in the Pacific war, some senior officers raised the possibility of destroying Japan's rice crop by germ warfare. According to Leahy, "spirited discussion" ensued in which he objected on both moral and deterrence grounds: "Mr. President, this would violate every Christian ethic I have ever heard of and all of the known laws of war. It would be an attack on the noncombatant population of the enemy. The reaction can be foretold—if we use it, the enemy will use it."[13]

Leahy's objections comported with the organizational interests of his career service, the navy. Use of chemical and biological weapons, whether strategically or tactically, to weaken Japan's defenses was a complement to the army's strategy of invading Japan's home islands, which the navy opposed. Leahy did not express similar reservations about a campaign of naval blockade and bombardment, which would have attacked Japan's population less indirectly and no less indiscriminately, at least in the Japanese cities subjected to bombing. Chemical and biological warfare also affected air force interests adversely. It would divert scarce resources from its campaign of strategic bombing using incendiary bombs and high explosives. Bombers would have to be reassigned from conventional bombing missions to dropping chemical munitions. And bomb casings, in short supply after the introduction of the larger-payload B-29s, would have to be reallocated from the air force's incendiary and high explosive

[12]Presidential authorization was required for any use of CBW since 1942, when Marshall rescinded a 1934 standing order permitting retaliatory use by field commanders and directed that the authority to do so rested with him, only to have Roosevelt supersede him that December and reserve the decision for himself (according to SIPRI, *Rise of CB Weapons*, p. 316). This was further formalized and clarified by U.S. acceptance of a British proposal in the Combined Chiefs of Staff Meeting on December 31, 1943 (Moon, "Chemical Weapons and Deterrence," p. 15).

[13]Leahy, *I Was There*, p. 440. Roosevelt remained noncommittal throughout the conversation.

[164]

programs to the army's toxic bomb-making, to prepare for even retaliatory use of chemical agents. Above all, strategic use of CBW might weaken the air force's claim that strategic bombing with conventional bombs was the winning strategy against Japan. Army interests were less clear-cut. Despite the Chemical Warfare Services' enthusiasm for its mission, chemical and biological warfare was subordinate to the army's organizational essence, ground combat. Strategic use of CBW to soften up Japan for invasion only invited Japanese retaliation against the army's invading force as it hit the beaches, forcing troops to don defensive gear that would impede a landing, if not make it much more hazardous. Besides, though only a handful of senior army officers knew it, another weapon was under development that could perform this mission much more devastatingly with no risk of retaliation in kind. In contrast, once the army invaders had secured a beachhead on Japan proper, tactical use of chemical weapons against well-entrenched defenders might hold down American casualties. If, however, the Japanese were to respond in kind, a net assessment might not prove promising, especially in view of the army's exaggerated estimate of Japan's CBW capabilities. With these interests at stake, it was difficult to get the chiefs of staff to approve even the readiness needed for retaliatory use, let alone to propose to the president that he authorize first use of chemical and biological weapons.

Every battle in the Pacific became a pretext for the Chemical Warfare Services to press for first use. In November 1943, after intensive fighting on Tarawa, it had tried and failed. In early 1945, in the aftermath of the costly campaign to take Iwo Jima, the Joint Chiefs of Staff considered a proposal to use chemical weapons in the forthcoming landing on Okinawa, but no formal proposal for use was forwarded to the president. By the spring of 1945, advocates of gas warfare began pressing against two deadlines. The ultimate deadline was November 1, the target date proposed to President Truman for the invasion of Japan. By then production, stockpiling, and logistical preparations had to be completed for the contingency of use. The more proximate deadline was the Potsdam Conference, where the Allies could be consulted about initiating use. In advance of a presidential go-ahead for its invasion plans, however, the army had to proceed with caution lest the CBW issue raise broader questions about its strategy for ending the war. On May 10 General Joseph Stilwell, commander of army ground forces, recommended that Army Chief of Staff Marshall consider using chemical weapons in the invasion of Japan. The recommendation emphasized introducing chemical mortar and artillery rounds, as well as increased use of flame throwers, rather than chemical bombing, thereby sidestepping potential air force objections. A copy of Stilwell's recommendation was forwarded to

Air Force Chief of Staff Arnold for comment.[14] Neither he nor Marshall was in any hurry to proceed. On May 30, a day after Marshall had broached the subject with Stimson, Arnold's office finally drafted a response, which stood firmly for procrastination: "The Army Air Forces together with the Chemical Warfare Services are continuing to study both the strategic and tactical employment of gas by air."[15]

While Arnold may not have been prepared to take on the army openly, he was not equally restrained in his reaction to proposals from within his own service. On June 1 the Air Technical Service Command briefed him on plans for "a quick knockout of Japan from the air by concentrating on sources of food," to include spraying ammonium thiocyanate or mustard gas on the rice-producing areas that supplied Japan's six largest cities, sowing mines in the main fishing grounds, and low-altitude bombing of large schools of fish. Arnold referred the plan to the director of the Joint Target Group, planners whose eyes were clearly focused on the air force's essence. The reply was not long in coming: "Our general attitude toward this question is that the effort required to do a good job against food would be better expended against material objectives having earlier and more certain impact."[16] Nothing could divert the air force from strategic bombing of cities, surely not chemical strikes against fish and rice paddies.

The army did not want to hold its strategy of invasion hostage to a reversal of CBW policy, but once the Joint Chiefs had reached agreement on June 14–15 to proceed with invasion plans, along with bombing and blockade, the army felt freer to approach the other services for approval of preparations for CBW use. The shift in army priorities is evident in the contrast between a June 4 OPD memorandum, which refrained from endorsing the use of gas as decisive for the invasion, and a June 14 OPD paper, which Marshall circulated to his colleagues on the Joint Chiefs of Staff, proposing that they order accelerated production of chemical weapons and take up the ban on first use "informally" with the president before he met the Allies at Potsdam. The June 14 paper made the case for first use openly, endorsing toxic gas as the one weapon not yet used

[14]Memorandum from Stilwell to Chief of Staff, May 10, 1945, Box 115, SAS 385 (Japan), Arnold Papers, Library of Congress; and Leo P. Brophy and George J. B. Fisher, *Organizing for War*, vol. 1 of U.S. Department of the Army, Office of the Chief of Military History, *The U.S. Army in World War II*, Ser. XI: The Technical Services, VII: Chemical Warfare Services (Washington, D.C., 1959), p. 86.

[15]Memorandum for the Chief of Staff, "Comments on Air Aspects of General Stilwell's Memorandum Relative to the Invasion of Japan," May 30, 1945, Box 115, SAS 385 (Japan), Arnold Papers.

[16]Brigadier General John A. Samford (Director of the Joint Target Group) to Major General V. E. Bertrandias (Air Technical Service Command), June 4, 1945, Box 115, SAS 385 (Japan), Arnold Papers.

"which assuredly can greatly decrease the cost in American lives and should materially shorten the war." The value of CBW seemed to appreciate the more the enemy was dehumanized: "He resists fanatically down to the last individual, burrowing into the ground and forcing our troops to engage in costly, time-consuming, and what amount to diversionary operations." The paper went on to challenge one of the more obvious counterarguments to first use—the postwar value of continued restraint. Conceding that first use would make the United States "liable to attack by chemical and biological warfare on the opening day of any future war," it dismissed that liability with the assertion that the next war would be all-out anyway: "[A] realistic military assessment must recognize that if the U.S. is ever again attacked, we will be attacked without warning and with the immediate employment of all weapons known in an effort to crush this nation before it can mobilize its tremendous latent power."[17] Military realism in the harness of organizational interests can be notoriously shortsighted, not to say unrealistic.

The paper recognized that two constituencies had to be placated before the United States could initiate use of chemical and biological weapons. One was the allies of the United States, who felt vulnerable to Japanese retaliation. The paper suggested discussing the change of policy with Stalin at Potsdam and with Chiang at a later date; it did not mention the British or other allies. Another was the American people, "conditioned against the use of chemical warfare," who might be disabused of their conditioning by publicizing the claim that gas was not as "terrible" as the "jelly bomb" or the flame thrower already in use: "If put to the people properly, they should approve." A campaign in the press, under way since early 1944, had already begun registering results in public opinion, especially after Iwo Jima and Okinawa, A September 1944 poll had found 23 percent of respondents in favor of using gas against Japan's cities; by June 1945, some 40 percent favored "using poison gas against the Japanese if doing so would reduce the number of American soldiers who are killed and wounded." Yet 49 percent remained opposed.[18]

Admiral Leahy responded to Marshall on June 20. As far as he was concerned, Roosevelt's 1943 reaffirmation of no first use had settled the matter, but he did not object to having Marshall reopen it with Roosevelt's successor. He suggested an approach: seek standing authority from Truman for retaliatory use, which would allow shipment of chemical munitions to the theater. "I have no doubt," Leahy surmised, "that

[17]Marshall to King, "U.S. Chemical Warfare Policy," June 14, 1945, Records of the War Department, General and Specific Staffs, Operations Decimal File, 1945, OPD 385, TS, RG 165, National Archives. Cf. Brophy and Fisher, *Organizing for War*, p. 87.
[18]Brown, *Chemical Warfare*, p. 287; SIPRI, *Rise of CB Weapons*, p. 321.

the President would approve" a recommendation from the Joint Chiefs to grant that authority.[19] Yet retaliatory use, even if it took the form of strategic retaliation against "enemy populations" rather than tactical use on the battlefield, was not the same as first use, and Marshall did not believe that diversion of scarce logistical capacity to transport chemical munitions within range of Japan was warranted for that purpose. He replied to Leahy the next day, "Because of the very considerable requirements in service troops, storage facilities, port capacity and shipping involved in providing forward stock[s] equal to our greatly increased capabilities [a reference to the larger B-29 payload], there is a serious question in my mind that a military justification exists" for the deployment "unless we are contemplating its use on other than a retaliatory basis."[20]

The Joint Chiefs took up the question of readiness to wage chemical and biological warfare on June 19, one day after Truman authorized invasion plans. They approved production of "sufficient chemical warfare munitions" by November 1945 "to conduct retaliatory gas warfare." They also agreed in principle on the need to ship those munitions to the Pacific, but deferred cutting orders to implement that deployment. Competing logistical requirements still had priority.[21]

When Truman set sail for Potsdam, the armed services had yet to recommend a policy of first use or to break its deadlock over forward deployment of chemical munitions. The OPD briefing book for Potsdam says only that "the advisability of changing the policy to permit the use of gas against the Japanese has been discussed informally by the JCS." Because the Allies were thought likely to oppose that change, "a decision to initiate use of gas must be taken on the highest level."[22] No recommendation or decision to do so was forthcoming prior to the end of the war.

In his study of chemical warfare, Frederic Brown concludes that "a lack of assimilation of toxic agents within the military profession" was the key to restraint: "Aside from those military leaders institutionally committed to toxic agents, the military establishment as a whole was opposed to their use." But Brown may exceed his evidence when he asserts that "the outcome of JCS consideration of chemical warfare was to limit severely, if not preclude, the chance of a subsequent decision to initiate had the war

[19]Leahy memorandum to Marshall, June 20, 1945, Operations Decimal File, 1945, OPD 385, TS, RG 165, National Archives.

[20]Brown, *Chemical Warfare*, pp. 273–74.

[21]Ibid., p. 273.

[22]U.S. Department of War, OPD, "Compilation of Subjects for Possible Discussion at Terminal," Tab 60, "Change in Chemical Warfare Policy," Item 21a, Exec. 5, Records of the War Department, General and Special Staffs, RG 165, National Archives.

continued into the fall and winter of 1945."[23] Once a landing on Kyushu was effected, service interests would change in subtle ways, loosening inhibitions on American initiation of chemical warfare. The landing would have outflanked the strategy of blockade and bombardment, leaving the U.S. navy with no compelling organizational interest in opposing chemical warfare other than its potential use against ships' crews in the future. By then too the U.S. air force would have all but exhausted its target list for strategic bombing with conventional munitions.[24] Production and logistical bottlenecks might also have eased enough to permit deployment of chemical munitions stocks large enough for tactical, if not strategic, use.

In any event, concern about retaliation against the Allies was no longer a critical consideration by the summer of 1945, judging from the frequency and substance of internal U.S. discussions of chemical use. Brown's point about the critical role of bureaucratic politics is thus well taken. Conscious strategic calculation of the potential Axis reaction had stayed America's hand until Germany's capitulation, but thereafter organizational interests supplanted balance-of-power considerations in restraining initiation of chemical warfare in the Pacific by the United States.

ESCALATING THE CONVENTIONAL BOMBING OF JAPAN

Intrawar deterrence may have helped forestall early introduction of toxic gas into the war against Japan by the United States, but no equivalent restraint was available to inhibit escalation of conventional bombing by the Americans. Moreover, bombing was thoroughly integrated into air force and navy standard operating procedures. Only small adjustments in air force procedures would lead to a substantial expansion in death and destruction. Above all, conventional bombing had what chemical warfare lacked: determined advocacy in senior military quarters. To most high-ranking officers in the army air forces, strategic bombing with conventional munitions was not just another mission; it was the raison d'être of an autonomous air force in the postwar American military establishment. Nothing could tame their ambitions for strategic bombing, whatever the consequences for Japan's internal struggle to surrender. Exploiting its substantial autonomy in the theaters of war out

[23]Brown, *Chemical Warfare*, pp. 288, 293–94, 271.
[24]Air force resistance to chemical warfare missions had already softened enough by early August to set in motion plans for a test destruction of crops from the air at Eglin Field (Memorandum from Lieutenant General Ira C. Eaker [deputy commander of the Army Air Forces] to the deputy chief of the Air Staff, "Experiment in Destruction of Crops by Air," August 3, 1945, Box 115, SAS 385 (Japan), Arnold Papers, Library of Congress).

of reach of Washington, the air force proceeded to bomb the Japanese home islands with impunity, ignoring opportunities to raise or lower the intensity of its attacks with a view toward strengthening the hand of those in Tokyo who were looking for a way out of the war.

Sustained American bombing of Japanese cities commenced in June 1944. Using high explosives, air force B-29s from Saipan concentrated on demolishing aircraft plants spreading relatively little havoc beyond the immediate vicinity of the plants. By early 1945 these attacks, like comparable ones against Germany, were proving inconclusive, disappointing some in the army air forces who had hoped for more spectacular results. Nevertheless, the so-called "bomber radicals" in air force ranks resisted any change in tactics and targets, preferring instead to press on with precision bombing—or what passed for precision bombing at the time.

Bombing was never very accurate in World War II, even after the deployment of long-range fighter escorts and other measures to protect the bombers in flight, or the introduction of a primitive radar to permit bombing runs in bad weather. What has been called precision bombing was, more or less, area bombing in which the size and shape of the area struck was a function of the size and shape of the mission itself—how many bombers flying how many sorties in what formation. What made precision bombing at all precise was the coincidence of the target area and the flying pattern. In the words of Walt Rostow, a target planner in the European theater, "Only in the case of a few targets (e.g., synthetic oil plants) was the plant area larger than the minimum bomb pattern, so that, in most instances, the physical center of the plant could serve as an adequate operational aiming point."[25] Otherwise, even when the aim point was hit, collateral damage in the form of death and destruction to whatever lay in the vicinity was unavoidable. The response of Britain's Bomber Command was to make a virtue out of necessity. Because it was uneconomical to "waste" collateral damage on small area targets with precise aim points, the Bomber Command's solution was to strike at larger area targets.[26] It was but a stone's throw from targeting cities per se. Basil Liddell Hart's characterization of the change is right on target: "Inaccuracy of weapon aim fostered inhumanity of war aim."[27]

Japan's war-related industry was concentrated in a few large congested cities, in neighborhoods full of highly combustible residential structures, some of which housed small manufacturing plants. As long ago as October 1943, intelligence analyses had reached the conclusion that Japan was consequently more vulnerable to incendiary bombing

---

[25]Walt W. Rostow, *Pre-Invasion Bombing Strategy* (Austin, Tex., 1981), p. 21.

[26]This consideration is evident in Sir Solly Zuckerman's assessment of the British bombing of transport before the invasion of Sicily, see ibid., p. 12.

[27]B. H. Liddell Hart, *The Revolution in Warfare* (London, 1946), p. 31.

than Germany. Not only would incendiary attacks disrupt its "cottage" industries camouflaged in residential areas, but they might also destroy adjacent fire-resistant plants in any general conflagration that ensued. Of course, they would also destroy nearby residences and kill innocent civilians. By October 1944 a few officers on General Arnold's staff began urging that the Twenty-first Bomber Command conduct trial raids on Japanese cities, dropping incendiary bombs instead of high explosives, but the commander of the Twenty-first General Haywood S. Hansell, a prototypical "bomber radical," was slow to respond.

In January 1945 General Curtis LeMay was dispatched to Guam to replace Hansell. The change of command was a sign that a change of tactics was in the offing. So too was the participation of American bombers in British raids on German cities in early February—the most savage of them against Dresden on February 13–15, which killed 135,000 people. When newspapers in the United States reported the attacks, General Carl Spaatz, commander of the bombers, hastened to defend U.S. involvement as confined to precision bombing of military targets.[28]

Later that month, following trial raids against Nagoya and Kobe, Arnold approved a new target directive. It modified the previous strategy of delaying any incendiary bombing of Japan until the air force could synchronize attacks on all Japan's cities, it moved incendiary bombing up to second in priority behind precision bombing of aircraft engine factories, and it designated Nagoya, Osaka, Kawasaki, and Tokyo as primary targets for the new pattern of attacks.[29] The air force's justification for the new directive placed emphasis on continuity with its customary bombing mission—counterforce strikes against enemy military capacity in support of the army's invasion plans—but implementation of the directive led to a radical change of mission: countervalue attacks on Japan's population and socioeconomic structure. Proponents hoped that the new bombing strategy would prove decisive in ending the war, obviating the need for further ground-force operations against Japan. Because counterforce and countervalue targets are seldom as distin-

[28]George Quester, *Deterrence before Hiroshima* (New York, 1966), p. 150. Quester (pp. 127–29, 145–49) offers a succinct discussion of bombing doctrine prior to 1945. Poor visibility and high loss rates over Germany led gradually to a change of mission, according to David MacIsaac, *Strategic Bombing in World War II* (New York, 1976), pp. 78–80. At Yalta the Joint Chiefs of Staff even toyed with using war-worn aircraft as drones to attack German cities by radio control, but the proposal ran afoul of objections in the Combined Chiefs of Staff, where British sensitivity to retaliation by German V-bombers prevailed. See Minutes, 190th meeting of JCS, February 8, 1945, CCS 334, 2–2–45, Records of U.S. Joint Chiefs of Staff, RG 218, National Archives.

[29]Wesley F. Craven and James L. Cate, *The Pacific: Matterhorn to Nagasaki, June 1944 to August 1945*, vol. 5 of U.S. Air Force, Historical Division of Research Studies, *The Army Air Forces in World War II* (Chicago: 1953), pp. 608–11. Cf. Strategic Bombing Survey (Pacific), *Effects of Strategic Bombing*, p. 63.

guishable in fact as they are in theory, the air force was able to accomplish the change without attracting undue attention in Washington, either from its parent service—the army—or from senior officials in the War Department, most notably Stimson, who were anxious to hold down civilian casualties in Japan.

The U.S. Strategic Bombing Survey acknowledges the subtlety of the change: "With the benefit of hindsight, it appears that the twin objectives of surrender without invasion and reduction of Japan's capacity and will to resist an invasion, should the first not succeed, called for basically the same type of attack." The proper target for either, says the survey, was "the basic economic and social fabric of the country."[30] Yet some distinctions may have been worth preserving—in particular, those between the noncombatant population of Japan and, say, its rail and transportation network. The air force chose to attack Japan's people. "Although urban area attacks were initiated in force in March 1945," the survey notes, "the railroad attack was just getting under way when the war ended." And by replacing high explosives with incendiary bombs, the air force assured that the bombing would be indiscriminate. Incendiaries, however, would also assure that the change in bombing practices would not remain invisible for long in Washington.

How the air force made this change says a good deal about why the change was made. Authority to work out the operational details of the new directive was delegated to the commander in the field, General LeMay, an exponent of strategic bombing. LeMay contemplated four changes in tactics. First, the bombers would fly low—at altitudes of 5,000–9,000 feet instead of 20,000–30,000 feet. Second, they would make individual bombing runs on their targets instead of flying in formation, eliminating the need to rendezvous en route. Third, they would carry no armament. All three changes saved fuel, and hence weight, enabling the planes to carry a heavier bomb load. Yet they also combined to make the bombers more vulnerable to Japanese air defenses—only partially offset by American seizure of Iwo Jima in late March, which shortened Japan's warning time and curtailed its ability to intercept American bombers en route to their targets. The net increase in vulnerability led LeMay to institute yet another change: attacking at night, when Japan's fighter planes, performing without benefit of radar, could least mount effective opposition. Even in daylight, visual bombing had proven inaccurate because of normal weather conditions over Japan, but nighttime raids exposed cities as the only discernible targets and made pinpoint accuracy impossible. LeMay's four tactical innovations amounted to a stra-

[30]U.S. Strategic Bombing Survey (Pacific), *Summary Report*, Report No. 1 (Washington, D.C., 1946), p. 16.

tegic revolution. The consequence was a gross increase in both civilian casualties and damage to nonmilitary installations.[31] As the first mission to adopt the new tactics was airborne, LeMay spoke of his hopes for strategic bombing: "If this raid works the way I think it will, we can shorten the war."[32] At another time and another place LeMay would use an earthier expression to describe what he was doing: stop "swatting at the flies" and go after "the manure pile."[33]

Secretary of War Stimson learned of the impending changes before they were put into practice and just after reading reports of the destruction of Dresden. The Dresden firebombing seemed to him "on its face terrible and probably unnecessary." He summoned Assistant Secretary of War for Air Robert A. Lovett to his office on March 5 and expressed his opposition to escalation of the air war. He elicited a promise from Lovett that the army air forces would employ "only precision bombing" in Japan against purely military targets. He also struck Kyoto from the list of targets.[34] Yet it was a measure of Stimson's influence at the time that his injunction had little effect on the conduct of the bombing. The air force did spare Kyoto for the moment, but it went ahead with plans to escalate the bombing. Orders were cut on March 7. The first mission, 334 B-29s laden with about 2,000 tons of bombs, took place on the night of March 9–10, Japan time. The bombers struck Tokyo, setting off a firestorm that all but leveled an area of 15.8 square miles, consuming nearly one of every four buildings in the capital and much of its largest residential neighborhoods. The attack killed 83,793 people and injured another 40,918. American losses were fourteen B-29s downed and forty-two damaged, all by enemy flak; Japanese fighters did not shoot down any.[35] Incendiary bombing of three other Japanese metropolises—Nagoya, Osaka, and Kobe—followed in rapid succession.

On June 1 Stimson renewed his opposition to escalation of the air war. He told Arnold of Lovett's promise to do "only precision bombing." Arnold replied that the proximity of industrial areas to employees' homes in Japan's cities made it "practically impossible to destroy the war output

---

[31]For LeMay's changes, Craven and Cate, *The Pacific*, pp. 612–14; Brooks E. Kleber and Dale Birdsell, *Chemicals in Combat*, vol. 3 of U.S. Department of the Army, Office of the Chief of Military History, *The U.S. Army in World War II*, Ser. XI: The Technical Services, VII: Chemical Warfare Services (Washington, D.C., 1966), pp. 626–27; Strategic Bombing Survey (Pacific), *Summary Report*, pp. 16–17; and St. Clair McKelway, "A Reporter with the B-29s," *The New Yorker*, June 23, 1945, pp. 28–30, 34–35.
[32]McKelway, "A Reporter with the B-29s," p. 36.
[33]David Halberstam, *The Best and the Brightest* (Greenwich, Conn., 1973), p. 560.
[34]Stimson diary, March 5, 1945, Yale University Library. Anticipated opposition from Stimson may account for LeMay's delay in informing Arnold of his intention to introduce his new tactics in the first mission of the pre-Okinawa bombing campaign. See Craven and Cate, *Men and Planes*, p. 614.
[35]Craven and Cate, *The Pacific*, pp. 615–17.

of Japan without doing more damage to civilians connected to that output than in Europe." He assured Stimson that the air force was trying to keep civilian casualties "down as far as possible." Stimson then repeated his injunction that Kyoto not be bombed without his permission.[36] Over Stimson's protestations the bombing continued unabated. The commander of the Far East Air Force, General George E. Kenney, went so far as to assert publicly that nothing was out of bounds for American bombing—"and that goes for the Emperor's palace, as far as I'm concerned."[37] In fact, part of the palace was struck.

On June 8 Marshall raised a different objection to the bombing campaign. Why, he wondered, had LeMay's Twentieth Air Force been striking the same target concentrations over and over again—the Nagoya area, the Kobe–Osaka area, and the Tokyo Bay area, which encompassed Tokyo, Kawasaki, and Yokohama? All were strategic targets, not necessarily the ones the army wanted struck in a campaign to reduce Japan's capacity to meet its planned invasion.[38]

Meanwhile, naval aviators, whose gradual ascendancy was manifesting itself more and more in personnel and doctrinal changes in the navy, became fearful of air force assertions of control over postwar aviation and took steps to head it off. Not to be outdone, the navy began running carrier-based air strikes against Japan.

On June 17, after destroying most major metropolitan areas in Japan, LeMay's bombers began turning their attention to its lesser cities. In late July they began calling their shots, dropping leaflets to warn cities of impending attack, then striking several of those they had warned.[39] By war's end they had flown some sixty missions against fifty-eight cities and towns. Only five of Japan's cities escaped largely unscathed from the conventional bombing: Kokura, Hiroshima, Niigata, Nagasaki, and Kyoto. Little better was in store for them.

A major escalation of the conventional bombing thus took place in March 1945, causing unprecedented civilian casualties and devastation

[36]Stimson diary, June 1, 1945. Cf. Stimson letter to Arnold, June 11, 1945, and reply from Arnold's deputy, General Ira C. Eaker, of the same date, Box 46, Folder 173, Arnold Papers.

[37]Remarks to newsmen, June 24, 1945, in F. M. Brewer, "Emperor of Japan," *Editorial Research Reports*, August 14, 1945, p. 125. Cf. letter of February 26 from Senator Brien McMahon, Democrat from Connecticut, asking whether the Imperial Palace had been placed off-limits to bombing, and a March 7 reply from the deputy chief of the Air Staff: "No directive has been issued to units of the Twentieth Air Force to bomb the Imperial Palace nor has any directive to the contrary been issued" (Brigadier General Ray L. Owens to McMahon, March 7, 1945, Box 115, SAS 385 [Japan], Arnold Papers).

[38]Memorandum from AC/AS Plans to Arnold, June 9, 1945, Box 115, SAS 385 (Japan), Arnold Papers.

[39]Craven and Cate, *The Pacific*, pp. 656, 674–75. Cf. U.S. Army, *Imperial Japanese Headquarters Army High Command Record*, pp. 203–4 and chart 16.

in Japan. A new air force targeting directive set the escalation in motion, but its implementation, the choice of tactics and targets, was left to the commander in the field, who had the greatest stake in demonstrating the impact of his strategy without considering its political ramifications with regard to the struggle within Japan over war termination. The escalation had one obvious consequence: it eroded whatever was left of the distinction between military and civilian targets. Although the air force used the proximity of war-related industry and residential areas as a pretext for its change in targeting and tactics, by 1944 home industry was no longer contributing substantially to Japan's war production while the more well constructed of its factory buildings were able to withstand the firestorms. [40] The air force attacks did not qualify as counterforce bombing: its targets were the cities and the people in them. Details of implementation saw to that.

"Authority fades with distance and with the speed of light," Dean Acheson once observed. [41] General LeMay's autonomy in the field allowed the erosion of any restraints on conventional bombing to pass virtually unnoticed by civilian authorities back in Washington. This is evident in a May 16 memorandum to the president from Stimson, who had earlier protested the extent of civilian bombing casualties. Now he discussed bombing operations as if no major escalation had already transpired: "I am anxious," he told Truman, "to hold our Air Force, so far as possible, to the 'precision' bombing which it has done so well in Europe. I am told that it is possible and adequate." He had much more than conventional bombing in mind: "I believe the same rule of sparing the civilian population should be applied as far as possible to the use of any new weapons." [42] It was. As a result, Stimson would have no more success in limiting the atomic bombing than he had had with the conventional bombing.

THE ATOMIC BOMBINGS—A FOREGONE CONCLUSION?

The decision to use the atomic bomb was a foregone conclusion. On this point the testimony of senior participants is unanimous. That conclusion was a legacy of Franklin D. Roosevelt, as those in a position to know chose to interpret that legacy for his successor, Harry S Truman. "At no time, from 1941 to 1945," writes Stimson, "did I ever hear it suggested by the President, or by any other responsible member of the

---

[40]Strategic Bombing Survey (Pacific), *Summary Report*, p. 18.
[41]Dean Acheson, *Sketches from Life of Men I Have Known* (New York, 1961), p. 48.
[42]Memorandum to Truman, Stimson diary, May 16, 1945.

government, that atomic energy should not be used in the war."[43] His qualifier, "responsible," is well chosen, for it highlights the distinction between those who occupied formal positions of authority for the atomic bomb program and those who did not—among them, a handful of scientists working the Manhattan Project, none of them senior administrators, who spearheaded opposition to using the bomb on Japanese cities without warning. The very fact that they were not "responsible members of government" limited their ability to influence those who were. They lacked both access and standing to intervene in the decisions about use of the bomb. Confined by official secrecy, they often lacked detailed knowledge of plans. What knowledge they had was sometimes informally obtained, restricting its use.

Even if use of the bomb was a foregone conclusion for the officials responsible, how to use it—what limits, if any, to place on its use—was not. The targets to be struck and the precise aim points, the number of bombs to be dropped and the time interval between them, and whether to precede or accompany the bombings with warnings were all matters of controversy within the U.S. government. Truman may never have been fully apprised of all the alternatives to dropping atomic bombs on Japan's cities without warning. Procedures for deciding about the bomb's use suggest why this was so: they left the choices of options in the hands of subordinate officials with the greatest stake in showing off the bomb to maximum effect—those responsible for building it and delivering it on target.

In the former group were those in charge of the Manhattan Engineering District (MED), the code name for the project to explore uses for atomic energy in the war and eventually to build the atomic bomb. Having expended nearly $2 billion—a vast sum by the standards of the day, even in wartime—and having done so with only the loosest internal fiscal controls and little or no congressional scrutiny, they were very anxious to have something to show for the money. As Leslie R. Groves, the MED's commanding general, remarked to his staff on Christmas Eve 1944, "If this weapon fizzles, each of you can look forward to a lifetime of testifying before congressional investigating committees."[44]

---

[43]Stimson, "Decision," p. 98.

[44]Fletcher Knebel and Charles W. Bailey, *No High Ground* (New York: Harper, 1960), p. 75. For additional evidence of this concern, see Vannevar Bush, *Pieces of the Action* (New York, 1970), pp. 278–79; Committee on Postwar Policy, Memorandum of December 28, 1944, MED, TS of Interest to Groves, folder 3, RG 77, National Archives, p. 5; Byrnes, Memorandum to the President, March 3, 1945, MED, TS of Interest to Groves, Folder 17, RG 77, National Archives; Lilienthal, *Journals*, II: 200; Leslie R. Groves, *Now It Can Be Told* (New York, 1962), pp. 70, 360; William L. Laurence, *Dawn over Zero: The Story of the Atomic Bomb* (New York, 1946), pp. 92–93; William L. Laurence, *Men and Atoms* (New York, 1959), p. 108; Memorandum from Under Secretary of War Patterson to General William Styer,

For the scientists administering the MED laboratories, even more was at stake. While many in the scientific community still clung to an older monastic tradition, that was not the case with the MED's Ernest O. Lawrence, Harold C. Urey, Arthur H. Compton, or J. Robert Oppenheimer. They were, in the words of Vannevar Bush, "scientific politicians" who had mastered the art of academic and bureaucratic politics and did not shrink from applying them to get their way.[45] A major concern for all of them was the impermanence of government support for science, especially for basic research as opposed to mission-oriented research. They wanted a civilian agency established after the war to fund basic research on a multiyear basis, rather than annually as is the custom with congressional appropriations. That meant an agency controlled by the scientists themselves, who alone, in their view, had the expertise to evaluate basic research. It also meant release from the military security apparatus and the compartmentation it imposed on freedom of inquiry. The blueprint for these scientific entrepreneurs was a 1945 report entitled *Science: The Endless Frontier*. So immodest were the report's goals that they prompted Budget Director Harold Smith to wonder whether "endless frontier" really meant "endless expenditure."[46] Skeptics notwithstanding, nuclear weapons, by contributing to American victory in war, could provide a rationale for government support of science in peace. The Bomb was the dowry for the marriage of Science to Government.

The organization responsible for delivering the bomb on target—the air force—was more ambivalent about atomic bombing. Still part of the army, it had an overriding interest in securing autonomy. Ever since the days of Billy Mitchell, army airmen had dreamed of forming a separate armed service in control of all land-based aviation. Autonomy would entitle the air force to its own service secretary equal in stature to those of the army and the navy, its own service academy, and above all its own career line insulated from the army's.

To justify autonomy, the army airmen formulated a strategic doctrine all their own, a doctrine that stressed the decisiveness of strategic bombing, specifically punitive bombing of the enemy heartland. While tactical bombing claimed some adherents, if the air force's essential missions were to remain those of close air support of ground forces and inter-

February 15, 1945, MED, TS of Interest to Groves, Folder 1, RG 77, National Archives; I. I. Rabi, "The Physicist Returns from the War," *The Atlantic* 176 (October 1945): 113; and James B. Conant, *My Several Lives* (New York, 1970), p. 294.

[45]Bush, *Pieces of the Action*, p. 140.

[46]Daniel J. Kevles, "The National Science Foundation and the Debate over Postwar Research Policy, 1942–1945: A Political Interpretation of *Science: The Endless Frontier*," *Isis* 68 (March 1977): 23.

diction of enemy lines of supply and communication, they would hardly provide a compelling reason for the airmen to separate from the army. Only strategic bombing would serve the air force interest in autonomy.[47] Yet strategic bombing was more than a means to other ends; it was an end in itself. And the bomber was more than mere capability. The uninitiated could never fully appreciate its significance. It meant as much to the airman as the horse did to the cavalryman, even more. It was nothing less than the weapon of the future in the service of the future.

Strategic bombing was the strategy of the army air forces for ending the war with Japan. Yet, as essential as strategic bombing was to army airmen, the atomic bomb did not yet loom large in their plans for peace. Partly this was due to the secrecy shrouding the project: the bomb's very existence was known to but a few high-ranking officers, and even they harbored doubts about the efficacy of a still untried weapon. But air force coolness toward the bomb had a more important source. Atomic bombing would not keep enough bombers flying. Airmen were seeking a seventy–group peacetime air force and a network of bases circling the globe, capabilities that could best be predicated upon conventional bombing. For the sake of air force capabilities, the Bomber, not the Bomb, had to win the war. This would be underscored shortly after V-J Day, when three B-29s made a well-publicized nonstop flight from Japan to Washington in order to demonstrate the air force's reach. At a press conference heralding their arrival, the mission commander, General Curtis LeMay, fumed at the inevitable question about the importance of the atomic bomb, calling the new weapon "the worst thing that ever happened" to the army air forces. Conventional bombing had already won the war, he insisted: "Even without the atomic bomb and the Russian entry into the war, Japan would have surrendered in two weeks."[48] Like many an official assertion about the causes of Japan's surrender, LeMay's reflected a keener appreciation of America's politics than of Japan's.

The bomb's potential for justifying deep reductions in the size of peacetime forces concerned the other armed services as well. Each also had its own preferred strategies for ending the war, and the atomic bomb played no essential role in either one. The army's essence was ground combat not strategic bombing, and the atomic bomb was at most an adjunct to, not a substitute for, its strategy of invasion. The navy's ships, especially its aircraft carriers, were vulnerable to the bomb, which strengthened the air force's case for the dominance of the heavy bomb-

---

[47]Perry McCoy Smith, *The Air Force Plans for Peace, 1943–1945* (Baltimore, 1970), fully documents air force interest in strategic bombing for the sake of autonomy at war's end.
[48]*New York Times*, "Giles Would Rule Japan a Century," September 21, 1945, p. 4. Cf. Curtis LeMay with MacKinlay Kantor, *Mission with LeMay* (Garden City, N.Y., 1965), p. 393.

er. The navy way to win the war was blockade and bombardment, a strategy that accommodated the interests of naval traditionalists aboard battleships and cruisers, as well as those of their new intraservice rivals, the submariners and carrier-based aviators.[49] Postwar service interests were institutional imperatives shaping military strategies for ending the war with Japan.

NARROWING THE OPTIONS

In the evolution of the choice of how to use the bomb, six options received consideration somewhere inside the government. Noncombatant casualties and destruction varied considerably from option to option. So did the premises—largely unexamined—of how each might affect Japan's internal struggle to surrender.

One option, favored by a handful of army planners privy to the secret, was to use the atomic bomb tactically, to attack Japan's preparations to counter the invasion. This option meant targeting military installations and troop concentrations, and rail and logistics networks, instead of cities, holding collateral damage to an unavoidable minimum, given the bomb's explosive force. As many as nine bombs were expected to be available for such use by November 1, the planning date for the invasion, and another five within the following month.[50] Early estimates of the expected yield of the weapon made this option seem more feasible than would the July test results at Alamogordo. "As late as May 1945," says Groves, "the responsible heads of Los Alamos felt that the explosive force of the first implosion type bombs would fall somewhere between 700 and 1,500 tons," well below the 20,000 tons of TNT of the test shot.[51]

All the other options used the bomb more or less as a strategic weapon. The option least likely to cause high noncombatant casualties and destruction of property was to demonstrate the bomb over, but not on, Japanese territory or elsewhere before a team of international observers,

[49]Vincent Davis, *Postwar Defense Policy and the U.S. Navy, 1943–1945* (Chapel Hill, N.C., 1966), describes internal differences over the navy's organizational essence at the time.
[50]Memorandum to Army Chief of Staff, July 30, 1945, bearing handwritten notation "shown to Gen. Marshall 8/1/45," MED, Groves' General Correspondence, Folder 1, Tab 5, RG 77, National Archives. Cf. Cable 37350 from Harrison to Stimson, MED, TS, Folder 5E. Marshall's recollection of this option appears in Lilienthal, *Journals*, II: 198–99, and in John P. Sutherland, "The Story General Marshall Told Me," *U.S. News & World Report*, November 2, 1959, p. 53. Confirmation of sorts appears in an anonymously written article, "The Balance of Military Power," *The Atlantic* 187 (June 1951): 23.
[51]Groves, letter to the editor, *Science*, December 4, 1959, p. 1593; cf. Oppenheimer letter, ibid., pp. 1530, 1592.

possibly including Japanese scientists or officials, in hopes that the threat of further use would compel Japan's surrender. The demonstration option had some proponents among the MED scientists, none of whom was a senior administrator.[52]

A variant of the second option was to demonstrate the bomb against a purely military target, one sufficiently demarcated from civilian areas to limit death and destruction to noncombatants. Perhaps the purest form of military demonstration would have been to use it against what remained of the Japanese fleet at sea or at anchor, a possibility mentioned by Marshall to Stimson on May 29, 1945.[53] This use had the added benefit to the army and the air force of highlighting the vulnerability of naval vessels, especially aircraft carriers, to nuclear attack.

The explosive force of the atomic bomb was so great, and military installations on the Japanese home islands were so intermingled with industrial and residential areas, that striking any other military target might have been virtually indistinguishable in practice from another option—hitting a target that consisted primarily, though not exclusively, of military installations. Yet few such targets remained to be struck after the intensive campaign of conventional bombing in the spring and summer of 1945.

A final pair of options deliberately targeted Japanese cities—one with prior warning, the other without it. Although some military installations and industries essential for war production might be situated within the city limits, the city itself would be the target. Massive collateral damage from such an attack was unavoidable, and little effort would be made to avoid it. Yet civilian casualties could be appreciably reduced if the attack were preceded by a specific warning. In his May 29 conversation with Stimson, Marshall seems to have had this option in mind for a second phase of a campaign of atomic bombings as a precursor to invasion. To avert the possibility that the Japanese, forewarned of attack, might mass their air defenses against it, Marshall suggested designating several cities for attack, much as LeMay was to do in a few late-July conventional bombing raids, "so that the Japs would not know exactly where we were to hit."[54] A version of this option was tentatively endorsed by Roosevelt and Churchill at Hyde Park on September 19, 1944, just after the Quebec Conference. An aide mémoire initialed by the two leaders says that "when a 'bomb' is finally available, it might perhaps, after mature con-

---

[52]The "Franck Report," e.g., proposed this option. See Alice K. Smith, *A Peril and a Hope: The Scientists' Movement in America, 1945–47* (Chicago, 1965), appendix B.

[53]Assistant Secretary of War John J. McCloy, also present at the May 29 meeting, transcribed Marshall's remarks in a memorandum of conversation; quoted in Knebel and Bailey, "The Fight over the A-Bomb," p. 23.

[54]Ibid.

sideration, be used against the Japanese, who should be warned that this bombardment will be repeated until they surrender."[55]

Dropping atomic bombs on Japan's cities without prior warning was the option preferred by MED administrators and air force planners. The object of this option was to destroy the cities and sap the morale of the survivors, which might somehow compel Japan's surrender or, failing that, soften it up for invasion. Since the war, much has been made of the shock effect of the bomb, but that possibility became clear only in retrospect. At the time, although there were occasional suggestions that one or two atomic bombs might suffice to shock Japan into submission, this possibility did not figure prominently in official plans for use of the bomb.

The last option was the one Truman chose. Yet it is not clear that he ever knew what the alternatives were, or exactly which option he had chosen, because the options were never clearly delineated, formally arrayed, and systematically compared. Not much "mature consideration" was given to the effects that various forms of bombing might have on Japan's decision to surrender. The president merely chose to proceed with atomic bombings and never expressed second thoughts about his decision.

The policy process helps explain why Truman was never exposed to a detailed presentation of alternatives, why he decided as he did, and why opposition to that decision was so muted at the time. In the absence of regular action channels for deciding on use of the bomb, proponents of the last option seized the opportunity to set up procedures of their own, which they exploited to outmaneuver potential opposition. They tried to circumvent consideration by the Joint Chiefs of Staff and to foreclose access to senior officials by dissident scientists in the MED, thereby limiting the options, information, and arguments that came to the president's attention. A few opponents succeeded in running the procedural roadblocks and reaching the president, but some muted their objections in the belief that they were too late to reverse the decision, while others had their stands discounted because of their parochial interests in the result.

[55] Annex 28 to the Diplomatic History of the Manhattan Project, MED, HB, Folder 111, RG 77, National Archives. Truman did not learn of the existence of the Hyde Park agreement until Potsdam. Neither Groves nor Stimson saw fit to notify him, perhaps because of their own coolness to, or anticipation of congressional concern about, postwar nuclear collaboration with the British, to which it committed the United States. The British had not forgotten, of course, and were able to produce a photocopy of the aide mémoire at Stimson's request. The U.S. copy seems to have been misfiled among navy documents included in Roosevelt's personal papers and did not turn up until years later. See *FRUS: Conference of Berlin*, II: 1371n; Smith, *A Peril and a Hope*, p. 11n; and Stimson diary, June 24, 1945. Cf. U.S. Congress, House, Committee on Military Affairs, *Atomic Energy: Hearings*, 79th Cong., 1st sess., 1945, p. 79; and Leahy, *I Was There*, p. 265.

The consequences of organizational interests and procedural improvisation can be inferred from a detailed examination of three ad hoc arrangements: a Target Committee, put together by Groves on Marshall's authority to select the targets for the atomic bombing; the Interim Committee and its Scientific Advisory Panel, established to recommend postwar policy and organization for atomic energy but exploited to outflank and undercut the dissident scientists in the MED who opposed attacking Japanese cities without warning; and a chain of command that left execution in the hands of the MED's commanding general and the air force. Together these ad hoc procedures and the compartmentation imposed by MED secrecy insulated the decision on use from other, related decisions on war termination.

GROVES' COMMITTEE CHOOSES THE TARGETS

Setting up action channels as he went along, the officer in charge of the Manhattan Project, General Leslie R. Groves, was in a position to ensure that the targets for the atomic bombings met his own specifications. Those specifications gave bureaucratic and technical considerations precedence over terminating the war with a minimum of gratuitous death and devastation. They meant, above all, that Groves would have something to show for expenditures on research and development of the bomb.

A Military Policy Committee, established in September 1942 "to consider and plan military policy" for the bomb, including "production, strategic and tactical problems and research and development relating thereto," acted as a sounding board for Groves, who formally served as its executive officer. Vannevar Bush, director of the Office of Scientific Research and Development (OSRD), chaired the body, with his deputy at OSRD, James Conant, as his alternate. Lieutenant General Wilhelm D. Styer represented the army, and Rear Admiral William R. Purnell represented the navy.[56] Late in 1944 Groves discussed his criteria for target selection with the committee. He then consulted with ordnance experts, meteorologists, and theoretical physicists at Los Alamos, among them J. Robert Oppenheimer, and checked his conclusions with his deputy, General Thomas Farrell, and the chief of staff of the newly constituted Strategic Air Force, General Lauris Norstad.

Groves' search procedure ensured that the criteria would meet his own specifications. The criterion that he later says was uppermost in his mind was that the targets be ones that might bring about Japan's sur-

[56]Memorandum A, September 23, 1942, MED, HB, Folder 6, RG 77, National Archives.

render. To Groves that meant attacking Japanese morale: "I had set as the governing factor that the targets chosen should be places the bombing of which would most adversely affect the will of the Japanese people to continue the war." Yet that criterion—and the targets that would satisfy it—was clearer to Groves in retrospect than it was at the time; even he did not expect the bombings to shock Japan into prompt surrender. "Beyond that," he stipulated, the targets "should be military in nature, consisting either of important headquarters or troop concentrations, or centers of production of military equipment and supplies." As his wording suggests, this criterion was secondary. Almost any Japanese city could satisfy it. His two other criteria had a direct bearing on the interests of the MED, an organization whose raison d'être was construction of an untried experimental weapon: "To enable us to assess accurately the effects of the bomb, the targets should not have been previously damaged by air raids. It was also desirable that the first target be of such size that the damage would be confined within it, so that we could more definitely determine the power of the bomb."[57] These two criteria would dominate the choice of targets. No purely military target could satisfy them, nor could a demonstration shot—whatever its psychological effects. Only attacking previously intact cities could. Doing that would also make a dramatic enough impression to convince even hardened skeptics that building the bomb had been worth the money spent.

Another consideration in Groves' plans for the bomb were traced to an idea first advanced by the navy representative on the Military Policy Committee, Admiral Purnell. According to Groves, Purnell believed that two bombs might suffice to end the war. Groves recalls that he and Purnell "often discussed the importance of having the second blow follow the first one quickly, so that the Japanese would not have time to recover their balance."[58] However primitive the notion of knocking Japan off "balance," and whatever the consequences of imbalance on Japan's internal politics of war termination, Purnell's notion did satisfy an organizational need. The MED was constructing two different types of bombs. One, a gun-type, used uranium-235 as its fissionable material and generated its force by firing a projectile consisting of a subcritical mass of U_{235} against another subcritical mass of U_{235} to create a supercritical mass, which would instantaneously and spontaneously set off an uncontrolled chain reaction. The triggering mechanism was simple enough to give its designers the confidence to try the gun-type bomb without first test-firing it. The problem lay in producing the requisite amount of

[57]Groves, *Now It Can Be Told*, p. 267.
[58]Ibid., p. 342.

weapons-grade U_{235} by separating it from other isotopes of uranium. The second bomb, an implosion-type, substituted plutonium-239, which was proving quicker to produce than U_{235} once production facilities began operation. But MED physicists were less sure about the mechanics of generating a supercritical mass of Pu_{239}—surrounding a hollow sphere of Pu_{239} with explosive charges that, when detonated, would compress the sphere, compacting the Pu_{239} and forcing free neutrons into closer proximity with the plutonium atoms, setting off an uncontrolled chain reaction. They did not dare use the implosion-type bomb without first testing it at Alamogordo.

Yet no test could substitute for combat use. MED scientists never lost sight of what some called the "Jesus factor," a reference to what could go wrong with a nuclear device outside the controlled environment of a laboratory or even a test site. Nor did Groves. Alamogordo would not "set aside all doubts about the bomb," he writes. "It proved merely that one implosion-type, plutonium bomb had worked; it did not prove that another would or that a uranium bomb of the gun type would."[59] Above all, it did not show his countrymen what havoc either type could wreak on the enemy. Nothing short of dropping two bombs on Japanese cities would silence doubts at home about the necessity of building both types.

A MED report released after the war listed four criteria that governed the choice of targets. None resembled Groves' "governing condition"— the psychological effects on the Japanese people and government. One loosely fit Groves' second criterion—that the target be "military in nature." The other three dealt specifically with the bomb's measurable physical effects on a Japanese city:

> A. Since the atomic bomb was expected to produce its greatest amount of damage by primary blast effect, and next greatest by fires, the targets should contain a large percentage of closely-built frame buildings and other construction that would be most susceptible to damage by blast and fire.
> B. The maximum blast effect of the bomb was calculated to extend over an area of approximately one mile in radius; therefore the selected targets should contain a densely built-up area of at least this size.
> C. The selected targets should have a high military strategic value.
> D. The first target should be relatively untouched by previous bombing, in order that the effect of a single atomic bomb could be determined.[60]

These considerations were not mere technicalities. They reflected the MED's organizational interests in enhancing the impression of the

[59]Ibid., p. 305.
[60]U.S., Manhattan Engineering District, *The Atomic Bombings of Hiroshima and Nagasaki* (Washington, D.C., 1946), p. 6.

bomb's physical effects in the United States and all but dictated the most extreme option for its use—striking the heart of large Japanese cities, because the concentration of buildings would enhance the impact of the bomb's shock wave and heat wave, and without warning—because advance notice might alert defenders and throw off bombing accuracy, if not cause cancellation of the mission altogether.

Selection of specific target cities was the next step. Before taking it, Groves undertook to coordinate preparations for delivering the bomb. He asked Army Chief of Staff Marshall to designate an air force officer in the OPD to serve as liaison with the MED. "After a moment's hesitation," recalls Groves, "General Marshall replied: 'I don't like to bring too many people into this matter. Is there any reason why you can't take this over and do it yourself?' My 'No, sir, I will' concluded the conversation, which constituted the only directive that I ever received or needed." Secrecy was one reason to circumvent the OPD, but Groves had another. The OPD did more than draw up plans; its coordinating functions involved it intimately in defining the roles and missions of the army and its air forces. Circumventing the OPD might avoid potential opposition to Groves' plans for the bomb. He needed no further prompting to make his own arrangements, and he immediately informed Air Force Chief of Staff Arnold of Marshall's wishes. The two set in motion the transfer of the 509th Composite Group with its specially modified B-29s to Tinian, where it could begin training under combat conditions for its unprecedented mission. Yet Groves drew the line at sharing authority with the air force over the choice of targets: "Our most pressing job was to select the bomb targets. This would be my responsibility."[61] Groves might be willing to take advice, but he intended to decide on his own what to recommend to his superiors—Marshall, Stimson, and in turn, the president.

To designate specific targets, Groves set up an ad hoc Target Committee. How the committee was constituted was one measure of his control over the process; another was his discreet but ongoing involvement in its deliberations. Three of its members came from the MED, three came from the office of the air force chief of staff, and Groves' deputy, General Farrell, was its chairman. "I was kept constantly informed of the committee's progress, by Farrell and the others from the MED," says Groves, "particularly [John] von Neumann, with whom I frequently discussed the many scientific and technical problems with which we were faced."[62] Influencing the politics of war termination in Japan was ostensibly not its concern.

[61]Groves, *Now It Can Be Told*, p. 267.
[62]Ibid., p. 268.

The Target Committee convened for the first time on April 27, 1945. Groves himself opened the session. He told members they should initially draw up a list of four targets. He also passed along for their consideration his own version of an option suggested by the army chief of staff—striking enemy ships in port: "I emphasized General Marshall's opinion that the ports on the west coast of Japan should not be ignored as possible targets, since they were vital to the Japanese communications with the Asiatic mainland."[63]

After Groves' departure the committee established some basic parameters, among them the probable range of a bomb-laden B-29, the need for visual bombing to assure pinpoint accuracy in order to enhance the bomb's blast effects, the weather conditions required for that visual bombing, and the consequent need to designate one primary target and two alternates for every bombing mission. Weather was the critical variable for two reasons, according to a memorandum prepared earlier that month by committee member D. M. Dennison. Heavy rain or thick fog at ground level could reduce the blast effects by half. Inclement weather could also interfere with bombing accuracy. Hitting the precise aim point was essential because the blast generated a wave motion and "the contour of the terrain with a radius of a mile or so from the point of detonation will have a controlling effect on the character and extent of the damage." With these considerations in mind, Dennison concluded, bombing should take place "only in daylight using visual methods."[64] Summing up committee discussion, Farrell deemed it "absolutely essential that we get a good day for the initial mission." The difficulty was that, as the Twentieth Air Force's chief meteorologist made all too clear, from June to September the weather over most of Japan was generally appalling: "Only once in five years have there been two successive good visual days [over] Tokyo." Worse yet for flight planners, Japan's weather was mercurial: forecasting "flyable" days with any confidence could be done no more than twenty-four hours in advance, and "the longest safe period" for calling off a mission was forty-eight hours ahead.[65]

Another difficulty was the availability of targets. According to Colonel William P. Fisher, an air force representative on the committee, target directives already in effect had the Twenty-first Bomber Command "systematically bombing out" Tokyo, Yokohama, Nagoya, Osaka, Kyoto, Kobe, Yawata, and Nagasaki "with the prime purpose in mind of not leaving one stone lying on another." And Fisher left no doubt what had

---

[63]Ibid. Cf. "Notes on Initial Meeting of Target Committee," transcribed May 2, 1945, MED, TS, Folder 5D2, RG 77, National Archives.

[64]Dennison to Captain William S. Parsons, navy ordnance expert on detail to the MED, April 6, 1945, MED, TS, Folder 5D4, RG 77, National Archives.

[65]"Notes on Initial Meeting of Target Committee."

priority for the air force—conventional bombing, not atomic bombing. "It should be remembered," he told the rest of the committee, "that in our selection of any target, the Twentieth Air Force is operating primarily to lay waste all the main Japanese cities, and that they do not propose to save some important primary target for us if it interferes with the operation of the war from their point of view."[66] Hiroshima was the largest unscathed city not yet on Twenty-first Bomber Command's priority list.

The same day, Twentieth Air Force targeters were directed to supply the committee with a list of possible targets to satisfy its specifications: they "should not be less than three miles in diameter," should be "located in a reasonably large urban area" between Tokyo and Nagasaki, and should "possess high strategic value." Among the places mentioned as suitable were Tokyo Bay, Kawasaki, Yokohama, Nagoya, Osaka, Kobe, Kyoto, Hiroshima, Kure, Yawata, Kokura, Shimonoseki, Yamaguchi, Kumamoto, Fukuoka, Nagasaki, and Sasebo. "The destruction," noted the directive, "will primarily be accomplished by the air blast effect and the selection should be made with this thought in mind."[67] Air force targeters responded on May 5 with a list of twenty-two possibilities, all but one with an area 1.5 miles or more in radius. Not about to let the atomic bomb upstage conventional bombing, they also recommended a coordinated strike using incendiaries.[68]

A day before the second meeting of the Target Committee, Dennison completed a report on procedures for dropping the bomb. It put renewed emphasis on visual bombing for the sake of accuracy to optimize blast effects. Accuracy too would improve with practice: "It is imperative that the crews should have at least one month's operational experience over Japanese target areas. They should drop a considerable number of pumpkins on enemy targets and the accuracy of their hits should be recorded." Weather was still a concern. It meant that the day of the strike could not be "preset with any exactness," and even then a sudden change of conditions could force the bomber to return to base with its cargo on board unless there were "strong reasons for not further delaying the strike, for example, the last of *n* days of grace or some damage to the [aircraft] which would make landing difficult." Under those circumstances, "the drop could be made by radar." From his desk at Los Alamos, Dennison's reasoning was no doubt based on an unexceptional premise: "In the bombing missions which have been flown heretofore,

[66]Ibid. Fisher was wrong about Kyoto.
[67]General Lauris Norstad to Director of Joint Target Group, April 28, 1945, MED, TS, Folder 5C3, Tab 1.B, RG 77, National Archives.
[68]Director of Joint Target Group to Norstad, May 5, 1945, MED, TS, Folder 5C3, Tab 1.B, RG 77, National Archives.

the crew is more valuable than the aircraft, and the aircraft more valuable than the bomb load. In the present case the bomb is far more valuable than the aircraft."[69] But on a bomber about to return to base with a fully armed atomic bomb on board, the crew might take exception to Dennison's new order.

The Target Committee reconvened at Los Alamos on May 10–11. Over the two days, Oppenheimer and several other MED scientists joined the discussion of targeting and related issues. One issue was the height of the detonation over ground zero. Again, obtaining the maximum blast effect was the primary consideration: detonation at 40 percent below the optimum height or 14 percent above it could reduce the area of damage by 25 percent. Radiation effects did not seem to enter the calculations. After hearing Dennison's report on bombing procedures, the committee prescribed training the crews for landing with a bomb on board, but noted that even with training such a landing "inevitably involved some risk to the base." It also endorsed Dennison's recommendation to rehearse bombing runs over Japan. It turned down the air force targeters' proposal for a coordinated strike with incendiaries and instead called for a day's delay in bombing to permit photo reconnaissance of the damage caused by the atomic bomb.[70] Nothing would get in the MED's way when it came to displaying the bomb to best effect.

An Air Force representative on the committee, J. C. Stearns, then reported on the choice of targets. The three criteria he had applied in making his selections were that "(1) they be important targets in a large urban area of more than three miles [in] diameter, (2) they be capable of being damaged effectively by a blast, and (3) they are likely to be unattacked by next August." He then listed, in order of priority, five targets "which the Air Force would be willing to reserve for our use unless unforeseen circumstances arise." Kyoto and Hiroshima were ranked at the top, Yokohama and Kokura arsenal next, and Niigata last. Stearns' brief descriptions of the targets highlighted topographical features that would amplify or interfere with blast effects. He made only passing mention of the cities' advantages as military targets. In Kyoto's case there were none. It could be justified only on other grounds: "From the psychological point of view there is the advantage that Kyoto is an intellectual center for Japan and the people there are more apt to appreciate the significance of such a weapon as a gadget." Many, of course, would never realize what hit them. The principal advantage of Kyoto lay else-

[69]Dennison, "Preliminary Report on Operational Procedures," May 9, 1945, MED, TS, Folder 5D4, RG 77, National Archives.

[70]Memorandum for Groves by Major J. A. Derry and N. F. Ramsey, "Summary of Target Committee Meetings of 10 and 11 May 1945," dated May 12, MED, TS, Folder 5D2, Tab B, RG 77, National Archives.

where: its topography and the wood construction of most of its buildings made it especially susceptible to blast effects. Hiroshima was characterized as "an important army depot and port of embarkation in the middle of an urban industrial area." More to the point, it would show the bomb to good effect: "It is a good radar target and it is of such a size that a large part of the city could be extensively damaged. There are adjacent hills which are likely to produce a focusing effect which would considerably increase the blast damage." More important to air force targeters, Hiroshima, transected by several branches of the Ota River, was "not a good incendiary target." That made it easier to reserve for atomic bombing.

Stearns' mention of "psychological" considerations led the committee to consider targeting the emperor's palace in Tokyo, but members refrained from recommending it, noting that any such action "should come from authorities on military policy."[71] It was the only point in the discussion at which the politics of war termination in Japan seemed to intrude, at least tangentially.

The committee accepted the first four targets on Stearns' list. "Psychological factors," it noted, were "of great importance" in its choice. By that it meant not only "obtaining the greatest psychological effect against Japan," which it did not spell out, but also "making the initial use sufficiently spectacular for the importance of the weapon to be internationally recognized when publicity on it is released." Morale and recognition were the larger targets of the atomic bombings. The military worth of a target shrank by comparison: "It was agreed that for the initial use of the weapon any small and strictly military objective should be located in a much larger area subject to blast damage in order to avoid undue risks of the weapon['s] being lost due to bad placing of the bomb."[72] Collateral damage would still make the most of a near miss. A report to the committee's next session detailing the results of the 509th Group's practice runs confirmed this judgment. Half of all hits had landed within 500 feet of their aim points. The widest miss had fallen 2,300 feet away. Drops within 1,000 feet of the aim point, the Group's commander felt, were "practically certain." The committee then decided not to designate industrial areas as aim points because these areas were "small, spread on fringes of cities and quite dispersed," but instead "to endeavor to place [the] first gadget in [the] center of [the] selected city."[73] The objective of maximizing blast effects thus had a corollary—maximum gratuitous death and destruction. Again, as in the case of conventional bombing, "inaccuracy of weapon aim" was fostering "inhumanity of war aim."

[71] Ibid.
[72] Ibid.
[73] "Minutes of Third Target Committee Meeting—Washington, 28 May 1945," MED, TS, Folder 5D2, Tab C, RG 77, National Archives.

The priority that Groves' Target Committee attached to the amplitude of the blast and the consequent imperative to do visual bombing would ultimately leave the selection of target and aim point to those on board the aircraft carrying out the bombing. That was still not enough to satisfy air force interests in reserving choice targets for conventional bombing and assuring its autonomy in executing the first nuclear mission. On May 17 an order went out from air force headquarters to General LeMay of Twenty-first Bomber Command placing just three, not four, targets on reserve for the 509th Composite Group and replacing Yokohama and Kokura with Niigata.[74] This prompted a threat from Groves to call in higher authority in order to reassert his control over atomic bombing arrangements. At its third meeting, on May 28, Groves informed the committee: "General Arnold and I had concluded that control over the use of the weapon should reside, for the present, in Washington." The announcement "was necessary because some of the Air Force people on the committee had displayed a total lack of comprehension of what was involved. They had assumed that the atomic bomb would be handled like any other new weapon; that when it was ready for combat use it would be turned over to the commander in the field, and though he might be given a list of recommended targets, he would have complete freedom of action in every respect." Groves doubted his superiors would approve a delegation of authority. The atomic bomb was "too complicated and all important a matter to be treated so casually."[75] What mattered to Groves was not merely that command-and-control remain in Washington, but that it remain in his own office. The reason he opposed autonomy for air force field commanders was that he could not trust them to show the bomb to best advantage—even to use it as soon as it became available and above all before conventional bombing or alternative strategies had brought the war to an end.

Groves had a willing accomplice in General Arnold. Autonomy for field commanders ran counter to air force organizational interests, as Arnold understood them at this time. The air force's future as a separate service depended on strategic bombing. As chief of staff, Arnold had succeeded in establishing a separate chain of command for the fledgling Strategic Air Force that circumvented the Joint Chiefs of Staff, where

[74]Cable from COMAF to Commanding General, Bomber Command (LeMay eyes only), May 17, 1945, MED, TS, Folder 5C2, RG 77, National Archives. Kokura was not added to the list until June 27. Cable from Colonel J. T. Posey to Commanding General, Bomber Command, Folder 25-O.

[75]Groves, *Now It Can Be Told*, p. 271. Arthur Compton, a MED laboratory director, disputes Groves' assertion that the bomb, by its very nature, dictated centralized command-and-control: "If we could have made a bomb the equivalent of, say, 500 tons of TNT, it would have been available for military use without restriction." (Compton, *Atomic Quest*, p. 234).

navy aviators might block air force missions. He did not want overly assertive field commanders to jeopardize this arrangement. "Reinforcing my impression that control would not be passed to the field," writes Groves, "was General Arnold's strong desire to retain personal control over the Strategic Air Force, keeping Norstad, its chief of staff, in Washington, where he could closely supervise his activities."[76] Arnold was prepared to tolerate interference with Groves "for the present," even to spare atomic bombing targets from conventional attack, secure in the knowledge that he would still have a hand in drafting any bombing directive and that one of his field commanders would ultimately execute it, so now was hardly the time to fight for autonomy.

By May 1945, officials concerned primarily with demonstrating the effectiveness of the atomic bomb as an instrument of war had made the initial choice of targets, foreclosing most options for its use. Throughout the minutes and reports of the Target Committee, apart from passing reference to the need for higher authority to target the emperor's palace, there is no discussion of how the atomic bombings might affect the politics of war termination in Japan. Much has since been made of the bomb's psychological impact, but that received only cursory mention in one committee session—three sentences in a seven-page single-spaced memorandum of conversation, to be exact. The impact was never spelled out. Nor was its bearing on war termination. Physical, not psychological, effects were the principal preoccupations of the committee. Technical, not political, considerations dominated its deliberations. When politics intruded, it was bureaucratic politics at home, not international politics or Japanese politics. Indeed, Japan entered into the discussion mainly as a physical place to destroy, not a political entity to influence. Institutionally disinclined to use the bomb in a restrained way to affect Japan's struggle to surrender, the committee blurred the distinction between military and nonmilitary targets and imposed almost no restraints on the bomb's use. If those involved thought at all about bargaining in war termination—and there is no record that they did—they took it for granted that the only way

---

[76]Groves, *Now It Can Be Told*, p. 272. Nothing could be more demeaning to the service of the future than having to fly defense suppression missions in support of navy aviators' attacks on the Japanese home islands. On one recorded occasion in 1945, that assignment drew a bitter complaint from LeMay to Admiral William F. Halsey: "How's about our supporting you by bombing strategic targets in the areas involved?" He received a terse reply, not from Halsey, but from Arnold: "Support Halsey in any way he asks." Much more was at stake for Arnold than a wartime mission. Peacetime autonomy meant "We must not get the navy mad at us right now." Yet LeMay was not easy to rein in. "O.K.," he told Halsey. "If the weather is suitable, I will bomb those airdromes in the vicinity which you intend to strike. But if we can't do precision bombing, we'll have to bomb by radar. We cannot bomb *tactical* targets by radar. If the weather compels me to resort to radar, I'll hit the targets I *can* hit: *strategic* targets." See Arnold, *Global Mission*, p. 563; and LeMay, *Mission with LeMay*, p. 377 (emphasis in the original).

to end the war was to escalate it to the limits of America's war-making capacity.

THE SECRETARY OF WAR SPARES HIS "PET CITY"—FOR THE MOMENT

Officials elsewhere in the U.S. government did not all share that unexamined assumption. They took a broader view of relations with other nations and had a more restrained idea of the use of military force in war termination. One of them, Secretary of War Stimson, did succeed in imposing at least one limit on the use of the bomb. And political considerations in Japan did enter into his reasons for doing so. But the limit was marginal at best, and perhaps no more than temporary.

With the Target Committee's list in hand, Groves' next task was to gain his superiors' approval for the choice of targets. He anticipated little interference at the very top: "Naturally, I expected that the President also would share in the control, not so much by making original decisions as by approving or disapproving the plans made by the War Department."[77] To ensure approval rather than disapproval, Groves sought to head off potential opposition en route to presidential authorization. In the chain of command two hurdles stood in his way: the Joint Chiefs of Staff and the secretary of war.

Groves intended to use Marshall's impromptu instructions to work out the details of atomic bombing operations on his own. He saw ad hoc coordination with Air Force Chief of Staff Arnold as a means of sidestepping formal action on the bombing by the Joint Chiefs of Staff, where navy opposition was almost certain to surface. It was "quite evident by now," at least to Groves, that his plans "would not be formally considered and acted upon by either the Joint Chiefs of Staff or the Combined Chiefs." The need to preserve secrecy is "one of the reasons" Groves gives for this, but "equally important," to say the least, "was Admiral Leahy's disbelief in the weapon and its hoped-for effectiveness; this would have made action by the Joint Chiefs quite difficult."[78]

He still needed the backing of his immediate superior, General Marshall. Only too well aware that the army had its own preferred strategy for ending the war, Groves in his conversations with Marshall construed his plans for the bomb in a way that minimized conflict with that strategy: dropping as many as nine atomic bombs by November 1 would weaken Japan's defenses against the army's invasion. If Groves ever believed that the shock of just two atomic bombs would suffice to end the war without the need to invade, he did not make much of that belief in the first six

[77]Groves, *Now It Can Be Told*, p. 271.
[78]Ibid.

months of 1945.[79] Marshall himself was of two minds about the invasion; he recognized what it might cost in lives, but he did not believe that unconditional surrender was attainable short of the physical conquest of Japan's home islands, with or without atomic bombing. And settling for less than unconditional surrender was a political judgment—not for him to make. Moreover, his snap decision to bar OPD involvement in planning for the atomic bombing operations had the unintended consequence of limiting his own exposure to options and arguments from sources other than Groves. Overseeing the final defeat and occupation of Japan gave him little time to think about the bomb. Without staffwork he was left to his own devices—and those of Groves.

On the basis of the Target Committee's recommendations, Groves drew up plans for atomic bombing operations for Marshall's approval, but before he had a chance to clear them with his immediate superior, Stimson intervened. On May 30, during a meeting on an unrelated matter, Stimson asked Groves whether he had selected any targets yet. Groves replied that he had and that he was hoping to submit a report to Marshall on the choice the next morning. When Stimson asked to see it, Groves demurred: "I said that I would rather not show it to him without having first discussed it with General Marshall, since this was a military operational matter." But Stimson was not to be put off by bureaucratic formalities: "This is a question I am settling myself. Marshall is not making that decision." Groves tried stalling for time, but Stimson persisted: "He said that he had all morning and that I should use his phone and get it over right away."

While the two awaited delivery of the report, Groves at Stimson's insistence ran down the list of targets. When he came to Kyoto, Stimson immediately objected that "he would not approve it." Groves suggested he might change his mind once he appreciated how well situated a target it was, but Stimson was unmoved: "He was sure that he would not." Stimson's objection, reports Groves, was that "Kyoto was the ancient capital of Japan, a historical city, and one that was of great religious significance to the Japanese." Having visited the city, Stimson was "very much impressed by its ancient culture." Groves, drawing on the description of Kyoto in his report, which had arrived in the interim, pointed out that "it had a population of over a million" and that "any city of that size in Japan must be involved in a tremendous amount of war work even if there were but a few large factories."[80]

[79] An example is Groves' memorandum to Marshall, "Atomic Fission Bombs," excerpted in FRUS: Malta and Yalta, pp. 383–84.

[80] Groves, Now It Can Be Told, pp. 273–74. The date can be inferred from Stimson's diary entry for May 30, reporting that he met with Groves "for most of the morning, calling in Marshall for part of the time."

Groves' recitation of the arguments on both sides do not do full justice to either man's reasoning. Stimson believed that destroying Kyoto might only stiffen Japan's will to resist, while sparing it might be taken as a sign of America's intention not to impose a Carthaginian peace on Japan, once it surrendered. Why that reasoning did not apply with equal force to the rest of Japan's cities Stimson never made clear. Groves had singled out Kyoto as being special for quite a different reason: "It was large enough in area for us to gain complete knowledge of the effects of the atomic bomb. Hiroshima was not nearly so satisfactory in this respect."[81] Straddling six strips of land separated by branches of the Ota River, which could impede the spread of fires, Hiroshima was topographically not as well situated to show the bomb to maximum effect.

Stimson then summoned Marshall and repeated his reasons for turning down Kyoto. Marshall perused the target description but avoided taking sides in the dispute. "It was my impression," says Groves, "that he believed it did not make too much difference either way." Embarrassed and outflanked by Stimson's intervention, Groves was in no position to rally Marshall to his side. "After some discussion," recalls Groves, "during which it was impossible for me discreetly to let General Marshall know how I had been trapped into bypassing him, the Secretary said that he stuck by his decision."[82] Later that day Groves alerted Norstad that "the Secretary of War and the Chief of Staff did *not* approve the three targets we had selected, particularly Kyoto."[83]

Having lost the first round, Groves did not give up, but "continued on a number of occasions afterward to urge" restoring Kyoto to the target list. Nor did Stimson dally in pressing his advantage. Two days later he called Arnold into his office to inquire about the indiscriminate bombing of Tokyo. In the course of the conversation, he identified "one city that they must not bomb without my permission and that was Kyoto."[84] Arnold acceded to the request, but only for the moment.

Next Stimson took the matter up with Truman. He did so in the context of a discussion about indiscriminate conventional bombing in which he accepted the major premise of the air force's rationale for doing so: "I told him how I was trying to hold the Air Force down to precision bombing but that with the Japanese method of scattering its manufacturing it was rather difficult to prevent area bombing." He gave two reasons for trying to be somewhat more punctilious: first, "I did not

[81]Groves, *Now It Can Be Told*, p. 275.

[82]Ibid., p. 274.

[83]Groves to Norstad, May 30, 1945, MED, Groves' General Correspondence, Box 3, Folder 5B, RG 77, National Archives (emphasis in the original).

[84]Stimson diary, June 1, 1945. Stimson seems to have tried to pass the message earlier through his assistant secretary for air, Robert Lovett.

want to have the United States get the reputation of outdoing Hitler in atrocities; and second, I was a little fearful that before we could get ready, the Air Force might have Japan so thoroughly bombed out that the new weapon would not have a fair background to show its strength. He laughed and said he understood."[85] The president's reaction was all the authorization Stimson needed to order five Japanese cities set aside as sanctuaries from conventional bombing, keeping them intact for atomic bombing. Yet, by not singling out Kyoto as a special case among the five, he failed to get presidential backing to spare it permanently.

On June 14 Groves submitted a revised target list to Marshall. On it were Kokura, Hiroshima, and Niigata. On June 27 Arnold's office cabled LeMay to amend its May 15 directive sparing three cities from conventional bombing by adding Kokura to the list.[86] Kyoto remained on the list. On July 3, despite Groves' best efforts to keep the issue away from the Joint Chiefs of Staff, they took up the question of the atomic bombing of Kyoto at an informal discussion over lunch. On the agenda was the designation of targets to reserve for atomic bombing. That required coordination with navy aviation. For discussion the Air Staff had armed Arnold with talking points taking issue with Stimson and recommending that "Kyoto be reserved as a target for the 509th Composite Group."[87] After hearing Arnold's arguments, the Chiefs radioed orders to Army and navy commanders in the Pacific declaring Kyoto, Hiroshima, Kokura, and Niigata off-limits to conventional bombing. The orders arguably contravened the stated wishes of Stimson.

On July 21 Groves began a last-ditch effort to designate Kyoto as the primary target for the first atomic bombing. From Interim Committee Acting Chairman George L. Harrison in Washington he stimulated a cable to Stimson in Potsdam: "All your local military advisers engaged in preparation definitely favor your pet city and would like to feel free to use it as first choice if those on the ride select it out of four possible spots in the light of local conditions at the time."[88] The message perturbed Stimson. Recently intercepted cable traffic on Japan's diplomatic exchanges in Moscow, which had come to his attention on July 16, as well as his impression of the Russians' behavior at Potsdam, had only strengthened his conviction about the need to spare Kyoto, both to induce Japan's surrender before the Soviet Union became too deeply engaged in the war

[85]Ibid., June 6, 1945. At this point Stimson seems to have conceded the fight to prevent the air force from eroding any distinction between military and nonmilitary targets.

[86]Cable from Colonel J. T. Posey to Commanding General, 21st Bomber Command, June 27, 1945, Groves' General Correspondence, Box 10, Folder 25-O, RG 77, National Archives. Groves' list appears in Hewlett and Anderson, *The New World*, p. 365.

[87]Knebel and Bailey, *No High Ground*, pp. 121–22. Cf. directive of July 24, 1945, to General Thomas Handy, in Giovannitti and Freed, *Decision to Drop the Bomb*, p. 252.

[88]*FRUS: Conference of Berlin*, II: 1372. Cf. Groves, *Now It Can Be Told*, p. 275.

and to avoid permanently alienating Japan in hopes of turning it into a bastion against Soviet expansion in the Far East once the war was over. Stimson wired Harrison: "Aware of no factors to change my decision. On the contrary new factors here tend to confirm it."[89]

The next morning Stimson took the precaution of again bringing up the point of sparing Kyoto with Truman, who according to Stimson "said he felt the same way."[90] After lunch he summoned Arnold to a meeting with Marshall and McCloy, showed him the exchange of cables with Harrison, and asked for Arnold's views. "He told me," Stimson noted in his diary, "that he agreed with me about the target which I struck off the program." Yet Arnold managed to exact a price for his concurrence. He won Stimson's permission to have the commander of the Twentieth Air Force, General Spaatz, "make the actual selection of targets" for each mission and "coordinate his decision" with Groves.[91] Arnold thereby reestablished the principle of autonomy for theater commanders over target selection and extended it to atomic bombing.

With Kyoto again temporarily ruled out, Arnold wasted little time asserting his newly gained authority. He sent instructions by messenger to aides back in Washington to add a city to the target list—Nagasaki.[92] A densely populated city of 230,000 situated along the Urakami River on the west coast of Kyushu, Nagasaki had a harbor of secondary importance. By American estimates Nagasaki's four Mitsubishi plants accounted for 96 percent of the city's industrial output, primarily shipbuilding, naval ordnance, and steel. Yet for bomb-makers in the MED, the city had two major drawbacks as a target: a series of undulating ridges and valleys made its terrain unsuited for amplifying the bomb's shock wave, and the damage it had already sustained from three conventional bombing raids would complicate precise measurement of the bomb's effects. Back in Washington, Groves' deputy, General Farrell, was quick to point out these drawbacks, but his objection was overruled and Nagasaki went on the target list.[93] Like Kyoto, Nagasaki was of historic importance, the site of many early Japanese contacts with the West and the center of Japanese Christianity. Unlike Kyoto, it was not to be the object of efforts to spare it on symbolic grounds.

[89]*FRUS: Conference of Berlin*, II: 1372. Cf. Stimson diary, July 16 and 21, 1945, and notes by his aide-de-camp, Colonel Kyle, Stimson Papers, Group 465, Series 11, Box 172, Folder 19, Yale University Library.

[90]Stimson diary, July 22, 1945, excerpted in *FRUS: Conference of Berlin*, II: 1373n. Stimson raised the matter "on short notice." Cf. Kyle's notes and Arnold's journal, "Terminal Conference," Box 272, Arnold Papers.

[91]Arnold, *Global Mission*, p. 589; cf. p. 585.

[92]Knebel and Bailey, *No High Ground*, p. 124; Arnold, *Global Mission*, p. 589; and Arnold's journal, "Terminal Conference."

[93]Giovannitti and Freed, *Decision to Drop the Bomb*, pp. 247–48. Cf. Groves, *Now It Can Be Told*, p. 275.

The next morning Stimson took the precaution of cabling Harrison once more to remind him about "excluding the particular place against which I have decided," adding, "My decision has been confirmed by highest authority." Groves took this message as the last word on the subject: "There was no further talk about Kyoto after that."[94] Maybe not within earshot of Groves, but Kyoto came up again at Potsdam.

Following a July 23 meeting of the Joint Chiefs of Staff, General Arnold made one more try at targeting the city. He recounts discussing the bomb's blast effects with Stimson that day. "There was no doubt," he argued, "that the effect of the atomic bomb would be much severer if it were exploded over an area in a valley, with high ridges on both sides to concentrate the effect of the blast, than if dropped over a coastal plain or over a large, flat area inland." Kyoto lay in just such a cup-shaped depression. Arnold later adverted to an option raised earlier by Marshall, one well suited to demonstrating the vulnerability of navies—and carrier-based aviation—in the coming age of air power: "To me it seemed of the utmost importance, and I presented the idea, that we should try to find out what the explosive effect would be if an atomic bomb were dropped in a harbor."[95] Stimson interpreted Arnold's initial remarks as signaling a reopening of the Kyoto decision and moved to head Arnold off. He met with President Truman first thing the next morning. This time he cast his argument explicitly in terms of postwar relations. Truman accepted Stimson's contention that if Kyoto were struck the ensuing "bitterness" from this "wanton act" might "make it impossible during the postwar period to reconcile the Japanese to us in that area rather than to the Russians."[96] If Stimson's impression of the conversation is correct—and a July 25 journal entry of Truman's suggests it was—he may have forestalled the atomic bombing of Kyoto, at least until other available targets had been exhausted. Nonetheless, Kyoto remained on the air force target list, fifth in order behind Hiroshima, Kokura, Niigata, and Nagasaki.[97]

Stimson thus successfully maneuvered Truman into accepting one limit on the use of the atomic bomb—sparing Kyoto. He did so in order to induce Japan's surrender and postwar reconciliation. The same reasoning would seem to imply avoiding cities altogether in the atomic

[94]Stimson cable to Harrison, July 22, 1945, *FRUS: Conference of Berlin*, II: 1373; Kyle's notes; and Groves, *Now It Can Be Told*, p. 275.

[95]Arnold, *Global Mission*, p. 590, and his journal, "Terminal Conference."

[96]Stimson diary, July 24, 1945, and Truman journal, quoted in Gregg Herken, *The Winning Weapon* (New York, 1980), p. 20n. Truman's journal entry of July 25 noting his conversation with Stimson says, "Even if the Japs are savages, ruthless, merciless, and fanatic, we as the leaders of the world for the common welfare cannot drop this terrible bomb on the old capital or the new." See Robert H. Ferrell, *Off the Record: The Private Papers of Harry S Truman* (Baltimore, 1980), pp. 55–56.

[97]Handwritten note, dated July 25, 1945, filed under "Atom Bomb, 1945," Box 223, Arnold Papers.

bombing of Japan, but Stimson did not take it that far. Others did—for instance, Leahy and Forrestal—but the navy's organizational interest may have fortified them in their stand against the bombing. Stimson's responsibility for the Manhattan Project dictated maximizing the bomb's impact. That conflicted with his ideological distrust of the Soviet Union. Stimson seems to have tried to resolve this value conflict by bombing other Japanese cities without warning but sparing Kyoto. That may have been the most he could achieve in the political climate in Washington at war's end. And even that limited achievement came at some sacrifice: he conceded all other limits on American bombing of Japan, conventional as well as nuclear.

Despite repeated decisions to place Kyoto off limits to all bombing, it was struck at least five times. On January 6, April 16, and June 26, lone bombers dropped bombs on the city, killing a total of 81 people and injuring 388. On two occasions after that, fighter planes strafed factories on the city's outskirts.[98]

There is no evidence to suggest whether or not sparing Kyoto had any effect on Japan's decision to surrender.

DEFLECTING DISSIDENT SCIENTISTS IN THE MED

Groves had now cleared all hurdles on the way to presidential authorization of the atomic bombing. He had little reason to doubt the outcome, but he was not about to take any chances. As opposition to dropping the bomb on Japanese cities without warning began welling up among the scientists at the MED, its commanding general took firm steps to keep it from seeping out into policy-making channels.

What aroused the scientists has often been misconstrued. Concern about the social and political implications of nuclear weapons since the war has drawn analysts' attention to scientific protest against using the atomic bomb during the war. Yet what first drew the MED's dissident scientists together was not so much the issue of wartime use as it was control of postwar research. Some did make a connection between the two. Recognizing the tension between their desires for generous government support of research and for freedom of inquiry unfettered by gov-

[98]U.S. Strategic Bombing Survey (Pacific), *Effects of Air Attacks on Osaka-Kobe-Kyoto*, Report No. 58 (Washington, D.C., 1947), p. 246. Two of these attacks took place before Stimson's campaign to spare Kyoto. The survey concludes that all three resulted from "accident or navigational error," but among the sites struck was a Mitsubishi aircraft plant it described as "one of the key units in that industry." Nagasaki was struck five times after it was placed on reserve status, according to the official air force history of the war, Craven and Cate, *The Pacific*, p. 719.

ernment secrecy and compartmentation, they looked to international control of atomic energy as a way out. Since national sovereignty over the bomb would necessarily lead to government control of nuclear research at home, they reasoned, domestic controls could be eased only if international controls were put in their place. Only gradually did a few dissident scientists make another connection, this one between peacetime control and wartime use of the bomb: while use of the bomb in some way during the war was essential to demonstrate the value of government support for science, they came to the realization that dropping atomic bombs on Japanese cities without prior warning might jeopardize chances for achieving international control of atomic energy and thereby relaxing domestic controls after the war.

At that point those who ran the MED intervened. Secretary of War Stimson had established a committee to advise him "on the whole problem of temporary war controls and later publicity" and to recommend arrangements for "postwar research, development, and controls, as well as legislation necessary to effectuate them."[99] As its mandate makes clear, the committee was to have no say over wartime use, only postwar research. As its name suggests, the "Interim Committee" was to serve until Congress provided for a permanent agency to oversee atomic energy programs. Once the scientific protest gained momentum, Groves with the help of others put the committee to a different use—to deflect and undercut that protest. If some MED scientists were questioning his plans for dropping the bomb, he could find others to endorse them.[100]

A Scientific Advisory Panel was set up, consisting of J. Robert Oppenheimer, Arthur H. Compton, Ernest O. Lawrence, and Enrico Fermi, all of them MED administrators, to act as surrogates for other scientists in the MED. On May 31 the panel met with the Interim Committee to discuss arrangements for postwar control of atomic energy. In the course of the morning's discussion, Oppenheimer proposed "to exchange information before the bomb was actually used." Interim Committee members expressed skepticism. When talk turned to notifying Russians about the bomb's existence, James F. Byrnes, whom Stimson had invited to serve on the committee as the president's personal representative and whom Truman had already asked to take over as secretary of state, came out against scientific interchange with the Soviet Union as a step toward international control of atomic energy.

[99]Stimson letter of May 4, 1945, invited members to the first meeting, Walter S. Schoenberger, *Decision of Destiny* (Athens, Ohio, 1969), p. 124.
[100]For a fuller treatment of the role of the Interim Committee in the policy process, see Leon V. Sigal, "Bureaucratic Politics and Tactical Use of Committees: The Interim Committee and the Decision to Drop the Atomic Bomb," *Polity* 10 (Spring 1978): 326–64. Permission to draw on this material is gratefully acknowledged.

In conversations over lunch, Byrnes asked Ernest Lawrence to elaborate on a suggestion he had briefly made during the morning that the United States demonstrate the bomb's effectiveness before using it on Japan. After lunch Stimson took the lead. Only the notion of shocking Japan could ease members' qualms about striking Japanese cities without warning, and he seized it:

> After much discussion concerning the various types of targets and the effects to be produced, *the Secretary expressed the conclusion, on which there was general agreement, that we could not give the Japanese any warning; that we could not concentrate on a civilian area; but that we should seek to make a profound psychological impression on as many of its inhabitants as possible. At the suggestion of Dr. Conant the Secretary agreed that the most desirable target would be a vital war plant employing a large number of workers and closely surrounded by workers' houses.*[101]

Stimson's summary, without Conant's qualification, was a way of casting the Target Committee's choice in the best possible light and endorsing it. Reference to "general agreement" suggests that not all qualms were eased. Again, as had the Target Committee in ranking Kyoto at the top of its list, the notion of psychological shock came to the rescue of a troubling targeting policy—deliberately aiming at noncombatants with only tangential involvement in the war effort. Again too the psychological effect was taken as a given without specifying what that effect might be on the politics of war termination in Japan.

Strategists before and since have sought to distinguish between bombing pressure that gradually erodes morale and abrupt escalation that shocks the body politic into war termination. As Basil Liddell Hart contends, "Decisive results come sooner from sudden shocks than long drawn out pressure. Shock throws the opponent off balance. Pressure allows him time to adjust to it."[102] Whatever its validity, this contention has become an article of faith in the air force and elsewhere in strategic circles since the war. How far Stimson's notion of making "a profound psychological impression" was from a strategic doctrine of abrupt escalation can be discerned from the ensuing discussion. When Oppenheimer, picking up Stimson's notion, proposed several simultaneous atomic attacks, General Groves quickly intervened to reject a strategy of shock. He posed three objections: "(1) We would lose the advantage of gaining additional knowledge concerning the weapon at each successive bombing; (2) such a program would require a rush job on the part of those

---

[101]"Notes of an Interim Committee Meeting—Thursday 31 May 1945," MED, HB, Folder 100, RG 77, National Archives, pp. 13–14 (emphasis in the original).
[102]Liddell Hart, *Revolution in Warfare*, p. 31.

assembling the bombs and might, therefore, be ineffective; (3) the effect would not be sufficiently distinct from our regular Air Force program."[103] Groves' third objection, however dubious, reveals his abiding interest in showing off the bomb. The second objection alludes to an important drawback for the MED in Oppenheimer's proposal: waiting for several bombs to be ready would delay the start of the bombing at least two weeks, raising the possibility that the war might end before the bomb could be used on Japan at all. The first objection strongly implies that Groves did not have a program of shock in mind, but rather a series of combat tests. Two bombings were essential, one to try each type of bomb, but at least five bombings would be useful to vary key parameters for the sake of comparison. A shock attack along Oppenheimer's lines would interfere with using the bomb as soon as possible and demonstrating the bomb's physical effects, and Groves was quick to head it off.

The next day, the Interim Committee, meeting in executive session without its Scientific Advisory Panel, formally adopted a resolution endorsing wartime use of the atomic bomb: "*Mr. Byrnes* recommended, and the Committee *agreed*, that the Secretary of War should be advised that, while recognizing that the final selection of the target was essentially a military decision, the present view of the Committee was that the bomb should be used against Japan as soon as possible; that it be used on a war plant surrounded by workers' homes; and that it be used without prior warning."[104] Rewording Conant's qualification made it possible to square the Interim Committee's endorsement with the Target Committee's choice of aim point—the "center of [the] selected city," not "a vital war plant."

Renewed opposition from scientists at the MED's laboratory in Chicago led to further tactical exploitation of the Scientific Advisory Panel in support of the Target Committee's selections. An informal committee of scientists at the laboratory drafted a report on the social and political implications of atomic energy. Commonly known as the Franck Report after the committee's chairman, James Franck, it started from the premise that domestic control and international control of atomic energy were inseparable: "All present plans for the organization of research, scientific and industrial development, and publication in the field of nucleonics are conditioned by the political and military climate in which one expects those plans to be carried out." For scientific inquiry to proceed relatively unfettered at home, it was essential to avoid arms competition abroad and the military control of research that would in-

---

[103]Ibid.
[104]"Notes of the Interim Committee Meeting—Friday, 1 June 1945," MED, HB, Folder 100, RG 77, National Archives, pp. 9–10 (emphasis in the original).

evitably accompany it. The report proposed "an international agreement barring a nuclear armaments race." But how could insecure and suspicious states reach such an agreement? At this point the Franck Report directly challenged plans to bomb Japan:

> If we consider international agreement on total prevention of nuclear warfare as the paramount objective, and believe that it can be achieved, this kind of introduction of atomic weapons to the world may easily destroy all our chances of success. Russia, and even allied countries which bear less mistrust of our ways and intentions, as well as neutral countries may be deeply shocked. It will be very difficult to persuade the world that a nation which was capable of secretly preparing and suddenly releasing a weapon as indiscriminate as the rocket bomb and a million times more destructive, is to be trusted in its proclaimed desire of having such weapons abolished by international agreement.[105]

Yet refraining from using the bomb at all could jeopardize postwar government funding for research. So Franck proposed first demonstrating it "before the eyes of representatives of the United Nations, on the desert or a barren island." Then, he conceded, "the weapon might perhaps be used against Japan if the sanction of the United Nations (and of public opinion at home) were obtained, perhaps after a preliminary ultimatum to Japan to surrender or at least to evacuate certain regions as an alternative to their total destruction." If an arms race proved unavoidable, the report argued, some wartime use of the bomb, by dramatizing the benefits from the vast sums spent on atomic energy research, would enable scientists "to obtain adequate support for further intensive development of nucleonics in this country" and avoid the danger that "enough information might leak out" to spur rival powers to develop the bomb while lack of public support for continued expenditures slowed America's advance and narrowed its lead in the competition.[106]

Instead of bringing the Franck Report to the immediate attention of the Interim Committee or the secretary of war, Acting Chairman George Harrison had it referred to the Scientific Advisory Panel for consideration at its June 16 meeting. Lest the panel misconstrue its mandate, Harrison defined it narrowly. "We were asked," Compton recalls, "to prepare a report as to whether we could devise any kind of demonstration that would seem likely to bring the war to an end without using the bomb against a live target."[107] Whether these were Harrison's exact words or just Compton's recollection of them, the instructions set as the panel's paramount objective not the prevention of a postwar arms race

[105]Franck Report, June 11, 1945, in Smith, *A Peril and a Hope*, p. 566.
[106]Ibid., pp. 567–68, 571.
[107]Compton, *Atomic Quest*, p. 239.

but the end of the war. They also ruled out considering whether to use the bomb at all, as well as options other than a demonstration. The text of the Franck Report was never sent to the panel, but as director of the MED laboratory in Chicago, Compton, for one, was familiar with its contents. The panel's four-paragraph report reads like an attempt to be responsive to Franck within the confines of its own mandate. It underscored the lack of consensus within the scientific community:

> Those who advocate a purely technical demonstration would wish to outlaw the use of atomic weapons and have feared that if we use the weapons now our position in future negotiations will be prejudiced. Others emphasize the opportunity of saving American lives by immediate military use, and believe that such use will improve the international prospects, in that they are more concerned with the prevention of war than with the elimination of this specific weapon. We find ourselves closer to these latter views; we can propose no technical demonstration likely to bring an end to the war; we see no acceptable alternative to direct military use. [108]

While rejecting a demonstration, the panel did recommend that "before the weapons are used, not only Britain, but also Russia, France, and China be advised that we have made considerable progress in our work on atomic weapons, that these may be ready to work during the present war, and that we would welcome suggestions as to how we can cooperate in making this development contribute to improved international relations."

The panel forwarded the short statement to Harrison on June 16 along with two lengthier reports it had completed that day. One report proposed a wide-ranging program of studies, from military, industrial, and medical applications of atomic energy to basic research, at a cost of $1 billion a year; another recommended extending the MED's authority into the immediate postwar period, with funding at an annual rate of $20 million. In the context of a crash effort to polish the rationale for vast government expenditures on postwar research, it would hardly be surprising if the panel gave only perfunctory consideration to Harrison's last-minute request to review wartime use. In its letter of transmittal, members acknowledged as much: "Because of the urgency of this matter, the Panel was not able to devote as extended a collective deliberation to the problem as it undoubtedly warrants."[109]

---

[108]"Report of the Scientific Advisory Panel," MED, HB, Folder 76, RG 77, National Archives, reprinted in Martin J. Sherwin, *A World Destroyed* (New York, 1975), pp. 304–5.
[109]Cover letter from Scientific Advisory Panel to Secretary of War, June 16, 1945, MED, HB, Folder 76, RG 77, National Archives. Oppenheimer's postwar testimony on the panel's activities has even more of a disarming frankness about it. See U.S. Atomic Energy Commission, *In the Matter of J. Robert Oppenheimer*, Transcript of Hearing before Personnel Security Board, April 12–May 6, 1954 (Washington, D.C., 1954), p. 100.

Five days later the Interim Committee reconvened in executive session to review all three reports. Explaining the need for yet another discussion of the bomb's use, Harrison told his colleagues he had received "a report from a group of scientists at Chicago recommending, among other things, that the weapon not be used in this war but that a purely technical test be conducted which would be made known to other countries"—not quite what Franck had written. Harrison noted that he had referred it to the Scientific Advisory Panel for "study and recommendation." The committee, faced with no new alternative, only the panel's endorsement of its own earlier recommendation on wartime use, simply "reaffirmed" the conclusion it had already reached. The panel's recommendation that the United States notify its allies about the bomb's existence before dropping it on Japan occasioned a lengthy discussion, after which the committee reached the unanimous conclusion that the president tell the Russians at Potsdam that the United States was working on a bomb that it expected to use against Japan, but provide no further details.[110] The committee thereupon adjourned. The Target Committee's option was now thrice-blessed.

Counting his blessings, Groves moved to quell scientific protest inside the MED and to prevent options other than his own from reaching the president. When one MED scientist, Leo Szilard, tried to solicit endorsement of the Franck Report from other scientists in the Chicago laboratory, MED security officers declared the report classified and barred its circulation.[111] When Szilard drew up a petition opposing use of the bomb against Japanese cities, Groves himself ordered the petition classified and shown only to those scientists cleared to receive the information in Szilard's possession, thereby restricting its dissemination.[112] When Szilard turned over a sheaf of signed petitions to Arthur Compton on July 17, it took eight days for them to reach Groves' office in Washington and another week for the general to forward the packet to Stimson's office. It never did reach the president. In a memorandum for the record written a year later, the secretary of the Interim Committee, Lieutenant R. Gordon Arneson, used its deliberations and those of its Scientific Advisory Panel to justify the disposition of the petition:

    a. The question of the use of the bomb had already been fully considered and settled by the proper authorities.

    b. As far as the scientists employed on the project were concerned, they

[110]"Notes of an Interim Committee Meeting—Thursday, 21 June 1945," MED, TS of Interest to Groves, Folder 3, RG 77, National Archives, pp. 6–8.

[111]Smith, *A Peril and a Hope*, p. 46.

[112]Memorandum from Major Grover C. Thompson to Colonel John Lansdale, July 11, 1945, MED, HB, Folder 76, RG 77, National Archives.

had been given adequate opportunity to express their views on this or any other question relating to the project to the Interim Committee through the Scientific Panel.

In view of the foregoing, it was decided that no useful purpose would be served by transmitting either the petition or any of the other attached documents to the White House, particularly since the President was not then in the country.[113]

The ad hoc policy process could justify keeping advice from the president rather than forwarding it to him.

The Interim Committee and its Scientific Advisory Panel thus played only an ancillary role in the decision to drop the bomb. Neither had any authority over wartime use because neither was in the military chain of command. Had they chosen to intervene in the bombing decision, they might have had the political influence, though not the mandate, to affect the result. That neither tried to do so is testament to the care their founders exercised in choosing their membership and arranging their agenda and procedures. One member who was to become involved in the decision as secretary of state, James F. Byrnes, came away impressed enough to tell the president about the committee's conclusions even before Groves and Stimson could. On June 1, before its first endorsement of the Target Committee's option had been formally transcribed, he went to see Truman. The two discussed the strategy of invasion and the toll it could take. Byrnes cited a military estimate he had heard that put American casualties at one million. He then recounted the Interim Committee's deliberations. Truman, says Byrnes, "expressed the opinion that, regrettable as it might be, so far as he could see, the only reasonable conclusion was to use the bomb."[114] Byrnes took away another impression from his committee service. "In this age," he remarked at the time, "it appears, every man must have his own physicist."[115]

Only one man succeeded in running the security blockade to reach the president with a dissent from Groves' option, and he was not a physicist but a civilian—the Navy Department's under secretary and its representative on the Interim Committee, Ralph Bard. Although Bard had initially joined in the committee's endorsement of dropping the bomb on Japanese cities without warning, by late June he was having second thoughts. "The whole thing was engineered by Stimson and Groves," he told interviewers after the war. "We didn't know a damned thing about

---

[113]"Memorandum for the Files," 24 May 1946, MED, HB, Folder 76, RG 77, National Archives, p. 4.

[114]Byrnes, *Speaking Frankly*, p. 262. For the correct date of the conversation, see *All in One Lifetime*, p. 286.

[115]Michael Amrine, *The Great Decision* (New York, 1959), p. 98.

this business. For quite a while I couldn't tell what the hell was going on." Back at the Navy Department there were many who thought blockade would suffice to compel Japan's surrender. Bard subscribed to that view. If use of the bomb was fast becoming an alternative to the army's strategy of invasion, the navy's strategy of blockade in his judgment had already made both superfluous: "The Pacific War was a Navy war. The Army didn't know what the hell was going on there. The Navy had sewed up those islands so that nothing was coming in or going out. The Navy knew the Japanese were licked. The Army wanted to be in on the kill."[116] On June 27 Bard sent a memorandum to Harrison urging that "Japan should have some preliminary warning for, say, two or three days in advance of use." He also recommended a prior effort to negotiate a settlement of the war by means of explicit threats of American atomic bombings and Soviet entry into the war, as well as a promise to spare the Japanese emperor.[117] Bard resigned from the government on July 1, but at the suggestion of Forrestal he arranged for an interview with the president. "For God's sake," he recalls telling Truman, "don't organize an army to go into Japan. Kill a million people? It's ridiculous."[118] To Truman, two weeks after giving preliminary approval to army plans for invasion, Bard could well have sounded like a navy partisan, a parochial reclaimant for a strategy he had already rejected as inadequate for achieving prompt and unconditional surrender. The president assured Bard that he had given careful consideration to invading and to offering Japan a chance to surrender before dropping the bomb.

Truman Does Not Interfere with Groves' Plans

Only two questions still remained unanswered: would the bombs be ready in time to be used before the war was over, and would the president authorize their use? Groves would not take no for an answer to either.

Based on calculations made in late May, he expected the MED to amass enough U_{235} by July 24 to assemble the first gun-type bomb. Production of Pu_{239} was proceeding even faster than anticipated, but the implosion-type bomb required testing before it could be used under combat conditions. A test was scheduled for 4 a.m. on July 16 at Alamogordo, New Mexico. Technical difficulties with last-minute preparations

[116]Nuel P. Davis, *Lawrence and Oppenheimer* (New York, 1968), pp. 245, 247.
[117]"Memorandum on the Use of the S-1 Bomb," June 25, 1945, in Knebel and Bailey, *No High Ground*, pp. 109–10.
[118]Davis, *Lawrence and Oppenheimer*, p. 247. Cf. Giovannitti and Freed, *Decision to Drop the Bomb*, pp. 144–45.

prompted Oppenheimer to request a postponement, but Groves turned him down. As the appointed hour approached, rain threatened to interfere with the test. Again Groves refused to call it off, although he did hold it up until 5:30. "I was extremely anxious to have the test carried off on schedule," Groves acknowledges. The source of his anxiety, however tortured his reasoning, was that the war might end before he could show off the bomb: "I knew the effect that a successful test would have on the issuance and wording of the Potsdam ultimatum." But its issuance, not its wording, was his concern: "A delay in issuing the Potsdam ultimatum could result in a delay in the Japanese reaction, with a further delay to the atomic attack on Japan."[119] Three days after the successful test at Alamogordo, Oppenheimer renewed his pleas for delay, this time to permit modifications in the bomb's design, but Groves was not about to slow the tempo of bomb production for anything. He ordered Oppenheimer to proceed on schedule: "It is necessary to drop the first Little Boy and the first Fat Man and probably a second one in accordance with our original plans. It may be that as many as three of the latter in their best present form may have to be dropped to conform with planned strategic operations."[120] Those "planned strategic operations," softening up Japan for the army's invasion, called for dropping as many atomic bombs as the MED could produce as fast as it could produce them. Readiness would not be a problem if Groves had anything to say about it.

Nor would the president's assent. Before leaving for Potsdam, Stimson had set up special communications links with Groves to expedite transmission of reports from Alamogordo. Five hours after the test, the first report arrived: "Operated on this morning. Diagnosis not yet complete but results seem satisfactory and already exceed expectations."[121] Stimson immediately brought it to Truman. The next day a second message arrived, expressing assurance that "the Little Boy is as husky as his big brother," a cryptic way of saying that the plutonium implosion-type bomb was as powerful as the uranium gun-type.[122] This message had the desired effect on Truman, according to Stimson, but Groves was not a man to leave well enough alone. He and his deputy, General Farrell, worked until midnight drafting a full report on the test, page after page of graphic detail, and had it sped to Potsdam by courier. They did not spare the hyperbole: "For the first time in history there was a nuclear

---

[119]Groves, *Now It Can Be Told*, pp. 292–93. On the May production schedule, see ibid., p. 124.
[120]Groves to Oppenheimer, July 19, 1945, in Knebel and Bailey, "The Fight over the A-Bomb," p. 23. Cf. Davis, *Lawrence and Oppenheimer*, p. 249.
[121]War 32887, in *FRUS: Conference of Berlin*, II, p. 1360.
[122]War 33556, in ibid., pp. 1360–61.

explosion. And what an explosion!"[123] Stimson found it "an immensely powerful document" when he received it on July 21. He read portions of it aloud to Truman and Byrnes. "The President," he says, "was tremendously pepped up by it and spoke to me of it again and again when I saw him." Yet Stimson may have exaggerated the impact of the report. Byrnes, for one, was not that impressed.[124]

Immediately after hearing Groves' report, Truman invited the Joint Chiefs of Staff to join Byrnes and Stimson in his quarters. "We reviewed our military strategy in the light of the revolutionary development," recalls Truman. But the development may not have seemed quite that "revolutionary" to the Joint Chiefs, for the only result of the afternoon's discussion was to confirm the president's order of June 18 to proceed with invasion plans.[125] On June 24, having dispensed with the formality of obtaining British acquiescence, Truman and Byrnes met once more with the Joint Chiefs. At the close of the meeting Truman formally authorized the atomic bombing of Japan. The decision preceded the issuance of the Potsdam Declaration by two days. Truman attached just one stipulation: that the first bombing not take place until after he had left Potsdam.

Despite Groves' best efforts, he had failed to circumvent the Joint Chiefs of Staff. Although he did keep them from playing a formal, corporate role in the chain of command, the president exercised his prerogative to seek their military advice on an informal basis. Had the chiefs of staff been both united and vigorous in their opposition when he polled them, they might have altered the course of the war. They were neither. They seem to have regarded the bomb's use as a foregone conclusion and, in any event, not likely to have a profound effect on war termination. Indeed, accounts of the events of July 21–24 by those who took part make little mention of the series of meetings preceding Truman's formal assent to the atomic bombings. With no official record of the proceedings, it is necessary to reconstruct what transpired from the sketchy details that participants have provided.

While Truman's recollection is that "the top military advisers to the President recommended its use," he may have mistaken grudging acceptance for affirmation.[126] There is no evidence in the public record to confirm that Admirals Leahy and King ever reversed their objections to

---

[123]Memorandum for Secretary of War from Commanding General, MED, "The Test," July 18, 1945, in ibid., p. 1362.

[124]On the divergent reactions to the report, see Stimson diary, July 21, 1945; Byrnes, *Speaking Frankly*, p. 262.

[125]Truman, *Year of Decisions*, p. 415.

[126]Ibid., p. 419. Cf. Margaret Truman, *Harry S Truman*, pp. 273–74; Knebel and Bailey, *No High Ground*, p. 120.

the bomb, and if anything, General Arnold hardened his reluctance to use it. The military adviser to the president, Leahy was outspoken in his opposition to use of "this barbarous weapon." It was, he later insisted, "of no material assistance" in ending the war: "The Japanese were already defeated and ready to surrender because of the effective sea blockade and the successful bombing with conventional weapons." He saw an ulterior motive in MED pressure to drop the bomb on Japan: "It was my reaction that the scientists and others wanted to make this test because of the vast sums that had been spent on the project. Truman knew that, and so did the other people involved."[127] Leahy was joined in opposition by the navy chief of staff, Admiral King, who felt that, "had we been willing to wait, the effective naval blockade would, in the course of time, have starved the Japanese into submission."[128] Yet Truman was already well aware of the admirals' strategic preferences and had rejected them. Had they expressed their opposition to atomic bombing in these terms, the president might well have discounted it as an attempt to reopen his June 18 decision, to proceed with plans for invasion while continuing the blockade and bombing. The air force chief of staff, General Arnold, along with other army airmen, was convinced that conventional bombing would suffice to compel Japan's surrender. "Accordingly," he writes, "it always appeared to us that, atomic bomb or no atomic bomb, the Japanese were already on the verge of collapse."[129] He took a stand that gingerly sidestepped the issue: "Whether or not the atomic bomb should be dropped was not for the Air Force to decide, but explosion of the bomb was not necessary to win the war."[130] The army chief of staff, General Marshall, believed that nothing short of invasion would compel unconditional surrender. His main interest was to forestall renewed opposition to the army's strategy or delay in its execution. He saw no inconsistency between that strategy and the atomic bombings: the determined Japanese resistance that he anticipated made the bomb "a wonderful weapon as a protection and preparation for landings," an impression that Groves had been careful to nurture.[131]

To President Truman, barely one hundred days in office, the choice had been clear-cut from the outset: "Let there be no mistake about it. I regarded the bomb as a military weapon and never had any doubt that it should be used."[132] Truman's certitude may have been his way of com-

---

[127]Leahy, *I Was There*, p. 441.
[128]King and Whitehead, *Fleet Admiral King* (New York, 1952), p. 621.
[129]Arnold, *Global Mission*, p. 598.
[130]Conversation with his deputy, General Eaker, paraphrased in Knebel and Bailey, *No High Ground*, p. 111.
[131]Lilienthal, *The Atomic Energy Years*, p. 198.
[132]Truman, *Year of Decisions*, p. 419.

pensating for feelings that at first others were not that sure about him. "No one knows what the President's views are—at least I don't," Stimson confided to his diary on April 12. "But we all feel that there is nothing to do but close in and make a solid phalanx along the pattern that has been followed hitherto."[133] When fitness to rule is in doubt, successors take refuge in continuity. So Truman pledged himself to fulfill Roosevelt's wishes insofar as he knew them—or insofar as holdovers from the Roosevelt administration chose to impart them. To Truman the Rooseveltian legacy meant, above all, achieving unconditional surrender as soon as possible. And maximum speed dictated maximum force. As of May, Truman recalls, "The thought now uppermost in my mind was how soon we could wind up the war in the Pacific, and it was natural for me to turn to General Marshall and Secretary of War Stimson."[134] But the army's invasion, Truman knew, would cost untold lives. He could easily anticipate the domestic political reaction if it were subsequently disclosed that he had had a secret and powerful weapon available but had refrained from using it and gone ahead with the invasion. As Stimson would later put it, "In the light of the alternatives which, on a fair estimate, were open to us I believe that no man, in our position and subject to our responsibilities, holding in his hands a weapon of such possibilities for accomplishing this purpose and saving those lives, could have failed to use it and afterwards looked his countrymen in the face."[135]

Truman's recent accession to power had other subtle consequences as well. Roosevelt's aversion to formal lines of process, to established channels for decision and action at the top, only compounded the difficulties normally attendant to presidential transitions. It enabled advocates of atomic bombing to seize the initiative and set up decision-making procedures of their own. These procedures allowed them to control the flow of information and options to the new president and to limit the access of those who might have opposed their plans. And Truman's own style of making decisions further aggravated the procedural constraints on his freedom of action. Perhaps out of unsureness, perhaps out of a belief that it was the way presidents were supposed to act, Truman affected an air of decisiveness. "The buck stops here" was more than a pose, however. It had the consequence of closing off deliberation prematurely. Again, to quote Stimson's private assessment of the novice in the White House, "He made the impression of a man who is willing and anxious to learn and to do his best but who is necessarily laboring with the terrific handicap of coming into such an office where the threads of information

133Stimson diary, April 12, 1945.
134Truman, *Year of Decisions*, p. 235.
135Stimson, "Decision," p. 106.

were so multitudinous that only long previous familiarity could allow him to control them."[136]

Whether or not the bomb's use was taken for granted, how to use it was hardly a matter of unanimity among Truman's advisers. Some may have tempered their opposition in the belief that the President was already inclined to drop it on Japan's cities without warning. Truman himself may have been inclined to discount the counsel of those who preferred other strategies for ending the war, since he had already resolved that issue. And his air of decisiveness was hardly conducive to probing his advisers for latent disagreement, let alone reaching beyond them for additional information and options. Security procedures got in his way; so did the president's own inexperience. In the end it is doubtful whether he ever fully appreciated exactly what the plans for atomic bombing called for. "I have told the Sec[retary] of War, Mr. Stimson, to use it so that military objectives and soldiers and sailors are the target and not women and children," reads his journal entry for July 25. "He and I are in accord. The target will be a purely military one."[137]

Insulated from the controversy swirling below him, hearing mostly muted objections from some around him and disregarding others, Truman could well have concluded, as he did, about dropping the bomb: "That was not any decision you had to worry about."[138] Once the various alternatives were excluded, using the bomb became a yes or no decision. By then Truman was, in Groves' words, "like a little boy on a toboggan. He never had the opportunity to say 'we *will* drop the bomb.' All he could do was say 'no.'"[139]

'TWIXT DECISION AND EXECUTION

Truman's way of deciding not only precluded careful scrutiny of limits on the use of force for bargaining purposes, but also left such critical operational details as the number of bombs to be dropped, the interval between them, and the particular cities and aim points to target in the hands of organizations in charge of implementing his decision—the

---

[136]Stimson diary, April 13, 1945. Henry Wallace, perhaps less inclined than Stimson to be favorably impressed, also sensed the new president's insecurity at a meeting two weeks later: "Truman was exceedingly eager to agree with everything I said. He also seemed eager to make decisions of every kind with the greatest promptness. Everything he said was decisive. It almost seemed as though he was eager to decide in advance of thinking." See Wallace diary entry of April 27, 1945, in John Morton Blum, ed., *The Price of Vision: The Diaries of Henry A. Wallace, 1942–1946* (Boston, 1973), p. 437.
[137]Ferrell, *Off the Record*, pp. 55–56.
[138]Harry S Truman, *Truman Speaks* (New York, 1960), p. 93.
[139]Knebel and Bailey, *No High Ground*, p. 244 (emphasis in the original).

MED and the Army Air Forces. "As far as I was concerned," says Groves, "his decision was one of noninterference—basically, a decision not to upset the existing plans."[140] That decision set in motion the use of as many atomic bombs as the MED could produce as fast as it could ship them to the Pacific until someone qualified or countermanded standing orders.

The directive authorizing the bombings allowed the air force and the MED to follow their own set procedures. On July 22 Arnold had coaxed from Stimson a substantial grant of authority for his field commander, General Spaatz, over the final choice of targets for the bomb: "It was left up to him, depending on weather, tactical situations, and any other factors that might influence his operations, which ones he should attack, that is, once it was determined that the atomic bomb was actually to be dropped at all."[141] Yet too much autonomy could be risky for a field commander. Before taking off for Guam, Spaatz asked General Thomas Handy, acting chief of staff of the army in Marshall's absence, for authorization in writing to conduct the atomic bombings. "Listen, Tom," he reportedly told Handy, "if I'm going to kill 100,000 people, I'm not going to do it on verbal [sic] orders. I want a piece of paper." In military parlance, Spaatz was "covering his ass" and the air force's. The absence of a written order, Handy tried to reassure him, was no ploy to shift responsibility, but in the end he conceded the point: "If a fellow thinks he might blow up the whole end of Japan, he ought to have a piece of paper."[142]

On July 23, after consulting with Spaatz, Groves drafted the order for Handy's signature. The following day he forwarded a request for final approval of bombing operations to Marshall, along with a sheaf of cover documents. A two-page memorandum put the probable date of the initial strike "between the first and tenth of August," or as soon after final assembly of the first gun-type bomb as weather would permit. It also gave the probable date that the next implosion bomb would be ready, allowing three days between bombs for final assembly, and went on "to forecast our delivery rates after the third bomb." The memorandum also diagramed a makeshift chain of command framed in accordance with the prior agreement between Groves and Arnold, specifying that all bombing directives would be issued through the commanding general of the U.S. Army Air Forces, which Groves says he intended to be "a clear indication to General Marshall that the orders for our operations against Japan would originate with me, be approved by him, and

---

[140]Groves, *Now It Can Be Told*, p. 265.
[141]Arnold, *Global Mission*, p. 492.
[142]Knebel and Bailey, *No High Ground*, pp. 95–96.

be issued to Spaatz over Arnold's signature."[143] It was anything but clear. It left up to Arnold whether there would be a return to the standard operating procedures previously governing the introduction of new weapons to the battlefield, delegation of authority over use to the field commander. Among the other attachments were a one-page description of each of the four target cities, a small map of Japan clipped from *National Geographic* magazine, and a draft order releasing the previously reserved targets—Hiroshima, Kokura, and Niigata—for attack only by the 509th Composite Group.[144]

There were three oversights. Hiroshima was not designated the primary target—a slip that was subsequently corrected. Nagasaki was left off the target list altogether. Arnold's courier had just arrived in Potsdam with oral instructions to add it to the list; in the rush to transmit the documents to Marshall its omission may have been a coincidence. It is more difficult to account for the third oversight: among the four target descriptions was one for Kyoto.

On the evening of July 24 Harrison alerted Stimson that the draft directive was en route from Washington and recommended that he approve it the next day even if he thought further modifications were necessary, lest operations be held up. Stimson did so by priority message the next morning.[145] Later that day General Handy turned over the action copy of the bombing order to General Spaatz:

1. The 509th Composite Group, 20th Air Force, will deliver its first special bomb as soon as weather will permit visual bombing after about 3 August 1945 on one of the targets: Hiroshima, Kokura, Niigata, and Nagasaki. . . .

2. Additional bombs will be delivered on the above targets as soon as made ready by the project staff. Further instructions will be issued concerning targets other than those listed above.[146]

Perhaps Truman and Secretaries Byrnes and Stimson hoped that one or two atomic bombs might shock Japan into accepting the terms of Potsdam, but nothing in the bombing directive contradicts the option Marshall believed he had accepted—a prolonged campaign of atomic bomb-

---

[143]Groves, *Now It Can Be Told*, pp. 309–11.

[144]War 37683, from Handy to Marshall, July 24, 1945, MED, HB, Folder 64, RG 77, National Archives, excerpted in Giovannitti and Freed, *Decision to Drop the Bomb*, p. 252. In Margaret Truman, *Harry S Truman*, p. 274, George Elsey, who worked in the "map room" at Potsdam, says he received written authorization from Truman for the bomb's use, but no copy of it has turned up.

[145]War 37750, from Harrison to Secretary of War, July 24, 1945, MED, HB, Folder 64, RG 77, National Archives; Knebel and Bailey, *No High Ground*, p. 126. Cf. Hewlett and Anderson, *The New World*, p. 394.

[146]Directive from Handy to Spaatz, July 25, 1945, reproduced in Craven and Cate, *The Pacific*, facing p. 697.

ing intended to soften up Japan for invasion. But this was softening up with a vengeance, aimed at destroying cities, not military forces. Groves too still seems to have been thinking about a longer bombing campaign in support of the army's strategy. Debriefing MED scientists on the results of the Alamogordo test, he noted that "tanks could have gone through our area after 30 minutes" and "we think we can move troops right through," conditions consistent with preinvasion strikes on Japan's defenses.[147]

Although the Potsdam Declaration was not issued until July 26—July 27 on Tinian and in Japan—the order permitted the Twentieth Air Force to drop the first atomic bomb "after about 3 August," or as early as July 30, Hiroshima time, or July 29, Potsdam and Washington time. "The difference in dates between Japan and Washington," explains Groves, "was overlooked in all of our arrangements." Less explicable was the use of "about," which Groves himself acknowledges was "thoroughly understood in the American Army. Official travel regulations of that period even defined 'about' as normally including a period of four days before and four days after the specific date cited."[148] In his haste to proceed, Groves drafted an order that, weather and the bomb's readiness permitting, would have allowed the 509th Composite Group to begin atomic bombing just three days after the issuance of the Potsdam Declaration, leaving little time for the Japanese to reflect on and respond to the ultimatum—and two days before Truman would leave Potsdam. Coincidence nearly intervened, but not quite. On July 31 Stimson asked the president to review a draft statement to be released to the public at the time of the first bombing. "The reason for the haste," he noted, "is that I was informed only yesterday that, weather permitting, it is likely that the weapon will be used as early as August 1st, Pacific Ocean Time, which is as you know a good many hours ahead of Washington time." Stimson too was off by a day, but his timing was close enough to alert Truman, who cabled back, "Release when ready but not sooner than 2 August."[149] Yet no record has been found that Spaatz' orders were ever countermanded. To military men, an order is an order, and those eager to obey it already had all the authority they needed to proceed.

No other orders were needed to bomb the rest of the targets on the list either, and no provision was made for a pause between atomic bombings to give Japan time to deliberate. It does not appear that Truman understood this. "Still no surrender order came" after Hiroshima, he writes in

[147]Groves' notes on his meeting with Oppenheimer and Tolman in Chicago, July 24, 1945, MED, TS, Folder 5, Tab I, RG 77, National Archives.

[148]Groves, *Now It Can Be Told*, pp. 311–12.

[149]War 41011 and Truman's reply, July 31, 1945, MED, HB, Folder 64, RG 77, National Archives.

his memoirs. "An order was issued to General Spaatz to continue operations as planned unless otherwise instructed."[150] No such order has ever been found. None was necessary. Truman's daughter understands why, more or less. "Some people have wondered why this second bomb was dropped so soon," she writes in her biography of the president. "This was in accordance with my father's original order, which he signed on July 24."[151] Not exactly his, but Groves', and it is possible he never got around to signing it, but the MED director saw to it that it was carried out anyway, and without delay.

Nor was additional presidential authority needed to bomb cities besides the ones already on the target list. Groves and Arnold could add to the list on their own. They considered doing so when efforts were renewed to drop the less than optimal target, Nagasaki, from the list. On July 31 Spaatz cabled Marshall with an unverified report that a prisoner-of-war camp had been located a mile from the city's center. None was said to be found in Hiroshima. Groves' reply reaffirmed the previously designated targets, citing Washington intelligence that "practically every major Japanese city" had such camps—but not before he had drafted an alternative response, listing three cities as possible replacements for Nagasaki: Osaka, Amagasaki, and Omuta.[152] Groves was not the only one thinking about additional targets; officers on Tinian were contemplating adding Tokyo to the list, along with a waiver of the requirement of visual bombing to permit a nighttime drop.[153]

Drawing up orders to field commanders was one thing; having them carried out as issued was quite another. At that point air force standard operating procedures took over, violating both the spirit and the letter of those orders, with some bearing on the timing of the bombings and the death and destruction they caused.

Weather conditions gave Japan a one-week reprieve. A mishap in the delivery of U_{235} to Tinian also set back assembly of the first bomb at least a day, then cloud cover obstructed visual bombing until August 6, Japan time.[154] Despite the inclement weather, formations of three planes continued making daily practice runs over the four target cities to drop projectiles that were exact replicas of the atomic bomb in every respect except one: they contained only small conventional explosive charges to mark the spot where they had landed. These missions had another

[150]Truman, *Year of Decisions*, p. 423.

[151]Margaret Truman, *Harry S Truman*, p. 283.

[152]Cable from Colonel H. M. Pasco (secretary to the general staff) to Spaatz, July 31, 1945, replying to Spaatz' 1005 and 1027 of the same date, MED, TS, Folder 5D3, RG 77, National Archives, and draft of a cable from Handy to Spaatz, Folder 5B. According to a handwritten notation on 1005, Groves was the action officer for the reply.

[153]Knebel and Bailey, *No High Ground*, p. 219.

[154]On the mishap, see Laurence, *Dawn over Zero*, pp. 203–4.

purpose besides improving bombing accuracy: conditioning enemy defenders to expect small formations of planes overhead that dropped bombs causing no appreciable damage. The drill worked so well that Tokyo Rose began deriding the 509th Group by name in Japanese propaganda broadcasts: "You are now reduced to small missions of three planes, and the bombs they drop are just duds."[155] Yet the practice runs had an unintended consequence far more devastating than lulling the defenders into not scrambling their fighter squadrons. When the *Enola Gay* and its two companion planes appeared over Hiroshima on the morning of August 6 and air raid sirens sounded, few inhabitants bothered to take cover. As many as 80,000 people lost their lives in the atomic bombing and its aftermath.[156]

In the absence of orders for a bombing pause, organizational interests and routines determined that there would be barely a two-day interval between atomic attacks. Availability of the implosion bomb depended on the rate of plutonium production, and Groves stepped up the tempo. Based on the rate at the end of July, the date of the second bombing had been advanced from August 20 to August 11. By August 7 Groves was able to advance it one more day. Then, on the basis of a long-range forecast of fair weather on August 9 and unfavorable flying weather for five days thereafter, Groves decided to rush preparations for dropping the second bomb, over the objections of scientists who had to assemble it. William L. Laurence, a reporter for the *New York Times* who had been detailed to the MED to help draft press releases on the bombings and who flew on board the second mission, later commented, "It is quite possible, though I have no direct knowledge of it, that the forecast of bad weather came all the way from Potsdam." Laurence's hunch may not have been off the mark by much. According to the commander of the 509th Composite Group, the forecast originated in Washington.[157] However inspired the forecast, Groves was able to use it to advance rather than postpone the second atomic bombing.

Only two cities were on the planned route of that mission—Kokura as the primary target and Nagasaki as the backup. Niigata was too far off

---

[155]Laurence, *Men and Atoms*, p. 164.

[156]The death toll has been a matter of some contention. The MED's own internal estimate was 78,000, see "Final Report of Finding of the Manhattan Engineering District Atomic Bomb Investigating Groups at Hiroshima and Nagasaki," April 19, 1946, MED History, Box 23, RG 374, National Archives. That figure was revised downward in the MED's public report, *Atomic Bombings of Hiroshima and Nagasaki*, p. 18. Both reports are based on fatality estimates prepared immediately after the bombings and underestimate the number of subsequent deaths, particularly from long-term radiation effects.

[157]On the bombing schedule, see Groves, *Now It Can Be Told*, pp. 341–42. On the advance forecast, see Laurence, *Dawn over Zero*, p. 226; and Craven and Cate, *The Pacific*, p. 709.

course for a bomb-laden B-29 to reach it and the other target cities and still have enough fuel to return to base. To increase the odds of hitting Kokura, instead of the less bomb-worthy Nagasaki, the crew was instructed to disregard reports from the weather plane flying out ahead of the mission and to pass close enough to the primary target to see for itself whether visual bombing was conceivable, before flying on to the secondary target.[158] This seemingly minor change in itinerary would help ensure that the implosion bomb had a combat test before war's end, but it would frustrate Groves' hopes for optimum blast effects.

The commander and the crew on board had no mean incentive to get rid of their deadly cargo before returning to base: a rough landing could endanger their lives, not to mention the immediate vicinity. That was manifest in a last-minute change in arrangements. Because of peculiarities in the bomb's design, the crew had been under orders to complete final assembly of the bomb on the ground and to load it on board fully armed. Yet the commander, with General Farrell's approval, decided to disregard those orders and arm the bomb in flight.[159] The bomb and fuel were a heavy load to lift on takeoff and the number of burnt-out bomber hulks scattered around North Field, Tinian, bore mute testimony to the crew's concern. If the crew worried about crashing on takeoff, how would they have felt about landing with a fully armed atomic bomb on board?

The urgency of using the second bomb as soon as possible was also impressed upon the crew at the last moment. When mechanics reported a defective fuel pump on board, Groves reports, Farrell decided on his own authority to proceed with the flight, even though it meant that the plane would not be able to draw on all its fuel reserves.[160]

The plane thus took off slightly low on fuel, circled too long waiting for a companion plane to arrive at their rendezvous, arrived over Kokura to find it clouded over, circled over the primary target until driven off by Japanese defenders, and flew on to Nagasaki. En route the crew calculated that the plane had just enough fuel to make one run over the target and still return to its alternate landing site—two runs and it would have to ditch at sea. When the bomber finally reached Nagasaki, the city was covered by thick overcast. The senior officers on board, says Groves, "decided that despite their positive orders to the contrary, they had no choice but to attempt radar bombing."[161] The plane made its entire bombing run by radar. William Laurence, who was on board, claims that an opening appeared in the clouds at the very last moment, but the

---

[158]Groves, *Now It Can Be Told*, pp. 342–43.
[159]Ibid., p. 317; cf. pp. 343–44 for a different version of events.
[160]Ibid., p. 344.
[161]Ibid., p. 345.

initial after-action report to the War Department suggests otherwise: "Cloud cover was bad at [the] strike and it will be necessary to await photographs to give [the] exact point of [the] strike and [the] damage."[162] If the bombardier ever did obtain a clear view, it was not of his aim point, for the bomb landed 1.5 miles to the north of it, far off the performance record on practice runs.

"No fire storm arose," reports the U.S. Strategic Bombing Survey, "and the uneven terrain of the city confined the maximum intensity of damage to the valley over which the bomb exploded."[163] Years later Groves could still not contain his disappointment at the results: "While the blast and resulting fire inflicted heavy destruction on Nagasaki and its population, the damage was not nearly [as] heavy as it would have been if the correct aiming point had been used."[164] The bombing destroyed less than half the city and claimed some 38,000 lives. The Mitsubishi dockyards and electric works, located on the outskirts of the city, were left standing.

Attempts to wrest control from Washington did not stop with lax execution of Groves' targeting directive. A day after the Hiroshima strike the ranking officers on Tinian—General Farrell, Admiral Purnell, and Captain William Parsons—conferred at Guam with the senior commanders in the Pacific theater, Admiral Nimitz and General Spaatz, about future targets for the atomic bomb. The outcome was nothing less than a broad unilateral reassertion of autonomy over the choice of targets by commanders in the field, as a memorandum from Farrell to Groves after the war makes clear: "A message was sent to you recommending that the question of targets should be reviewed, that larger targets should be provided, that visual bombing should be no longer required, and that the target list should be revised to include several large cities. It was requested that the region of Tokyo be included as a target because of its great psychological value."[165]

LEASHING THE DOGS OF WAR

Organizational considerations rather than national purpose dominated the planning and execution, if not the decision, to use the atomic bomb,

---

[162]Laurence, *Men and Atoms*, p. 158; Cable from Commander, 313th Bomber Wing, Tinian, to War Department, MED, HB, Folder 7, RG 77, National Archives.

[163]Strategic Bombing Survey (Pacific), *Effects of Atomic Bombs on Hiroshima and Nagasaki*, p. 5.

[164]Groves, *Now It Can Be Told*, p. 346.

[165]Memorandum from Farrell to Groves, "Report on Overseas Operations—Atomic Bomb," September 27, 1945, in Anthony Cave Brown and Charles B. MacDonald, *The Secret History of the Atomic Bomb* (New York, 1977), p. 531.

much as they did the introduction of toxic gas and the escalation of the conventional bombing of Japan. Seldom did conscious strategic calculation guide the United States. Seldom too did the politics of war termination in Japan enter explicitly into American deliberations.

The United States could have taken a number of steps besides banning gas warfare and sparing Kyoto to mitigate the use of force without demonstrably reducing the chances of an acceptable end to the war—for instance, limiting the use of incendiary bombs, staging a noncombat demonstration of the atomic bomb, delaying further atomic bombing or ceasing all hostile acts from the air to give Japan time to reconsider and sue for peace. It did not try any of these steps. At worst, withholding force might have prolonged the war for a while at a time when little combat was taking place; it would not have altered the final result. Yet restraint could have significantly reduced the gratuitous suffering on both sides, especially for noncombatants.

In rational-choice terms, it can be argued that the United States behaved as if the objective of inducing Japan to surrender was subordinated to another objective—in Stimson's words, that of exerting "maximum force with maximum speed."[166] American policy was guided by an implicit assumption that only the escalation of military pressure could bring the war to a rapid conclusion. That assumption confuses the physics of brute force with the politics of power.

Truman may well have acted on that assumption and pursued that objective, but close scrutiny of American actions at war's end suggests that others did not. Stimson himself did not when he tried first to limit civilian casualties from conventional bombing and then to spare Kyoto as inducements to Japanese cooperation. Nor did Marshall when he tried to divert the army air forces from strategic bombing. Nor did Leahy and King when they opposed using either toxic gas or the atomic bomb. Nor did Bard and the dissident scientists in the MED when they resisted dropping atomic bombs on Japanese cities without warning. Yet in each instance the opponents of escalation, for various reasons, favored other means of putting military pressure on Japan. And with the possible exception of gas warfare, those who favored escalation won. The rational-choice approach thus captures the thrust of American policy but not the conflicts or the motivations of those who made it.

Rational-choice accounts, following the lead of some participants, have dwelled on the use of the atomic bomb for its psychological effect. That was arguably rational, given the goal of prompt and unconditional surrender. Yet close scrutiny of the details of the decision suggests that few U.S. officials had psychology clearly in mind. Truman, Byrnes, and

[166]Stimson and Bundy, *On Active Service*, p. 629.

Stimson may have hoped that the shock of the bomb would spare them the pain of invasion, but others more familiar with the weapon were not as optimistic. They saw a campaign of atomic bombings as a precursor to a landing on the Japanese home islands. In the course of the internal American deliberations, the few references to the psychological impact of the bomb may have been intended to ease qualms about its physical impact, but may only have blurred precise thinking about its political impact.

Working within the rational-choice approach, Paul Kecskemeti's *Strategic Surrender* takes issue with the objective of applying "maximum force with maximum speed." Once the outcome of battle is clear and irreversible, Kecskemeti argues, "a rational economy of warfare prescribes the quickest and least costly transition from violence to nonviolence, and this aim is not likely to be achieved by intensifying the destructiveness of the war during its terminal stage."[167] In bargaining at war's end it may be prudent to withhold force, but that is precisely what the United States and Japan found it politically difficult to do. In practice, war may be too emotional, chaotic, and inexorable to satisfy the requirements for "a rational economy of warfare" in theory. Yet acting on Sherman's dictum that "war is hell" appeases only those who refuse to consider any limitations on the use of force and blinds others to the realization that war termination is a political act.

From Clausewitz to Kecskemeti, the intellectual tradition of a calculus of war conceives of force as a tool of bargaining between states, but what Clausewitz calls "friction" keeps getting in the way. Two of the most abrasive sources of friction are internal politics and organizational routines. They ground rational calculation to a halt at nearly every turn during the end of the war between the United States and Japan.

Over the spring and summer of 1945, as U.S. officials considered how much force to apply in order to bring about Japan's surrender, bureaucratic and domestic politics, not international politics, shaped military plans and the decisions to proceed with them. Hawks and doves may differ on the utility of military pressure, but what often concerns the armed services is the form that pressure takes. To some military men the use of force is just a nasty job someone has to do, to some it is the raison d'être of their service, but to others it is the means to organizational ends—desired roles and missions, increased budget shares and prestige, enhanced capabilities, more officer billets and promotions, improved morale. The services have a large stake in the strategies states adopt.

Those in charge of the Manhattan Project had no less of a stake in their preferred weapon and strategy for ending the war than did the army air

---

[167]Kecskemeti, *Strategic Surrender*, p. 196.

forces in strategic bombing with conventional munitions; if anything, the MED's uneasiness about justifying the vast sums it had expended in secret with only the loosest fiscal accountability made its stake all the greater. As Stimson quipped to his two assistant secretaries, John Mc-Cloy and Harvey Bundy, after getting word of the test at Alamogordo, "Well, I have been responsible for spending two billions of dollars on this atomic venture. Now that it is successful I shall not be sent to prison in Fort Leavenworth."[168] While perhaps overly marked by his own preoccupations, Groves reminiscences are nonetheless indicative of the political reasons for pressing ahead with the atomic bombings:

> I said that they could not fail to use this bomb because if they didn't use it, they would immediately cast a lot of reflection on Mr. Roosevelt, [raising questions like] why did you spend all this money and all this effort and then when you got it, why didn't you use it? Also it would have come out sooner or later in a Congressional hearing, if nowhere else, just when we could have dropped the bomb if we didn't use it. And then, knowing American politics, you know as well as I do that there would have been elections fought on the basis that every mother whose son was killed after such and such a date [might feel] the blood was on the head of the President.[169]

To Groves and the scientist administrators in the MED, only successful wartime use of the bomb would justify both past appropriations and continued support for research into the atom. In contrast to conventional and atomic bombing, gas warfare was not a major role and mission of any powerful military organization. Its use was easier to limit.

Groves also had the political will and skill to see the project through and to get his way on plans for the bomb's use. Latent opposition to those plans arose within the armed services and among the scientists working in the MED laboratories. Why that opposition failed to alter Groves' plans at all seems inexplicable without some appreciation of his bureaucratic maneuvering. In the end, President Truman might have gone along with Groves even if he had heard a full debate of the alternatives, but Groves saw to it that he never got the chance.

Groves' shrewdness may be peculiar to the circumstances of this case, but compartmentation imposed by security procedures, a critical feature of the wartime policy process, is likely to recur at other times and places. That compartmentation excluded all but a few officials from detailed knowledge of war plans and widened the already radical separation

---

[168]Harvey H. Bundy, "Remembered Words," *The Atlantic* 199 (March 1957): 57.
[169]Giovannitti and Freed, *Decision to Drop the Bomb*, p. 322. New York Republican Representative Clare Booth Luce posed such questions to Groves in hearings on October 9, 1945; see U.S. Congress, House, Committee on Military Affairs, *Atomic Energy*, p. 28.

between those whose job it was to consider the political consequences of American actions for relations with Japan and those whose job it was to develop and deploy weapons. Only at the very apex of the government would it have been possible to do what rational choice demands, to integrate those two concerns and pursue a coherent bargaining strategy, using both escalation and deescalation, to induce the enemy to lay down its arms. This, American leaders did not do.

A *decision* to drop atomic bombs, moreover, is not the same as an *order* to do so. And neither may correspond to *implementation*. The control of military forces in the field requires perspicacious attention to operational detail by leaders or those who serve them—drawing up precise orders and investing time, energy, and political capital to monitor and induce compliance with them. Even had the president and his civilian advisers intended to use military force to influence the Japanese, they left execution of the conventional and atomic bombing to the armed services and the MED. They thereby put themselves—and the Japanese—at the mercy of organizations whose standard operating procedures for waging war did not facilitate limits on force, whose very conceptions of force ruled out its sensitive employment to induce the enemy to quit fighting and aimed instead at the destruction of enemy war-making capacity, as if the enemy would fight on unless and until it no longer could.

When Secretary of War Stimson did attempt to impose some limits on the bombing, it took sustained bargaining with those in the armed forces who supposedly served him. In the end Stimson had to content himself with maintaining the illusion of control while conceding much of its reality. He succeeded in sparing Kyoto only after conceding control over all other bombing to the air force chief of staff, a concession that might have made even that limited success short-lived had the war not concluded when it did. General Arnold and General Groves hardly had more success than Stimson in controlling the use of force. Nor did their putative commander-in-chief, the president of the United States. Yet Truman insists in his memoirs, "The final decision of where and when to use the atomic bomb was up to me."[170] If he thought so, he was deceiving himself. If he did not, he was perpetuating the illusion of control. In waging war, delegation is ultimately unavoidable. And that makes centralized command-and-control of military forces tenuous at best—the more extensive the forces, the more tenuous the control. Leaders may rightly be held responsible for knowing this and failing to assert control, but those who write about war termination dare not base their conclusions on the assumption that leaders will behave as they are supposed to and can succeed if they try.

[170]Truman, *Year of Decisions*, p. 419.

[222]

For many strategy-makers in Washington, Japan did not exist as political entity, only as a target to be hit. Insofar as American decisions to use force took political considerations into account, politics stopped at the water's edge. It is the misfortune of war that the acts that followed these decisions did not stop there as well. Nothing reveals more clearly the internal preoccupations of those who drew up plans for the atomic bomb than the public statements issued immediately after the bombing of Hiroshima. The White House press release was typical. Painstakingly drafted by Groves' staff and cleared by the president, it ran more than a thousand words in length. Scarcely one in five concerned Japan or the world beyond the bureaucracy. The rest extolled America's victory in "the battle of the laboratories," paid tribute to the scientific community, private industry, and the army for "the greatest achievement of organized science in history," and foresaw "a long period of intensive research" on atomic energy. Scientists may wonder whether such statements are true; politicians wonder why they were issued. To those who harbored doubts about the secret project, who saw "great quantities of materials going in" and "nothing coming out of these plants," Groves, in the president's name, could now offer reassurance: "We have spent two billion dollars on the greatest scientific gamble in history—and won."[171]

---

[171]White House press release, August 6, 1945, in FRUS, *Conference of Berlin*, II: 1376–78. The secretary of war, in a parallel release issued at the same time, mainfested similar preoccupations.

[5]

The Struggle for Compliance:
Japan Sues for Peace

How can you treat on its merits in this quiet room, a question
which will not be treated on its merits when it gets out of this
room?
—Woodrow Wilson (1919)

On the morning of August 6, 1945, the *Enola Gay*, a B-29 specially
modified for the purpose, dropped an atomic bomb over Hiroshima.
The blast shattered all but a handful of buildings located within 2,000
feet of ground zero, even many of those built to withstand the shock of
an earthquake. An ensuing wave of thermal radiation set off a firestorm
with winds of up to 40 miles per hour that consumed much of the rubble
and almost completely burned out some 4.4 square miles of the city
center. The combination of blast and fire destroyed 62,000 of the 90,000
buildings in the metropolitan area and severely damaged another 6,000.
Minutes after the blast, rain began to fall, bringing radioactive dust
down with it. An estimated 71,000 people died that day, roughly 30
percent of the city's population; about an equal number suffered serious
injuries. Subsequent deaths directly attributable to the bombing and its
aftermath pushed the toll past 80,000.[1]

American radio broadcasts monitored in Tokyo the next day carried a
statement by President Truman: "It is an atomic bomb. It is a harnessing
of the basic power of the universe." Recalling that Japanese leaders had
rejected the "the ultimatum of July 26" designed "to spare the Japanese
people from utter destruction," the president warned, "If they do not
now accept our terms, they may expect a rain of ruin from the air, the
like of which has never been seen on this earth. Behind this air attack
will follow sea and land forces in such numbers and power as they have

[1] All data except casualty figures are drawn from Strategic Bombing Survey (Pacific),
Effects of Atomic Bombs, pp. 3, 5–6, 9.

not yet seen, and with the fighting skill of which they are already well aware."[2]

Since the war, much has been made of the psychological impact of the atomic bombing on Japan. In its most exaggerated form, the claim is that the bomb shocked Japan into surrendering, a classic case of *post hoc, ergo propter hoc* reasoning. Disaggregating the state to examine the reactions of Japan's leaders one by one calls this reasoning into question. Not a single senior official involved in high-level decision-making circles changed his prior stand on war termination after the atomic bombing. The Big Six remained deadlocked. So did the cabinet. The bombing of Hiroshima did have one significant political impact. It reinforced Emperor Hirohito's previous conviction that the time had come for Japan to sue for peace and it redoubled his sense of urgency. Upon learning of the attack on Hiroshima, recalls Privy Seal Kido, the emperor told him, "Under these circumstances, we must bow to the inevitable. No matter what happens to my safety, we must put an end to this war as speedily as possible so that this tragedy will not be repeated."[3]

One reason why the bombing had less of a psychological impact than usually assumed is that the shock was confined largely to the immediate vicinity of Hiroshima. The U.S. Strategic Bombing Survey says as much: "It is apparent that the effect of the atomic bombings on the confidence of the Japanese civilian population was remarkably localized. Outside of the target cities, it was subordinate to other demoralizing experiences."[4] So physically devastating was the attack on Hiroshima that it virtually cut the city off from the outside world for days. In the meantime the Japanese army tried to confine the impact of the bombing and downplay its significance. It disputed characterizations of the weapon as an atomic bomb, dismissed reports of the devastation as exaggerated, and exuded optimism about countermeasures to ameliorate its effects. Even within official circles, appreciation of what had befallen Hiroshima was localized. Army Vice-Chief of Staff Torashiro Kawabe recalls, "Since Tokyo was not directly affected by the bombing, the full force of the shock was not felt." Officials too "had become accustomed to bombings" because of "frequent raids by B-29s." Kawabe himself was one of the few high-ranking officers at Imperial General Headquarters who had some familiarity with the potential of atomic energy: "Actually, a majority in the Army did not realize at first that what had been dropped was an atomic bomb, and they were not familiar with the terrible nature of the atomic bomb. It was only in a gradual manner that the horrible wreckage which had been made of

---

[2]Statement by the President, August 6, 1945, in *FRUS: Conference of Berlin*, II: 1377.
[3]Kido, in "Statements," II, no. 61541, p. 176; cf. p. 196. Cf. also Tōgō, ibid., IV, no. 50304, p. 268.
[4]Strategic Bombing Survey (Pacific), *Effects of Atomic Bombs*, p. 22.

Hiroshima became known."[5] For military men schooled to believe in the superiority of the moral over the material, it was still conceivable to think of fighting on. And few officials, civilian or military, were ready to consider unconditional surrender.

"In comparison," says General Kawabe, "the Soviet entry into the war was a great shock when it actually came," on August 8, two days after the Hiroshima bombing. Soviet Foreign Minister Molotov summoned Ambassador Satō and read him the Soviet declaration of war. One passage made the futility of Japan's approach to Moscow all too plain: "The demand of the three powers, the United States, Great Britain and China, of July 26 for the unconditional surrender of the Japanese armed forces was rejected by Japan. Thus the proposal made by the Japanese Government to the Soviet Union for mediation in the Far East has lost all foundation."[6] Satō's reporting cable was delayed in transmission, but a Domei news agency dispatch on the Soviet move arrived at the Foreign Ministry shortly after midnight. At about the same time, word reached the capital through Japanese army channels that the Kwantung army in Manchuria was under attack. Reports described Soviet forces "as invading in swarms," recalls Kawabe. "It gave us all the more severe shock and alarm because we had been in constant fear" that "the vast Red Army forces in Europe were now being turned against us."[7] Stripped of vital manpower to reinforce the home islands, the Kwantung army was no match for its adversary. As soon as Prime Minister Suzuki learned of the fighting, he consulted Lieutenant General Sumihasa Ikeda, chief of the Cabinet Planning Board and just back from Manchuria, to find out whether Japanese forces there were capable of repulsing the attack. "The Kwantung Army is hopeless," reported Ikeda. "Within two weeks Hsinking [Chang-chun] will be occupied." "Is the Kwantung Army that weak?" the prime minister sighed. "Then the game is up."[8]

The attack dashed army hopes of continued Soviet neutrality, let alone active support, and dulled the attraction of a circuitous approach to the Allies through Moscow. It also made the army strategy of threatening last-ditch resistance in hopes of winning Allies concessions seem less compelling. Of perhaps greater moment, as soon as the Soviet declaration of war began circulating, its explicit reference to Japan's proposal "for mediation" would alert the diehards to the back-channel negotiations. No longer would the concern about preserving secrecy inhibit a direct

[5]Kawabe, in "Statements," II, no. 52608, p. 97.

[6]USSR, *Information Bulletin*, August 11, 1945, p. 1. Cf. Kase, *Journey to the Missouri*, p. 224.

[7]Kawabe, in "Statements," II, no. 52608, p. 97. Cf. Toyoda, in ibid., IV, no. 61340, p. 395.

[8]Ikeda, in ibid., I, no. 54479, p. 543.

approach to the United States or Great Britain; if anything, impending announcement of Soviet entry prompted the government to act before the diehards could react.

Under these circumstances War Minister Anami and Army Chief of Staff Umezu could not remain adamant in their opposition to direct negotiations. Yet the Japanese army leadership was not prepared to accept the terms of Potsdam. Nor was the government. Even after most senior officials in Tokyo had abandoned all hope of successfully resisting an Allied invasion of the homeland, or credibly threatening to do so, none was about to advocate surrender without some assurance that the throne would remain in place. And the threat to exact a high toll of American invaders, even if it could not beat them back, still left Japan with some bargaining leverage.

Behind the Japanese army's opposition to unconditional surrender, and ultimately the government's as well, lay a predicament of military command-and-control that states often face in war termination. At no time is command-and-control more imperative—or more precarious— than at war's end, when any untoward incident can jeopardize efforts to coordinate diplomatic and military strategy or, worse yet, prolong the war and add to its death and destruction. At no other time is the potential for conflict between service morale and compliance greater. The army threat to resist the invasion would give Japan bargaining leverage only if the atomic bombing and Soviet entry into the war did not produce a collapse of morale among the rank and file. Yet, for every soldier who might break and run under the pressure of the American onslaught, there were many others, especially in the officer corps, prepared to fight on to uphold the honor of the service and the nation. Only an honorable settlement of the war could appease them. That meant, at a minimum, preserving the throne. Far from collapsing, they might disobey orders and fight on rather than accept unconditional surrender. Morale was thus a two-edged sword.

Orders to surrender, moreover, are not necessarily self-executing. They require a willingness among subordinates to comply. Without it the war may go on despite the best intentions at the top. Worse yet, insubordination may take the form of a coup d'état, removing those at the top. That would be likely to interfere with implementation of a decision on war termination. It could also overturn that decision. Orderly termination of a war requires that senior officers take precautions to avoid insubordination by the zealous as well as the timid, and above all to forestall any coup d'état by those determined to continue the war or halt it at all costs.

Forestalling a coup means staging a countercoup. Participating in a coup resembles fleeing a rout: no one wants to be the first to join, but above all no one wants to be left behind. Yet coups typically lack the spontaneity of a rout. Staging a coup requires planning and coordination beforehand; mutual trust and discipline alone will not suffice. Reliable comrades in arms must be well positioned in command of pivotal units and at critical nodes of communication. Like staging a coup, preventing a coup requires prior conspiracy. Those in command of the armed forces cannot simply issue orders against coup attempts; they must line up key subordinates by bargaining and persuasion, for if the orders they issue are disobeyed, they too could be numbered among the plotters' victims. Preventing a coup is only the most extreme predicament of compliance that leaders face in exercising command-and-control at war's end.

Curbing unprofessional conduct, whether by an excess of zeal or timidity among subordinates, is the institutional responsibility of senior generals and admirals. While those in command of Japan's armed forces had not always acted to uphold that responsibility during the war, those in authority by late summer 1945, Generals Anami and Umezu and Admirals Yonai and Toyoda, were military professionals, not zealots. Even though War Minister Anami and both chiefs of staff had pressed for adopting the strategy of decisive battle for the homeland as the most effective means of terminating the war to Japan's advantage, they were by no means diehards. Nor were most of their top-ranking subordinates. The views of General Shuichi Miyazaki, chief of the army's Operations Division, typified the army's stand at war's end: "Having learned since the spring of [1944] that the problem of Japan's national structure was being discussed in the American press and radio, I had a good many reasons to fear that were we to surrender, the question of our national polity would be placed beyond our control. To me such [an] eventuality was the most painful consequence associated with Japan's defeat, and to all Japanese military men it was a common problem of the utmost gravity."[9] Victory "was beyond all expectation," Miyazaki believed. "The best we could hope for" was to inflict "a major blow on the enemy. I, therefore, held that we should not sue for peace without making a final effort toward that end, and do all in our power to make the decisive homeland operation a great success." Lieutenant General Seizō Arisue, chief of the army's Intelligence Bureau, took a similar view: "If we could defeat the enemy in Kyushu or inflict tremendous losses, forcing him to realize the strong fighting spirit of the Japanese Army and people, it would be possible, we hoped, to bring about the termination of hostilities on comparatively favorable terms."[10] The staunch commitment of

[9]Miyazaki, in ibid., II, no. 54478, pp. 544–45.
[10]Arisue, in ibid., I, no. 52506, p. 64.

the army officer corps to a strategy of decisive battle did not give Japan's leadership much room for maneuver; accepting anything like the terms of Potsdam would seem tantamount to capitulation, prompting army zealots to topple the government.

In the course of the Big Six deliberations, the high command of the Japanese army had heard more determined advocacy than ever before from those taking a dovish stand. Foreign Minister Tōgō contended that these deliberations reconciled Anami and Umezu to surrender and to efforts at assuring army compliance: "As the result of frank talk at the meetings," everyone present, "including the soldiers, became prepared psychologically for termination of the war; without such a unity of feeling it might well have proved that in the great unrest immediately preceding the surrender the military leaders would have turned obstinate" and the army, spurred on by overzealous subordinates, "would have been impossible to control."[11] While available evidence does not support the contention that the high command underwent an intellectual conversion, their behavior from mid-July on presupposes no irreconcilable commitment to a decisive battle for the homeland, only the precariousness of their hold on those below them.[12]

Arranging for key subordinates to comply with an order to surrender took time. In the meantime, reticence was the order of the day for the high command. Disclosing word of the atomic bombing and the Soviet declaration of war might have shaken confidence in the populace and stirred unrest in the ranks, but it would hardly have swayed diehard officers prepared to stick to their guns, secure in the conviction that only victory or death could uphold their honor. Publicizing these events would only have alerted the diehards to Japan's response and incited them to rebellion, while demoralizing the rank and file at home and at the front. So service leaders opted for reticence and carried the government with them.

Compliance also required a convincing demonstration that army leaders had done everything in their power to obtain peace with honor. So they retreated to a new stand, permitting negotiations to open immediately on the basis of the terms of Potsdam, but attaching four conditions to their acceptance: (1) preservation of the throne, (2) disarmament and demobilization of Japan's armed forces under their own supervision; (3) disposition of war criminals under Japanese law; and (4) no

---

[11]Tōgō, *Cause of Japan*, p. 284. Cf. Suzuki, in "Interrogations," II, no. 531, p. 312.

[12]In contrast to Tōgō's conversion thesis, see Kazuo Kawai, "Militarist Activity between Japan's Two Surrender Decisions," *Pacific Historical Review* 22 (November 1953): 383–89, depicts the Japanese army high command as a monolithic group of diehard hawks. Both understate the problem of command-and-control that army leaders faced. Neither can account for Anami's refusal to join the coup or to bring down the government by resigning.

occupation of the home islands, or else confining the army of occupation to a minimum number of troops at a few locations outside Japan's cities. Lieutenant General Masao Yoshizumi, chief of the Military Affairs Bureau, sums up the army's new stand: "Even if we are to decide to terminate the war without fighting the homeland battle, we should submit the four conditions of peace, and we must resolve to go on with the battle of the homeland in case these conditions are not met."[13] Yet Japanese insistence on these four conditions, given Allied insistence on unconditional surrender, set up a test of will that assured continued prosecution of the war.

Military compliance with orders to surrender ultimately required artful use of imperial authority. It was the emperor's intervention, carefully arranged by a handful of palace officials, that made surrender politically possible. As one close observer, former foreign minister Mamoru Shigemitsu, later put it, "Our plans to restore peace" were premised on awaiting "the right moment when the Emperor could issue a direct command. Meanwhile we should foster a state of mind in the Army and the Navy ensuring obedience thereto, in order that no serious obstacle should arise."[14] Yet intervention by the emperor, despite his prestige, could itself create a "serious obstacle" because it constituted a gross breach of court etiquette and constitutional practice.

THE PALACE PLOTS FOR PEACE

The Meiji constitution cloaked the emperor's role in ambiguity, but there was no ambiguity on one point: his authority was not that of an absolute monarch. According to Article IV, he embodied all state authority, "combining in himself the rights of sovereignty," but he was enjoined to exercise those rights "according to the provisions of the present constitution." Among those provisions were Article V, stipulating that he "exercises the legislative power with the consent of the Imperial Diet," and Article LV, providing that "all Laws, Imperial Ordinances, and Imperial Rescripts of whatever kind, that relate to the affairs of the State, require the countersignature of a Minister of State."[15] These provisions are consistent with the conception of the emperor either as chief of state in form only, merely legitimating whatever decisions the government makes, or at most a constitutional monarch, involved more or

[13]Yoshizumi, in "Statements," IV, no. 54484, p. 603. Cf. Tōgō, *Cause of Japan*, pp. 316–17.

[14]Shigemitsu, *Japan and Her Destiny*, p. 334.

[15]Official translation of the Meiji constitution, in George E. Uyehara, *The Political Development of Japan, 1867–1909* (New York, 1910), appendix.

less actively, albeit unobtrusively, in trying to influence cabinet politics.

Under Hirohito, imperial practice corresponded to constitutional doctrine. In his youth Hirohito was tutored in his duties by Prince Kimmochi Saionji, last of the surviving *genro*, or founding fathers of the Meiji Restoration, who is said to have "thought it most important for the Emperor to guard his position as constitutional monarch zealously." Consistent with this principle, "he guided the Emperor, vigilantly guarding against [having] any responsibility shifted onto" him for government policy.[16] To Kido the scope of the emperor's role was just as limited: the emperor "may give words of advice and caution to the government, but once the government has decided on a certain policy, it has been the consistent attitude of emperors since the Meiji Era not to veto any such measure."[17] Hirohito's posture, though consistent, had very different consequences in different political contexts. When the armed services dominated Japan's policy process, his transcendence served their dominance, just as it had served the cabinet's in an earlier period of his reign.

Although palace bureaucrats sought to avoid putting the emperor in a politically exposed position in order to maintain his neutrality and transcendence as symbol of the nation's unity, his protected position did not rule out all involvement in the policy process. The emperor—and the palace bureaucrats who acted in his name—performed two essential functions in that process: ratifier of decisions made elsewhere, and catalyst for crystallizing a consensus. These two functions had very different implications for integrating and coordinating diplomatic and military strategy among the army, the navy, and the cabinet and preventing autonomous action in the trifurcated policy process of wartime Japan.

Ratification avoided involvement in controversy. When either armed service came before the emperor to seek approval of its plans, he was obliged to grant it; the same was the case for cabinet policies. Yet mere ratification of decisions made elsewhere could not resolve contradictions among the army, the navy, and the government. Similar inhibitions limited the emperor's role in matters of war termination that required joint decision among the services and the cabinet. Once participants had reached agreement in the Supreme Council for the Direction of the War (SCDW), they requested an imperial conference to obtain the emperor's consent. On those occasions the imperial conference consisted of a formal rehearsal of the SCDW deliberations at which the emperor was

---

[16]Deposition of Count Nobuaki Makino, in *IMTFE*, Defense Document 2247, p. 4.
[17]Cross-examination in *IMTFE*, pp. 31329–30. James B. Crowley, *Japan's Quest for Autonomy* (Princeton, N.J., 1966), p. 151, dates the origins of this pattern to 1913. For a comparative perspective on the tension between political legitimation and political action, and the importance of charisma to both, see Hans H. Gerth and C. Wright Mills, eds., *From Max Weber: Essays in Sociology* (New York, 1958), pp. 263–64.

constrained from delving too deeply into the substance of the decision beyond reassuring himself that a valid consensus existed for him to ratify. [18] That consensus need not have reconciled underlying contradictions. Ratification by the emperor was pro forma. No imperial conference could even be convened without prior approval in writing from each of the chiefs of staff and the prime minister. For the government to request an imperial conference to report its inability to reach agreement on a policy matter was tantamount to tendering its resignation.

The emperor could involve himself more obtrusively in the policy process by acting as a catalyst when no consensus existed. Because such involvement was necessarily more controversial, it was undertaken either indirectly by having palace bureaucrats solicit information and make suggestions to ministers and service chiefs, or privately by the emperor in audiences with one or two of the principals. Private audiences were typically formal affairs, conducted in the presence of a chamberlain, with the chief aide-de-camp present on military matters and the privy seal on government issues, but the emperor could request those in attendance to approach the throne, inviting palace bureaucrats to withdraw and leave him alone with the others for less formal conversations. By circumspect questioning, sometimes by guarded and elliptical statements, the emperor could convey his personal wishes. Yet those in attendance were free to ignore or "misinterpret" him. [19] Although the use of court bureaucrats to crystallize consensus in backstage negotiations could help break down the barriers of trifurcation in the policy process, it was contrary to court practice for cabinet ministers to attend audiences in the company of the service chiefs, thus limiting the utility of the audience, not just the imperial conference, as an integrative or coordinating mechanism. [20] But in exercising his right to pose questions and offer suggestions either on his own or through those around the throne, the emperor could step beyond neutral ratification and involve the palace more actively in policy formation.

It would be a far more overt intrusion—and one carrying far greater risk to his stance of neutrality—for the emperor to express his policy

[18]E.g., in the fall of 1941, when Hirohito informed Kido of his intention to inquire about the substance of policy at the next imperial conference, Kido discouraged that overt an intrusion into the political process (see David A. Titus, *Palace and Politics in Prewar Japan* [New York, 1974], pp. 263–64).

[19]E.g., on New Year's Eve 1945, Hirohito had addressed an unusually blunt question to Prime Minister Koiso, asking how he proposed to retrieve the worsening war situation after the events at Leyte. Some observers took this gesture as a sign of Hirohito's lack of confidence in the government, but Koiso did not tender his resignation at the time (see Kase, *Journey to the Missouri*, p. 98).

[20]The importance of backstage bargaining to the Japanese is depicted in Michael Blaker, *Japanese International Negotiating Style* (New York, 1977), pp. 64–67.

preferences openly at an imperial conference and to involve the court and the imperial family actively in trying to achieve cabinet and service compliance with those preferences. Such a course of action would not only transgress the bounds of constitution and custom observed by the court, it could also endanger the palace policy process itself, exposing those around the throne to violent retribution. As symbols of the nation, the emperor and his family enjoyed enormous prestige. The emperor's place in the Shinto pantheon sanctified his orders to the troops, transforming war into a crusade in his name. Yet his intervention might not succeed if those outside the palace walls became convinced that he was in the thrall of a parochial cabal within the court. Nevertheless, some around the throne had come to believe, such an overt intrusion into politics might be the only way to break the deadlock over war termination.

Emperor Hirohito had kept abreast of military trends at the front and political maneuvering at home. Information flowed into the palace from a variety of sources, dovish as well as hawkish, partly as a by-product of the court's role as broker among the army, navy, and cabinet, partly as a result of the emperor's own discussions with officials in individual audiences. On the basis of this information Hirohito gradually became convinced that a prompt end to the war was now imperative.

The principal channel through which pessimistic assessments reached the emperor was Privy Seal Kido. His willingness to pass them along was indicative not necessarily of Kido's personal commitment to an early settlement, but only of the privy seal's official responsibility for gathering political intelligence for the throne. As early as March 30, 1943, after Japan's costly defeat at Guadalcanal, Kido noted in his diary that he had held an "unusually long" audience with the emperor "about the outlook on the war," at which he had submitted his "frank" views to the throne. These views, Kido later elaborated, echoed Prince Konoye's fear of "the Red peril," a resurgence of communism at home, made possible by the domestic strains of a prolonged war.[21] On May 14, 1943, after discussing the war's prognosis with Shigemitsu, Kido raised the possibility of involving the imperial family in the event of a peace move during an audience with the emperor's younger brother, Prince Takamatsu. Anticipating difficulty reconciling "the fighting services' demands with the peace terms," Kido observed that "in such a contingency, His Highness [the Prince] will be requested to redouble his efforts."[22] It was the first inkling of future palace plans for war termination.

---

[21]Kido diary, February 4 and March 30, 1943, excerpted and interpolated in *IMTFE* testimony, pp. 31068–69. Cf. Kido, "Statements," II, no. 61541, p. 175.
[22]Kido diary, May 14, 1943, *IMTFE* testimony, p. 31070.

As the war dragged on, the emperor reached out for more diverse sources of information and advice. On January 6, 1945, at the time of the American landing on Luzon, he proposed holding an audience with the senior statesmen to solicit their views. Kido, fearful of army resentment at the unorthodox procedure, counseled delay. When the emperor decided to proceed, instead of inviting the senior statesmen as a group—which would have meant including the newest of the former premiers, General Hideki Tōjō—court officials scheduled a series of individual audiences for them between February 7 and 26. Despite precautions to assure frankness and confidentiality, only Prince Konoye spoke out in favor of ending the war "as speedily as possible." In Konoye's view, prolonging the war would place the national polity at risk of revolution: "The question would be different if there were even some slight hope of the fighting taking a turn for the better, but with defeat staring us in the face we shall simply be playing into the hands of the Communists if we elect to continue a war [with] no prospect of victory." As a first step, he recommended cashiering the existing army high command and replacing them with officers loyal to the throne: "Although the military men have already lost confidence in their ability to prosecute the war to a successful conclusion, they are likely to continue fighting to the very end merely to save face." He also proposed a purge of the "extremist element" within the armed forces "as a prerequisite" to war termination: "Should we endeavor to stop the war abruptly without first rooting out the extremists, I fear that they—supported by sympathizers within both the right and left wings—might perpetrate internal disorder, thus making it difficult for us to achieve our desired goal."[23]

Following his audiences with the senior statesmen, the emperor commissioned Admiral Kiyoshi Hasegawa to assess Japan's naval capabilities. Hasegawa reported back on June 12, four days after an imperial conference had ratified the army's "fundamental policy" of unabated prosecution of the war. His assessment catalogued the deficiencies in naval preparedness: shortages of war matériel, shoddy production, gross inadequacies in the training and supply of kamikaze forces, losses to American bombing, and delays in implementing directives of the general staff to meet the expected invasion of Japan.[24] With the emperor's encouragement, Kido also widened his search for dovish options and infor-

---

[23]Konoye memorial to the throne, in Butow, *Japan's Decision to Surrender*, pp. 47–50. Konoye's own views of revolutionary tendencies within the army were less orthodox or sectarian than the appellation "communist" usually implies: "It is immaterial whether we call this revolution-minded group right-wing or left-wing, for in reality the rightists are nothing more than Communists masquerading in the dress of the national polity-ists."

[24]Hasegawa, in "Statements," I, no. 57667, pp. 272–73; Tōgō, in ibid., IV, no. 50304, p. 257.

mation. He arranged for Tōgō to report directly to the emperor.[25] He also arranged for his own chief secretary, Marquis Yasumasa Matsudaira, to act as liaison to four senior statesmen who conferred from time to time on ways to end the war and as a member of the four-man secretariat that generated alternative estimates and proposals from the War, Navy, and Foreign ministries.[26]

While Hirohito's exposure to dovish views was increasing, he still gave few indications of his own policy preferences, confining himself mostly to cryptic allusions to peace in private audiences. In a February 1942 audience with Tōjō, less than three months after the attack on Pearl Harbor, he had spoken "in abstract terms" about his desire for "an early restoration of peace." Again that July he expressed similar sentiments to Tōgō. Yet the timing and vagueness of the emperor's pronouncements leave them open to the interpretation that he was hoping for a swift settlement on terms commensurate with Japan's military ascendancy at the time. By the spring of 1945, when such expressions of preference had an altogether different significance, Hirohito was becoming increasingly outspoken about his desire for peace, but only to palace functionaries.[27] He continued to stop short of any overt intrusion into the policy process.

In the aftermath of the June 8 imperial conference, however, Kido had privately begun drawing up plans for eventual "Imperial intervention" to arrange a negotiated settlement of the war. On June 20, after the Big Six had resolved to sound out the Soviet Union on possible mediation, but without committing themselves to a negotiating position, Kido arranged an imperial audience for the Big Six as a group. At that audience Hirohito expressed the desire that they "study concrete means" for ending the war and "strive for their prompt realization." This occasion is the first on record at which he expressed that preference to a group that included the service chiefs, but he still refrained from proposing modalities or terms of settlement. On July 7 Hirohito went a step further. In an audience with Prime Minister Suzuki, he suggested that the government dispatch a special envoy to Moscow bearing a personal message from him, a step the Big Six was already considering. Five days later, in an unusually long audience with Prince Konoye, the envoy designate, he gave Konoye carte blanche on the terms to seek and in-

---

[25]Tōgō, *Cause of Japan*, p. 276.
[26]Matsudaira, in "Statements," II, no. 60745, p. 427; Kido, in ibid., no. 61541, p. 175, and in *IMTFE* testimony, pp. 31055–57; and Tōgō, in ibid., p. 35740.
[27]Shigeru Hasunuma (chief aide-de-camp), in "Interrogations," I, no. 58225, p. 301; Kido, in "Statements," II, no. 61541, pp. 175–76. There is no corroboration for Kido's claim that Hirohito expressed his desire for peace in granting imperial commands to Koiso and Suzuki to form new governments.

structions to report to him personally on the mission. The emperor had gone about as far as he could go, short of direct political intervention.

DELAY AND DEADLOCK

It took until late afternoon of August 6 for official word to reach Tokyo of what had befallen Hiroshima. A cable arrived at the Home Ministry indicating that a small number of enemy planes had dropped "an unknown type of bomb" on the city, "causing a tremendous number of deaths."[28] At dawn the next day Army Vice-Chief of Staff Kawabe received a report that "the whole city of Hiroshima was destroyed instantly by a single bomb."[29] Shortly thereafter, a partial text of President Truman's radio broadcast was distributed, stating that an atomic bomb had caused the destruction. The reports sparked official inquiries into the nature of the attack; they did not break the political deadlock in Tokyo.

Lieutenant General Seizō Arisue, chief of the army's Intelligence Bureau, took personal command of one team of investigators dispatched to Hiroshima. The team was to have included Japan's leading nuclear scientist, Yoshio Nishina, but his flight was grounded overnight by engine trouble. On August 8 Arisue sent back a preliminary report, acknowledging that a "special bomb" had been used but insisting that countermeasures were possible. The only specific countermeasure he mentioned was wearing white clothing to protect against flash burns. He also passed along a rumor that Tokyo was scheduled to be hit August 12.[30] That same day Nishina finally made his way to Hiroshima. Surveying the stricken city from the air, he recalls, "I decided at a glance that nothing but an atomic bomb could have done such damage."[31] After conferring with navy investigators, some of whom were still maintaining that the bomb had not been a fission device, the team returned to Tokyo on August 11, five days after Hiroshima's destruction, to attest to its cause.[32]

Meanwhile, back in Tokyo, there was pressure for delay. A cabinet-

[28]Home Minister Genki Abe, quoted in Giovannitti and Freed, *Decision to Drop the Bomb,* p. 266. Cf. Sakomizu, in "Interrogations," II, unnumbered, April 21, 1949, p. 123.
[29]Kawabe, in "Statements," II, no. 61539, p. 99.
[30]Arisue, in ibid., I, no. 61411, p. 74; Nishina, in ibid., II, no. 60246, pp. 705–6.
[31]Nishina, in "Statements," II, no. 60245, pp. 699–700. Nishina was himself working on various methods for uranium separation under Japanese navy sponsorship. See Deborah Shapley, "Nuclear Weapons History: Japan's Wartime Bomb Projects Revealed," *Science,* January 13, 1978, pp. 152–57; and Charles Weiner, "Retroactive Saber Rattling?" *Bulletin of the Atomic Scientists* 34 (April 1978): 10–12.
[32]The team's arrival was preceded by a message from a physicist on the navy investigating team stating categorically that an atomic bomb had been used and that there was no known defense against the weapon (Brooks, *Behind Japan's Surrender,* p. 194).

[236]

level Atomic Bomb Countermeasure Committee was formed. It held its first meeting on the afternoon of August 7 in an atmosphere of sketchy reports, enemy hyperbole, and rampant rumor. Tōgō, citing Truman's prediction that the bomb would "revolutionize" warfare and his warning that "more bombs would be dropped," argued in a "roundabout" way for acceptance of the terms of Potsdam, but Anami, insisting that they wait for the investigators' reports, carried the day.[33]

The issue was what to tell the Japanese people in the meantime. Technical Board representatives, claiming that an atomic bomb would be too "unstable" to transport across the Pacific, suggested referring to the weapon as "a new type of bomb" without further specifying its nature. Imperial General Headquarters used these words in a communiqué it issued that day, stating that an attack "by a small number of B-29s" had caused "considerable damage" to Hiroshima and adding, "The explosive power of the bomb is now under investigation, but it is considered that it should not be made light of."[34] More than a suspension of judgment amid technical uncertainty dictated the careful wording. "The military," says Home Minister Genki Abe, "did not wish to publicize that it had been an atomic bomb, if it was, simply because they were afraid that such an announcement would affect the morale of the military forces."[35]

On August 8 Foreign Minister Tōgō arranged for an audience with the emperor to relay information gathered at the scene of the bombing and from Allied broadcasts and to "impress him with the urgency of the situation."[36] At Hirohito's request, Tōgō went to see Prime Minister Suzuki to renew Hirohito's plea for prompt settlement of the war. Tōgō asked Suzuki to convene a meeting of the Big Six, but the unavailability of some members forced postponement until the next day.

Overnight the Foreign Office monitored Radio Moscow's announcement of the Soviet declaration of war. No longer was there any pretext for delaying a direct suit for peace. The services agreed to open talks on the basis of the Potsdam Declaration. The only issue that remained for the Big Six to resolve was Japan's negotiating position in those talks.

Suzuki began the meeting by proposing that Japan accept the terms of Potsdam. A long silence ensued, broken at last by a question from Yonai: "If we accept the Potsdam Declaration, should we accept it unconditionally or should we attach certain conditions?" He raised four possible conditions: the emperor, disarmament, treatment of war crimi-

---

[33]Ikeda, in "Statements," I, no. 54479, pp. 545–46; Tōgō, in ibid., IV, no. 50304, pp. 267–68; Sakomizu, in "Interrogations," II, unnumbered, April 21, 1949, p. 123.
[34]Kase, *Journey to the Missouri*, p. 212; Ikeda, in "Statements," I, no. 54479, p. 545.
[35]Giovannitti and Freed, *Decision to Drop the Bomb*, p. 267.
[36]Tōgō, in "Statements," IV, no. 50304, p. 268.

nals, and occupation.[37] Tōgō then reviewed the latest developments at considerable length and proposed limiting Japan's conditions to just one, on the argument that "since the present situation was so critical as to preclude all hope of victory, I felt it essential to sue for peace and accept the Potsdam Declaration immediately; that, since the welfare of the Imperial family must be secured at all costs, we must obtain a guarantee in that respect; but that, since the recent attitude of the United States, Great Britain, China, and the USSR indicated that they would reject our proposals outright and refuse to negotiate further if we attempted to exact a large number of concessions, we should reduce our conditions to bare minimum."[38]

Yonai immediately seconded Tōgō, but War Minister Anami and the service chiefs insisted on attaching additional conditions to Japan's acceptance of the terms of Potsdam. Umezu was especially vehement on the question of limiting the scope of the occupation, demanding that the size of the occupying army and the area to be occupied be held to a minimum. He and Anami both objected to the victors' presiding over war crimes trials, recommending instead that they be conducted before Japanese tribunals. Toyoda, while not siding with Yonai, confined himself for the most part to insisting on a disarmament proviso: "I felt that if we were to effectuate Japan's surrender smoothly and peacefully," the warring parties "would have to exercise extreme caution in carrying out the terms of surrender." Tōgō, he says, "understood my point very well," but preferred to work out the arrangements "at an opportune moment" rather than proposing that Japan's armed forces be permitted to disarm themselves "as a surrender condition." Toyoda, along with Anami and Umezu, rejected Tōgō's counterproposal even though it appeared to meet Toyoda's stated concern about command-and-control.

Much more was at stake in Toyoda's proposal than the modalities of stacking arms: having Japan disarm itself would preserve a token measure of dignity and autonomy for the armed services and enhance morale. It would also avert an army-navy split. Toyoda's own explanation for his stand suggest his broader concerns. He later testified that even in navy circles, especially the general staff, "some elements were strongly opposed to the peace arrangement, but I was fully confident of my ability to keep them under control."[39] Notwithstanding Toyoda's confidence, his hawkish deputy, Admiral Ōnishi, reportedly burst into the meeting

---

[37]Toyoda, in ibid., no. 57670, pp. 379–80. Cf. Sakomizu, in "Interrogations," II, unnumbered, May 3, 1949, pp. 125–26; and Tōgō, in "Statements," IV, no. 50304, p. 271.
[38]Tōgō, in "Statements," IV, no. 50304, pp. 269–70.
[39]Toyoda, in ibid., no. 57670, pp. 380–81; cf. pp. 391–92.

and called Anami out of the room to exhort him to stand firm on continued prosecution of the war and denounce Yonai as "weak-kneed."[40] Interservice considerations reinforced intraservice considerations in Toyoda's stand: "I felt that if a conflict developed between the Army and the Navy, the termination of the war would not be successfully realized. I thought that in order to prevent the Army from revolting, it was imperative for the Navy to show a sympathetic attitude toward the Army, and to persuade the Army by saying that since the Navy was making a great concession in agreeing to the peace, the Army should also join in the move."[41] An army-navy split not only might encourage diehards on the naval general staff to join forces with army insurgents, but would also leave the navy open to army charges of betrayal.

Tōgō tried to rebut the military stand by predicting that insistence on the four conditions would cause a breakdown of negotiations, leading to a fight to the death: "I asked whether we could expect to win the war if the peace talks collapsed, to which they replied that, although they were not certain of ultimate victory, they were capable of one more campaign. I then asked whether or not they believed they could ward off an invasion of the homeland and the Army Chief of Staff replied that, if we were lucky, we could repulse the invaders before they landed, but that all he could say with assurance was that we could destroy the major part of an invading army."[42] Tōgō's penetrating questions succeeded in getting to the crux of the disagreement, though not in resolving it. His argument was that the Allies saw negotiations and fighting as an either-or proposition. In contrast, the army, backed by the navy chief of staff, believed "there was still room for further negotiations" while the fighting continued. While Tōgō emphasized that prolonging the war would only cost Japan more than it would the Allies and weaken its military position relative to theirs, the high command's retort was that what counted was not relative cost or relative strength, but the willingness of the Americans to bear the costs of invasion in order to avoid any concessions. Toyoda later put it, "I believed at the time that the Allied nations were not necessarily bent upon further continuation of the war and that it would be against their desire to see further bloodshed."[43] At this point the dispute recapitulated the endless if sterile doctrinal debate over whether it is calculations of relative capability or the risk of unacceptable damage that coerces a hostile state—with the usual result. "All in all," says

---

[40]Vice-Admiral Zenshiro Hoshina (chief of the Naval Affairs Bureau), in ibid., I, no. 61978, p. 478.
[41]Toyoda, in ibid., IV, no. 57670, pp. 381–82; cf. p. 394.
[42]Tōgō, in ibid., no. 50304, p. 270.
[43]Toyoda, in ibid., no. 57670, p. 381.

Tōgō, "it was an extremely heated discussion, but it accomplished nothing."[44]

At 11:02 that morning the United States dropped a second atomic bomb on a Japanese city. Nagasaki was partially destroyed, killing an estimated 38,000 people and injuring a somewhat larger number. Air raid sirens had sounded a full alert earlier, then the alert was called off, and even though the city remained on warning alert only about 400 people were still in air raid shelters when the blast wave struck. Because of the city's topography, no general conflagration ensued, but the blast and fires completely destroyed 14,146 of its 52,000 residential units and partly damaged another 5,441. Of the 558 nonresidential structures in the built-up area of the city, only 12 percent of the usable floor area survived intact, but the Mitsubishi dockyards and electric works, located on the outskirts, escaped largely unscathed.[45]

Unlike Hiroshima, the report that Nagasaki had suffered a similar fate was not long in arriving. Not even that was enough to break the Big Six deadlock. It seemed that neither calculations of relative capability nor risk of unacceptable damage could compel Japan's leaders to surrender unconditionally. After two hours the Big Six adjourned so that four of the six could attend a cabinet meeting scheduled for that afternoon. No minds had been changed; no decision had been reached.

The cabinet meeting turned out to be, in Tōgō's words, "a repeat performance." He and Yonai fought War Minister Anami over the same ground, again to a standstill. The ministers of agriculture, transportation, munitions, and commerce, pointing in turn to the poorest rice crop since 1931, havoc caused by the bombing, and declining morale and productivity, called for an end to the war, while Home Minister Abe, supporting Anami, warned that he could not assure popular compliance if Japan capitulated. When Prime Minister Suzuki finally called the question at ten o'clock that evening, he and three others sided with Tōgō and Yonai in favor of accepting the terms of Potsdam with the sole reservation that the throne be preserved, two ministers voted with Anami to attach four conditions to surrender, and five others abstained, while voicing various misgivings about insisting on that many conditions.[46]

At Suzuki's request, Tōgō accompanied him to the palace to report to the emperor on the inconclusive result. By custom, a deadlock in the cabinet, once reported to the throne, required the cabinet's resignation. But not this time. Anticipating the deadlock, Tōgō had told Suzuki ear-

[44]Tōgō, in ibid., no. 50304, p. 270. Kido, who was not present, misconstrues the Big Six outcome in his diary, see *IMTFE* testimony, pp. 11393, 31175, 35593–94.

[45]Strategic Bombing Survey (Pacific), *Effects of Atomic Bombs*, pp. 3, 13, 15.

[46]Tōgō, in "Statements," IV, no. 50304, p. 270; Pacific War Research Society, *Japan's Longest Day*, pp. 26–28; Ikeda, in "Statements," I, no. 54483, p. 552.

lier in the day that an imperial conference might be the way to break it. The task of rounding up the required signatures of the Big Six was left to Chief Cabinet Secretary Sakomizu, who did so on the pretext of expediting decision-making. The ploy stirred army resentment, since it was the practice to call an imperial conference only after the Big Six had reached accord. But again not this time. Now Suzuki formally requested an imperial conference in the absence of a decision, and the emperor gave his consent.[47] Because further delay was not advisable, the conference was scheduled for midnight. The time had come for the emperor's descent from transcendence.

THE EMPEROR CALLS FOR SURRENDER

Joining the Big Six in the imperial presence were the SCDW secretariat, Chief Cabinet Secretary Sakomizu, Naval Affairs Bureau Chief Hoshina, Military Affairs Bureau Chief Yoshizumi, and Cabinet Planning Board Director Ikeda, along with Chief Aide-de-Camp Shigeru Hasunuma and Privy Council President Kiichirō Hiranuma. After Prime Minister Suzuki opened the meeting with a review of the day's deliberations, each of the Big Six rehearsed his previous stand. Hiranuma immediately launched into a prolonged interrogation, first of Foreign Minister Tōgō regarding the Moscow talks and Soviet entry into the war, then of the servicemen about "the aggravation of internal disorder which might result from concluding the war." Expressing qualified endorsement of Tōgō's proposal to accept the terms of Potsdam on just one condition, Hiranuma then provided a detailed exegesis of the nature of sovereignty under Japan's constitution in order to show why the phrasing of the Potsdam Declaration was "not appropriate." The understanding that it did not include any demand for a change "in the position of the Emperor as provided for in the national laws," he insisted be reworded to read: on the understanding that it "comprised no demand which would prejudice the prerogatives of the Emperor as sovereign ruler." After proposing that attaching any additional conditions to Japan's acceptance of the Potsdam Declaration be left to the emperor, bearing in mind the critical need to maintain public order, he sat down.[48] Navy Chief of Staff Toyoda, whom Suzuki had overlooked in his canvass of Big Six views, repeated his endorsement of the army stand. Then the prime minister, expressing

[47]Sakomizu, in "Interrogations," II, unnumbered, May 3, 1949, p. 125; Tōgō, *Cause of Japan*, p. 319; Toyoda, in "Statements," IV, no. 57670, p. 394.

[48]Paraphrased in informal notes kept by Ikeda, in "Statements," I, no. 54483, pp. 555–56. Cf. Tōgō, *Cause of Japan*, p. 320; and Hiranuma, in "Interrogations," I, no. 55127, pp. 150–52.

regret that the Big Six had failed to reach agreement, approached the throne and entreated the emperor for his opinion.

It was past two o'clock in the morning when the emperor spoke. "I agree with the proposal of the Foreign Minister," he said in no uncertain terms. Citing the unreliability of previous military estimates of the course of the war, the still unfinished fortifications at likely sites of an enemy landing, the gap between planning and results in the production of critical matériel, specifically aircraft, Hirohito questioned the likelihood of repelling the invasion. The intensifying air raids, he noted, were only adding to popular distress. Addressing himself directly to the conditions proposed by the armed services, he was sympathetic but unyielding. As unbearable as it might be to have his troops disarmed by the enemy or to have men unswerving in their loyalty to him be punished as responsible for the war, "now," he insisted, "is the time to bear the unbearable."[49]

The decision was still up to the cabinet. As the Emperor was making his exit, Suzuki gave instructions to reconvene the ministers at his official residence at 3 A.M. At this juncture, War Minister Anami and his fellow hawks could have brought down the government by blocking the decision or by resigning. They did not do so. It took those in favor of suing for peace just over an hour to prevail upon their colleagues, even the reluctant Home Minister Abe, to affix their seals to the motion: "Based on the Imperial desire, it is hereby decided that the Potsdam Declaration will be accepted on the one condition."[50] The emperor's intervention had broken the political deadlock.

Tōgō hurried to the Foreign Ministry to draft telegrams notifying the Allies, those to the United States and China to Ambassador Kase in Berne for transmittal through Swiss intermediaries, those to Great Britain and the Soviet Union to Ambassador Okamoto in Stockholm for transmittal through the Swedish government. The operant paragraphs read:

The Japanese Government are ready to accept the terms enumerated in the joint declaration which was issued at Potsdam on July 26th, 1945, by the heads of the Governments of the United States, Great Britain, and China, and later subscribed by the Soviet Government, with the understanding that the said declaration does not comprise any demand which prejudices the prerogatives of His Majesty as a Sovereign Ruler.

The Japanese Government sincerely hope that this understanding is warranted and desire keenly that *an explicit indication* to this effect will be speedily forthcoming.[51]

[49]Kido diary, *IMTFE* testimony, pp. 31178–79; Ikeda, in "Statements," I, no. 54483, pp. 556–57; Tōgō, *Cause of Japan*, p. 321, and in "Statements," IV, no. 50304, p. 271.
[50]Sakomizu, in "Interrogations," II, unnumbered, May 3, 1949, p. 127.
[51]Official text of Japan's reply, August 10, 1945, in *FRUS*, 1945, VI: 627 (emphasis

Having decided to sue for peace, the war, navy, and foreign ministers reconvened that afternoon to consider making that step public. The morning newspapers, by publishing the Soviet declaration of war, had alerted the diehards to Japan's earlier request for mediation. Now official acknowledgment of Japan's conditional acceptance of the terms of Potsdam could set off uncontrollable tremors in service ranks, shattering the morale of troops on the front lines before the Allies had accepted Japan's condition for surrender and generating secondary shocks in the upper echelons of the army strong enough to topple the government before officers loyal to the emperor could reassert control. In the end, Anami, Yonai, and Tōgō concluded that the risk of undoing the government's decision by publicizing it outweighed the benefits of openly committing the government to ending the war and preparing the Japanese people for that eventuality. Yet official reticence could give Japan's diehards time to reverse the decision while leaving the Allies in doubt about the firmness of Japan's commitment to it.

Instead of acknowledging the suit for peace, the three ministers drafted an announcement for transmission on the evening news broadcast and publication in morning newspapers that alluded almost imperceptibly to the prospect of an end to the war while making obligatory references to the need for staunch determination in the face of enemy escalation and impending invasion: "In truth, we cannot but recognize that we are now beset with the worst possible situation. Just as the government is exerting its utmost efforts to defend the homeland, safeguard the polity, and preserve the honor of the nation, so too must the people rise to the occasion and overcome all manner of difficulties in order to protect the [national polity]."[52]

Conflicting responsibilities for sustaining troop morale up to the moment of surrender yet ensuring compliance with cease-fire orders thereafter posed a dilemma for the army high command. Diehards in high-ranking military posts were able to exploit that dilemma in maneuvering to undermine the decision for conditional acceptance of the Potsdam Declaration. They did so by taking action plausibly designed to shore up morale, but in ways that made eventual command-and-control more precarious. Immediately after the early morning cabinet decision, Anami assembled all officers in the War Ministry and related what had trans-

---

added). The precise origins of the second paragraph are obscure, but it was added in the Foreign Ministry. Shunichi Matsumoto (vice-minister of foreign affairs), "Statements," in II, no. 61451, p. 451; and Tōgō, *Cause of Japan*, p. 321.

[52]*Nippon Times*, August 11, 1945, quoted in Butow, *Japan's Decision to Surrender*, p. 182.

pired overnight. "I do not know what excuse to make to you," he told them, "but since it is the Emperor's decision, it cannot be helped. The important thing is that the Army shall act in an organized manner. Individual feelings must be disregarded. This decision, however, was made on the condition that the upholding of our national polity be guaranteed. Consequently, it does not mean that the war was ended. The Army must be prepared for either war or peace." When a few of the colonels protested that surrender was unthinkable, Anami snapped, "I have no excuse to offer for the fact that peace has been decided upon. However, those among you who are dissatisfied and wish to stave it off will have to do it over my dead body."[53]

Upon hearing Anami's injunction to maintain readiness "for either war or peace," Lieutenant Colonel Masao Inaba, chief of the Budget Subsection of the Military Affairs Bureau, returned to his office convinced that "some sort of encouragement" to troops at the front, especially the Kwantung army under Soviet attack, "was needed as a stop-gap measure." He drafted a rousing call to arms and made the rounds of his superiors to obtain their concurrence. Having located all but Anami, who was then engaged in drafting the government announcement, Inaba was marking time when he encountered Lieutenant Colonel Masahiko Takeshita, chief of the Home Affairs Subsection and brother-in-law of General Anami, and a companion. The pair suggested broadcasting Inaba's announcement on the evening news so that it would reach the fighting fronts at once. On the pretext of meeting the 4 P.M. news deadline, they rushed off to the Information Board without getting Anami's authorization for their makeshift draft.[54] Issuing instructions to the troops through routine military channels, while somewhat slower, would have minimized chances that other audiences, in Japan and abroad, might get the wrong idea, but that was no concern of theirs. For Inaba and Takeshita the hasty announcement was a happy coincidence of organizational interest and personal predilection: later that week they would join a conspiracy to overthrow the government.

Announcement in hand, the director of the Information Board telephoned General Anami to ask him to withdraw it, but the war minister, after a moment's hesitation, refused. A later attempt to withhold the announcement, this time by Military Affairs Bureau Chief Yoshizumi,

---

[53]Takeshita, in "Statements," IV, no. 50025A, p. 71; cf. p. 77, and Inaba, in ibid., I, no. 57692, p. 579. The same day, orders were dispatched over Umezu's signature saying, "The Imperial Army and Navy shall by no means return the sword to the scabbard" and calling on all units to "insure that the fighting morale is maintained at all costs" (CINCUSFLT, Pacific Strategic Intelligence Section, "Japanese Surrender Maneuvers," August 29, 1945, NSA Records, SRH 090, Box 4, RG 457, National Archives, p. 22).

[54]Inaba, in "Statements," I, no. 57692, p. 580; Takeshita, in ibid., IV, no. 50025A, p. 72.

came too close to deadline to halt its publication in the newspapers without suppressing the morning editions altogether.[55] As a result, the army's announcement preceded the government's on the evening news broadcast of August 10, and the two ran side-by-side on most front pages of the next morning's newspapers. Calling upon the troops for unflagging zeal in the "holy war" to save their "sacred land," it drew its words of inspiration from Anami himself, "Even though we have to eat grass, swallow dirt, and lie in the fields, we shall fight on to the bitter end, ever firm in our faith that we shall find life in death."[56] When the emperor rebuked the war minister the next day, Anami defended the announcement as necessary for troop morale and did not bother to admonish his zealous subordinates.[57] In so doing he was playing into the hands of the diehards.

In contrast to the War Ministry's concern with morale at the front, the Foreign Ministry's attention was directed elsewhere—to the reaction of enemy interlocutors. On the morning of August 10, Yoshizumi awakened Shunichi Matsumoto, the vice-minister of foreign affairs, and prevailed upon him not to refer to Japan's suit for peace in Foreign Ministry propaganda broadcasts beamed at East Asia. Once he learned of the army's announcement, however, Tōgō interceded and had the Domei news agency confirm Japan's conditional acceptance of the Potsdam Declaration in Morse code transmissions elsewhere overseas.[58]

Although the war, navy, and foreign ministers had decided not to disclose Japan's suit for peace out of concern for command-and-control of the armed forces, action did not correspond to decision. The army's interest in bolstering morale at the front gave the diehards an excuse for escalating the rhetoric. That in turn provoked the Foreign Ministry, anxious about an adverse effect on negotiations, to issue a quasi-public announcement of Japan's conditional surrender on its own. Organizational implementation thereby turned a high-level decision for reticence into cacophony.

BYRNES REPLIES

Japan's leaders had opted for reticence, but in demanding an explicit guarantee on the future of the throne, they were asking America's lead-

---

[55]Information Board Director Hiroshi Shimomura, in "Interrogations," II, no. 57668, p. 236; Yoshizumi, in "Statements," IV, no. 54484, p. 610. While Shimomura inferred that Anami was in a "tight spot" with his subordinates, the evidence suggests that the War Minister too saw the need to encourage front-line forces.

[56]*Nippon Times*, August 12, 1945, quoted in Butow, *Japan's Decision to Surrender*, p. 183.

[57]Inaba, in "Statements," I, no. 57692, p. 580; Takeshita, in ibid., IV, no. 50025A, p. 72.

[58]Matsumoto, in ibid., II, no. 61451, p. 451; Pacific War Research Society, *Japan's Longest Day*, p. 42.

ers to do what they had felt unable to do themselves—take domestic political risks for peace.

The confusing signals emanating from Tokyo had no effect on Washington because U.S. officials were not paying close attention. They were more attuned to reaction at home and in Allied capitals, and they showed little awareness of Japan's reticence or the reasons for it. The competing concerns that had dictated the wording of the Potsdam Declaration continued to influence the politics of America's response to Japan's conditional suit for peace: the army's interest in autonomy to run the occupation, and its consequent desire to retain the emperor as a means of securing Japanese compliance with surrender and administering the occupation, collided with countervailing pressures from domestic and Allied publics, who insisted on unconditional surrender and retribution against the emperor. Truman's desire to hold down American casualties, the navy's interest in ending the war before the army could go ahead with its strategy of invasion, and Grew's, Forrestal's, and Stimson's concern about reaching a settlement before the Red Army could advance much deeper into the Far East all lent urgency to ending the war quickly, but none could outweigh domestic political opposition to offering Japan any concessions.

While many of the principals were still en route home from Potsdam, the dispute over the terms of surrender raged unabated back in Washington. As Under Secretary of State Grew had anticipated in May, time was strengthening the case for preserving the throne on grounds of administrative convenience. On August 2 the British chargé in Washington, on an informal basis, passed Grew a memorandum based on the observations of George Sansom, a noted authority on Japanese history. "Total and protracted military occupation," it pointed out, "combined with the assumption of all the functions of government, is likely to be a strain on both manpower and physical resources." While careful not to commit Great Britain or the Commonwealth to any alternative to American policy, the "non-paper," a diplomatic term of art to reflect the memorandum's unofficial status, questioned whether it might be "preferable" for the Allies "to work through a Japanese administration, using economic sanctions to secure compliance."[59]

American officials were raising the same question. Two days later Stimson sent Grew "a remarkably good paper" he had received "outside channels."[60] Written by an air force colonel, de Forest Van Slyck, the

---

[59]Notes from British Chargé to Acting Secretary of State, "Observations by the Foreign Office on Notes by Sir George Sansom Regarding United States Policy in Respect of Japan," August 1, 1945, in *FRUS, 1945*, VI: 583–84.

[60]Its precise origins were not noted. "Memorandum of Telephone Conversation by the Acting Secretary of State," August 4, 1945, in ibid., pp. 584, 585n; Stimson diary, August 2 and 4, 1945.

paper attempted to undercut the reason for opposing retention of the emperor—public clamor for retribution. "To be realistic," Van Slyck argued, "post-hostilities policy toward Japan" had to anticipate not only the immediate popular outcry but also "the probable reaction of the American public *over a period of time*." Sustaining domestic support for a "prolonged occupation" would be difficult: the American public would soon grow "restive" with the "burdens of governing" Japan. "Demands for withdrawal," he predicted, "are likely to begin within six months after the surrender of Japan and thereafter to build up increasing political pressure to that end." The passage of time would also make this dilemma of occupation increasingly poignant: while an occupying power could not "impose its form of government, ideals, or way of life upon a conquered nation except by permanent military occupation and immigration," the exercise of "direct political and military control over a vanquished nation" would "inevitably" arouse its resentment. That made it essential, Van Slyck concluded, to "avoid to the maximum extent possible policies dictated by current war hysteria which subsequently the American public will repudiate or which will involve commitments which the American public will be unwilling to fulfill." He proposed retention of the emperor and Japan's civil administration, replacement of the present cabinet with a "liberal" one, establishment of a Supreme Allied Council which would "issue its directives through the regularly constituted government," and inclusion of a pledge in the terms of surrender to maintain the imperial line "only so long as it cooperated fully with the Council."[61]

Grew passed along the paper to the department's Office of Far Eastern Affairs for comment. In its August 6 response the office agreed that the premise of planning for a short occupation was questionable: if "a genuine democratic movement" failed to develop in Japan, then the Allies would face the choice of having to step in and assume "more control" or else leaving the Japanese "to develop internally as they see fit." An occupation was also essential to bring home to the Japanese "the extent of their defeat" in order to discredit militarism "completely and permanently." In an unusually explicit way, it went on to raise domestic political considerations: "Recent public opinion surveys in this country show that a third of those questioned advocate the execution of the Emperor after the war, a fifth voted for his imprisonment or exile, a sixth wanted a court to decide his fate, while only three percent supported his use by the Allies." Under these conditions it questioned "whether or not it would be politically practicable for the Allies to use the Emperor to the extent suggested" by Van Slyck. It then raised a "compromise" under consideration in SWNCC's Subcommittee for the Far East: a three-phased occupation to

[61]Memorandum to the War Department, "Observations on Post-Hostilities Policy toward Japan," in *FRUS*, 1945, VI: 585–86 (emphasis in the original).

be instituted in the event that Japan surrendered before being invaded. In the first phase, which "would probably not exceed 18 months," the Supreme Allied Commander would assume authority over Japan but use Japan's administrative structure "to the fullest possible extent," facilitating army autonomy in running the occupation without straining resources or relying on Allied assistance. During this phase, it noted, "the Emperor and his immediate family would be placed under protective custody so that the Institution of the Emperor would, in reality, be continued." During a second phase, also "limited in duration," the Supreme Allied Commander would cede authority to an Allied Supervisory Commission, composed of civilian representatives of the Allies at war with Japan. Implementation of the commission's directives would be left up to the Japanese themselves, with only a limited occupation force on hand to ensure compliance. A third phase would gradually devolve control to the Japanese.[62] Most important, this plan would postpone any public commitment to preserve the throne until wartime fervor for vengeance dissipated in the United States yet leave the person and institution of the emperor intact in the meantime.

Liberals opposed to preserving the throne were not about to wait for public fervor to die down, but they were prepared to exploit that fervor in order to force the issue now. On the pretext of providing guidance to the Office of War Information, Archibald MacLeish, assistant secretary of state for public affairs, began prodding the Office of Far Eastern Affairs for a statement of policy on war criminals. The August 8 reply from the Office of Far Eastern Affairs was noncommittal.[63] On August 4 a cable arrived from Ambassador Patrick Hurley seeking instructions in the event that the question of naming the emperor as a war criminal were to arise during deliberations of the United Nations War Crimes Subcommission for the Far East, then sitting in Chungking.[64] Hurley's cable elicited an opinion from the State Department's legal adviser, Green H. Hackworth, requesting an immediate decision and warning that the department would be subjected to considerable criticism if the impression were to get out that it was hedging on the status of the emperor. But Under Secretary Grew covered Hackworth's memorandum with one of his own and sent both to Secretary Byrnes on August 7. Grew cited Ambassador Satō's reports from Moscow, intercepted and decoded by

[62]Memorandum from Director of Office of Far Eastern Affairs to Under Secretary of State, "Comments on Memorandum Forwarded by Secretary of War Henry L. Stimson on 'Observations on Post-Hostilities Policy toward Japan,'" August 6, 1945, in ibid., pp. 587–89.

[63]Memorandum from Director of the Office of Far Eastern Affairs to Assistant Secretary of State MacLeish, August 8, 1945, in ibid., p. 591.

[64]Cable from Ambassador in China to Secretary of State, August 4, 1945, in ibid., p. 902.

the ONI, as evidence of efforts in Tokyo to order surrender by imperial rescript. "Short of fighting to the last ditch within Japan itself," Grew argued, "it is not believed that the war is likely to come to an end in any other way as it is improbable that the Japanese armies in China, Manchuria, and elsewhere would obey such an order from any Japanese Government without the sanction of the Emperor." Grew sought to have Byrnes hold off any discussion in Chungking about putting Hirohito on trial: "If it now becomes known that we have agreed to the listing of the Emperor as a war criminal—and if we take such a position it will almost certainly leak to the public in short order—the effect in Japan would in all probability be to nip in the bud any movement toward unconditional surrender and peace. The result, in all probability, would be to consolidate the determination of the Japanese people as a whole to fight on to the bitter end."[65]

The internal struggle over the emperor's fate was gradually emerging into the public domain. As it did, it put Grew and his allies at a distinct political disadvantage by arousing American opponents of a compromise peace while underscoring the arguments of Japanese diehards.[66] But by diverting public attention from the issue, the atomic bombing gave American officials leeway to postpone its resolution.

In these domestic and bureaucratic political circumstances, Stimson arranged to see Truman on August 8. After showing the president reports of atomic bomb damage in Hiroshima, Stimson handed him the Van Slyck memorandum, along with two other papers dealing with the surrender and occupation and the usefulness of the emperor in accomplishing both. Calling for "kindness or tact" in dealing with Japan, Stimson tried a homespun appeal: "When you punish your dog, you don't keep souring on him all day after the punishment is over" if the aim is "to keep his affection." It was "same way with Japan," he said. "They naturally are a smiling people and we have to get on those terms with them."[67] Afterward Stimson also showed the Van Slyck paper to Marshall and Byrnes.

Early in the morning of August 10 first word of Japan's suit for peace reached Washington when monitors picked up shortwave radio transmissions from Tokyo. Two hours later Byrnes, Stimson, Forrestal, and

[65]Memorandum for Secretary of State from Under Secretary, August 7, 1945, in ibid., pp. 905–6.

[66]Concern with the risk of publicity had led Grew a week earlier to seek cancellation of an Army Air Force Day speech by General Arnold which contained, in Grew's view, "virtually a new ultimatum to Japan" (Stimson diary, July 31, 1945, Yale University Library).

[67]Ibid., August 8, 1945. Toward the close of the meeting Stimson brought up two other impending departmental concerns, "the effect of the atomic bomb on the necessary size of the Army" and his own intention to resign upon the advice of physicians.

Leahy met with the president in the Oval Office to frame an American response.[68] Now, as in July, domestic political considerations took precedence over strategic ones in deciding what to say about the future of the throne. Leahy, maintaining the navy's and his own long-held stand, supported prompt acceptance of Japan's offer. "This did not mean," he recalls, "that I favored the emperor's retaining all his prerogatives. I had no feelings about little Hirohito, but was convinced that it would be necessary to use him in effecting the surrender." Had those demanding the emperor's execution prevailed, Leahy felt, "his subjects would probably have fought on until every loyal Japanese was dead, and at that moment there were more than five million Japanese soldiers in the field."[69] Byrnes spearheaded the opposition to Leahy. Accepting Japan's terms, he declared, could lead to "crucifixion of the President." Byrnes wanted no concessions now. "I do not see why we should retreat from our demand for unconditional surrender," he insisted. "If any conditions are to be accepted, I want the United States and not Japan to state the conditions."[70]

Forrestal then offered a way around Byrnes' objection—"an affirmative statement on our part in which we could see to it that the language of surrender accorded fully with our intent and view."[71] The president then called on Stimson, who said that "even if the question hadn't been raised by the Japanese we would have to continue the Emperor ourselves" in order to get "the many scattered armies of the Japanese" to lay down their arms. But Stimson stopped short of recommending explicit assurances now on the future of the throne. Instead he went along with Forrestal on the grounds that as time passed "something like an armistice over the settlement of the question was inevitable."[72] Obfuscation might facilitate an "armistice" in the bureaucratic battle over the emperor's fate, while, as Van Slyck had argued, public passions had time to subside.

Truman then directed Byrnes to frame a reply to Japan along the lines Forrestal had laid out. Byrnes' aide, Benjamin Cohen, prepared a draft with some unsolicited advice from Grew, Dooman, and Ballantine.

[68]Millis, *The Forrestal Diaries*, p. 83, notes the presence of John Snyder, director of the Office of War Mobilization, along with several military aides to the president.

[69]Leahy, *I Was There*, p. 434. Contrary to Leahy's impression, no one present proposed executing the emperor. Rather, the issue was whether to accept Japan's offer, as Leahy proposed, or to postpone any public commitment on the emperor's fate that Americans could interpret as a "retreat" from unconditional surrender.

[70]Walter Brown's notes, August 10, 1945, in Barton J. Bernstein, "The Perils and Politics of Surrender: Ending the War with Japan and Avoiding the Third Atomic Bomb," *Pacific Historical Review* 44 (February 1977): 5; and Byrnes, *Speaking Frankly*, p. 209. Byrnes offers a different rationale in *All in One Lifetime*, p. 305.

[71]Millis, *Forrestal Diaries*, p. 83.

[72]Stimson diary, August 10, 1945.

Byrnes cleared it with Stimson and reviewed it over lunch with Truman and Leahy. Without directly addressing the Japanese government's "understanding," the draft seemed to imply that the emperor would continue to play a role for the moment, but it made no explicit commitment for the future:

> From the moment of surrender the authority of the Emperor and the Japanese Government to rule the state shall be subject to the Supreme Commander of the Allied Powers who will take such steps as he deems proper to effectuate the surrender terms.
>
> The Emperor and the Japanese High Command will be required to sign the surrender terms necessary to carry out the provisions of the Potsdam Declaration, to issue orders to all the armed forces of Japan to cease hostilities and to surrender their arms, and to issue such other orders as the Supreme Commander may require to give effect to the surrender terms.[73]

The reply went on to repeat that "the ultimate form of government of Japan shall, in accordance with the Potsdam Declaration, be established by the freely expressed will of the Japanese people."

Byrnes presented the draft to the cabinet that afternoon. He and Truman, notes Forrestal, "emphasized the fact that they had used the term 'Supreme Commander' rather than 'Supreme Command' so that it would be quite clear that the United States would run this particular business and avoid a situation of composite responsibility such as had plagued us in Germany." Noting that he had already transmitted the text to Allied governments for their approval, Truman said "he expected we might not hear" from the Russians, but in that event he intended to "act without them."[74] The reason for the unseemly haste had nothing to do with the struggle in Japan. When Stimson surmised that the Russians might stall to permit the Red Army to "push as far into Manchuria as possible," Truman declared it "to our interest" that the Russians "not push too far."[75] Had his main concern been to forestall Soviet gains in the Far East, he could have opted for a concession on the emperor in hopes of hastening the end of the war, but even then there was little to stop the Red Army from advancing had it sought to. At bottom, Soviet desires mattered less than American ones in framing the reply to Japan. As if to underscore the point, Truman himself introduced new evidence of public

[73]Truman, *Year of Decisions*, p. 429. Edward G. Miller, Jr., special assistant to Under Secretary of State Acheson and author of the State Department's legal analysis of the reply, argued that the wording "in effect rejected" Japan's interpretation and offered "exactly the situation that would prevail in the event of an unconditional surrender" (Memorandum to Cohen, August 21, 1945, in *FRUS*, 1945, VI, p. 682).

[74]Millis, *Forrestal Diaries*, p. 84.

[75]Blum, *Price of Vision*, p. 474; Stimson diary, August 10, 1945.

sentiment. In reaction to rumors of a compromise peace, he told the cabinet, the White House had received 170 telegrams overnight, 153 of them insisting on unconditional surrender.

When Ambassador Harriman presented the Byrnes reply the next day, the Russians did propose that the Allies "reach agreement on the candidate or candidacies" for the "Allied High Command," but when Harriman dismissed the proposal as "unacceptable," they did not press the issue and gave their assent.[76] The British reply questioned the propriety of having the emperor personally affix his seal to the instruments of surrender, and he proposed a revision that Byrnes, with minor emendation, accepted: "The Emperor will be required to authorize and ensure the signature by the Government of Japan and the Japanese Imperial Headquarters. . . ."[77]

The Byrnes reply fell short of Japan's request—or the hopes of Japanese doves—for an explicit commitment on the future of the throne.

AMERICAN BOMBING INTENSIFIES

If the modification of American terms of settlement was subtle and veiled, there was nothing subtle or veiled about American military pressure on Japan. At the morning meeting to discuss Japan's suit for peace, Stimson urged a bombing halt while negotiations were under way, citing a "growing feeling of apprehension and misgiving as to the effect of the atomic bomb even in our own country." Forrestal, concerned that "this nation would have to bear" the brunt of Japan's "hatred" after the war, rallied to Stimson's side. President Truman rejected their pleas for de-escalation as premature. Later that morning Forrestal telephoned Stimson to reinforce his stand against the bombing. "He told me," Stimson recorded, that naval aviators "were planning another big attack by [Admiral] Halsey and he was afraid this would go on."[78] The navy was not alone in pressing on with the bombing; the chiefs of staff unanimously opposed de-escalation.

At the cabinet meeting that afternoon Truman again ruled out a bombing halt, but with one exception. "The President observed," notes Forrestal, "that we would keep up the war at its present intensity until the

---

[76]Cable from the Ambassador in the Soviet Union to the Secretary of State, August 11, 1945, in *FRUS*, 1945, VI: 630–31; cf. p. 629; Harriman's recollections in Giovannitti and Freed, *Decision to Drop the Bomb*, p. 287.

[77]Cable from Ambassador in the United Kingdom to Secretary of State, August 11, 1945, in *FRUS*, 1945, VI: 628; cf. the final text, pp. 631–32; memorandum from Cohen to Byrnes, August 10, 1945, pp. 625–26; and Truman, *Year of Decisions*, pp. 429–31.

[78]Millis, *Forrestal Diaries*, p. 83; Stimson diary, August 10, 1945.

Japanese agreed to these terms, with the limitation, however, that there would be no further dropping of atomic bombs."[79] Marshall passed along Truman's instructions in a penciled notation to Groves directing that a third bomb was "not to be released on Japan without express authority from the President."[80]

Groves had already taken the initiative on his own. The next bomb was scheduled to be shipped to Tinian after August 17 or 18 and would be ready for delivery against Japan after August 24. Groves approached Marshall with the suggestion that further shipments of fissionable materials to Tinian be held up until August 13, to be resumed if Japan had not surrendered by that date. Groves writes, "I did not want to provide any basis for later claims that we had wantonly dropped a third bomb when it was obvious that the war was over." Perhaps, but Groves had another, more mundane reason for holding up shipment. With no bombs in reserve and no authority for the MED to continue bomb-making once the war was over, Groves, having field-tested both types of bombs, did not want to take any needless chance of losing more precious fissionable material in transit across the Pacific: "It seemed to me that under the circumstances it would be a terrible mistake for us to send overseas the ingredients of another bomb."[81] When August 13 came and went without definitive word from Tokyo, Stimson suggested resuming the shipments, but Groves continued to hold them up.[82]

Yet conventional bombing not only continued but also intensified. American escalation has often been attributed to the belief, by civilian and military leaders alike, that maximum military pressure on the enemy was conducive to maximum political influence over the enemy, but that belief was not shared. Even if Truman acted on that belief, details of the bombing from August 10 on suggest another explanation, one that had more to do with competing interests of rival organizations within the U.S. government than with its anticipated effect on decision-making in Japan. The only program that military organizations have for waging war is to apply force, according to the standard operating procedures each has for doing so. To air force and navy aviators, this meant more bombing. Moreover, both services were girding for a coming struggle over roles and missions and budget shares, especially with respect to air power, and demonstrations of service effectiveness could affect the outcome of that struggle. Bureaucratic politics did not end with Japan's suit for peace; it only intensified—and so did the bombing of Japan.

[79] Millis, *Forrestal Diaries*, p. 84. Cf. Blum, *Price of Vision*, p. 474.
[80] Note on memorandum from Groves to Marshall, August 10, 1945, MED, TS, Folder 5B, RG 77, National Archives.
[81] Groves, *Now It Can Be Told*, pp. 352–53.
[82] Groves' diary, August 13, 1945, National Archives.

Before the United States transmitted its reply to Japan's offer of surrender, General Spaatz had ordered Strategic Air Force bombers under
his command in the Pacific to restrict their missions to "precision" bombing of strategic targets, thereby curtailing incendiary raids against Japan's cities. When bad weather forced cancellation of scheduled air
strikes on August 10, the American press interpreted it as a cease-fire.
Rather than signal a breakdown in negotiations, President Truman then
ordered a halt to all strategic bombing operations and the recall of any
planes already airborne.

Yet attacks by tactical bomber wings of the Far East Air Force continued unabated for at least another day, and against targets that could
hardly be distinguished from "strategic" targets.[83] In doubt about
whether the president's directive covered them, the tactical aviators
then suspended operations for a day before resuming their attacks. But
as eager as the air force may have been to show what its tactical bombers
could do, senior airmen wanted even more to have LeMay's strategic
bombers resume their attacks: after all, strategic bombing with conventional munitions was, the raison d'être of an autonomous air force. The
air force became even more eager to resume bombing after navy aviators
under Admiral Halsey's command circumvented the bombing halt with
an August 13 attack on Tokyo. Using planes it designated as "tactical,"
and characterizing the strikes as "preliminaries" to the invasion of
Japan, the navy conducted one of its largest carrier-based raids of the
war against a target that seemed by air force standards to fit the designation "strategic."[84]

On August 13 the air force succeeded in having the ban on strategic
bombing rescinded. The president, reports his military adviser, Admiral
Leahy, "directed General Marshall to proceed with all planned offensive
operations against Japan, pending action by the Japanese Government
on our demand for a surrender."[85] Spaatz immediately proposed dropping an atomic bomb on Tokyo, but Air Force Chief of Staff Arnold
turned him down. Spaatz then recommended conventional attacks on
seven target cities, excluding Tokyo on the grounds that the navy raid
left the city center too battered to demonstrate the air force's effectiveness. This won Arnold's assent. According to the U.S. air force official
history of the war, "Arnold wanted as big a finale as possible." He
hoped that the Strategic Air Force "could hit the Tokyo area in a 1,000–
plane mission," duplicating a feat that the navy had accomplished on
July 10.[86] Intending to put 1,000 planes aloft by borrowing some from

[83]Craven and Cate, *The Pacific*, pp. 699, 732.
[84]King and Whitehill, *Fleet Admiral King*, p. 622.
[85]Leahy, *I Was There*, p. 435.
[86]Craven and Cate, *The Pacific*, pp. 732–33. Navy Chief of Staff King did not pass up the

the Eighth Air Force, but finding them otherwise engaged, Spaatz cut orders to appropriate seven bombers from the 509th Composite Group and send out 350 of his own Strategic Air Force bombers twice the same day. Adding 186 fighter escorts to his complement ran the total to 1,014, the largest mission of the war. The attack lasted fourteen hours, until past 2 A.M. on August 15—well after Radio Tokyo began broadcasting unofficial word of Japan's decision to surrender.[87]

Bombs were not all that American planes dropped over Japan after it had sued for peace. They also dropped leaflets. While the bombs caused considerable gratuitous suffering to a nation with whom American leaders intended to seek postwar reconciliation, the leaflets were potentially even more counterproductive. Alone among U.S. officials, Admiral Zacharias of the ONI observed "the fact that the surrender offer had not been announced on the home broadcasts of Radio Tokyo" and drew the correct inference that Japan's leaders "were playing a dangerous and delicate game, which would require that they prepare the ground and establish themselves firmly before they took the people of Japan into their confidence."[88] Instead of concluding that a halt in navy bombing would give Japan's leaders time to accomplish their "delicate" task, Zacharias confined his policy recommendations to his own area of responsibility, psychological warfare operations: "I advised that during this period Japan be left unharassed in order to prevent interference with the Emperor's efforts. There was no immediate need for a propaganda exploitation of the diplomatic note." Other U.S. agencies did not take Zacharias' advice. The army, acting at the request of Byrnes, followed up the bombing of Nagasaki with a leaflet barrage urging immediate surrender. The wording of the leaflets was left up to public information officers in the field. Millions of copies were scattered over Japan from August 14 on.[89]

American officials gave little if any thought to the political effects of the Byrnes reply, the bombing, or the leafleting on rival factions in Japan. Political preoccupations at home obscured their view of the en-

---

opportunity to boast that the navy had been the first to do so in his Second Official Report to the Secretary of the Navy; see Walter Millis, ed., *The War Reports of General of the Army George C. Marshall, General of the Army H. H. Arnold, and Fleet Admiral Ernest J. King* (Philadelphia, 1947), p. 679.

[87]*New York Times*, "'Superforts' Stage 6–Target Wind-Up," August 15, 1945, p. 8.

[88]Zacharias, *Secret Missions*, pp. 385–86. By contrast, Leahy (*I Was There*, p. 434) refers to an announcement "in plain language" over "their government radio in Tokyo," and Truman (*Year of Decisions*, p. 427) refers to a "news item being given out over Radio Tokyo," neglecting to distinguish between Morse code transmissions aimed at the Allies and radio broadcasts beamed at the armed forces and people of Japan.

[89]Note from Secretary of State to Secretary of War, August 11, 1945, in FRUS, 1945, VI: 633. Under Secretary of War Patterson's reply (ibid., p. 633n), says the leafleting was done on August 13 and 14, presumably Washington time. Cf. Laurence, *Dawn over Zero*, p. 214; and Zacharias, *Secret Missions*, p. 386.

emy camp. The American response to Japan's surrender offer did nothing to ease the predicament of those in Tokyo who were maneuvering to arrange an end to the war. "No direct answer to our request was made in this reply," Chief Cabinet Secretary Sakomizu told postwar interviewers. "This put us in a very awkward position. Frankly speaking, I wonder why America did not give more consideration to the standpoint of Japan and did not reply in a fashion that it would be easier for Japan to accept. If America was to agree to our proposition, why didn't she frankly say 'yes' then?"[90]

PUTTING THE NATIONAL POLITY AT RISK

In Japan, political deadlock seemed likely and military insubordination appeared inevitable. To some officials in the court, cabinet, and high command, only the emperor's personal intervention could conceivably break the political deadlock, only his active involvement could ensure an orderly surrender. But the American reply threatened to undercut the emperor's standing in Tokyo. If he moved to accept the reply as stated, without any explicit guarantees of his own future or that of the throne, he could call into question his own legitimacy as embodiment and defender of the national polity.

Shortly after midnight August 12, the Foreign Office picked up a Morse code transmission of the Byrnes reply. Chief Cabinet Secretary Sakomizu, Vice-Minister of Foreign Affairs Matsumoto, and Toshikazu Kase, a Foreign Ministry specialist on the United States, met over breakfast to pore over the unofficial translation. The trio, says Matsumoto, was "in low spirits, believing that it was probably impossible for Japan to accept the terms outlined in this reply."[91] Public attention in Japan would later rivet on the passage that said the emperor's authority would be "subject to" the Supreme Commander of the occupation forces, but they were more concerned with the stipulation, repeated from the Potsdam Declaration, that "the ultimate form of government," and presumably the future of the throne, would depend on "the freely expressed will of the Japanese people." Matsumoto then drove off to inform Foreign Minister Tōgō. Tōgō too balked at this wording. Matsumoto, seconded by the chiefs of the Political Affairs Bureau and the Treaties Bureau, tried to dissuade Tōgō from making an issue of the offending passage, because that would only play into the hands of the diehards. Instead, they argued, he should focus deliberations on the phrase "sub-

[90]Giovannitti and Freed, *Decision to Drop the Bomb*, p. 288.
[91]Matsumoto, in "Statements," II, no. 61451, p. 448.

ject to." In the meantime Foreign Ministry specialists were scouring their dictionaries in search of a suitable way to render "subject to" in Japanese without its offensive connotation "subordinate to." They finally hit upon "under the limitation of," which they incorporated into the ministry translation.[92]

Imperial General Headquarters had already obtained its own copy of the unofficial translation and found little reassuring about it. Some of the firebrands in senior ranks demanded immediate public denunciation of the American terms. The ferocity of their reaction was sufficient for the service chiefs to rush off to the palace in quest of an imperial audience to vent their opposition without taking the time to consult their respective ministers first.[93] "From my observations," says Chief Aide-de-Camp Hasunuma, who was present at the 8:20 A.M. audience, "both chiefs of staff seemed to be making their recommendations unwillingly on the request of their subordinates." Whatever their own misgivings, Toyoda and Umezu had good reason to fear an impending coup by unruly subordinates. The emperor was unmoved by the circumstances. He "displayed no strong emotion" and tried to play for time, saying that "no formal Allied answer [had] come yet." When it did and if, after careful scrutiny, it still proved unsatisfactory, Japan could "probably make another inquiry over those points still in doubt."[94] Hirohito's noncommittal stance, while constitutionally appropriate, may have reassured the chiefs of staff about the possibility of further bargaining with the Allies, but it would do little to assuage the diehards.

Three hours later the emperor shifted his stance. After consulting with Suzuki, Tōgō went to the palace to apprise the emperor of the Foreign Ministry's reading of Byrnes' reply. Hirohito, says Tōgō, deemed the reply "satisfactory" and instructed him to tell Prime Minister Suzuki that "we should accept it as it stood."[95] The emperor was prepared to surrender without any ironclad assurances about the future of the national polity.

On his way out of the audience, Tōgō dropped by Kido's office and warned Kido to expect trouble from "jealous" guardians of the national polity, who were certain to take umbrage at Allied insistence on the passage about "the ultimate form of government."[96] It did not take long for trouble to surface. While Tōgō was reporting the emperor's wishes to

---

[92]Brooks, *Behind Japan's Surrender*, p. 217.

[93]For this breach of protocol Yonai dressed down Toyoda later that day. See Hoshina, in "Statements," I, no. 61978, p. 479; cf. Toyoda, in ibid., IV, no. 57670, p. 382.

[94]Hasunuma, in ibid., I, no. 58225, p. 298. Hirohito himself, Hasunuma says, "seemed to sense that these were merely perfunctory recommendations," but the chiefs' urgent request for an audience hardly seems perfunctory.

[95]Tōgō, *Cause of Japan*, p. 325; Matsumoto, in "Statements," II, no. 61451, p. 449.

[96]Kido, in IMTFE testimony, p. 31184.

Suzuki, Privy Council President Hiranuma joined them. Ever the strict constructionist, Hiranuma expressed strong reservations about the two critical passages in the Byrnes reply, insisting that the question of sovereignty "was a vital matter" and "had to be fully confirmed before we gave our final reply." Hiranuma then proceeded to the palace to repeat his objections to Kido.[97]

Preservation of the national polity (*Kokutai*) was fast becoming a rallying cry, and not just for a handful of rightist constitutional theorists like Hiranuma. Like many a unifying political slogan, however, preservation of the national polity was a generality that concealed important differences among its adherents. At an irreducible minimum it meant maintaining the throne—on that point all senior Japanese officials would insist. As the symbol of Japan's unity and nationhood and the source of all constitutional and legal, if not spiritual, authority, the emperor was the object of deep and abiding reverence among his subjects.[98] In the hands of extreme nationalists, he had come to stand for much more. The emperor was head of the national family. As his descendants, the Japanese people shared in his special grace. So long as they displayed "sincerity of heart" toward him, their own actions were, by definition, virtuous, or at least justifiable.[99] Purity of motive could—and did—rationalize a multitude of sins by extremists. In August 1945 it could inspire a fight to the death. Even in its more restrictive sense, though, preserving the national polity meant different things to different people. Did the national polity embrace only the throne, or the person of Hirohito and the line of succession? Did it also encompass the right of supreme command, direct access by the armed service to the throne?

To Baron Hiranuma the answer was simple: "To uphold the national polity means to keep the Emperor's position unchanged." Thus, he could break with the service chiefs over the issues of war crimes trials and disarmament because "the position of the Emperor will not be changed in any way" by their resolution, yet oppose acceptance of the Byrnes reply on the grounds that the emperor's authority should neither depend on "the freely expressed will of the people" nor be "subject to" the Supreme Commander of the occupation forces.[100]

[97]Hiranuma, in "Interrogations," I, no. 55127, p. 146; cf. p. 147; Tōgō, *Cause of Japan*, p. 325; and Kido, in *IMTFE* testimony, p. 31184.

[98]Some schismatics in the Japanese Communist Party in the 1930s even tried to reconcile the preservation of the throne with Marxist doctrine. See George M. Beckmann, "The Radical Left and the Failure of Communism," in *Dilemmas of Growth in Prewar Japan*, ed. James Morley (Princeton, N.J., 1971), pp. 166–67.

[99]Richard Storry, *The Double Patriots* (London, 1957), p. 4. On the expanded conception of national polity, see Warren Tsuneishi, "The Japanese Emperor: A Study in Constitutional and Political Change" (Ph.D. diss., Yale University, 1960), pp. 165–66.

[100]Hiranuma, in "Interrogations," I, no. 55127, pp. 148, 150.

To palace bureaucrats the throne was at once their raison d'être and their source of political power. Organizational interests would have predisposed them to insist on an explicit Allied commitment to maintain the throne, if not its present incumbent and his line of succession, had it not been for Hirohito's own attitude. In his initial reaction to the atomic bombing, as Kido recorded it, and in his audience with the foreign minister, as Tōgō recalled it, the emperor showed his willingness to sacrifice organizational interests to the national interest, as he defined it: sparing the Japanese people from further suffering. "No matter what happens to my safety," he had told Kido, "we must put an end to this war as speedily as possible." Now, to Tōgō, Hirohito indicated his willingness to surrender without explicit assurances about the future of the throne. To the extent that Kido and his colleagues obeyed Hirohito's personal wishes, they were risking the court's institutional survival—by placing it into the hands of either the Americans or the extremists. But it was a chance they were prepared to take because continued prosecution of the war would probably lead to the destruction of the national polity, along with much of the nation.

For many officers at Imperial General Headquarters, constitutional prerogative coincided with organizational interest: to them the national polity was synonymous with the right of supreme command and direct access to the throne, the source of service morale and autonomy, which they were reluctant to concede. The willingness of the Foreign Ministry and its palace sympathizers to entertain acceptance of the Byrnes reply without seeking further assurances on the future of the throne seemed to them an act of treason. From their vantage point the emperor was either a captive of the capitulationists or a betrayer of his birthright. Either way, the self-anointed guardians of the national polity saw only one response, to stage a coup d'état in the name of the imperial institution. Lieutenant Colonel Takeshita, a branch chief in the War Ministry and brother-in-law of Anami, reasoned: "Although the result would be temporary disobedience of the present Emperor—a situation certainly to be avoided—to act in compliance with the wishes of his Imperial Ancestors would constitute a wiser and truer loyalty to the Throne in the final analysis."[101] Such a "final analysis" led to insubordination now, much as it had in the recent past.

PLOT AND COUNTERPLOT

A successful coup, however, required that plotters arm themselves with more than their own righteousness. The rebellious army officers,

---

[101]Takeshita, in "Statements," IV, no. 56367, p. 77.

serving as they did in the War Ministry or on the general staff, may have been well placed to find out about political and diplomatic maneuvering, but they were not in direct command of troops, especially the units needed to seize the palace and overthrow the government. Their positions shaped their plot. The plotters intended to win over the war minister and both service chiefs, to have them lead the coup, and to establish a military government headed by the war minister that would rule, like the shogunate, in the emperor's name. Without the active collaboration of Anami and Umezu, however, the plot would only cause disruption of the army command structure, impairing the very war effort that the plotters hoped to inspire.

On the morning of August 12, after details of the Allied reply began circulating in Imperial General Headquarters, along with rumors that it might be accepted, the plotting began in earnest. At the heart of the conspiracy were six field-grade officers in the Military Affairs Bureau of the War Ministry: Takeshita and two of his subordinates in the Home Affairs Branch, Major Kenji Hatanaka and Lieutenant Colonel Jiro Shiizaki; the chief of the Budget Branch and draftsman of War Minister Anami's speeches and press releases, Lieutenant Colonel Masao Inaba; a subordinate of Inaba's, Lieutenant Colonel Masataka Ida; and the chief of the Military Affairs Section of the bureau, Colonel Okikatsu Arao, the highest-ranking of the six, who may have been playing a double role.

The plan they drew up that morning was sketchy. It relied, in turn, on local garrison commanders to declare martial law on a provisional basis without imperial sanction, and then on the war minister to use his authority to dispatch local troops in an emergency. The conspirators intended to strike at midnight of August 13–14, seal off the palace, restrict the emperor's movements, and arrest Kido, Tōgō, Yonai, and "other advocates of peace." The military government under Anami would then resume negotiations with the Allies and refuse to surrender "until definite assurance was given as to our conditions regarding the Emperor."[102] The sole condition for proceeding was prior consent of the war minister, the army chief of staff, and the commanding officers of the Eastern District Army and the Imperial Guards Division, which controlled the environs of Tokyo and the palace, respectively. Sounding out officers in the Guards, the plotters found their commander firmly opposed to a coup, but they did manage to win over several of his junior officers.

---

[102]Inaba, in ibid., I, no. 57692, p. 582. Takeshita, in ibid., IV, no. 56367, p. 78, includes two colonels from the general staff among the ringleaders and says the plot began taking shape "around August 11" with the aim of separating "the Emperor from his peace-seeking advisers" in order to "persuade him to change his mind and continue the war." The plot bears some resemblance to the coup attempt of 1936, as described in Ben Ami Shillony, "The February 26 Affair: Politics of a Military Insurrection," in *Crisis Politics in Pre-War Japan*, ed. George M. Wilson (Tokyo, 1970), pp. 30–34.

In anticipation of just such a coup attempt, the palace had begun taking steps to forestall service unrest by assuring the loyalty of officers in command of key posts and preparing to transmit imperial commands directly to rank-and-file servicemen. The day before the plot took shape, Kido circulated a proposal in the palace to have Hirohito personally broadcast an imperial rescript announcing Japan's surrender and putting his full authority behind it. Kido broached the idea with the imperial household minister at a meeting that he characterizes as a "free and frank exchange of views," a diplomatic way of referring to the reluctance he encountered from palace functionaries at the thought of placing the emperor in so politically exposed a position. Immediately afterward Kido presented the plan to the throne and got Hirohito's approval. [103]

The same day, Hirohito had an audience with General Anami. After reprimanding him for his part in issuing the appeal for a "holy war" the previous day, the emperor, addressing him familiarly as "Anami," assured the war minister that preserving the national polity was his aim. The general, who had served as an aide-de-camp to Hirohito in the early 1930s, was very moved by the personal nature of the assurance. [104] From this point on, although he continued to hold out for rejection of the Byrnes reply and occasionally appeared to vacillate in his opposition to the conspiracy, Anami remained loyal to the emperor.

The next day, August 12, the plotters moved to win over the war minister. Trying an end-run around Yoshizumi, whom they considered unsympathetic, they spoke to Vice-Minister Tadaichi Wakamatsu, who alerted Anami. When they finally entered Anami's office, he was about to leave to confer with Suzuki about the Byrnes reply in advance of that afternoon's cabinet meeting. They hurriedly laid out their plot, but Anami left without revealing his feelings toward the coup. [105]

As Japan moved toward surrender, the lines of cleavage between officials generally coincided with the division of labor within the state. Army leaders, responsible for command-and-control of their forces and concerned about arranging an orderly surrender, yet eager to preserve what little they could of the service's honor and reputation for military professionalism, believed that holding out for firmer Allied assurances on the throne would make it easier to win over potentially rebellious subordinates and gain compliance with orders to surrender. Even if the war minister could not persuade his cabinet colleagues to hold out, he

[103]Kido diary, in *IMTFE* testimony, p. 31182; cf. pp 31180–81.
[104]Inaba, in "Statements," I, no. 57692, pp. 580–81, and Yoshizumi, in ibid., IV, no. 54484, p. 610, suggest that Anami may have confided in them about the audience. The chief aide-de-camp, rather than Hirohito himself, may have administered the reprimand.
[105]Takeshita, in ibid., IV, no. 56367, pp. 78–79, and no. 50025A, p. 73; Inaba, in ibid., I, no. 57672, pp. 582, 585.

could at least face subordinates back in the War Ministry, secure in the knowledge that he had done all he could. Upon learning of Suzuki's intention to accede to the emperor's wishes and accept the Byrnes reply, Yoshizumi, hardly a supporter of the coup, pleaded with the director of the Cabinet Planning Board, General Ikeda, "Please try to change the Premier's decision, because acceptance of the Potsdam Declaration will invite serious action by the military circles."[106] By contrast, the Foreign Ministry, charged with conducting diplomacy, concerned that rising intransigence in Allied capitals would lead to rejection of any Japanese counteroffer and fearful of a breakdown in negotiations and unending war, insisted that holding out would be worse than fruitless—it could be disastrous. The court bureaucracy—responsible for maintaining the imperial institution, concerned about a military takeover, and appalled at the prospect of losing control of the palace itself—believed that accepting Allied assurances for whatever they were worth and relying on imperial prestige to assure compliance with surrender held out the only possibility, however slim, of ending the war without precipitating domestic chaos and causing the emperor's downfall.

It was in the context of an impending insurrection that the cabinet convened to consider the Byrnes reply. At issue was how best to bring about surrender without inciting the diehards. Foreign Minister Tōgō opened the discussion. "The United States' response to our inquiry," he conceded, "could not be said to be entirely reassuring." Nevertheless, he insisted, "This was not unforeseen; it is inevitable that under a guarantee occupation the sovereignty of the state will be limited to the extent requisite to implement the surrender terms." Then, disregarding the advice of his subordinates, he turned to the "provision that the national polity of Japan was to be determined by the Japanese themselves," and construing it as best he could, he claimed it ran counter to "any suggestion" of "interference from without." Even if the Allies were to put the question to a referendum, "it was impossible to conceive that the overwhelming loyal majority of our people would not wish to preserve our traditional system," sidestepping the constitutional issue of whether that question could be put to a vote at all. Attempts to wring further assurances from the Allies, he warned, might lead them to break off negotiations. He saw "reasons to believe that much antagonism existed among the Allies to the Imperial system of Japan, but that Anglo-American leaders had managed to restrain it to the extent that Byrnes' reply evidenced." Under the circumstances, Tōgō concluded, continuing the war would be "intolerable even if not impossible."[107]

---

[106]Ikeda, in ibid., I, no. 54479, p. 548.
[107]Tōgō, *Cause of Japan*, pp. 325–27.

War Minister Anami responded, concentrating his fire on the two critical passages in the Allied text. Two or three ministers seconded him and Navy Minister Yonai rose to Tōgō's defense. Then Suzuki shocked the doves by siding with Anami. His preoccupation with military command-and-control was evident as he argued "in very strong terms that the Allied reply was unsatisfactory, that to be disarmed by the enemy would be unbearable for a soldier, and that under the circumstances there was no alternative to continuation of the war."[108] Suddenly fearing outright rejection of the Byrnes reply, Tōgō moved for adjournment of the pretext that Japan had yet to receive the official text of the Allied note through diplomatic channels.

Immediately after adjournment, Tōgō confronted Suzuki in the prime minister's office. "I was sufficiently aware of Prime Minister Suzuki's position as an arbitrator," Tōgō recounts, "to show adequate sympathy for the views of the opposing party, as well as for the insistence of the military, in order to prevent them from revolting." Yet, if a threat from military diehards was causing the old admiral to waver once again, the foreign minister was prepared to issue a threat of his own to redress the doves' bargaining disadvantage. If Suzuki persisted in holding up acceptance of the Allied reply, he warned, "I might be compelled to report *individually* to the Throne my dissenting view," in effect bringing down the government.[109] Later, Admiral Yonai associated himself with Tōgō's threat, prompting Anami, no ally of Yonai's, to try to dissuade him.[110] To Tōgō and Yonai, acceptance of the Allied terms came first, then asserting control over the armed forces; to Anami, the priorities were reversed. Yet none of the three could afford to carry out the threat of resignation: bringing down the Suzuki government would facilitate neither surrender nor command-and-control.

The threat of resignation was not the only tactic that the Foreign Ministry used to try to get its way. Officials there tried to reinterpret the meaning of "the ultimate form of government" to have it refer only to the cabinet, not the throne. At Vice-Minister Matsumoto's suggestion,

[108]Tōgō, in "Statements," IV, no. 50304, p. 273; cf. no. 54562, p. 287, and Tōgō, *Cause of Japan*, p. 327.

[109]Tōgō, *Cause of Japan*, p. 328 (emphasis added). Cf. Tōgō, in "Statements," IV, no. 54562, pp. 287–88; and Matsumoto, in ibid., II, no. 61451, p. 449. Learning of Suzuki's latest turnabout from Tōgō, Kido invited Suzuki to his office that evening to reinforce the message, stressing "the necessity for courageously accepting the Potsdam Declaration, even if a disturbance should break out in the country as a result." See Kido diary, in *IMTFE* testimony, p. 31187; cf. pp. 31185–86; Tōgō, *Cause of Japan*, p. 328, and Tōgō, in "Statements," IV, no. 50304, p. 274.

[110]Anami "not only sent a letter to Minister of State Sakonji soliciting his aid in persuading the Minister of [the] Navy to keep his post, but also came to us asking for help in the matter," says Hiroshi Shimomura (chief of the Cabinet Information Bureau), in "Interrogations," II, no. 57668, p. 233.

the Telegraph Office postdated receipt of the official Allied reply in order to buy more time for Suzuki to reconsider. In the interim, cables arrived from ambassadors in Berne and Stockholm lending support to Tōgō's contention that Japan had little to gain by prolonging the negotiations because Allied governments were coming under increasing public pressure to seek a still harsher settlement. Matsumoto personally delivered copies to the prime minister's residence around 1 A.M.[111] Whether or not the cables contained valid assessments of trends in Allied public opinion, the convenient timing of their arrival is circumstantial evidence that Foreign Ministry officials in Tokyo had solicited them via back channel.

August 13, says Kido, was "the most trying day in our peace move."[112] Amid mounting military unrest and continued political deadlock, the palace moved to assert control and forge a consensus. The previous afternoon, while the cabinet was in session, Hirohito had convened the royal princes "to ask them to unite solidly" behind his desire for surrender. The imperial family council lasted two hours and was not without rancor. When it was over, the princes pledged their fealty.[113] On the morning of August 13 Anami tried unsuccessfully to convince Kido of the need to seek Allied concessions in order to secure army compliance with surrender.[114] From there Anami proceeded to the Prime Minister's residence for a meeting of the Big Six, but Hirohito interrupted the meeting to summon the service chiefs to an audience. "A peace proposal is now being submitted to the Allies," he told them. "What is your plan for air operations to be conducted while the negotiations [are] in progress?" According to Admiral Toyoda, General Umezu replied for the two of them, saying that the services would "refrain" from initiating attacks but would "return fire."[115] What else Hirohito said is not clear from the record, but loyal senior officers quietly began taking precautions against untoward incidents.

---

[111]Butow, *Japan's Decision to Surrender*, p. 198; Matsumoto, in "Statements," II, no. 61451, pp. 449–50; Okamoto, in ibid., III, no. 61477, p. 143; Tsuneishi, "The Japanese Emperor," pp. 108–9n.

[112]Kido, in "Statements," II, no. 61476, p. 198.

[113]Kido, in *IMTFE* testimony, p. 31187, says the session was marked by "a very free and frank exchange of views." That evening Prince Mikasa, who had served in Army intelligence, upbraided Anami for trying to prolong the fighting in order to improve the terms of surrender. See Colonel Saburo Hayashi (Anami's secretary), in "Statements," I, no. 61436, p. 405; Takeshita, in ibid., IV, no. 50025A, p. 71; and Inaba, in ibid., I, no. 57692, p. 585.

[114]Kido, in *IMTFE* testimony, pp. 31188–89, and in "Statements," II, no. 61476, pp. 199–200.

[115]Toyoda, in "Statements," IV, no. 57670, p. 382. Despite Umezu's assurances, the orders were apparently not cut until two days later. See Order no. 1381, dated August 15, U.S., Army, *Imperial General Headquarters Army High Command Record*, Supplement II.

The navy was the first to act. Navy Minister Yonai had already drawn up contingency plans to call in marines from Yokosuka in the event of disorder. Now he and Tōgō alerted Tokyo's police chief to the possibility, circumventing Home Minister Abe, whom they considered unreliable.[116] Hearing rumors of an attempt on Yonai's life, Toyoda warned Ōnishi and other irreconcilables on the naval general staff "not to resort to indiscreet actions" while pledging to do his "utmost" to obtain the best surrender terms possible.

The situation inside the army was even more delicate, because senior officers had yet to ascertain where their fellow officers stood on the proposed coup. Early in the morning Anami had sent his secretary to sound out Umezu on a proposal to have Field Marshal Hata appeal to the emperor on the army's behalf to reject the Allied terms. Umezu, a firm believer in military discipline who had been brought in as vice-chief of staff to restore order in the army after the February 26 incident, replied unequivocally that he was prepared to accept the Potsdam Declaration and an end to the war—something he had yet to tell the Big Six and an indication to Anami that he was not about to countenance a coup.[117] Later that day Yoshizumi suggested to Vice-Minister of War Wakamatsu that the military police round up suspected plotters and place them in preventive detention, but the chief of military police refused to go along. Wakamatsu then notified the commander of the Imperial Guards Division, responsible for palace security, not to obey any order on troop movements unless he personally issued it by telephone.[118]

Meanwhile, Sakomizu, alarmed at signs of restiveness in the foreign press and hoping to stay the hand of the Allies, instructed the Domei news agency to transmit a report on its shortwave overseas broadcast that the cabinet had decided to accept the Allied terms and was currently debating procedures for implementing its decision. When American propaganda broadcasts beamed the Domei report back to Japan, army monitors picked up the report and several diehard officers stormed into Sakomizu's office to demand an explanation.[119]

In this frenzied atmosphere the Big Six, having resumed deliberations, adjourned in disagreement—with Suzuki, Yonai, and Tōgō in favor of immediate surrender, and Anami, Umezu, and Toyoda still opposed.[120] That afternoon the cabinet picked up where it had left off the previous

[116]Tōgō, in "Statements," IV, no. 50304, pp. 274–75.

[117]Hayashi, in ibid., I, no. 54482, p. 396; Pacific War Research Society, *Japan's Longest Day*, p. 51. On Umezu's professionalism, see Storry, *Double Patriots*, p. 230.

[118]Yoshizumi, in "Statements," IV, no. 61338, pp. 611–12; Ikeda, in ibid., I, no. 54479, p. 548. Yoshizumi informed Anami of the details. Cf. Takeshita, in ibid., IV, no. 56367, p. 80; and Inaba, in ibid., no. 57692, p. 583.

[119]Brooks, *Behind Japan's Surrender*, p. 240.

[120]Tōgō, *Cause of Japan*, pp. 328–29.

day. After three hours of debate and little progress toward consensus, Suzuki polled the members: eight ministers joined Tōgō and Yonai in supporting acceptance of the Allied terms; Anami, Home Minister Abe, and Justice Minister Hiromasa Matsuzaka remained opposed; Munitions Minister Sadajiro Toyoda was undecided, and Minister-without-Portfolio Heigoro Sakurai deferred his decision to the prime minister. Faced with an irreconcilable split, the cabinet was constitutionally obliged to resign, and some who favored surrender threatened to fulfill that obligation in order to dynamite the logjam and attain their end. In contrast, War Minister Anami, far from encouraging a constitutionally sanctioned overthrow of the government, seemed anxious to prevent it from collapsing. He also took advantage of a brief recess to calm subordinates back in the War Ministry by telephoning to report a "favorable turn" in the cabinet deliberations.[121]

Around eight o'clock that evening the army conspirators finally caught up with Anami. For over two hours they rehearsed their plot with him. He called the scheme "crude" and put them off until midnight, to give him time to consider it further. But from other cryptic remarks he made, Takeshita, for one, came away optimistic about getting his support. When the plotters departed, Colonel Saburo Hayashi, Anami's private secretary, asked whether he had intended to leave them with the impression that he backed the coup. "If you disapprove of the plan," Hayashi recalls saying, "it is necessary for you to say so definitely."[122] Yet Anami continued to play for time. At midnight, the appointed hour for the coup to begin, he summoned Colonel Arao and gave him a noncommittal reply. When Lieutenant Colonel Ida pressed his co-conspirators to set the coup in motion anyway, they procrastinated in hopes of shortly gaining Anami's approval. Instead, early the next morning, Anami, accompanied by Arao, sounded out Umezu, who objected to any coup.[123] Umezu's firm opposition ruled out any unified army seizure of power along the lines envisioned by the plotters.

Anticipating Anami's approval, the conspirators had scheduled a meeting of all section and bureau chiefs in the ministry for 9 A.M. and

[121]Yoshizumi, in "Statements," IV, no. 61338, p. 610; Sakomizu, in "Interrogations," II, unnumbered, May 3, 1949, p. 131. Tōgō, *Cause of Japan*, p. 311, identifies his eight other allies as Finance Minister Hosaku Hirose, Agriculture Minister Tadaatsu Ishiguro, Education Minister Saburo Ōta, Welfare Minister Tadahiko Okada, Transportation Minister Naoto Kobiyama, and Ministers without Portfolio Yasui, Sakonji, and Shimomura. Ōta initiated the move to resign (according to Brooks, *Behind Japan's Surrender*, p. 71).

[122]Hayashi, in "Statements," I, no. 61436, p. 406. Cf. Inaba, in ibid., no. 57692, p. 582; Takeshita, in ibid., IV, no. 56367, pp. 80–81.

[123]Ida, in ibid., I, no. 62348, pp. 513–14; Inaba, in ibid., no. 57692, p. 583; Takeshita, in ibid., IV, no. 56367, p. 81. Ikeda, who learned of the meeting from Umezu, is mistaken about its time, see ibid., I, no. 54479, p. 548.

had summoned the commanders of the Eastern District Army, the Imperial Guards Division, and the military police to the war minister's office. Upon his return to the ministry around 10 A.M., Anami found them all assembled. Meeting first with the three commanders in his office, he admonished them to take special precautions against any insurrection. Then he went outside to address the bureau and section chiefs, among them several of the conspirators. The army should act in unison, he declared. When one of the plotters protested, Anami stiffened: anyone attempting "arbitrary action" would have to kill him first.[124] Yet Anami's speech was still equivocal enough to leave listeners with differing impressions of his intentions.

THE EMPEROR AGAIN BREAKS THE POLITICAL DEADLOCK

Shortly after the cabinet adjourned in deadlock on August 13, Chief Cabinet Secretary Sakomizu began rounding up the required signatures on a petition to convene an imperial conference. This time the service chiefs balked, recalling that the doves had used just such a tactic four days ago to seek the emperor's involvement without prior government decision. What "probably seemed like interference," says Toyoda, was an insistence on form, on the obligation to make decisions before submitting them for the emperor's ratification. Toyoda's aim was "to counter the conspiring moves of the advocates of [an] immediate end [to the] war who were relying on Imperial decision for the settlement of the issue."[125] Toyoda and Umezu signed on only after obtaining firm assurances that they would be consulted again before the petition was presented to the throne. Then they, along with Anami, appealed for a two-day delay, but the palace bureaucracy intervened the next morning, short-circuiting the consensual process and convening an imperial conference on their own.

The immediate stimulus for court action was an American propaganda leaflet that a chamberlain brought Kido as he was awakening on the morning of August 14. Addressed "to the Japanese people," it announced that "American planes are dropping these leaflets instead [of bombs] because the Japanese government has offered to surrender and every Japanese has a right to know the terms of the offer and the reply made to it by the U.S. Government on behalf of itself, the British, Chinese and Russian [governments]." It then reprinted the texts of the

---

[124]Inaba, in ibid., I, no. 57692, p. 583. Cf. Ida, in ibid., no. 62348, pp. 514–15, confuses this meeting with another around midday. On the meeting with local commanders, see Takeshita, in ibid., IV, no. 56367, p. 81; and Hayashi, in ibid., I, no. 51436, pp. 407, 409.
[125]Toyoda, in ibid., IV, no. 61340, p. 394. Cf. Brooks, *Behind Japan's Surrender*, p. 251.

Japanese note of August 10 and Byrnes' reply.[126] The leaflet barrage, designed to inform and arouse a war-weary populace to pressure its government into surrendering, could not have been more ill-suited to the conditions of Japan that day. One glance "caused me to be stricken with consternation," says Kido. "Here, such leaflets were being distributed at this juncture! If they should fall into the hands of the troops and enrage them, a military coup d'état would become inevitable and make the execution of planned policy extremely difficult."[127] Only heightening Kido's consternation was the fear that if those who opposed surrender stood firm the cabinet might yield to them, and if those who favored it tried to ram through a decision, "the cabinet would collapse, followed by chaos." The only way out for Kido was to seek an imperial conference in the hope that "if the cabinet members heard the words directly from His Majesty's lips, they would abide by the Imperial opinion unless they were particularly strong in [their] opposition, and that the cabinet would reach an accord." An appeal from the emperor, Kido felt, would move Anami, for one. "In other words," he concludes, "I intended to take the maximum advantage of the Emperor's prestige."[128] Kido immediately petitioned for an audience with Hirohito At 8:30 A.M. he was ushered into Hirohito's chambers, related what had happened, and urged him "to command the government without further loss of time to go through the formalities for terminating the war."[129]

By coincidence Suzuki arrived just as Kido was leaving the imperial presence. After he and Kido exchanged notes about the services' efforts to hold up the imperial conference and Kido's audience with Hirohito Kido told him that he had "no alternative left to him but to petition the Emperor not only to convoke a joint Imperial conference" of the cabinet and the chiefs of staff, but also "to command the termination of the war and [the] drafting of an Imperial Rescript" to that effect.[130] Suzuki agreed and returned with Kido to the emperor's chambers to petition for an imperial conference on their own authority. After a short discussion Hirohito gave his consent to the unprecedented procedure.

Despite the short notice, the last of the conferees, in various states of dishabille, trooped into the underground conference room of the palace by 11 A.M. In addition to the cabinet ministers and chiefs of staff, those responding to the imperial summons included Privy Council President Hiranuma, Planning Board Director Ikeda, Metropolitan Police Chief Machimura, Chief Cabinet Secretary Sakomizu, Military Affairs Bureau

---

[126]Brooks, *Behind Japan's Surrender*, pp. 258–59.
[127]Kido, in "Statements," II, no. 61541, p. 176. Cf. *IMTFE* testimony, pp. 31189, 31192.
[128]Kido, in "Statements," II, no. 61476, p. 200.
[129]Kido, in *IMTFE* testimony, pp. 31189–90.
[130]Ibid., p. 31190. Cf. "Statements," II, no. 61451, p. 177.

Chief Yoshizumi, Naval Affairs Bureau Chief Hoshina, and Legislative Bureau Director Murase. Prime Minister Suzuki opened the conference with a brief review of the cabinet deadlock and the Big Six split. After recapitulating the foreign minister's arguments in favor of immediate acceptance of the Allied terms, he begged the emperor's indulgence and invited the three leading exponents of holding out for further concessions to present their case. Army Chief of Staff Umezu spoke briefly, arguing that accepting the terms of Potsdam as qualified by the Byrnes reply would endanger the national polity and that under the circumstances Japan had no recourse other than to continue fighting while bargaining for firmer assurances. Next Suzuki called on Navy Chief of Staff Toyoda, who spoke at greater length, expressing fears that the Japanese people, and by implication the military diehards, "would not readily accept the wording of the reply, which placed the Emperor in a position subordinate to that of the Supreme Commander of the occupation forces." Conceding that "in practice" a defeated power might have to undergo such humiliation, he still found that "language" difficult to accept. His voice broke as he asked why, once Japan had demonstrated the resolve to fight a decisive battle for the homeland, the Allies would prefer to break off negotiations rather than make the minor concession necessary to assure the emperor's position. After Toyoda had finished, War Minister Anami echoed Umezu's sentiments.[131]

Finally, the emperor himself spoke, "I have listened carefully to the various views expressed in opposition but my decision, as given previously, remains unchanged. After careful study of the world situation and conditions at home, I have arrived at the conclusion that it is pointless to continue the war any longer." Tears welled up in onlookers' eyes and sobs were audible as Hirohito went on to associate himself with Tōgō's interpretation of the Allied terms: "On the question of the national polity I am aware that there remains considerable doubt in your minds; but reading between the lines I interpret this reply to mean that they are quite sympathetic. Your suspicions about their attitude may be justified, but I for one do not wish to entertain any such doubts."[132] Here was the clearest expression yet of the Hirohito's willingness to run the risk of sacrificing the throne in order to avert further bloodshed. The national interest, as he defined it, transcended organizational interest. Marquis Yasumasa Matsudaira, chief secretary to Kido, has this assessment of the emperor's readiness to surrender without any firm assurances on the future of the throne: "He trusted the Allied Powers and

---

[131]Toyoda, in USSBS, *Interrogations*, II: 322. Cf. "Statements," IV, no. 61340, p. 393; and Tōgō, *Cause of Japan*, p. 334. Evidence of who said what at the conference, apart from Hirohito's speech, is very sketchy.

[132]Tsuneishi, "The Japanese Emperor," p. 3.

knew they would not do away with either the nation or the people. He just wanted to end the massacre of lives in the world. His feeling was that this was his only desire, and as long as this was accomplished, *he did not care about his position.*" Yet, as Matsudaira is quick to acknowledge, "This incident itself was the best excuse for those not favoring peace."[133]

The emperor went on to address the question of military compliance with his wishes. He expressed anguish at having "to turn over to the Allied authorities officers and men upon whom I have depended all the time as though they were parts of my own body." In words evocative of those used by his grandfather, Emperor Meiji, at the time of the Triple Intervention, he called upon those present to "bear the unbearable" and accept the terms of Potsdam.[134] He volunteered to "stand before a 'mike' at any time" and personally address the nation—an unprecedented breach of palace decorum. Because the decision to surrender would come as "an even greater shock" to the armed forces, he said, "undoubtedly it will be difficult to keep them under control, but I should like the War and Navy Ministers to understand fully how I feel and to cooperate and see to it that everything is settled smoothly." He was personally prepared, he added, to address the officers and men. "Since it will be necessary to issue an Imperial Rescript on this occasion," he concluded, "I should like to have the government draft it at once. These are my feelings."[135]

Never before had the emperor intervened that openly in the political process, or spoken that directly. Even on the rare occasions when he had offered advice or expressed his own preferences, he tended to do it in the sanctum of private audiences or through palace functionaries. On the two recorded exceptions when he had made his personal wishes known to a large gathering, at the time of the February 26 incident and at the August 9 imperial conference, he had spoken allusively. According to Matsudaira, Hirohito himself recalled "only two occasions during his reign when he was able to do something more than simply wish, advise, or suggest."[136]

[133]Matsudaira, in "Statements," II, no. 60745, p. 430. It is not clear whether Matsudaira was himself present at the conference or was briefed on it shortly afterward.

[134]Toyoda, in USSBS, *Interrogations*, II: 322. Cf. Tōgō, *Cause of Japan*, p. 334, and in "Statements," IV, no. 50304, p. 275.

[135]Tsuneishi, "The Japanese Emperor," p. 4. Cf. Hasunuma, in "Statements," I, no. 58225, p. 297; Toyoda, in USSBS, *Interrogations*, II: 323; and Hirohito, interview with C. L. Sulzberger, "Hirohito Favors a Visit by Nixon," *New York Times*, March 8, 1972, p. 2.

[136]Matsudaira, in "Statements," II, no. 60745, p. 430. Cf. ibid., p. 431; and Takashi Oka, "The Emperor Who Meets the President Today," *New York Times Magazine*, September 26, 1971, p. 59, quoting Grand Chamberlain Sukemasa Iriye. Hirohito himself, in a September 20, 1975, interview, told *Newsweek* correspondent Bernard Krisher: "At the time of the termination of the war, I made the decision on my own. That is because the Prime Minister failed to obtain agreement in the cabinet and asked my opinion. So, I stated my opinion and then made the decision according to my opinion."

When the emperor had withdrawn, the cabinet recessed for an hour, then reconvened to make its formal decision. Hirohito's intervention had had the desired effect: Anami reversed himself. With his about-face, opposition to surrender within the cabinet collapsed and all fifteen members signed the memorandum of decision to accept the Allied terms. Foreign Minister Tōgō instructed Vice-Minister Matsumoto to draft a surrender note to the Allies. The rest of the afternoon was taken up in preparing the imperial rescript. A draft that Sakomizu had been working on since August 10 served as the basis for discussion. Anami objected strenuously to one sentence in it, "The war situation grows more unfavorable to us every day." It was a conclusion certain to arouse army resentment. He proposed recasting it to read "The war situation has not turned in our favor." Navy Minister Yonai initially opposed the change, but eventually recognizing the force of Anami's objection he conceded the point. Anami also succeeded in inserting the phrase "having been able to safeguard and maintain the national polity," a face-saving way of implying that, whatever the results on the battlefield, the army had achieved peace with honor. At the request of the service ministers, copies were sent to their staffs for review. The war ministry responded by insisting that the Privy Council ratify the rescript prior to its promulgation, a delay other ministers opposed. In the end a compromise was arranged: the rescript would become effective that evening with its publication in the Official Gazette, but the Privy Council would review it the next morning. [137]

Meanwhile, the Foreign Ministry completed the official note of surrender. It also drafted a separate note to the Allies on the modalities of surrender, incorporating points raised earlier by the War Minister and the chiefs of staff in objecting to the Byrnes reply. In order to "forestall any unnecessary complications," it requested that "(a) in case of the entry of Allied fleets or troops in Japan proper, the Japanese Government be notified in advance, so that arrangements can be made for reception" and that "(b) the number of points in Japanese territory to be designated by the Allies for occupation be limited to [a] minimum number," the list of designated points "leave such a city as Tokyo unoccupied," and "the forces to be stationed at each point be made as small as possible." Because disarming Japan's armed forces was "a most delicate task," the note suggested that "the most effective method" would be, "under the command of His Majesty the Emperor," to allow them "to disarm themselves." Moreover, "since some forces are located in remote places," making it "difficult to communicate the Imperial order, it is desired that reasonable time be allowed before the cessation

---

[137]Tōgō, *Cause of Japan*, pp. 334–35; Brooks, *Behind Japan's Surrender*, pp. 293–97; and Pacific War Research Society, *Japan's Longest Day*, pp. 148–50, 155.

of hostilities."[138] Around eleven o'clock that evening, the ministers affixed their seals to the documents and adjourned. The rescript was sent to the palace, where the emperor recorded it for broadcast at noon the following day.[139]

At 6 P.M. August 14, Washington time, the Swiss chargé delivered the Japanese notes to the State Department. Within the hour President Truman announced their receipt. Playing to the home crowd, he made surrender seem somewhat more unconditional than it was: "I deem this reply a full acceptance of the Potsdam Declaration which specifies the unconditional surrender of Japan. In the reply there is no qualification." Reaction to the second of the notes was three days longer in coming. The note was first sent to the Supreme Commander of occupation forces, General Douglas MacArthur, who cabled back, "The suggested ameliorations would relieve Japan of much of the physical and psychological burdens of defeat. I believe that public opinion throughout the Allied world would not support favorable consideration of these stipulations."[140] It would not be the last time that MacArthur would raise the threat of setting off a public reaction to get his way. The American reply, drafted by the army, had the peremptory language of victor to vanquished: "Such information as the Japanese Government requires to carry out the surrender arrangements will be communicated by the Supreme Commander at appropriate times determined by him."[141]

The formalities were over. Japan's decision to surrender was now official. What remained to be done was to implement it. Once again, the United States would be of little help.

COPING WITH INSUBORDINATION

So long as the ranking officers in the Japanese army remained united in their opposition to any coup d'état, the plot in the Military Affairs Bureau was doomed to failure. Yet, having sounded each other out on the morning of August 14 and come to agreement not to join the conspiracy, War Minister Anami and Army Chief of Staff Umezu still had to

---

[138]Note from Swiss Chargé to Secretary of State, August 16, 1945, in *FRUS*, 1945, VI: 699. Cf. Tōgō, *Cause of Japan*, pp. 336–37.

[139]Sakomizu, in "Interrogations," II, unnumbered, April 21, 1949, p. 124. Kido, in *IMTFE* testimony, p. 38934, recalls discussing with others in the palace sometime early in August the possibility of an imperial broadcast to minimize internal "confusion" after surrender.

[140]Cable from MacArthur to Marshall, August 17, 1945 (Manila time), in *FRUS*, 1945, VI: 671.

[141]Note from Secretary of State to Swiss Chargé, August 17, 1945, in *FRUS*, 1945, VI: 671, cf. p. 670n; Truman, *Year of Decisions*, p. 456.

contend with the possibility that in desperation others might try to lead a coup in their stead.

Compliance with the will of the emperor and the decision of the government to surrender required army and navy leaders not only to anticipate and head off other plots but also to arrange an orderly stand-down in the field. They had to reach military units scattered throughout the Far East, operating under standing orders never to surrender, and countermand those orders over lines of communication that were at best physically tenuous and at worst politically unreliable, with many a zealot at key nodes in the chain of command. Of particular concern to the army general staff was the China Expeditionary Army, not always noted for past obedience to central authority. At the time "no part of the China theater appeared in danger of collapse," recalls Vice-Chief of Staff Kawabe, just back from a six-day tour of inspection there. Officers and men from "the commander, on down, still exhibited the high morale that characterizes victors."[142]

The palace had already taken steps of its own to avoid any irreparable breakdown in command-and-control. Just before the imperial conference, the emperor had summoned the three oldest senior officers on active duty, field marshals Gen Sugiyama and Shunroku Hata and Fleet Admiral Osami Nagano, to ask their help in securing compliance.[143] Immediately after the imperial conference, the emperor's chief aide-de-camp, General Hasunuma, followed up the emperor's offer to address the troops in person to exhort them to lay down their arms. Even after Anami and Yonai assured Hasunuma that "it was unnecessary to trouble the Emperor to do anything special," the palace made arrangements to deliver imperial rescripts to the various field commands.[144]

In the interval between the imperial conference and the cabinet meeting, Anami returned to the War Ministry. First, he rejected a plea from his brother-in-law, Lieutenant Colonel Takeshita, that he resign, bringing down the government. Then, acting on the advice of Military Affairs Section Chief Arao—no longer a co-conspirator, if indeed he ever was—Anami called in the two other members of the army's so-called "Big Three," Chief of Staff Umezu and Inspector General Doihara, as well as the commanders of the First and Second Armies, Field Marshals Sugiyama and Hata, and had them sign a pledge that "the Army will act in obedience to the Imperial decision to the last." Umezu, fearful of un-

---

[142]Kawabe, in "Statements," II, no. 50226, p. 105.

[143]U.S. Army, *Imperial General Headquarters Army High Command Record*, p. 252 (Hereafter, *Imperial Headquarters Record*).

[144]Hasunuma, in "Statements," I, no. 58225, p. 297. Cf. Matsudaira, in ibid., II, no. 69745, p. 431; and Kido, in *IMTFE* testimony, p. 31193.

toward acts by the army's air forces, recommended that its commander sign as well. Vice-Minister Wakamatsu immediately saw to it.[145]

Rumors of the surrender decision were spreading rapidly throughout the War Ministry, and about thirty officers, including all the bureau and section chiefs, converged on General Anami's conference room just as he came out of the meeting. Anami confirmed that it was the emperor's express desire to end the war and, in words reminiscent of those he had used four days before in similar circumstances, he told the crowd, "Even if it means sleeping on grass and eating stones, I ask you all to do your utmost to preserve the national polity," whatever that meant.[146] Umezu meanwhile began spreading word among the general staff that he would not tolerate acts of insubordination.

That afternoon the army cut orders to all field commanders co-signed by Anami and Umezu, again invoking the prestige of the emperor and the professionalism of the service to demand compliance with surrender: "The Emperor has made his decision. The Army expects you to obey the decision and make no unauthorized moves that would put to shame the glorious traditions of the Imperial Army and its many distinguished military services." The directive closed on a personal note: "The Minister of War and the Chief of Staff dispatch this order with grief in their hearts, and they expect you to appreciate the emotions of the Emperor when he himself broadcasts the Imperial Rescript terminating the war at twelve noon tomorrow."[147]

The navy's order came right to the point: "Further offensive operations against the United States, Great Britain, the USSR, and China will be suspended pending further orders." A companion cable to all naval commands from Yonai elaborated on the decision and the emperor's role in it: "His, and only his, decision" was that "for the Empire's future, the only thing to do was to accept the Potsdam Declaration on condition that the structure of the nation be left intact." Citing Hirohito's expressed readiness "personally to talk to the Army and Navy if necessary," Yonai pointedly recalled that he and Anami had "advised him that we would assume the duty of controlling and maintaining order within our respective departments." The message ended by invok-

---

[145]Kawabe, in "Statements," II, no. 50224, pp. 101–2. Cf. Ikeda, in ibid., I, no. 54479, pp. 547–48; Inaba, in ibid., I, no. 57692, p. 583; and *Imperial Headquarters Record*, pp. 252–53.

[146]Takeshita, in "Statements," IV, no. 56367, p. 82. Cf. Lieutenant Colonel Shiro Hara, in "Interrogations," I, no. 50563, p. 224; Yoshizumi, in "Statements," IV, no. 59277, p. 604.

[147]Pacific War Research Society, *Japan's Longest Day*, p. 174. Cf. Kawabe, in "Statements," II, no. 50226, p. 106; and *Imperial Headquarters Record*, p. 253, and Supplement 2, p. 14.

ing the emperor's name once again, "These are the Emperor's wishes, and the Emperor can best be served by obeying these orders."[148]

Yet at the very moment that senior military officers were issuing orders to comply with the decision to surrender, others not quite as senior were suborning them. No sooner had Generals Umezu and Anami agreed to not to lead an army coup than some conspirators renewed efforts to start one. Hearing reports of the generals' agreement, Lieutenant Colonel Inaba went at once to his cohorts in the Operations Section of the general staff and urged them to appeal to Umezu to reconsider, while Lieutenant Colonel Takeshita attempted to convert his brother-in-law Anami. Acting under the illusion that the Anami's course was not yet unalterable, Takeshita then drew up new plans for a coup. While neither he nor Inaba appeared willing to proceed without the war minister's express backing, not all their co-conspirators were that punctilious. Ignoring Anami's injunction against insubordination, perhaps on the assumption that once a coup was set in motion he and other senior officers would fall in with it, Hatanaka and Shiizaki pressed ahead with a plot to seal off the palace, seize the radio station, and prevent the broadcast of the imperial rescript.[149]

Late in the afternoon of August 14, they broached the scheme to Lieutenant Colonel Ida, who, momentarily preferring suicide over rebellion, refused to join. Around ten o'clock that evening they renewed their effort and so "inspired" Ida with their ardor that he agreed to line up support for the plot. Hatanaka awakened Takeshita at midnight and convinced him to make another try at winning over Anami. The trio then proceeded to the headquarters of the Imperial Guards Division to draw in its commander, Lieutenant General Takeshi Mori, but Mori resisted their entreaties. Bursting with impatience at the time-consuming discussion, Hatanaka shot and killed Mori and used the general's seal to forge orders for the regimental commanders to seize control of the palace. Ida then dashed off to Eastern District Army headquarters to try to gain the support of its commander.[150]

---

[148]Naval Order no. 47, August 14, 1945, U.S. Army, Far East Command, Military History Section, Japanese Research Division, "Translations of Japanese Documents," Document no. 63042; and CINCUSFLT, Pacific Strategic Intelligence Section, "Japanese Surrender Maneuvers," August 29, 1945, NSA Records, Box 4, SRH 090, RG 457, National Archives, pp. 23–24.

[149]Inaba, in "Statements," I, no. 57692, p. 584; Takeshita, in ibid., IV, no. 56367, pp. 81–82. The new plot is discernible, at least in broad outline, from Imperial Guards Division Strategic Order no. 584, dated 2 A.M., August 15, 1945, in Pacific War Research Society, *Japan's Longest Day*, pp. 226–27. Inaba and Takeshita both report that Colonel Hiroshi Hosoda had sounded out Umezu and felt that he was "not opposed to the plot"—a mistaken impression.

[150]Ida, in "Statements," I, no. 62348, pp. 511–13, 516; Takeshita, in ibid., IV, unnumbered, February 28, 1950, p. 84; Kido, in *IMTFE* testimony, p. 31198; Lieutenant Colonel

Takeshita, meanwhile, arrived at Anami's home still hoping to convince him to join the coup, but found him instead contemplating suicide. Three hours of conversation followed, and then, fortified by saki, War Minister Anami committed *seppuku*.[151] To view Anami as a diehard militarist makes the inconsistency of his behavior inexplicable. To view him instead as a professional soldier pulled in different directions by conflicting obligations—obedience to the emperor who commanded the army to comply with surrender, and loyalty to his closest subordinates who asked him to join the coup—draws attention to his official responsibility. That responsibility, to maintain the morale of his service, required at once that he try to secure peace with honor and that he uphold the code of military professionalism by preventing acts of insubordination. In the end, torn apart by these competing claims, he died a traditional samurai death.[152] While the form of his death may have been uniquely Japanese, as was the force of his obligations, the role conflict that he experienced was not: it was that of many a military commander at war's end.

Since the support of the army high command was critical to the plotters' success, the combination of Umezu's unswerving loyalty to the throne and Anami's suicide had the effect of decapitating the coup d'état.[153] No other high-ranking officers joined the conspiracy. By the time Ida arrived at Eastern District Army headquarters, a telephone call from the Imperial Guards Division had alerted its commander, who moved at once to crush the rebellion. Rushing to the palace, he personally reprimanded the commanders of the insurgent regiments and restored order by morning.

Hiroshi Fuwa (staff officer of the Eastern District Army), in "Statements," I, no. 62238, p. 191; and *Imperial Headquarters Record*, pp. 253–54.

[151]Takeshita, in "Statements," IV, no. 50025A, pp. 73–74.

[152]Four different conceptions of Anami's behavior in the final hours of his life underlie subsequent accounts of those around him: first, that he was doing his duty, adopting a time-honored Japanese way of accepting responsibility for failure; second, that he was apologizing for having given tacit encouragement to the coup; third, that he was expressing the strongest dissent possible from the decision to surrender and absolving himself of any responsibility for its consequences; and fourth, that he was cutting the ties that bound him. Exponents of the first include Inaba ("Statements," I, no. 57692, p. 584); Takeshita (ibid., IV, unnumbered, February 28, 1950, p. 84); Yoshizumi, (ibid., IV, no. 61338, p. 611); and Ida (ibid., I, no. 62348, p. 512). Anami's private secretary, Colonel Hayashi, provides some support for the second (ibid., I, no. 61436, pp. 403–5). The third appears in Kase, *Journey to the Missouri*, p. 262, not always a reliable account. Evidence for the fourth comes from Anami's opponents and associates alike, among them, Tōgō, in ibid., IV, no. 50304, p. 276; Kido, in ibid., II, no. 61476, pp. 199–200; Admiral Kishaburo Nomura, in USSBS, *Interrogations*, II: 391; Kawabe, in "Statements," II, no. 52608, pp. 94–96; Sakomizu, in "Interrogations," II, unnumbered, May 3, 1949, p. 131; and Interior Minister Abe, in Giovannitti and Freed, *Decision to Drop the Bomb*, p. 299.

[153]Ikeda, in "Statements," I, no. 54479, p. 548. A cultural explanation of small-group structure in Japan, emphasizing the disruptiveness of changes in leadership, is suggestive of the conspirators' behavior. See Chie Nakane, *Japanese Society* (Berkeley, Calif., 1970), pp. 44–45, 53.

A recording of the imperial rescript, stowed out of reach of the conspirators, survived the night intact. Delayed by the unrest, the Privy Council did not convene until noon, then recessed to listen to the emperor's broadcast before it had time to give its formal approval to the rescript.[154] At noon Japanese citizens tuned in to hear an extraordinary appeal by the emperor himself for compliance with Japan's decision to surrender. To many listeners his message seemed all but incomprehensible. His language was court Japanese, archaic and formal, alien to vernacular of commoners. Euphemisms inserted into the text at the insistence of the army further obscured his meaning. But at least to listeners who had been paying close attention to the events of the past week, his second sentence was unambiguous: "We have ordered our Government to communicate to the Governments of the United States, Great Britain, China, and the Soviet Union that our Empire accepts the provisions of the Joint Declaration."[155]

That afternoon, as American bombers were still raining their loads on Japan, the Suzuki cabinet resigned en bloc. After conferring with Privy Council President Hiranuma, Privy Seal Kido recommended that Prince Higashikuni form a new government.[156] Calling upon a member of the royal family to serve as prime minister for the first time in the sixty-year history of cabinet government in Japan was just one of several steps that the palace took to invoke the prestige of the emperor at war's end. On August 17 and again on August 22, the palace addressed imperial rescripts to the field commands ordering an immediate cease-fire and appealing for compliance. It also dispatched three princes overseas with personal messages from the emperor for the troops. Four more were scheduled to depart August 22, when the palace got word they were no longer needed.[157]

The services too issued cease-fire orders to various theaters of war from August 15 until August 25 and warned against "rash actions." They managed to devise a face-saving formula to reconcile these orders with the doctrine of never surrendering: "None of the Japanese Army personnel and civilian employees coming under the control of enemy forces after the promulgation of the imperial rescript will be considered prisoners of war."[158]

[154]Tōgō, *Cause of Japan*, pp. 337–38.

[155]Butow, *Japan's Decision to Surrender*, appendix 1. Abe, who heard the broadcast at the Home Ministry, recalls: "Most of the lower-rank officials thought at first that this message was intended to encourage the nation so that the people might be ready to fight on the homeland." Giovannitti and Freed, *Decision to Drop the Bomb*, p. 305.

[156]Tōgō, *Cause of Japan*, p. 338; Kido, in *IMTFE* testimony, pp. 31199–201.

[157]Hasunuma, in "Statements," I, no. 58225, p. 297. The text of the August 17 rescript appears in F. C. Jones, *Japan's New Order in East Asia* (London, 1954), pp. 475–76.

[158]Army Order no. 1385, August 18, 1945, U.S. Army, "Translations of Japanese Documents," III. Cf. Naval Order no. 50, August 19, 1945, Document no. 63045; and Yonai, in USSBS, *Interrogations*, II: p. 332.

Despite these precautions, scores of isolated incidents of insubordination took place during the two weeks following Japan's decision to surrender. Even the stacking of arms was not uneventful. In Korea, American forces supervising the disarming of Japanese troops had to rearm some of them with rifles and three or four rounds of ammunition, so that they could protect themselves and their mates against reprisals by the Koreans.

IMPLEMENTING A DECISION TO SURRENDER

The accepted wisdom on the end of the war between the United States and Japan is that the atomic bombings shocked Japan into surrendering unconditionally. That is wrong. And when the wisdom of shocking the enemy into surrender is applied to ending other wars, it may be dangerously misleading. Close scrutiny of the details of the public and bureaucratic reaction to the bombings reveals that the shock effects were largely physical, not psychological.

The atomic bombings did not add much to the defeatism already widespread in the populace. Data presented in the U.S. Strategic Bombing Survey indicates that by July 1 some 47 percent of the Japanese polled "had become certain that a Japanese victory was impossible, and 34 percent felt that they could not go on with the war." A survey taken shortly after the war found that the demoralizing effects of the atomic bombings were "remarkably localized." In Hiroshima and Nagasaki only 25 percent of the survivors felt "certain of defeat" because of the atomic bomb. That percentage dropped to 23 percent for the cities nearest to the target cities, to 15 percent in cities nearby, to 8 percent in cities farther away, and to 6 percent in cities farthest from Hiroshima and Nagasaki. The import of the Strategic Bombing Survey is that sheer physical destructiveness is not be confused with psychological impact or political efficacy: "Even in the target cities, it must be emphasized, the atomic bombs did not uniformly destroy the Japanese fighting spirit. Hiroshima and Nagasaki, when compared with other Japanese cities, were not more defeatist than the average."[159]

Nor did the atomic bombings shock those making decisions in Tokyo. Distance cushioned their impact. If anything, Soviet entry into the war was more shocking than the bomb to most senior Japanese officials, especially army officers. Nonetheless, the evidence is that neither the atomic bombings nor Soviet entry caused anyone in the cabinet or the high command to change his convictions about war termination. The

---

[159]Strategic Bombing Survey (Pacific), *Effects of Atomic Bombs*, pp. 21–22.

atomic bombings did have an effect on the palace, giving the emperor a new sense of urgency about ending the war and providing those who wanted to sue for peace a pretext for involving him in the policy process.

High-ranking Japanese military officers, like their American counterparts, continued to believe that nothing short of invasion and outright conquest of Japan's home islands could compel capitulation. The calculus of war suggested that in the test of will at war's end the losers still had scope and leverage for bargaining with the winners over the terms and conditions of surrender. The Japanese could threaten to exact a price for invasion, a price the Americans might prefer to avoid by granting concessions. The unambiguous shift in the military balance during the war did not go unnoticed on either side of the Pacific, but in the end it did not matter inside Japan. What is now called "escalation dominance" did not alter Japan's calculations appreciably enough for it to accept unconditional surrender. The American bomb and the Soviet attack did diminish its threat to resist invasion and its leverage to strike a better bargain with the Allies, but they did not eliminate that threat and the resulting leverage altogether. If the advent of nuclear weapons made these calculations somewhat less appropriate, neither side had yet had time to absorb the implications of the new weapon and reach that conclusion.

Although atomic bombing and Soviet entry did not convert hawks into doves in the government or the high command, they did not cause complete immobility either. Soviet entry forced the army to shift its stand, if not its beliefs or objectives, and to allow direct negotiations with the Allies on the basis of the terms of Potsdam. The events also reinforced the conviction of those favoring an immediate end to hostilities that now was the time for the emperor to intervene openly in the policy process. Admiral Toyoda, who favored holding out for better terms, saw Soviet entry as providing a suitable political context for imperial intervention, "Apart from the intervention of Soviet Russia, it is difficult for me to say [if,] at any time prior to the actual termination of the war, the Emperor had issued a rescript terminating the war, the Navy would have been willing to say that is not a mistake, because so long as one feels there is any chance left, it is very difficult to say that the time to quit [has come]."[160] The emperor himself seems to have seen the bomb too as providing the context for intervening in the policy process. In the end it was his intervention, not the atomic bombings or Soviet entry, that was decisive. Kido puts the point succinctly, "The only reason the Japanese Army stopped fighting was [that] the Emperor ordered

---

[160]Toyoda, in *Interrogations*, II, p. 320. For a diehard's view of the bomb's effect on the palace, see Inaba, in "Statements," I, no. 57692, p. 585.

them to do so."[161] Another atomic bombing, with Tokyo as its target, far from prompting a decision to surrender, might have precluded it.

Even as Hirohito was intervening on August 9 and 14 to break the political deadlock over the terms of Potsdam, the problem facing Japan's leaders was how best to assure army compliance with orders to cease hostilities. The political deadlock in Tokyo was partly due to differences between those who thought that Allied concessions would facilitate compliance and those who feared that holding out longer would only jeopardize it. While the zeal of Japan's armed forces may have been extreme, the difficulties of command-and-control during war termination were not. Execution seldom follows from decision automatically, especially at war's end.

The United States did little to ease Japan's predicament. If the atomic attack on Nagasaki, barely three days after Hiroshima, and the last-minute conventional bombing of Japanese cities both seem gratuitous, and the leafleting operations inappropriate, the proposal to target Tokyo for the next atomic bombing was potentially self-defeating. Striking the capital was like shocking Japan by destroying its central nervous system. It endangered the lives of the very people who alone could authoritatively commit Japan to surrender. It threatened to shatter command-and-control over Japan's widely scattered forces, virtually assuring non-compliance with any order to cease hostilities. That would have prolonged a war that both governments were now trying to end.

Nor was Washington in any mood to make the concessions that might have eased Japan's surrender. Some have argued that Japan's residual war-making capacity counted enough in the calculations of U.S. officials to compel them eventually to provide Japanese leaders with explicit assurances on the future of the throne.[162] They did not. The United States offered no such assurances, nor did Japan think it had. Indeed, the heat of domestic politics all but precluded cool calculation on both sides. In the end it was not Japan's residual military strength but its political weakness that prolonged war termination— the inability of Japanese leaders to resolve divisions within the cabinet and the Big Six and the tenuousness of their command-and-control over the armed forces.

Still, there were Americans who remained dissatisfied with the terms of surrender. On September 2, on board the battleship *Missouri* in Tokyo

---

[161]Giovannitti and Freed, *Decision to Drop the Bomb*, p. 335. Cf. Kido, in *IMTFE* testimony, p. 31204. A number of American accounts, trying to justify the atomic bombings by the impact they had on Japan, draw inferences that do not seem warranted by the evidence, among them, Compton, "If the Atomic Bomb Had Not Been Used," p. 55; Samuel Eliot Morison, "Why Japan Surrendered," *The Atlantic* 206 (October 1960): 47; and Feis, *Atomic Bomb*, 195.

[162]E.g., Kecskemeti, *Strategic Surrender*, p. 210.

Bay, Japan signed the instruments of surrender.[163] On September 18 Richard Russell, Democrat of Georgia, rose to denounce the peace settlement on the Senate floor. He called for resumption of the bombing: "Our people have not forgotten that the Japanese struck us the first blow in the war without the slightest warning. They believe that we should continue to strike the Japanese until they are brought grovelling to their knees." In Russell's view, there should be no limits on the use of force: "If we do not have a sufficient number of atomic bombs with which to finish the job immediately, let us carry on with TNT and fire bombs until we can produce them." He tried to reduce the politics of war termination to the physics of pounding the enemy into submission: "The next plea for peace should come from an utterly destroyed Tokyo."[164] At the dawn of the nuclear age, domestic politics more than ever dictated the peace of the dead.

[163]The day the Japanese surrender note arrived, Forrestal launched a campaign to have Admiral Nimitz share equal billing with MacArthur at the surrender ceremonies, but he had to settle for holding those ceremonies on board the *Missouri* (Byrnes, *All in One Lifetime*, p. 307).

[164]U.S. Congress, Senate, *Congressional Record* 91 (September 18, 1945): 8816.

[6]

War Termination
Then and Now

> There is an inexorability about war. It is a little unbridled for
> the realist's rather nice sense of purposive social control. . . .
> For the inexorable abolishes choices, and it is the essence of
> the realist's creed to have, in every situation, alternatives be-
> fore him.
>
> —Randolph Bourne, "A War Diary"

Thinking about war termination in the rational-choice approach, by
analogy to chess, assumes that during the terminal stage of a war a state,
pursuing its national interests or goals, will prudently calculate the probable consequence of alternative courses of action, choose the one that
maximizes its interests, and act accordingly. At war's end, it should be as
clear as it ever will be, especially on the losing side, what interests the
state should be prepared to sacrifice rather than fight on. Indeed, the
national interest could be operationally defined as the goals for which a
state would prefer to keep waging a lost war rather than concede.

Preserving the throne was ostensibly such a goal for Japan. Yet in the
end the emperor himself was prepared to surrender without firm assurances that he or his throne would be spared, and his wishes prevailed in Tokyo. Similarly, U.S. officials agreed that sparing the throne
was in the interests of the United States, at least in order to facilitate the
surrender and occupation of Japan and at most to avoid alienating Japan
permanently and preclude postwar reconciliation. But in the face of
these interests, which they themselves affirmed, U.S. officials insisted
on unconditional surrender for reasons of domestic politics.

A rational economy of force, in the tradition of Clausewitz, would also
have suggested bringing war to a close with a minimum of gratuitous
loss of life and property once its outcome was clear to both sides. Yet
few officials on either side of the Pacific sought to do so. Of those who
did—Stimson and Grew in Washington, Tōgō and Yonai in Japan—
none succeeded in getting the state to follow their lead.

Near the end of World War II, when each of the belligerent states should have been united in its purpose, closing ranks behind its strategy, neither the United States nor Japan was. Quite the contrary, the two contenders sometimes behaved as if each of their pieces on the board—armies, navies, air forces, diplomats—was acting on its own volition, moving according to its own program. There was, in short, no Pacific endgame.

PEACEMAKING BEGINS AT HOME

As a rule, armies do not end wars; states do. Except in cases of outright conquest, rare in this century, war termination is fundamentally a political act, not a military one. Seemingly decisive military advantage or disadvantage does not promptly or automatically produce an end to hostilities any more than stalemate does. Translating results on the battlefield into war termination requires political agreement—within governments, among allies, and between the opposing sides. Contrary to those who write as if politics ends once war begins, it is the thesis of this study that analysts cannot ignore the fundamentally political character of war termination.

Once officials on both sides conclude that the war has been won, lost, or stalemated, their situation is somewhat analogous to that of union leaders who have decided to settle with management but who have to get their membership to ratify the new contract. From then on, the hardest bargaining may take place in the union hall, not at the negotiating table, and labor and management may behave like tacit allies against the union rank and file in trying to secure ratification. Even though they may have a common interest in reaching accord, labor and management first have to satisfy their respective constituencies in order to consolidate their own organizational base. So it is with the leaders of contending sides near war's end. They have to make common cause with their counterparts in the enemy camp, but in so doing they may jeopardize their political standing where it counts—back home.

From this perspective, war termination begins and ends at home. Stakes and stands are rooted in domestic and bureaucratic politics. That may obscure the identity of potential "allies" behind enemy lines and may make it difficult to ascertain their motives. That may also make it politically unpalatable or organizationally impracticable for officials on one side who want to end the war to deliver what their allies on the other side need from them. For one thing, it puts the organization usually responsible for managing relations with the enemy, a regional bureau or country desk in the foreign office, at a considerable disadvantage

[283]

because the outbreak of war has disrupted diplomatic discourse, and with it the flow of cable traffic that assures that organization access to the policy process. Politically too diplomats may be doubly suspect once war breaks out, both for their failure to prevent it and for their proposals to end it: any bureau or faction that advocates accommodation with the enemy leaves itself open to attack by rivals at home. Diplomats may thus have some incentive to try to bring home a favorable settlement, but avoid responsibility for negotiating an unfavorable one. Tōgō's reluctance to go to Moscow himself may be seen in this light. At the same time, rival armed services, trying to protect their own preferred roles and missions, autonomy, and budget shares, may be fighting over the choice of strategy for ending the war. The stands they take on the war at the front may depend on the stakes they see in battles at home. Diplomacy for them may be only a means to furthering their strategy preferences. That was the case with the army and navy in Japan in deciding to approach Moscow. The consequence was that at war's end intransigents on one side made common cause with intransigents in the enemy camp in order to defeat those on both sides who sought accommodation. There were occasional but rare exceptions: after Japan's suit for peace, Americans opposed to concessions to Japan, by insisting on unconditional surrender, impelled Japanese trying to arrange an end to the war to resist pressures in Tokyo to negotiate over the terms of Potsdam.

According to the internal-politics approach, whatever happens abroad is of little concern to officials back home unless it impinges directly on their bureaucratic responsibilities or their political constituencies. The self-absorption, sometimes to the point of autism, with which states wage war in this approach stands in sharp contrast to the assumption of conscious strategic interaction among states that is the mark of rational-choice accounts of war termination. Obviously, the premises of both approaches may be overdrawn for the sake of simplicity. Nevertheless, it is instructive to keep these contrasting perspectives in mind in thinking about international politics, and especially about war termination.

Moreover, when war begins it sets off organizational routines. Once in motion they are difficult to alter, let alone to stop altogether. It is no longer possible then, if ever, to set policy and assume that execution will follow automatically. During a war, to the contrary, the operations are the policy. That is especially true of bombing. What the quasi-autonomous organizational entities within the state do routinely to wage war affects how readily the war can be terminated. As a consequence, war-making, even more than most government programs, may be easier to start than to stop.

War may only numb what little sensitivity states normally exhibit outside their borders. Uncertain about what is happening inside the enemy state and how to get it to do what they want, officials may go by the book, preferring the familiarity and certitude of organizational routine to the unknowns and unknowables of creative statesmanship. In the dark about what is best for the nation, leaders may steer by the light of organizational interest or head wherever prevailing political winds may be blowing them. So the army air forces kept up the conventional bombing of Japanese cities despite Stimson's efforts to curb it. So too Truman and Byrnes were reluctant to give any public commitment to sparing the emperor.

Self-absorption has perverse consequences for war termination. On a few occasions officials on one side or the other deliberately initiated actions on their own in hopes of eliciting an appropriate response from the other side that would help them move their own government toward war termination. Yet even when they tried to make common cause with the enemy, they failed. The clear signals they intended to send were lost amid the noise of conflicting acts by the large and unwieldy organizations that comprise the state. And even when the other side received their signals and interpreted them correctly, it failed to respond with the diplomatic initiative or unilateral concession or military de-escalation that was sought. Those in the U.S. government who desired a prompt cessation of hostilities were hoping that Japan would sue for peace on terms not far short of unconditional surrender so that they could get the United States to reciprocate with concessions of its own; but the Japanese could only reach internal agreement on an indirect approach to Moscow without specifying the terms of settlement they were prepared to accept. Similarly, those in Japan anxious to end the war needed clear public assurances from the United States about the future of the throne in order to have any chance of getting internal agreement on surrender; but U.S. officials, while recognizing the need to preserve the throne in order to gain Japanese compliance with surrender and occupation, were nonetheless unwilling to court domestic displeasure by granting any explicit concessions to Japan.

Unity was hardly the order of the day in either Japan or the United States at war's end. Vehement, even violent, disagreement was common in the highest councils. So was persistent parochialism. Organizational interests often displaced national interests and in the process became ends in themselves. Many officials on both sides took resolute stands in defense of their organization's interests and resisted changes in their organization's routines. There were some notable exceptions. In Japan, for example, the emperor was willing to accept unconditional surrender at some risk to his future and that of the throne. In contrast, however, there were army officers who regarded his willingness to do so as tantamount to treason—if not by the emperor himself then by some in his entourage—and who identified preservation of the throne with maintaining the army's special relationship to it: the right of supreme command. Similarly, Grew and briefly Stimson were prepared to concede the commitment to preserve the throne. Yet the battle within the U.S. government to spell out conditions of unconditional surrender was subordinated to a struggle over military strategy that took place amid intensified competition among the armed services over roles and missions, capabilities, and budget shares. In that competition each service anticipated that a favorable decision on strategy would benefit it over its rivals after the war by strengthening its claim to credit for victory.

With so much at stake, those claims were not long in coming once the war ended. The chief of naval operations, Admiral King, saw the key to victory in the struggle of navy against navy. In his final war report King asserted, "Japan's armies were intact and undefeated and her air forces only weakened when she surrendered, but her navy had been destroyed and her merchant marine had been fatally crippled." Yet for every admiral who agreed with King that "Japan lost the war because she lost command of the sea, and in doing so lost—to us—the islands bases from which her factories and cities could be destroyed by air," there were army airmen prepared to respond, as did Arnold in his final war report, by relegating the other services to distinctly subservient roles: "Fully recognizing the indispensable contributions of other arms, I feel that air power's part may fairly be called decisive."[1] Others were prepared to put the air force case more forcefully. "The Navy," testified General James H. Doolittle, "had the transport to make the invasion of Japan possible; the Ground Forces had the power to make it successful; and the B-29 made it unnecessary."[2] Against this combined onslaught, the most the army could muster was to highlight its role in Europe while fighting a rearguard action about the part it had played in victory over Japan. The army recalled its campaign of island-hopping across the Pacific that brought it to the verge of invading Japan proper and dwelt on the potency of the threat that its invasion posed. After all, there is nothing as potent as an unexecuted threat—or as successful as an untried strategy.

Yet there was unanimity among the armed services on one key point: the atomic bomb had not been necessary for victory. Even to Arnold, conventional bombing had won the war: "Without attempting to mini-

---

[1]King, "Second Official Report to the Secretary of the Navy," in Millis, *War Reports*, p. 654; and Arnold, "Third Report" in ibid., p. 437. The validity of the competing claims is difficult to assess because Japan's military defeat is overdetermined.

[2]U.S. Congress, Senate, Committee on Military Affairs, *Department of Armed Forces, Department of Military Security*, Hearings on S. 84 and S. 1482, 79th Cong., 1st sess., 1945, p. 290.

mize the appalling and far-reaching results of the atomic bomb, we have good reason to believe that its actual use provided a way out for the Japanese government. The fact is that the Japanese could not have held out long, because they had lost control of the air." Atomic bombing could hardly justify the planes and pilots for a seventy-group air force on bases circling the globe that the army airmen were seeking at war's end, but Arnold could put it to good use against the navy by claiming that "the only known effective means of delivering atomic bombs in their present stage of development is the very heavy bomber," one presumably too heavy to take off from the deck of an aircraft carrier. This allowed Arnold to conclude, "The influence of atomic energy on Air Power can be stated very simply. It has made Air Power all-important."[3] In the face of repeated service efforts to downplay the bomb's role in the victory over Japan and to question the need for its use, Groves and others in charge of the Manhattan Project propagated a novel doctrine to justify the atomic bombings. That doctrine stressed the bomb's shock effect on Japan's body politic.

Service propaganda may have fueled the historians' debate about the atomic bomb, but it did little to shape the perceptions of the public, the Congress, or civilian policy-makers. Hiroshima and Nagasaki made a profound impression on them. It convinced most in 1945 that the atomic bombings and the end of the war were cause and effect. Nothing that service partisans said could shake that conviction, whatever its validity.

RETHINKING THE UNTHINKABLE

While war termination has been a recurrent difficulty throughout history, the advent of nuclear weapons has made the difficulty all the more acute. As Thomas Schelling has cogently pointed out, "Earlier wars, like World Wars I and II or the Franco-Prussian War, were limited by *termination*, by an ending that occurred before the period of greatest potential violence, by negotiation that brought the *threat* of pain and privation to bear but often precluded the massive *exercise* of civilian violence. With nuclear weapons available, the restraint of violence cannot await the

[3] Arnold, "Third Report," pp. 438, 462, 464. The U.S. Strategic Bombing Survey, which Arnold had hoped would end all doubts about the primacy of conventional bombing in winning the war, tended to follow his lead in downplaying the significance of the atomic bomb. According to Arnold, *Global Mission*, p. 490, when he and Robert Lovett (assistant secretary of war for air), commissioned a blue-ribbon panel of civilians in 1944 to assess the effectiveness of strategic bombing, "We both knew that following World War I everybody claimed to have won it. Finally, to stop further arguments, people used to say the Great War had been won by the chaplains." MacIsaac, *Strategic Bombing* chap. 3, has a different view of the survey's origins.

outcome of a contest of military strength; restraint, to occur at all, must occur during the war itself."[4]

Shortly after World War II it became the policy of the United States to use nuclear weapons first, if need be, to deter conventional attack not only upon itself but also upon its allies in Western Europe and elsewhere. But the implicit assumption of that policy, that the greater the prospective costs of war the more a state will be deterred from starting one, is a legacy of pre-nuclear thought. Once the Soviet Union acquired nuclear weapons of its own and the means of delivering them on the United States, it became difficult to raise the cost of war to one side without also doing so for the other. Under this condition of nuclear interdependence, deterrence no longer means increasing the cost of war to a potential foe, but instead manipulating the shared risk of a war neither side can afford. Yet the fundamental change in the strategic balance did not prompt an equally fundamental reconsideration of American nuclear doctrine away from first use of nuclear weapons. That doctrine still poses a deliberate risk of nuclear war today.

The very existence of nuclear weapons and the latent threat of escalation that they pose may reduce the likelihood of premeditated war between the superpowers. Yet what Schelling has called "the threat that leaves something to chance" does not satisfy those who want to make the doctrine of deliberate first use somehow more credible by seeking ever more forces and more options for waging and "winning" nuclear war. The United States has consequently embraced force postures and operating practices that increase the likelihood of preemptive or inadvertent war in a crisis. But the deliberate threat of first use is irrational unless it satisfies either of two conditions: if the United States could deny the Soviet Union the means of nuclear retaliation by a combination of a disarming first-strike and comprehensive defenses against nuclear attack, or else if nuclear war could somehow be limited, once it began. The technical infeasibility of satisfying the first condition has directed attention toward trying to meet the second. Yet the very idea of a limited nuclear war, if it is not an utter absurdity, presumes that nuclear war, once under way, could be stopped well short of mutual annihilation.

The theory of limited nuclear war, like the rest of nuclear doctrine, is largely deductive, almost axiomatic. As such it is ahistorical. It consists of a set of logical deductions from simple assumptions about state behavior. But logic alone seems incapable of sustaining this or any other theory. This is especially so in the case of current nuclear doctrine insofar as its logic rests on a central paradox: how can a state deter its rival by

[4]Thomas C. Schelling, *Arms and Influence* (New Haven, 1966), p. 20 (emphasis in the original).

nuclear threats that it manifestly prefers not to carry out? Ultimately, the only way to invalidate the claims of theory is to test them empirically. Yet nuclear weapons, by their very nature, rule that out. As Fred Iklé puts it, "Our entire structure of thinking about deterrence lacks empiricism. Like no other field of human endeavor, nuclear deterrence is unique in demanding—absolutely compellingly—that we work out successful solutions without directly relevant experience, without experimentation. There can be no trial and error here, no real learning." The contrast to strategizing about conventional war is particularly stark to Iklé: "Curiously, when we confront the task of calculating traditional conventional military campaigns, we are far more modest than with our calculations about nuclear deterrence. In fact, the more battle experience military analysts have, the more modest they become in predicting the course of conventional war."[5]

What light, if any, can war termination in the Pacific shed on nuclear war termination today? Is the experience of Hiroshima and Nagasaki at all germane?

Two caveats are in order. First, a single case can hardly invalidate a theory. At most it can have heuristic value, suggesting alternative hypotheses that may prove vital in informing a rethinking of nuclear doctrine. Second, any comparisons across time and space make sense only if the fundamental differences are kept in mind. At least three stand out. The constituent organizations of the superpowers and their routine practices differ in detail from those of World War II. So too does the internal politics of the states involved. Above all, the military balance of power between the United States and the Soviet Union operates today in a way that is fundamentally different from the one between the United States and Japan at the end of World War II. Because at least part of the nuclear arsenals of either superpower would survive any attack intact, the possibility of further and uncontrolled nuclear retaliation will hang over all decisions and actions to end a war between them.

Yet the issue is not whether nuclear war termination would be comparable to the end of the war in the Pacific, but in what respects they may be comparable. For instance, technical means, standard operating procedures, and political arrangements for the command-and-control of military forces may have changed in detail, but could comparable problems recur? Organizational interests may differ, but would officials still be motivated by such interests—or not? The mutual vulnerability of today's superpowers to rapid devastation may call into question the relevance of the American experience at the end of World War II, but

---

[5]Fred Iklé, "The Prevention of Nuclear War in a World of Uncertainty," in U.S. Department of State, *Bulletin*, March 25, 1974, p. 314.

what about the Japanese experience, in view of its vulnerability to further atomic bombing?

While strategists have not grounded the doctrine of limited nuclear war in the concreteness of history, historical experience may suggest the need for closer scrutiny of the doctrine's central premises. Nowhere may that doctrine stand in greater need of closer scrutiny than in the way it conceives of war termination.

War Termination as Rational Choice

A major premise of theorizing about limited nuclear war is that rational calculation will guide states during war termination. That same premise was implicit in the way that officials and historians portrayed the decision to drop the atomic bomb in World War II—as the product of cool deliberation, prudent calculation, and careful weighing of all alternatives. Yet upon closer examination that description and explanation of the atomic bombings of Japan seems misconceived. No such deliberation ever took place. A reconstruction of what officials may have reckoned had they undertaken careful calculations suggests that dropping the second bomb on a Japanese city, if not the first, was a miscalculation. Indeed, that miscalculation occurred despite an extraordinary intelligence breakthrough that provided the United States with intimate knowledge of Japan's intentions, thereby reducing, though by no means eliminating, the endemic uncertainty that is the curse of calculation.

Disaggregating the state into its constituent organizations, as the organizational-process and internal-politics approaches do, calls into question the possibility of calculating costs and benefits that is so central to the rational-choice approach. Organizational processes may lead to a radical separation between the costs and benefits of the war. Some organizations may be primarily concerned with monitoring and assessing the benefits, or the attainment of war aims; others may be concerned with monitoring and assessing the costs, or casualties and destruction imposed by enemy attacks. And the very costs and benefits may themselves be organizationally defined and evaluated.

Wartime secrecy also imposed compartmentation on the policy process, which interfered with comprehensive evaluation of the alternative courses of action available to the United States for ending the war and inhibited explicit recognition of trade-offs that is the crux of rational choice. Compartmentation excluded all but a handful of officials from detailed knowledge of war plans for the bomb, widening the already radical separation between those whose job it was to develop and deploy weapons and those responsible for anticipating the consequences of American actions for relations with the enemy state. Decentralization of the ultimate choice of bombing targets further constrained rational choice. Compartmentation and decentralization are recurrent features of superpower war-making as well. The dispersal of the leadership and the disruption of internal communication in the course of a nuclear war may only further insulate diplomats and military commanders from each other and from political leaders.

Yet some strategists insist that under the pressure of nuclear war rational choice is especially likely to govern state behavior. Unlike large-scale conventional wars, Herman Kahn speculates, in which emotion can overwhelm calculation and "realism easily becomes the victim of morale" or political myth-making, "euphoria is difficult in a nuclear environment: the presence of nuclear weapons is likely to prove a powerful inducement to clear and/or cautious thinking."[6]

The premise that rational calculation will exert its compelling logic during nuclear war and that prudence will prevail has a corollary—that domestic and bureaucratic politics will have little or no effect on state behavior in nuclear war termination. In Kahn's view, the outbreak of nuclear war will insulate leaders from the strains of internal politics: "Such a war most likely would be relatively technical, run by government authorities and technicians, with little or no attention paid to the immediate problems of support from, or the morale of, the civilian population." Politics would not interfere with calculation in nuclear war: "It would probably be fought relatively coolly, and be guided by considerations of national interest little affected by propaganda or popular emotion."[7] Similarly, the unifying force of nuclear attack would overwhelm differences in organizational interests within and among the armed services, the diplomatic corps, and domestic agencies. Nuclear war would bring about internal political peace. Doctrinal differences among the armed services, for instance, would have little bearing on war termination. As Defense Secretary James Schlesinger testified at a 1974 Senate hearing, "Doctrines control the minds of men only in periods of non-emergency. They do not necessarily control the minds of men during periods of emergency."[8]

The question whether international or internal politics governs states, whether the imperatives of the balance of power or those of organiza-

---

[6]Herman Kahn, "Issues of Thermonuclear War Termination," *How Wars End: Annals of the American Academy of Political and Social Science* 392 (November 1970): 166. Rare among exponents of limited nuclear war, Kahn explicitly addresses the subject of war termination and articulates assumptions about state behavior that others leave unstated. That assumption is at least partially shared by Schelling in *Arms and Influence*, p. 20.

[7]Herman Kahn, *On Escalation: Metaphors and Scenarios* (Baltimore, 1968), p. 201.

[8]U.S. Congress, Senate, Committee on Foreign Relations, Subcommittee on Arms Control, International Law and Organizations, *Nuclear Weapons and Foreign Policy: Hearings*, 93d Cong., 2d sess., 1974, p. 160.

tional interest and domestic politics motivate leaders, may be ultimately unanswerable because of the level-of-analysis problem. But the experience of the end of the war in the Pacific suggests caution in applying rational calculation alone to thinking about war termination.

Instead of the constant pursuit of clearly defined national interests that rational-choice approaches expect of states engaged in war termination, both Japan and the United States often appeared to move in several different directions at once, as befits states whose constituent organizations sometimes do as they please and other times bargain and logroll to reach decisions—compromise decisions that are not optimal by anyone's calculations. American plans for Operation Olympic, the Japanese approach to Moscow, and the American bombing campaign in August 1945 all had this character. Internal politics at least interfered with—at most defeated—either side in applying a rational economy of force in pursuit of a coherent strategy of war termination.

The deadlock, doubts, passion, and violence that marked Japan's response to the atomic bombings belie the assumption of coolly rational choice under nuclear threat. While the intensity of Japan's divisions may be extreme, its internal conflict is by no means unique, as struggles within the German army and between it and the government during both world wars attest. Japan's protracted transition from war to peace hardly bodes well for nuclear war termination today, when time may be on no one's side.

Command-and-Control

Some strategists assert that a high degree of centralization of command-and-control over nuclear forces would persist in nuclear war and facilitate bargaining in ways that have not occurred in conventional wars of the past. They argue that the combatants would be willing and able to exercise restraint in their use of force and that each side would be able to recognize the restraint that its rival intends to show. Far from subjecting command, control, and communications to unprecedented strain, says Kahn, uncertainty and chaos, "which are very great in sustained high-intensity nuclear wars, are very much reduced in slow-motion exchanges that are limited and deliberate."[9] Organizational routines and interests would not interfere with that deliberateness. Military forces, however widely dispersed and intensely engaged they are, would do as they are told, no more and no less. Even breakdowns in communication would prove manageable, according to Kahn, who conceives of a leader or a field commander steering through the "fog of war" by "dead

[9]Kahn, *On Escalation*, p. 147.

reckoning." With some knowledge of how the war began and prevailing conditions at that time, he could estimate his initial position. "From this point forward," Kahn writes, "even though he is completely cut off from all information external to his own organization and forces, and perhaps even from much of that, he may still have enough of an idea of events and their timetable, at least in outline, and a sufficient judgment of what the other side is trying to accomplish (through knowledge of its logistics, forces, doctrine, and other constraints) to 'play' both sides hypothetically by dead reckoning—adding and correcting with whatever information comes in."[10]

The experience of the war in the Pacific raises major doubts about command, control, and communication arrangements for military forces and calls attention to the organizational and political as well as the technical aspects of these arrangements. In the use and control of military force, the connection between decision and execution can be very tenuous indeed. Getting Japanese army units to comply with orders to stand down at war's end took extraordinary political efforts by the high command, the government, and the palace—with less than complete success. Arranging a nuclear stand-down could be even more fraught with difficulty because of the greater dispersion of weapons and resulting decentralization of control that would occur once a nuclear war is under way.

Moreover, command-and-control arrangements for the atomic bombings in World War II were highly centralized by the standards of that day. Yet control ultimately devolved to the commanders on board the aircraft delivering the bombs, much to the dismay of General Groves, when the strict procedures he had devised for dropping the bomb were circumvented. Despite persistent efforts by Groves, Secretary of War Stimson, and Air Force Chief of Staff Arnold to control the bombing from Washington, the only arrangement that worked was physical possession, withholding the weapons from the theater, a precaution Groves was willing to take only after two bombs had been dropped on Japan and a third was ready for shipment for Tinian.

Much greater decentralization of control would be the rule in a nuclear war today. Once war seems imminent, some nuclear forces would be dispersed to protect them against conventional attack. The mobility and concealment that both superpowers rely on to reduce the vulnerability of their nuclear forces would inevitably lead to some devolution of control over those forces. Indeed, the flushing of nuclear weapons from their storage sites in crisis or conventional war, far from deterring nuclear war, may instead signal its imminence and trigger preemptive

[10]Ibid., p. 212.

attack. The prime targets for that attack are the weapons themselves and the communications links that connect them to central command posts. If the object of attack is to disrupt coherent retaliation, the time to strike those targets comes before dispersal has taken place. Yet once communications are disrupted and forces dispersed, central control would not be easy to restore.

At that point, standard operating procedures may well dictate whether it is possible for the war to be limited or terminated at all. Four sets of procedures are critical: intelligence collection and assessment, standing authority to release and fire nuclear weapons, nuclear rules of engagement, and prior plans and training for targeting and retargeting nuclear weapons. These procedures operate very differently during peacetime, crisis, and wartime.

Under peacetime conditions, organizational procedures are optimized to prevent unauthorized use of the weapons. Intelligence collection and assessment are centralized, subjecting detection of any unusual military activity by the other side to cross-checking against numerous other sensors. The strong presumption in assessing the threat is that no attack is under way. Only the president can authorize the use of nuclear weapons; military commanders, even if they are under attack, may not have the authority to retaliate with the nuclear forces under their command. Targeting and retargeting of weapons are subject to central direction, if not always control.

All these arrangements begin to break down in a crisis. As nuclear forces are dispersed, some of the checks on their use give way. Others loosen. Perhaps the most important peacetime check is the strong presumption that attack is utterly implausible. In crisis conditions, especially in the field, that inference of impossibility may give way to credulity about an attack. Pressures may begin to build for authority to preempt before the enemy attacks.

Once nuclear war is under way, organizational procedures are likely to undergo radical transformation. With forces dispersed undersea and on land and surviving communications networks drastically overloaded, if not interrupted, intelligence collection would become segmented and assessment decentralized. Commanders in the field may be left to draw their own conclusions about the course of the war. Perceptions and interests may vary widely from theater to theater and between the field and the national command authority, or what is left of it. Some predelegation of authority is a possibility. If, on the one hand, those who command nuclear forces in the field could not launch them without positive authorization from above, then an enemy attack that decapitates the national command authority or disconnects it from the field could effectively disarm the state. If, on the other hand, field commanders may launch with something less than positive authorization, then the likelihood of retaliation would rise as the chances of reasserting central command-and-control decline. In the United States some measure of pre-delegated authority was standard operating procedure in the mid-1960s. As one report describes arrangements then extant, "The realities of command-and-control in the nuclear age would seem to increase the necessity for prior delegation under certain carefully defined conditions. For example, in the event that a president were disabled in a surprise attack and his lawful successor were not immediately accessible, a contingency plan, containing a delegation of authority to order the use of nuclear weapons under certain conditions, would seem to be a logical and prudent precaution—perhaps necessary to national survival."[11] Some of these "carefully defined conditions" may be spelled out in rules of engagement. Commanders of ballistic missile submarines on either side, for instance, may have authorization to launch during nuclear war if they come under attack by enemy antisubmarine forces.[12]

Once nuclear war erupts and triggers organizational routines, central command-and-control may become untenable and the deft use of military force to bargain for an acceptable peace settlement may be illusory. At that point it will be difficult for either side to determine whether its rival is deliberately exercising self-restraint, whether the latest attack was authorized—indeed, whether anyone purporting to negotiate on behalf of the enemy can stop the fighting even if he agrees to do so. So Japanese officials did not attach any political significance to the sparing of Kyoto: after Hiroshima and Nagasaki how were they to know whether the cities that had yet to be struck were being deliberately spared, and why? The struggle over the official damage assessment of Hiroshima raises doubts whether any such assessment could be completed in a timely way and whether military commanders would reach the same conclusions as the political leaders. The extraordinary efforts that it took for Japan to secure compliance with surrender should stand as a warning to anyone who speaks cavalierly about waging limited nuclear war. And what if the American air forces had dropped the third atomic bomb on Tokyo, as proposed? Or if the Japanese army, insisting that Japan fight on in order to improve the terms of surrender, had had nuclear weapons at its disposal?

[11]U.S. Congressional Research Service, *Authority to Order the Use of Nuclear Weapons*, 94th Cong., 1st sess., 1975, pp. 3–4. Arrangements to protect the national command authority and its connectivity may not have improved significantly since the mid-1960s.
[12]On the escalatory risks of antisubmarine warfare, see Barry R. Posen, "Inadvertent Nuclear War?" *International Security* 7 (Fall 1982): 44. For an overview of current command-and-control practices, see Bruce Blair, *Strategic Command and Control* (Washington, D.C., 1985); Desmond Ball, "Can Nuclear War Be Controlled?" *Adelphi Papers* 169 (1981); and Paul J. Bracken, *Command and Control of Nuclear Forces* (New Haven, 1983).

Intrawar Deterrence

Even after nuclear war erupts, limited nuclear war theorists assert, deterrence would not cease to operate, but would continue to restrain the combatants from all-out attack. By their reckoning, intrawar deterrence would be reinforced by employing limited nuclear options or by holding out the threat of doing so. In the first instance, because war had broken out in spite of a deterrent threat, a single-shot demonstration might be used to restore deterrence, but once restored, deterrence would restrain further escalation by threatening still more escalation. That is the premise of the first nuclear step in NATO's flexible response, a nuclear "shot across the bow." In his classic exposition of the first use of nuclear weapons for "redress, warning, bargaining, punitive, fining, or deterrence purposes," Kahn offers this possibility: "One side is losing conventionally and decides to use nuclear weapons. It doesn't use them to damage the other side in a way that really hurts, because that could easily cause escalation to get out of control. But it might drop a bomb or two on some logistical target, such as a supply dump or railroad yard."[13] Should that shot fail to exert the desired effect, other less limited nuclear options would be needed. In other versions of the doctrine, limited nuclear options exist less to be used than to be held in abeyance, as a threat. That was the view of Schlesinger in advocating additional options at a 1974 hearing: "Should there be a breakdown of deterrence, there will be very powerful incentives on both sides to restrain the destructiveness of the use of nuclear weapons, and to come as rapidly as possible to the termination of not only the war but also the causes of war that led to, hopefully, small-scale use of nuclear weapons."[14]

The notion of "escalation dominance" combines actual use with holding it out as a threat, for purposes of both deterrence and compellence. Its exponents claim that if one side has an advantage in every category of nuclear force and an extensive array of options for their employment, then it can keep the other side from escalating, as well as terminate the war. "Strategic superiority," asserts Colin Gray, "translates into the ability to control a process of deliberate escalation in pursuit of acceptable terms for war termination."[15]

The contention that deterrence remains a viable restraint in war may need qualification in the light of the mixed experience of World War II. Neither side acted as if it felt bound by the threat of further escalation in its use of conventional force. Rather than mutual restraint, they seemed

[13]Kahn, *On Escalation*, p. 138.
[14]U.S. Senate Committee on Foreign Relations, *Nuclear Weapons and Foreign Policy*, p. 177.
[15]Colin Gray, "The Strategic Forces Triad: End of the Road?" *Foreign Affairs* 56 (July 1978): 774.

more in the grip of reciprocal escalation, ultimately spiraling into general war. The character of their interaction is captured in George Ball's warning about the risk of escalation in Vietnam: "It is in the nature of escalation that each move passes the option to the other side, while at the same time the party which seems to be losing will be tempted to keep raising the ante," Ball wrote in an October 1964 memorandum. "To the extent that the response to a move can be controlled, that move is probably ineffective. If the move is effective, it may not be possible to control—or accurately anticipate—the response."[16] During the terminal stages of a war, even if the weaker party cannot "raise the ante" it can fight on. If it is fighting with nuclear weapons, the costs of continuing can be catastrophic.

Japan was never wholly deterred from using chemical or biological weapons against China by the American threat to retaliate—at least until late in the war when Germany had surrendered and U.S. forces were drawing within striking distance of Japan proper. The United States, which may have previously been deterred from using gas by the Axis threat to retaliate against its allies, no longer considered itself so bound once the war in Europe ended—at least to judge from internal plans and discussions at war's end. The ancillary role of chemical and biological warfare in the armed services of both sides was perhaps a more significant restraint on their use than enemy deterrent threats. So remote were these forms of warfare from the organizational essence of the army—the only armed service on either side with any significant means to wage chemical or biological warfare—that the capabilities and doctrine for their use were never thoroughly integrated with the rest of the service. Yet that restraint would not be as likely to operate today inasmuch as nuclear weapons have come to be regarded as integral to the roles and missions, prestige, and doctrine of the armed services of both superpowers.

Of course, the threat of nuclear weapons did not hang over the actions of the two sides as it would in any superpower conflict today, and the war ended so soon after the atomic bombings that the Japanese had yet to absorb the full implications of the new weapon. Nevertheless, the atomic bombing in World War II did satisfy some of the conditions that strategists usually associate with intrawar deterrence. The bomb's use was wholly unanticipated. Its impact was devastating. And Truman's threat of more to come was also credible: rumors were circulating in Japanese official circles that Tokyo was the next city to be struck. Yet the shock effect on Japan was less than proponents of its use have since alleged, and not enough to shatter the political logjam in Tokyo. The

[16]George Ball, "A Light That Failed," *Atlantic* 230 (July 1972): 41.

threat of further atomic bombing did not inhibit the Japanese army from going ahead with preparations to meet the expected American bombing and invasion.

Moreover, the United States had had "escalation dominance" for more than a year without being able to compel Japan to sue for peace. Even in August 1945, after two atomic bombings and Soviet intervention, Japanese military men could still maintain that Japan's residual capacity to take its toll of American invaders gave it bargaining leverage to improve the terms of settlement of the war. Military men armed with nuclear weapons might be even more disposed to make that claim.

Escalation in the Pacific had less of the finely tuned and controlled use of force and much more inexorability about it than the exponents of limited nuclear war would like. That experience suggests that a ladder may be an appropriate metaphor for escalation, not in the sense of having discrete steps, clearly distinguishable to any would-be climber, but in three other ways: it has no clear and distinct stopping point other than the top or the bottom, it is easier to climb up than down, and the higher one rises, the greater the risk of falling off.

Military Force and Political Agreement

Most discussions of limited nuclear war assume a direct cause-and-effect relationship between the use of military force and the political settlement of the war. They seldom discuss the terms of settlement that might prove acceptable: a standstill cease-fire, restoration of the status quo ante, or a more one-sided outcome. Force, they assume, would dictate war termination without the need to translate the outcome on the battlefield into a political agreement—within governments, among allies, and between the enemy camps—to end the war. At times Kahn writes as if a victory of sorts is possible: "Once one accepts the idea that deterrence is not absolutely reliable and that it would be possible to survive a war, then [one] may be willing to buy insurance—to spend money on preparations to . . . get the best military result possible—at least 'to prevail' in some meaningful sense if [one] cannot win."[17] At other times he is prepared to settle for less: an ad hoc cease-fire is likely to follow a nuclear exchange, he asserts, because, among other things, "mutual shock reaction swamps politics."[18] Either way, the political settlement is the direct result of the military outcome. Politics would not intervene.

Yet the atomic bombings, far from setting off a shock that "swamped politics," only seemed to intensify Japan's internal struggle over war

---

[17]Herman Kahn, *On Thermonuclear War* (Princeton, N.J., 1961), p. 24.
[18]Kahn, "Issues of Thermonuclear War Termination," p. 158.

termination, a point often overlooked because of the emperor's intervention in the policy process. Bureaucratic politics, specifically interservice differences over strategy, precluded any limited and flexible use of military force for bargaining at war's end. And bureaucratic and domestic politics blocked agreement on terms.

The employment of military force, to the extent that it is the outcome of internal bargaining over strategy, may not proceed by discrete steps in one direction but may move in different directions at once: escalation on one front may accompany de-escalation on another; restraint in the use of one weapon may coincide with stepped-up use of another. So U.S. officials succeeded in halting further use of the atomic bomb after Nagasaki at the cost of lifting nearly all restrictions on the conventional bombing of Japan. Navy-air force rivalry over postwar aviation saw to it that bombing was carried out to the limit of available resources. So too Kyoto seems to have remained on the list of targets for atomic bombing, despite orders to the contrary.

To the extent that war-making is the routine output of military machines, even if leaders try to improvise options during wartime, the military organizations that must implement those options may not be willing or able to alter their standard operating procedures to accommodate improvisation. So the crew on its bombing run over Nagasaki, under orders to release only after visually sighting the precise aim point or else return to base with the atomic bomb on board, made a radar approach through heavy cloud cover and dropped the bomb way off the mark. Limited nuclear war requires organizations that have been trained for large-scale retaliation or preemption to conduct nuclear strikes with pinpoint accuracy and minimum collateral damage under wartime conditions. These organizations are not likely to. And paralysis, not creativity, would probably be the result of trying to improvise options in the heat of battle.

Compartmentation is apt to inhibit coordination and routines, to constrict flexibility. War plans are so recondite and political leaders are so absorbed in other matters that military organizations may remain free to determine which plans they implement and how, without the leaders' full awareness of the alternatives. So Truman was never fully aware of his options or of precisely what he was authorizing in approving plans for the atomic bombings. Some leaders are less informed than Truman, but try as they may, all leaders have to leave many operational details to subordinates. Few senior officials take the time to acquaint themselves with the intricacies of weapon systems and targeting plans, not to mention how these details might affect the limitation and termination of nuclear war—in short, to master what Harry Truman or Henry Stimson never did. War-gaming may be too important to leave to the strategists.

The doctrine of mutual assured destruction, whether or not it was ever government policy, may have led strategists astray by deflecting attention from what happens if deterrence fails and nuclear war breaks out, but doctrines of limited nuclear war have taken them no farther down the path of war termination. The experience of war termination in the Pacific raises troubling questions about those doctrines. Yet whatever doctrine the superpowers adopt, it is still essential for them to prepare for limiting and terminating nuclear war, should it ever occur. Indeed, war termination should be the starting point of any reconsideration of doctrine under current conditions of nuclear interdependence.

Terminating War Today: Some Hypotheses

Scrutiny of the behavior of the United States and Japan at the end of World War II suggests the need for much skepticism about prospects for terminating nuclear war once it begins. Yet the slim likelihood of stopping a nuclear war does not diminish the need to prepare to do so. There is no chance of success unless the difficulties are anticipated in advance. That is conceivable only by placing organizational and political questions at the center of any rethinking of war termination.

The Politics of War Aims

Karl von Clausewitz, who formulated a rational economy of warfare, reasoned that because war "is controlled by its political object" the value of that object should determine the measure of sacrifice by which it is purchased. [19] That dictated, above all, that the means employed should follow from and be limited by the ends that the warring parties sought. But what objective could sustain the full measure of sacrifice in nuclear war? Even if war aims are supposed to be what a war is about, not all wars begin as the result of well-defined aims. In deliberate or premeditated wars, the war aims of the belligerents, or at least of the aggressor, are likely to be specified in advance. But not all wars are premeditated. Many are preventive or preemptive. Premeditated war occurs when states are not deterred by the expectation that the cost of achieving their ends through war will exceed the benefits. Yet the threats posed by deterrents may not suffice to prevent war. Instead, they may provoke it. So it was in December 1941, when Japanese leaders believed war with the United States to be inevitable. Under that condition, a U.S. military buildup and oil embargo only spurred the Japanese to war sooner rather than later, when they believed they would be relatively worse off mili-

---

[19] Clausewitz, *On War*, p. 92.

tarily. So too in August 1914 alliance obligations undertaken to deter war helped bring it about, and mobilization ordered as a precaution against aggression prompted preemption once war came to be seen as imminent. Under present-day conditions of nuclear interdependence, as in the operation of a conventional balance of power, the possibility of preventive or preemptive war coexists with that of premeditated war.

Well-defined war aims can facilitate mutual adjustment, whether unilaterally or by negotiation, as a way of ending the war. In the absence of those aims, war may be more difficult to terminate. In a preventive or preemptive war, the war aims of the belligerents are less likely to have been spelled out and understood in advance than in a premeditated war. So in 1941 the Japanese belief in the inevitability of war with the United States arose more as a consequence of social psychology than of rational calculation. That belief does presume that the interests or goals of the two sides are antagonistic, but it need not presume that the attacker's aims were well-defined in advance. Insofar as Japan's were, they had more to do with holding onto gains in China and expanding into Southeast Asia and elsewhere to secure critical raw materials in anticipation of an attack by the United States. Regardless of the validity of Japan's beliefs, the preventive rather than premeditated nature of the war meant that Japan's war aims vis-a-vis the United States were ill-defined. Trying to define, and hence to limit, war aims proved difficult once the war began.

In 1914 too, Russia and Serbia, and in turn Russia and Austro-Hungary as well as France and Germany and ultimately England and Germany, all had antagonistic aims. During the crisis of July and August some leaders were even prepared to run the risk of local war, perhaps even of world war, to achieve those aims, but none intended to start a world war deliberately. Once war seemed imminent, however, the interaction of deterrent threats, alliance obligations, and precautionary mobilizations sparked preemption. Having anticipated at most a limited war in the Balkans and not a major war involving all the powers in Europe, the contenders lacked war aims commensurate with the new circumstances. As the war expanded, so did their war aims.

In 1945 unconditional surrender was an object worthy of all-out war, commanding an ever-greater expenditure of lives and resources, but all-out war may culminate in mutual exhaustion, especially once nuclear weapons come into play. By its very indiscriminateness the Bomb destroys its own rationale. Its sheer destructiveness may wipe out any meaningful distinction between winning and losing and invalidate the very idea of military strategy as the efficient employment of force to attain the state's aims. The introduction of nuclear weapons turns means-ends calculation, the crux of a rational economy of force, into an absurdity. At that point a war between the superpowers could turn into a pure test of resolve, but insofar as it did it could become endless—both aimless and limitless. That violates the basic premise of Clausewitz and his followers that war is a bounded form of violence. Once all bounds are crossed, war degenerates into sheer violence, into slaughter, which negates its very essence, as Clausewitz understood it. By imparting a preoccupation with saving face, nuclear war could generate its own ends as well as means. Both the indefiniteness of war aims and their inherent expansiveness makes nuclear war difficult to limit.

This logic has led some to call for a "convention" of victory and defeat in nuclear war in order to facilitate its termination.[20] Unconditional surrender is one such convention. In comparison with what Thomas Schelling calls "unconditional extermination," the convention of unconditional surrender does at least hold out some prospect of sparing both sides from gratuitous death and destruction by giving war an end.[21] But that end may well be too one-sided for nuclear war termination between the superpowers. In those circumstances it makes sense to adopt what might be called the "Aiken convention" after Vermont's Republican Senator George Aiken, who proposed that the best way for the United States to stop fighting in Vietnam was to declare victory and go home. Yet that convention may favor the side that shoots first in nuclear war by codifying the status quo on the battlefield. More fundamentally, the call for a convention of nuclear war termination only begs the question of how internal agreement could be reached on such a convention.

Internal political logic diverges from rational logic in thinking about war aims. By rational choice, states sue for peace as soon as the marginal costs exceed the marginal benefits of continuing the struggle. Yet instead of letting bygones be bygones and comparing marginal benefits to marginal costs, as rational calculation dictates, internal politics may demand recompense for past suffering. And no object may satisfy those who have endured nuclear war. War aims are often an expression of both bureaucratic compromise and public propaganda. Once spelled out, they provide a rationale for fighting according to the programs of some organizations and not others. Once promulgated, they serve as a rallying cry to the populace and an inspiration to the troops. Consequently, they resist softening. Only the U.S. army's strategy of invasion seemed equal to the task of compelling Japan's unconditional surrender, so the navy, seeking victory through blockade and bombing, favored moderating U.S. war aims in the Potsdam Declaration. But the attempt to qualify the unconditionality of surrender meant undoing a bureaucratic bargain in the face of expected popular outcry.

[20]Ian Clark, *Limited Nuclear War* (Princeton, N.J., 1982), pp. 102, 198.
[21]Schelling, *Arms and Influence*, p. 126.

Domestic divisions are certain to arise between those prepared for further sacrifice to achieve what they define as peace with honor and those prepared to reach a settlement. That settlement may satisfy some, but it may leave others with a thirst for vengeance—against domestic as well as foreign enemies. Anticipating adverse public or parliamentary reaction, politicians may be reluctant to compromise abroad, lest they be compromised at home. Even leaders with victory in their grasp may be chary of magnanimity for fear of domestic repercussions. So Truman and Byrnes, potential rivals for the presidency, insisted on unconditional surrender and refused to concede any public commitment to spare the emperor, while the Japanese cabinet refused to settle for anything less than that. Domestic politics made a settlement in the Pacific difficult to arrange.

While politicians seldom want to be seen opposing peace, the terms and conditions under which they are willing to accept it usually prolong wars. Conflicting political pressures account for the seeming contradiction. Governments tend to be deeply and passionately divided over the wisdom of any softening of war aims. So do publics. Cross-pressured by colleagues, anticipating adverse public and parliamentary reaction whichever way they turn, political leaders are inclined to float their concessions on a tide of threats. But moving in two directions at once in order to conceal the softening of terms from their own bureaucrats and publics and hold their governing coalitions together, they may only succeed in signalling intransigence when moderation was intended, or vice versa. So the Truman administration hinted at keeping the emperor in place to authorize the surrender and occupation at the same time that it stepped up the conventional bombing of Japan. So too the Nixon administration ordered the Christmas bombing of Hanoi to cover its acceptance of the Paris peace accords in 1972. Worse yet, states may take refuge in vagueness, as Japan did in approaching Moscow. The consequence in either case may be to confuse the other side, especially when the coordination of diplomatic and military action is loose, as in nuclear war.

Radical instability in the politics of war aims makes it imperative to spell out war aims well in advance of the war. This may be done unilaterally, but is best accomplished in cooperation with allies and the rival superpower. Regardless of the advantage it may give to the initiator of a war, the only war aim likely to pose any feasible limit to a nuclear war is that of stopping the war as soon as it starts—a cease-fire in place. A public declaration to that end might be of some utility.

The Politics of Negotiations

During a nuclear war it may be more difficult to arrange negotiations than to promulgate unilateral changes in war aims, but negotiations may be a politically less treacherous path to reaching a mutual accommodation. One possibility is to open talks while deferring disputes on the terms to be offered. The struggle to devise a negotiating position can thereby serve as an action-forcing process for forging internal agreement. Negotiations too can sometimes allow unilateral concessions to be made in private, postponing public scrutiny until they are disclosed as part of a package settlement along with enemy quid pro quos and a cessation of hostilities. But if negotiations do provide a temporary cover for softening war aims, they cannot substitute for the will to make concessions. Sooner or later, political leaders at war must face up to the need for compromise with the enemy. As Japan's fate suggests, the longer they wait, the heavier the war's toll. Use of nuclear weapons only adds to the pressure of time on both sides.

Negotiating without first reaching internal agreement on aims has another drawback. Peace feelers—quasi-official contacts with the enemy—can serve purposes other than advancing a settlement. Such contacts afford the opportunity to gather intelligence, especially to probe for political divisions within the enemy camp and to wage psychological warfare, exploiting those divisions to disrupt the enemy's war effort. Individuals who are eager to secure favorable postwar treatment for themselves and their causes may also initiate contact on their own. Such contacts are less likely to earn their initiators a Nobel Peace Prize than a death sentence for treason, sometimes deservedly so: however well intentioned, they may impede rather than expedite peacemaking.

Distinguishing bona fide negotiating approaches from ploys is difficult in the best of circumstances, but especially when the initiating party has no concrete and authoritative offer to make or is internally divided over the purpose of its démarche, as Japan was in its approach to Moscow. Given what the warring parties are already doing to each other, it is easy for the recipient to assume the worst. Nuclear war may only deepen the paranoia. Under those circumstances, talks can quickly degenerate into a propaganda exercise as each side tries to sow division in the enemy camp while consolidating its own ranks.

Nothing as formal and complex as a peace treaty need be negotiated in order to terminate a nuclear war. Agreement on a nuclear cease-fire might suffice. Yet some political quid pro quos could prove necessary, especially if a conventional cease-fire is to accompany the end of nuclear hostilities. If nuclear war termination is to be accomplished expeditiously, the political elements of any truce might have to be kept as simple as possible. They could take the form of a return to the status quo ante bellum or a standstill cease-fire, perhaps with minor adjustments on a reciprocal basis—swaps of territory to rectify defensible borders, exchanges of prisoners of war, and the like. Settlements outside the main theater of war might come later, theater by theater. Yet these mutual accommodations might not slake a popular thirst for vengeance—or at least the desire to see those responsible brought to justice. If so, the war may go on.

Nuclear war only compounds the difficulties of negotiating. Even conventional war tends to impede normal diplomatic intercourse, but nuclear war may hinder the reestablishment of channels even after they are disrupted. It puts a premium on direct exchanges between capitals, compared to third-party mediation or direct talks at a neutral site. Direct talks between capitals make fewer demands on communications facilities that, if unavailable or disrupted, could interfere with rapid, high-fidelity exchanges between the belligerents. One way to communicate directly is by hot line, but only if it survives or can be reconstituted. If not, open radio or telegraph communications may be possible, although their very openness can be a drawback, as Japan's diplomats learned to their distress: those opposed to a settlement can listen in and try to disrupt the negotiations. Publics and allies would also be privy to the talks, which might compel both sides to play to multiple audiences, much to the confusion of their interlocutors. That might interfere with delicate efforts to probe enemy positions and communicate nuanced proposals. While war termination may be politically too sensitive to conduct through open or formal channels, private back-channel communications, employing go-betweens like Prince Konoye who have personal ties to the leaders of the warring states, may be technically too demanding to arrange in the midst of a superpower nuclear war.[22]

Nevertheless, the venue and medium is less likely to prove an insuperable obstacle to negotiations than sorting out signals from noise. Discerning what constitutes an authoritative message from the other side involves more than establishing diplomatic bona fides: in nuclear war no one, however well connected and well intentioned, may be in a position to deliver on commitments and to coordinate diplomatic with military moves. Command-and-control, haphazard under the best of circumstances, may be all but impossible in the chaos of nuclear war. Leaders are seldom in a position to act alone. They have colleagues to consult and consensus to crystallize on matters of life and death for their governments, if not their nation and themselves. Relocation of officials

[22]E.g., in the Cuban missile crisis, while much of the negotiations were conducted in the clear, over the public airways, the most politically sensitive arrangements were handled through more private back channels: William Knox, president of Westinghouse International, Yuri Zhukov, a confidant of Nikita Khrushchev's, and John Scali, ABC's State Department correspondent, were used as extrabureaucratic emissaries, while President Kennedy entrusted the most delicate contacts with Soviet Ambassador Anatoly Dobrynin to his brother, Attorney General Robert Kennedy (Allison, *Essence of Decision*, pp. 124–25, 220–22, 228–30).

to dispersed or mobile shelters and dislocation of communications might make allied governments hard to find and even harder to deliver. Noncompliance, internal resistance, even incipient coups are all possibilities, as Japan's experience at war's end suggests.

The Politics of Military Force

Deploying new weapons for the purpose of waging limited nuclear war makes no sense unless their use can be shown to facilitate not only limits in the waging of war, but also its conclusion. It is at this point that the very idea of limited nuclear war suffers from terminal vagueness. Nuclear war can, at least in theory, be limited in four general ways:

In geographic scope. Nuclear war can be confined to the immediate battlefield, to lines of supply and communication beyond the battlefield, or to a particular theater of war—for instance, Central Europe.
In choice of targets. The targets to be struck can include only the nuclear forces of the other side, other purely military targets, or targets with some military potential that are not purely military in nature.
In intensity. The firepower or megatonnage expended and the rate of fire per hour or per day can be restrained.
In duration. The war can be stopped altogether within a reasonably short period of time.

In practice, however, it is difficult to specify any limits that are likely to hold, and it is even harder to see how limiting the geographic scope, targets, and intensity of the war would facilitate limiting its duration. Nuclear weapons are inherently indiscriminate, compared with weapons of past wars. And military machines have always been too unwieldy to make fine distinctions. Consequently, it is all but impossible to design discriminating nuclear attacks that the other side could clearly distinguish as such—to escalate in ways that unambiguously signal the intent to go only so far and no further. Moreover, many of the weapons more suitable for use in discriminating attacks are also the most threatening to the other side's nuclear forces and command-and-control—the very weapons likely to trigger preemption in a crisis, to set off nuclear escalation rather than control it.

Nuclear strategists have focused their attention on a few saliencies that might serve as the basis for limiting escalation: avoiding the enemy homeland altogether; no cities; striking purely military targets with low-yield weapons designed to minimize collateral damage; or confining attacks to the battlefield through the use of so-called tactical nuclear weapons—those with ranges below 100 kilometers. Yet during World War II in the Pacific, the only saliency that proved at all effective was a complete prohibition on certain classes of weapons—chemical and biological agents. Even that limitation did not prove completely effective, nor did it shorten the duration of the war.

That experience suggests that only saliencies of the utmost clarity and paramount importance may stand out enough to signal war termination once nuclear war erupts. Two saliencies may meet these demanding specifications. One is to spare the other side's command, control, and communications, including its national capital, from attack. The second is to stop all nuclear attacks everywhere as soon as possible. A temporary pause would have to be prolonged enough to provide a decent interval for moving toward war termination. The pause eventually might become permanent if appropriate political arrangements can be made. A clear stopping point might be of marginal help—the eleventh hour of the eleventh day of the eleventh month, for example—to facilitate coordination within as well as cooperation between the two sides.

Even so, the two sides would have to live with considerable ambiguity, especially if their capabilities for monitoring a nuclear cease-fire have been degraded during the war. A cease-fire would not likely include nuclear disarmament, because stacking nuclear arms may jeopardize the reestablishment of a balance of power, deterring the two sides from resuming hostilities and other states from taking advantage of the superpowers' predicament. Procedures for degenerating alerted forces—for instance, returning aircraft and mobile missiles to base—may be difficult to arrange in ways that do not increase susceptibility to attack in a one-sided way. Nuclear forces could still be subject to attack if a conventional cease-fire does not coincide with the nuclear standdown. Calling off antisubmarine warfare activities that threaten the reserve forces of the enemy in missile-carrying submarines may be especially difficult to arrange.

Yet the two saliencies most useful for war termination might be the most difficult to arrange politically because they offer the greatest military advantages, however marginal or temporary, to the side that ignores them. The very same communications links that would permit enemy leaders to exert command-and-control over their forces in moving to a nuclear stand-down could also transmit orders to fire. Consequently, just as the air force planned to target Tokyo for the next atomic bombing, military planners might press to execute attacks that decapitate the other side and segment enemy command-and-control arrangements in order to prevent coordinated counterattacks. If the difficulties that Japan experienced with compliance are at all instructive, doing so might jeopardize any chance of war termination. Similarly, field commanders might be unwilling to accede to a total cease-fire, fearing that the other side will take advantage of the lull to conduct a damage assessment, reconstitute and retarget its forces, and plan, if not launch, a renewed attack. Short of a total halt, however, other stopping points may be so ambiguous and nuclear forces so difficult to restrain that nuclear war termination could prove impossible.

If limits on war require stable points in the fighting, the dynamic of war makes such points hard to discern and harder to preserve. To the degree that states conceive of war as a competition in risk-taking, they may deliberately want to cross thresholds or saliencies of violence in ways that heighten risks, that raise doubts about future limits, in enemy minds. What makes a saliency salient and a limit limiting is no more than the expectations of the two sides, expectations that are notoriously slippery under the stress of war. Those expectations must also comport with organizational routines, a condition especially difficult to satisfy during nuclear war, according to Schelling: "Stable stopping points must not only be physically possible, in terms of momentum, gravity, and fuel supplies, and consistent with command arrangements, communications, the speed of decisions, and the information available; they must also be reasonably secure against double cross or resumption of the war."[23] War may have more in common with a commodity futures market than a grandfather clock when it comes to settling on stable stopping points.

Because of the division of labor within states, the use of force most directly involves those who may be least disposed to discontinue it—field commanders. Through them pass most reports on the situation at the front. From them come recommendations on the strategy to follow, which political leaders need not accept but dare not ignore. On them rests the ultimate responsibility for faithful execution of decisions to employ military force and the decision to lay down arms. Mediating between the field commanders and the political leadership is the military high command or general staff. If the Japanese experience is typical and the chiefs of staff back the field commanders, no armed service would be willing to call for de-escalation until its capacity for war-making is all but exhausted.

To the extent that field commanders prefer to use every weapon at their disposal rather than see their forces suffer even a temporary tactical reverse, acquiring more and more forces and options for waging limited nuclear war may be perverse. Moreover, the greater the variety of nuclear forces, the greater the pressures to diversify and enlarge the attack. Chiefs of staff may be unwilling to countenance a rival service's gaining authorization to use nuclear weapons unless they can secure it for their own service. "Since disputes about targets," Henry Kissinger once ob-

[23]Schelling, *Arms and Influence*, pp. 106–7, 157–58, 208.

[308]

served, "are usually settled by addition—by permitting each service to destroy what it considers essential to its mission—limited nuclear war fought in this manner may well become indistinguishable from all-out war."[24]

But not all the armed services are likely to oppose de-escalation with equal vigor. What concerns service leaders is not so much the level and intensity of force employed as the particular form that force takes and the strategy for its use. Institutionally and doctrinally, generals and admirals seldom see eye to eye on strategy. At war's end, organizational concerns may come to the fore. On the losing side, as morale begins to crumble, the armed services may resist stacking arms without some assurance of peace with honor, but they may also care about organizational maintenance, about retaining some forces in being after the war. So, as the Japanese navy saw its forces depleted it was left with little to fight for, as well as with, from late 1944 on. On the winning side, as the services gird for postwar scarcity each may push for a strategy that strengthens its claims to credit for victory and hence for a greater share of future resources. So the American navy and army air forces tried to show off their bombing. Generals and admirals may plan for the last war, but they fight for capabilities for the next one. Politicians who appreciate that may be able to play one service off against another in order to inform their strategic choices. Those who do not will permit the services to logroll and pursue several competing military strategies at once, only adding to the gratuitous violence and suffering of war. That was the case in the run up to Operation Olympic, the conventional and atomic bombing that preceded the planned invasion of Japan. Although the effects of organizational interests on the waging and limiting of nuclear war is difficult to foresee with any assurance, the desire to play a role in nuclear warfare and to secure peace with honor might add to escalatory pressures. The concern for organizational maintenance would make the services reluctant to initiate nuclear attack unless enemy preemption seems imminent, but once the war is under way that concern might reassert itself much too late to limit the war. In World War II, restraints on chemical and biological warfare were reinforced because military organizations did not deem these weapons part of their essential roles and missions or critical to their prestige. Taking nuclear weapons out of the hands of the army, navy, and air force, and assigning them to a new low-prestige military organization might have a similarly beneficial effect today.

Along with service interests, organizational routines may well hamper nuclear war termination. Habituated to carry out their own war-making

[24]Henry A. Kissinger, *Necessity for Choice* (New York, 1960), p. 82.

programs, the armed services tend to do more of the same day after day. And operational reflexes can often overwhelm strategic calculations in the mind-set of senior officers, especially field commanders, in the midst of the fighting. A mundane example is General Curtis LeMay's response to a request from his chief of staff, General H. H. Arnold, for a planning date for the end of the war with Japan: "Well, we had been so busy fighting it that we hadn't thought about a date for the end but we went back to some of the charts we had shown him about the rate of activity, the targets we were hitting, and it was completely evident that we were running out of targets along in September and by October there wouldn't be much to work on except possibly railroads or something of that sort. So we felt that if there were no targets left in Japan, certainly there wouldn't be much war left."[25] LeMay chose a date in October, preceding the army's planning date of November 1 for its invasion of Kyushu. Such habits of mind do more than reinforce interservice rivalry, however. They identify war termination with the physical destruction of the other side and ignore the political nature of a decision to sue for peace. It is a confusion that could make nuclear war termination impossible.

Those who think about ending wars often treat the enemy like a rival boxer to be pummeled into submission rather than like a politically unstable coalition to be threatened, cajoled, and helped to reach some mutual accommodation. At their worst, nuclear attacks could jeopardize war termination by destroying the very officials who can coalesce and authorize a settlement and the communications network that links them to each other and to the armed forces in the field. At best, nuclear attacks might do little to facilitate war termination efforts beyond reminding everyone involved what will happen if those efforts fail.

Peace-making, like war-making, begins at home. It requires building and sustaining a winning coalition, both in and out of government, in favor of ending a war with a minimum of gratuitous death and destruction. It takes consummate political will and skill to moderate war aims, restrain the use of military force, and open negotiations with a view toward mutual accommodation. Either side can take the first step on its own, but further progress requires cooperation between the belligerents. All too often, however, the political risk of unilateral steps toward cooperation instills caution in leaders. They see their own options as limited, while they attribute freedom of action to the other side. They prefer to wait on events, hoping for the enemy to make the first move, or else try to compel it to surrender. In the meantime, however, military plans may only expand war aims and foreclose peace talks. In nuclear

[25]Giovannitti and Freed, *Decision to Drop the Bomb*, pp. 35–36.

war between superpowers there is little prospect of victory and no place for Micawberism.

Deterrence alone cannot prevent nuclear war any more than it can terminate it. Indeed, some steps taken to bolster deterrence may reduce the likelihood of premeditated war only at a greater risk of preemptive or preventive war. The overall likelihood of war can be reduced only by increasing military stability—in particular, by cooperative efforts, negotiated and otherwise, to reduce the vulnerability of both sides' nuclear forces to attack. Conciliation is also needed to defuse, if not resolve, the political differences that could give rise to perceptions that war is imminent or inevitable. As difficult as cooperation between the superpowers seems today, once war breaks out, it may be too late to cooperate. The difficulties of imposing any restraints on nuclear war strongly suggest that the best time to stop it is before it begins.

Appendix:
Organizational Interests in the United States and Japan in 1945

DEPARTMENT/ SUBORGANIZATION	ORGANIZATIONAL INTERESTS*
	United States
War	
Army	Preserve its organizational essence (ground combat) Capability/Budget (peacetime standing army, Universal Military Training) Autonomy to perform roles and missions (occupation)
Army Air Forces	Autonomy (separate service from army) Organizational essence (strategic bombing) Capability (70–wing air force, hence conventional bombing)
MED	Organizational essence (basic research) Budget (postwar government funding on multiyear basis, $1 billion annually) Autonomy (freedom of inquiry, science, technology for its own sake)
Navy	Budget share Roles and missions (protect carrier aviation) Autonomy (no unification) Capabilities (300 ships, enough to defeat all navies combined and to project "sea-air power" around the globe, using flush-deck carriers, overseas bases)
State Department	Organizational essence (representation, reporting, avoid risk of negotiating peace settlement with Japan)
Far Eastern Affairs	Organizational essence (represent Japan vs. represent China)

Department/ suborganization	Organizational interests*
Public Affairs	Organizational essence (maintain public support for conduct of U.S. foreign relations)
Congressional Liaison	Organizational essence (maintain congressional support for conduct of U.S. foreign relations)

Japan	
Palace	Organizational essence (preserve the throne) Capability (no punishment of emperor)
Army	Morale (peace with honor: orderly surrender, self-disarmament, limited occupation, right of supreme command, limited cession of seized territory)
Navy	Autonomy (no unification) Capabilities (preserve surface fleet, naval aviation) Roles and missions ("special attack" forces)
Foreign Ministry	Organizational essence (preserve essential mission of negotiations by avoiding lead role in unsuccessful negotiations) Autonomy (preserve and restore freedom of action in conduct of reporting and negotiating)

*Listed in rank order of priority. Each organization seeks all its interests simultaneously, except when interests are in conflict, and then sequentially according to rank order.

SOURCES

United States

Army

On the organizational essence of the U.S. Army and its persistence to this day, *Infantry Journal*, "How Much Infantry?" February 1945, pp. 6–7; William R. Lucas and Raymond W. Dawson, *The Organizational Politics of Defense* (Pittsburgh: International Studies Association, 1974), pp. 28–29; Brian M. Jenkins, *The Unchangeable War* (Santa Monica, Calif.: Rand, 1972). On its peacetime capabilities, budgets, and budget shares, Michael S. Sherry, *Preparing for the Next War* (New Haven: Yale University Press, 1977), pp. 4, 78, 105–8; Demetrios Caraley, *The Politics of Military Unification* (New York: Columbia University Press, 1966), pp. 58–63, 66–69, 71; U.S. Congress, House, Select Committee on Postwar Military Policy, *Proposal to Establish a Single Department of Armed Forces: Hearings*, 78th Cong., 2d sess., 1944, Part II, p. 575; Vincent Davis, *Postwar Defense Policy and the U.S. Navy, 1943–1945* (Chapel Hill: University of North Carolina Press,

1966), p. 151; George C. Marshall, "Summary of Biennial Report of the Chief of Staff of the Army to the Secretary of War, September 1, 1945," in Walter Millis, ed., *The War Reports of General of the Army George C. Marshall, General of the Army H. H. Arnold and Fleet Admiral Ernest J. King* (Philadelphia: Lippincott, 1947), p. 294; Perry McCoy Smith, *The Air Force Plans for Peace, 1943–1945* (Baltimore: Johns Hopkins University Press, 1970), p. 67; U.S. Congress, Senate, Committee on Military Affairs, *Department of Armed Forces, Department of Military Security: Hearings on S. 84 and S. 1482*, 79th Cong., 1st sess., 1945, pp. 42–43, 50–52, 56–59, 164–65, 262–64. On autonomy in running the occupation of Japan and resulting manpower constraints, Henry H. Arnold, *Global Mission* (New York: Harper, 1949), p. 560.

Army Air Forces

On autonomy and its relationship to the organizational essence of the army air force, strategic bombing as opposed to close-air support, and other tactical roles and missions, Smith, *Air Force Plans for Peace*, pp. 15–19, 25, 27–28; Lucas and Dawson, *The Organizational Politics of Defense*, pp. 19–23; Curtis LeMay with MacKinlay Kantor, *Mission with LeMay* (Garden City, N.Y.: Doubleday, 1965), pp. 373, 376–77; Arnold, *Global Mission*, pp. 562–63; Senate Committee on Military Affairs, *Department of Armed Forces, Department of Military Security: Hearings*, pp. 68–69, 74, 76, 232–33, 272–73, 292–95, 301, 511, 548–51; memorandum by Colonel S. F. Griffin, "Future Trends in Air Fighting," November 25, 1944, Arnold Papers, Box 115 (Japan), SAS 385, Library of Congress. On the gradual assertion of autonomy, Wesley F. Craven and James Lea Cate, *The Pacific: Matterhorn to Nagasaki, June 1944 to August 1945*, vol. 5 of U.S. Air Force, Historical Division of Research Studies, *The Army Air Forces in World War II* (Chicago: University of Chicago Press, 1953), pp. 530–32, 679–85; Wesley F. Craven and James L. Cate, *Men and Planes*, vol. 6 of U.S. Air Force, Historical Division of Research Studies, *The Army Air Forces in World War II* (Chicago: University of Chicago Press, 1955), pp. 48–49; Caraley, *Politics of Military Unification*, pp. 16–18; William D. Leahy, *I Was There* (New York: McGraw-Hill, 1950), p. 261. On postwar capabilities, Arnold, *Global Mission*, pp. 536, 586–87; Smith, *Air Force Plans for Peace, 1943–1945*, pp. 67–72, 81, 88; Senate Committee on Military Affairs, *Department of Armed Services, Department of Military Security: Hearings*, pp. 301, 308–9.

Manhattan Engineering District (MED)

On the organizational essence of the MED, defined by scientist administrators, Warner R. Schilling, "Scientists, Foreign Policy, and Politics," *American Political Science Review* 56 (June 1962): 294–95; Robert Gilpin, *American Scientists and Nuclear Weapons Policy* (Princeton, N.J.: Princeton University Press, 1962), chaps. 1 and 10; J. Stefan Dupré and Sanford A. Lakoff, *Science and the Nation* (Englewood Cliffs, N.J.: Prentice-Hall, 1962), chap. 6; Dan Greenberg, *The Politics of Pure Science* (New York: New American Library, 1968). On government funding for peacetime research and justifying wartime expenditures, the works cited in note 44 to Chapter 4, above; Karl T. Compton, "Educational Effects and Implications of the Defense Program," *Science*, October 17, 1941, pp. 368–69; Vannevar Bush, *Science: The Endless Frontier* (Washington, D.C.: National Science Foundation Office of Research and Development, 1960), pp. 18, 31–33; Richard C. Hewlett and Oscar E. Anderson, Jr., *The New World, 1939–1945*, vol. 1 of *A History of the United States Atomic Energy Commission* (University Park: Pennsylvania State University Press, 1962), pp. 18–19, 38–43, 322–25; Vannevar Bush, *Pieces of the Action* (New York: Morrow, 1970), pp. 31, 42–43, 58–60; Committee on Postwar Policy, [Tolman] Report of December 28, 1944, MED, TS of Interest to Groves, Folder 3 RG 77, National Archives. On the MED's remoteness from the army's organizational essence, and its quest for autonomy and freedom of inquiry, Arthur H. Compton, *Atomic Quest* (New York: Oxford University Press, 1956), p. 283; J. Robert Oppenheimer, Talk to the Association of Los Alamos Scientists, November 2, 1945, *New York Times Book Review*, May 11, 1980, p. 9; Leslie R. Groves, *Now It Can Be Told* (New York: Harper 1962), pp. 3–4, 140; U.S. Congress, Senate, Special Committee on Atomic Energy, *Atomic Energy: Hearings Pursuant to S. Res. 179*, 79th Cong., 1st sess., 1945, Part II, pp. 14–15, 63–64, 290–95; Martin J. Sherwin, *A World Destroyed* (New York: Knopf, 1975), pp. 53, 56–60.

Navy

On the threat to the navy's budget share, the move to a "balanced force" within the navy, and the resulting competition for budget shares among surface, carrier, and submarine navies, Davis, *Postwar Defense Policy and the U.S. Navy, 1943–1945*, pp. 64, 112–14, 122–24, 132–33, 164–65, 194–97, 202, 228–29, 240–41; Robert G. Albion and Robert H. Connery, *Forrestal and the Navy* (New York: Columbia University Press, 1962), p. 151; Leahy diary, March 22, 1945, Library of Congress; U.S. Congress, House, Committee on Naval Affairs, *Composition of the Post-War Navy: Hearings on H. Con. Res. 80*, 79th Cong., 1st sess., 1945, pp. 1188–89, 1196–97; Senate Committee on Military Affairs, *Department of Armed Services, Department of Military Security: Hearings*, pp. 276, 584–85; Smith, *Air Force Plans for Peace*, pp. 19, 59–61. On the rise of carrier aviation within the navy and its response to the threat from outside, Davis, *Postwar Defense Policy and the U.S. Navy*, pp. 32, 42–45, 126–27, 188–91; 203–7, 217–19, 230–32; Senate Committee on Military Affairs, *Department of Armed Services, Department of Military Security: Hearings*, pp. 88–89, 276, 295–96, 298, 308–9, 504–7; Leahy, *I Was There*, p. 261; H. H. Arnold, "Second Report of the Commanding General of the Army Air Force to the Secretary of War," February 27, 1945, in Millis, *War Reports*, pp. 414, 416; Caraley, *Politics of Military Unification*, pp. 80, 82–83; Albion and Connery, *Forrestal and the Navy*, pp. 256, 260; U.S. Congress, Senate, Committee on Appropriations, *Navy Department Appropriations Bill for 1946*, 79th Cong., 1st sess., 1945, Part I, pp. 4–5; Sherry, *Preparing for the Next War*, p. 218. On opposition to unification, Davis, *Postwar Defense Policy and the U.S. Navy, 1943–1945*, pp. 141–46; Leahy, *I Was There*, p. 371; Caraley, *Politics of Military Unification*, p. 28, chap. 4; U.S. Congress, House, *Proposal to Establish a Single Department of Armed Forces*, 78th Cong., 2d sess., 1944, pp. 62, 75; Senate Committee on

Military Affairs, *Department of Armed Services, Department of Military Security: Hearings,* pp. 392, 570–71. On capabilities, Raymond Dennett, "The U.S. Navy and Dependent Areas," *Far Eastern Review,* April 25, 1945, pp. 93–95; William R. Louis, *Imperialism at Bay* (New York: Oxford University Press, 1978), pp. 259–68, 366, 373–77; Walter Millis, ed., *The Forrestal Diaries* (New York: Viking, 1951), pp. 8, 24.

State Department

On the organizational essence of the State Department, as defined by the Foreign Service, and on resistance to specialization and more technical roles and missions, *The Memoirs of Cordell Hull* (New York: Macmillan, 1948), I: 188–89; Charles W. Thayer, *Diplomat* (New York: Harper, 1959), p. 81; Robert D. Schulzinger, *The Making of the Diplomatic Mind* (Middletown, Conn.: Wesleyan University Press, 1975), pp. 101–3, 142–43; Dean Acheson, *Present at the Creation* (New York: Norton, 1969), p. 43; John Morton Blum, ed., *The Price of Vision: The Diary of Henry A. Wallace, 1942–1946* (Boston: Houghton Mifflin, 1973), pp. 419–20. On specialization by country desk and resulting differences of interest in the Office of Far Eastern Affairs, see James C. Thomson, Jr., "The Role of the Department of State," in Dorothy Borg and Shumpei Okamoto, eds., *Pearl Harbor As History* (New York: Columbia University Press, 1973), pp. 81–106; Hugh de Santis, *The Diplomacy of Silence* (Chicago: University of Chicago Press, 1980), pp. 15–16, 76–77; Joseph C. Grew, *Turbulent Era,* ed. Walter Johnson (Boston: Houghton Mifflin, 1952), II: 953–55; and "A New Far Eastern Policy? Japan Versus China," *Amerasia,* June 9, 1944, pp. 179–80.

JAPAN

Palace

On the role of the palace bureaucracy, David A. Titus, *Palace and Politics in Prewar Japan* (New York: Columbia University Press, 1974).

Army

On the declining importance of army factionalism after the February 26 incident, compared with the division of labor between the army general staff and the Ministry of War, between field commanders and Imperial General Headquarters, and between infantry and artillery, Lieutenant General Seizo Arisue, in "Interrogations," I, no. 49157, p. 26; Saburo Hayashi with Alvin D. Coox, *Kōgun: The Japanese Army in the Pacific War* (Quantico, Va.: Marine Corps Association, 1959), pp. 18, 23; General Akira Muto, International Military Tribunal for the Far East, *Record of Proceedings, 1946–1948* (Washington, D.C.: Library of Congress, 1974, microfilm), pp. 33102, 33106; James B. Crowley, *Japan's Quest for Autonomy* (Princeton, N.J.: Princeton University Press, 1966), pp. 84–85; James B. Crowley, "Japanese Army Factionalism in the Early 1930's," *Journal of Asian Studies* 21 (May 1962): 326. On the importance of morale, Hayashi, *Kōgun,* pp. 16,

151; Crowley, *Japan's Quest for Autonomy*, pp. 86, 203; Fujiwara Akira, "The Role of the Japanese Army," in *Pearl Harbor as History*, pp. 192–93; Fumimaro Ko-noye, "Memoirs with Appended Papers" (Tokyo: 5250th Technical Intelligence Co., SCAP, June 10, 1946, mimeographed), pp. 3, 66; Masao Maruyama, "The Theory and Psychology of Ultra-Nationalism, in Ivan Morris, ed., *Thought and Behavior in Modern Japanese Politics* (New York: Oxford University Press, 1963), p. 14.

Navy

On autonomy, U.S. Strategic Bombing Survey (Pacific) (USSBS), Naval Analysis Division, *Interrogations of Japanese Officials*, Report No. 72 (Washington, D.C., 1946), II: 313–14, 321, 329, 390, 394, 496; Hayashi, *Kōgun*, pp. 152–53; Mamoru Shigemtisu, *Japan and Her Destiny*, ed. F. S. G. Piggott (New York: Dutton, 1958), p. 354; Toshikazu Kase, *Journey to the Missouri*, ed. David Rowe (New Haven: Yale University Press, 1950), p. 52. On capabilities, especially naval aviation, Masuo Kato, *The Lost War* (New York: Knopf, 1946), p. 107; USSBS, *Interrogations*, II: 262, 285, 314–15, 324–25, 389, 392; Shuichi Miyazaki, in "Interrogations, unnumbered, May 20, 1949, p. 506; David Bergamini, *Japan's Imperial Conspiracy* (New York: Morrow, 1971), pp. 1002–3; Hayashi, *Kōgun*, pp. 116–17.

Foreign Ministry

On the risk to the organizational essence of the Foreign Ministry of taking the lead on surrender talks, Kase, *Journey to the Missouri*, pp. 16–17. On its loss of autonomy to new wartime agencies, Akira Iriye, *Power and Culture: The Japanese-American War, 1941–1945* (Cambridge, Mass.: Harvard University Press, 1981), pp. 68–70; F. C. Jones, *Japan's New Order for Asia* (London: Oxford University Press, 1954), pp. 85–86, 334–37; Kase, *Journey to the Missouri*, pp. 17–18; Robert Craigie, *Behind the Japanese Mask* (London: Hutchinson, 1946), pp. 80–81.

Bibliography

Acheson, Dean. *Present at the Creation: My Years in the State Department*. New York: W.W. Norton, 1969.
——. *Sketches from Life of the Men I Have Known*. New York: Harper, 1961.
Allison, Graham T. "Conceptual Models and the Cuban Missile Crisis." *American Political Science Review* 63 (September 1969): 689–718.
——. *Essence of Decision*. Boston: Little, Brown, 1971.
Alperovitz, Gar. *Atomic Diplomacy: Hiroshima and Potsdam*. New York: Vintage, 1967.
Amrine, Michael. *The Great Decision*. New York: Putnam, 1959.
Anon. "The Balance of Military Power," *The Atlantic*, 187 (June 1951), 21–27.
Arnold, Henry H. *Global Mission*. New York: Harper, 1949.
Aron, Raymond. *The Century of Total War*. Garden City, N.Y.: Doubleday, 1954.
Ball, Desmond. "Can Nuclear War Be Controlled?" *Adelphi Papers* 169 (1981).
Ball, George. "A Light That Failed," *The Atlantic* 230 (July 1972): 33–49.
Bergamini, David. *Japan's Imperial Conspiracy*. New York: Morrow, 1971.
Bernstein, Barton J. "The Perils and Politics of Surrender: Ending the War with Japan and Avoiding the Third Atomic Bomb." *Pacific Historical Review* 44 (February 1977): 1–27.
Blackett, P. M. S. *Fear, War and the Bomb: Military and Political Consequences*. New York: Whittlesey House, 1949.
Blair, Bruce. *Strategic Command and Control*. Washington, D.C.: Brookings Institution, 1985.
Blaker, Michael. *Japanese International Negotiating Style*. New York: Columbia University Press, 1977.
Blum, John Morton, ed.. *The Price of Vision: The Diary of Henry A. Wallace, 1942–1946*. Boston: Houghton Mifflin, 1973.
Bohlen, Charles E. *Witness to History, 1929–1969*. New York: Norton, 1973.
Borg, Dorothy and Shumpei Okamoto, eds. *Pearl Harbor as History*. New York: Columbia University Press, 1973.
Bourne, Randolph. *War and the Intellectuals*. Ed. by Carl Resek. New York: Harper & Row, 1964.
Bracken, Paul J. *The Command and Control of Nuclear Forces*. New Haven: Yale University Press, 1983.
Brewer, F. M. "Emperor of Japan." *Editorial Research Reports*, August 14, 1945, pp. 123–38.
Brooks, Lester. *Behind Japan's Surrender*. New York: McGraw-Hill, 1968.
Brophy, Leo P., and George J. B. Fisher. *Organizing for War*, vol. 1 of U.S. Department of the Army, Office of the Chief of Military History, *The U.S. Army in World War II*, Ser. XI: The Technical Services, VII: Chemical Warfare Services. Washington, D.C.: Government Printing Office, 1959.

[319]

Brown, Anthony Cave, and Charles B. MacDonald. *The Secret History of the Atomic Bomb.* New York: Dial, 1977.

Brown, Frederic J. *Chemical Warfare: A Study in Restraints.* Princeton, N.J.: Princeton University Press, 1968.

Bundy, Harvey H. "Remembered Words," *The Atlantic* 199 (March 1957): 56–57.

Bush, Vannevar. *Pieces of the Action.* New York: Morrow, 1970.

Butow, Robert J. C. *Japan's Decision to Surrender.* Stanford, Calif.: Stanford University Press, 1954.

Byrnes, James F. *All in One Lifetime.* New York: Harper, 1958.

——. *Speaking Frankly.* New York: Harper, 1947.

Calahan, H. A. *What Makes a War End?* New York: Vanguard, 1944.

Cantril, Hadley, ed. *Public Opinion, 1935–1946.* Princeton, N.J.: Princeton University Press, 1951.

Chase, James L. "Unconditional Surrender Reconsidered." *Political Science Quarterly* 70 (June 1955): 258–79.

Churchill, Winston. *Triumph and Tragedy.* Boston: Houghton Mifflin, 1953.

Clark, Ian. *Limited Nuclear War.* Princeton, N.J.: Princeton University Press, 1982.

Clausewitz, Karl von. *On War.* Ed. Michael Howard and Peter Paret. Princeton, N.J.: Princeton University Press, 1976.

Cline, Ray S. *Washington Command Post: The Operations Division,* vol. 2 of U.S. Department of the Army, Office of the Chief of Military History, *U.S. Army in World War II,* series I: The War Department. Washington, D.C.: Government Printing Office, 1951.

Compton, Arthur H. *Atomic Quest.* New York: Oxford University Press, 1956.

Compton, Karl T. "If the Atomic Bomb Had Not Been Used." *Atlantic Monthly* 178 (December 1946): 52–54.

Conant, James B. *My Several Lives.* New York: Harper & Row, 1970.

Coser, Lewis. "The Termination of Conflict." *Journal of Conflict Resolution* 5 (December 1961): 347–53.

Cousins, Norman, and Thomas K. Finletter. "A Beginning for Sanity." *Saturday Review of Literature,* June 15, 1946, pp. 7–8.

Craig, Gordon, and Alexander George. *Force and Statecraft: Diplomatic Problems of Our Time.* New York: Oxford University Press, 1983.

Craven, Wesley F., and James L. Cate. *Men and Planes,* vol. 6 of U.S. Air Force, Historical Division of Research Studies, *The Army Air Forces in World War II.* Chicago: University of Chicago Press, 1955.

——. *The Pacific: Matterhorn to Nagasaki, June 1944 to August 1945,* vol. 5 of U.S. Air Force, Historical Division of Research Studies, *The Army Air Forces in World War II.* Chicago: University of Chicago Press, 1953.

Crowley, James B. *Japan's Quest for Autonomy.* Princeton, N.J.: Princeton University Press, 1966.

Davis, Nuel Pharr. *Lawrence and Oppenheimer.* New York: Simon & Schuster, 1968.

Davis, Vincent. *Postwar Defense Policy and the U.S. Navy, 1943–1945.* Chapel Hill: University of North Carolina Press, 1966.

Deane, John R. *The Strange Alliance.* New York: Viking, 1947.

Ehrman, John, ed. *Grand Strategy,* vol. 6 of *History of the Second World War.* London: Her Majesty's Stationery Office, 1956.

Eisenhower, Dwight D. *Crusade in Europe.* Garden City, N.Y.: Doubleday, 1948.

Feis, Herbert. *The Atomic Bomb and the End of World War II.* 2d ed. rev. Princeton, N.J.: Princeton University Press, 1966.

——. "Some Notes on Historical Record-Keeping, the Role of Historians, and the Influence of Historical Memoirs during the Era of the Second World War." In *The Historian and the Diplomat,* ed. Francis Loewenheim. New York: Harper & Row, 1967.

Ferrell, Robert H. ed. *Off the Record: The Private Papers of Harry S Truman*. New York: Harper & Row, 1980.

Field, Harry H., and Louise M. Van Patten. "If the American People Made the Peace." *Public Opinion Quarterly* 8 (Winter 1944–45): 500–12.

Fishel, Wesley R. "A Japanese Peace Maneuver in 1944." *Far Eastern Quarterly* 8 (August 1949): 387–97.

Foster, James L., and Garry D. Brewer. "And the Clocks Were Striking Thirteen: The Termination of War." *Policy Sciences* 7 (June 1976): 225–43.

Gerth, Hans H., and C. Wright Mills, ed. *From Max Weber: Essays in Sociology*. New York: Oxford University Press, 1958.

Giovannitti, Len, and Fred Freed. *The Decision to Drop the Bomb*. New York: Coward-McCann, 1965.

Gray, Colin. "The Strategic Forces Triad: End of the Road?" *Foreign Affairs* 56 (July 1978): 771–89.

Grew, Joseph C. *Turbulent Era: A Diplomatic Record of Forty Years, 1904–1945*. Ed. Walter Johnson. 2 vols. Boston: Houghton Mifflin, 1952.

Groves, Leslie R. *Now It Can Be Told*. New York: Harper, 1962.

Halberstam, David. *The Best and the Brightest*. Greenwich, Conn.: Fawcett, 1973.

Halperin, Morton H. *Bureaucratic Politics and Foreign Policy*. Washington, D.C.: Brookings Institution, 1974.

——. *Limited War in the Nuclear Age*. New York: Wiley, 1963.

——. "Why Bureaucrats Play Games." *Foreign Policy* 2 (Spring 1971): 70–90.

Handel, Michael. "The Study of War Termination." *Journal of Strategic Studies* 1 (May 1978): 51–75.

Havens, Thomas R. H. *Valley of Darkness: The Japanese People and World War Two*. New York: Norton, 1978.

Hayashi, Saburo, with Alvin D. Coox. *Kōgun: The Japanese Army in the Pacific War*. Quantico, Va.: Marine Corps Association, 1959.

Herken, Gregg. *The Winning Weapon*. New York: Knopf, 1980.

Hewlett, Richard C., and Oscar E. Anderson, Jr. *The New World 1939–1945*, vol. 1 of *A History of the United States Atomic Energy Commission*. University Park: Pennsylvania State University, 1962.

Holborn, Louise W., ed. *The War and Peace Aims of the United Nations*. 2 vols. Boston: World Peace Foundation, 1943, 1948.

How Wars End. Annals of the American Academy of Social and Political Science 392 (November 1970).

Hull, Cordell. *The Memoirs of Cordell Hull*. 2 vols. New York: Macmillan, 1948.

Ike, Nobutake, ed. *Japan's Decision for War*. Stanford, Calif.: Stanford University Press, 1967.

Iklé, Fred C. *Every War Must End*. New York: Columbia University Press, 1971.

——. "The Prevention of Nuclear War in a World of Uncertainty." In U.S. Department of State, *Bulletin*, March 25, 1974, pp. 314–18.

International Military Tribunal for the Far East (IMTFE). *Record of Proceedings, 1946–1948*. Washington, D.C.: Library of Congress, 1974. Microfilm.

Iriye, Akira. *Power and Culture: The Japanese-American War, 1941–1945*. Cambridge, Mass.: Harvard University Press, 1981.

Ito, Masanori. *The End of the Imperial Japanese Navy*. Trans. Andrew Y. Kuroda and Roger Pineau. New York: Norton, 1956.

Jervis, Robert. *Perception and Misperception*. Princeton, N.J.: Princeton University Press, 1976.

Jones, F. C. *Japan's New Order in East Asia*. London: Oxford University Press, 1954.

Kahn, Herman. *On Escalation: Metaphors and Scenarios*. Baltimore: Penguin, 1968.

———. *On Thermonuclear War*. Princeton, N.J.: Princeton University Press, 1961.
———. *War Termination Issues and Concepts*. Croton-on-Hudson, N.Y.: Hudson Institute, 1968.
Kase, Toshikazu. *Journey to the Missouri*. Ed. David N. Rowe. New Haven: Yale University Press, 1950.
Katō, Masuo. *The Lost War: A Japanese Reporter's Inside Story*. New York: Knopf, 1946.
Kawai, Kazuo. "Militarist Activity between Japan's Two Surrender Decisions." *Pacific Historical Review* 22 (November 1953): 383–89.
———. "*Mokusatsu*, Japan's Response to the Potsdam Declaration," *Pacific Historical Review* 19 (November 1950): 409–14.
Kecskemeti, Paul. *Strategic Surrender*. New York: Atheneum, 1964.
Kevles, Daniel J. "The National Science Foundation and the Debate over Postwar Research Policy, 1942–1945: A Political Interpretation of *Science: The Endless Frontier*," *Isis* 68 (March 1977), 5–26.
King, Ernest J., and Walter Muir Whitehead. *Fleet Admiral King*. New York: Norton, 1952.
Kissinger, Henry A. *The Necessity for Choice*. New York: Harper, 1960.
Kleber, Brooks E., and Dale Birdsell. *Chemicals in Combat*, vol. 3 of U.S. Department of the Army, Office of the Chief of Military History, *The U.S. Army in World War II*, ser. XI: The Technical Services, VII: Chemical Warfare Services. Washington, D.C.: Government Printing Office, 1966.
Knebel, Fletcher, and Charles W. Bailey. *No High Ground*. New York: Harper, 1960.
———. "Secret: The Fight over the A-Bomb," *Look*, August 13, 1963, pp. 19–23.
Kuroki, Yukichi. "From War to Peace Cabinets," *Contemporary Japan* 14 (April-December 1945): 182–92.
Laurence, William L. *Dawn over Zero: The Story of the Atomic Bomb*. New York: Knopf, 1946.
———. *Men and Atoms*. New York: Simon & Schuster, 1959.
Leahy, William D. *I Was There: The Personal Story of the Chief of Staff to Presidents Roosevelt and Truman Based on His Notes and Diaries Made at the Time*. New York: McGraw-Hill, 1950.
Leighton, Alexander H., and Morris E. Opler. "Psychiatry and Applied Anthropology in Psychological Warfare against Japan," *American Journal of Psychoanalysis* 6 (1946): 20–34.
LeMay, Curtis E., with MacKinlay Kantor. *Mission with LeMay*. Garden City, N.Y.: Doubleday, 1965.
Liddell Hart, Basil H. *The Revolution in Warfare*. London: Faber & Faber, 1946.
Lilienthal, David E. *The Journals of David Lilienthal*, II: *The Atomic Energy Years*. New York: Harper & Row, 1964.
McCloy, John J. *The Challenge to American Foreign Policy*. Cambridge, Mass.: Harvard University Press, 1953.
MacIsaac, David. *Strategic Bombing in World War Two*. New York: Garland, 1976.
McKelway, St. Clair. "A Reporter with the B-29s," *The New Yorker*, June 23, 1945, pp. 26–39.
March, James G., and Herbert Simon. *Organizations*. New York: Wiley, 1968.
Maruyama, Masao. *Thought and Behavior in Modern Japanese Politics*. Ed. Ivan Morris. London: Oxford University Press, 1963.
Maxon, Yale C. *Control of Japanese Foreign Policy*. Berkeley: University of California Press, 1957.
Miller, David H. *The Drafting of the Covenant*. Vol. I. New York: Putnam, 1928.
Miller, Merle. *Plain Speaking: An Oral Biography of Harry S Truman*. New York: Berkley, 1974.
Millis, Walter, ed. *The Forrestal Diaries*. New York: Viking, 1951.
———. *The War Reports of General of the Army George C. Marshall, General of the Army H. H. Arnold, and Fleet Admiral Ernest J. King*. Philadelphia: Lippincott, 1947.

Moon, John. "Chemical Weapons and Deterrence: The World War II Experience." *International Security* 8 (Spring 1984): 3–35.

Morley, James W., ed. *Dilemmas of Growth in Prewar Japan*. Princeton, N.J.: Princeton University Press, 1971.

Morison, Samuel Eliot. "Why Japan Surrendered," *The Atlantic* 206 (October 1960): 41–47.

Nakane, Chie. *Japanese Society*. Berkeley: University of California Press, 1970.

"A New Far Eastern Policy? Japan versus China." *Amerasia*, June 9, 1944, pp. 179–89.

Notter, Harley A. *Post-War Foreign Policy Preparation, 1939–1945*. Washington, D.C.: Government Printing Office, 1949.

Pacific War Research Society. *Japan's Longest Day*. Tokyo: Kodansha, 1968.

Patterson, Robert P. "Leahy's Inside Story of the Business of Making War." *New York Times Book Review*, March 19, 1950, p. 3.

Pomeroy, Earl S. "Sentiment for a Strong Peace, 1917–1919." *South Atlantic Quarterly* 43 (October 1944): 325–37.

Posen, Barry R. "Inadvertent Nuclear War?" *International Security* 7 (Fall 1982): 3–31.

Powell, John W. "A Hidden Chapter in History." *Bulletin of the Atomic Scientists* 37 (October 1981): 44–52.

Quester, George. *Deterrence before Hiroshima*. New York: Wiley, 1966.

Rabi, I. I. "The Physicist Returns from the War." *The Atlantic* 176 (October 1945): 107–14.

Rapoport, Anatol. *Fights, Games, and Debates*. Binghamton, N.Y.: Vail-Baillou Press, 1960.

Reischauer, Edwin O. *The United States and Japan*. Cambridge, Mass.: Harvard University Press, 1950.

Richardson, Lewis F. "War Moods." *Psychometrica* 13 (September 1948): 147–74 and (December 1948): 197–232.

Roosevelt, Elliott. *As He Saw It*. New York: Duell, Sloan & Pearce, 1956.

Roosevelt Presidential Press Conferences. Hyde Park: Roosevelt Library, 1957. Microfilm.

Rose, Lisle A. *After Yalta*. New York: Scribner, 1973.

Rosenman, Samuel I. *Working with Roosevelt*. New York: Harper, 1952.

Rosenman, Samuel I., ed. *The Public Papers and Addresses of Franklin D. Roosevelt, 1943: The Tide Turns*. New York: Harper & Row, 1950.

Rostow, Walt W. *Pre-Invasion Bombing Strategy*. Austin: University of Texas Press, 1981.

Rowe, David N. "Ultimatum for Japan." *Far Eastern Survey*, August 15, 1945, pp. 217–19.

Rudin, Harry R. *Armistice 1918*. New Haven: Yale University Press, 1944.

Sallagar, Frederick M. *The Road to Total War*. Santa Monica, Calif.: RAND, 1969.

Schelling, Thomas C. *Arms and Influence*. New Haven: Yale University Press, 1966.

——. *The Strategy of Conflict*. New York: Oxford University Press, 1963.

Schoenberger, Walter S. *Decision of Destiny*. Athens: Ohio University Press, 1969.

Sekine, Gumpei. "America's Strategy against Japan," Trans. A. J. Grajdanzev. *Pacific Affairs* 14 (July 1941): 215–21.

Shapley, Deborah. "Nuclear Weapons History: Japan's Wartime Bomb Projects Revealed." *Science*, January 13, 1978, pp. 152–57.

Sherwin, Martin J. *A World Destroyed: The Atomic Bomb and the Grand Alliance*. New York: Knopf, 1975.

Sherwood, Robert E. *Roosevelt and Hopkins*. New York: Grossett & Dunlap, 1950.

Shigemitsu, Mamoru. *Japan and Her Destiny*. Edited by F. S. G. Piggott. New York: Dutton, 1958.

Sigal, Leon V. "Bureaucratic Politics and Tactical Use of Committees: The Interim Committee and the Decision to Drop the Atomic Bomb." *Polity* 10 (Spring 1978): 326–64.

Smith, Alice K. *A Peril and a Hope: The Scientists' Movement in America, 1945–1947*. Chicago: University of Chicago Press, 1965.

[323]

Smith, M. Brewster, Jerome S. Bruner, and Robert W. White. *Opinions and Personality*. New York: Wiley, 1964.

Smith, Perry McCoy. *The Air Force Plans for Peace, 1943–1945*. Baltimore: Johns Hopkins University Press, 1970.

Smoke, Richard. *War: Controlling Escalation*. Cambridge, Mass.: Harvard University Press, 1977.

Stein, Janice G. "War Termination and Conflict Resolution, or How Wars Should End." *Jerusalem Journal of International Relations* 1 (Fall 1975): 1–27.

Steinbruner, John. *The Cybernetic Theory of Decision: New Dimensions of Political Analysis*. Princeton, N.J.: Princeton University Press, 1974.

Stimson, Henry L. "The Decision to Use the Atomic Bomb," *Harper's* 194 (February 1947): 98–107.

Stimson, Henry L., and McGeorge Bundy. *On Active Service in Peace and War*. New York: Harper, 1948.

Stockholm International Peace Research Institute (SIPRI). *The Rise of CB Weapons*. Vol. 1 of *The Problems of Chemical and Biological Warfare*, by Julian Perry Robinson with Milton Leitenberg. Stockholm: Almqvist & Wicksell, 1981.

Storry, Richard. *The Double Patriots*. London: Chatto & Windus, 1957.

——. "Konoye Fumimaro, 'The Last of the Fujiwara.'" *Far Eastern Affairs* 2 (1960) (St. Antony's Papers no. 7): 9–23.

Strauss, Lewis L. *Men and Decisions*. New York: Doubleday, 1962.

Sutherland, John P. "The Story General Marshall Told Me." *U.S. News & World Report*, November 2, 1959, pp. 50–56.

Titus, David A. *Palace and Politics in Prewar Japan*. New York: Columbia University Press, 1974.

Tōgō, Shigenori. *The Cause of Japan*. New York: Simon & Schuster, 1956.

Toland, John. *The Rising Sun*. New York: Bantam, 1970.

Truman, Harry S. *Memoirs*, Vol. I: *Year of Decisions*. Garden City, N.Y.: Doubleday, 1955.

——. *Truman Speaks*. New York: Columbia University Press, 1960.

Truman, Margaret. *Harry S Truman*. New York: Morrow, 1973.

Tsuneishi, Warren M. "The Japanese Emperor: A Study in Constitutional Political Change." Ph.D. diss., Yale University, 1960.

U.S. Army. Far East Command. Military History Section. Japanese Research Division. *Imperial General Headquarters Army High Command Record*. Japanese Monograph No. 45. Mimeographed.

——. "Interrogations of Japanese Officials." 2 vols. Typescript.

——. "Statements of Japanese Officials." 4 vols. Typescript.

——, "Translations of Japanese Documents." 4 vols. Typescript.

U.S. Atomic Energy Commission. *In the Matter of J. Robert Oppenheimer*. Transcript of Hearing before Personnel Security Board, April 12–May 6, 1954. Washington, D.C.: Government Printing Office, 1954.

U.S. Congress. House. Committee on Military Affairs. *Atomic Energy. Hearings*. 79th Cong., 1st sess., 1945.

U.S. Congress. Senate. Committee on Foreign Relations. Subcommittee on Arms Control, International Law and Organizations. *Nuclear Weapons and Foreign Policy: Hearings*. 93d Cong., 2d sess., 1974.

U.S. Congress. Senate. Committee on Military Affairs. *Department of Armed Forces, Department of Military Security: Hearings on S. 84 and S. 1482*. 79th Cong., 1st sess., 1945.

U.S. Congressional Research Service. *Authority to Order the Use of Nuclear Weapons: Hearings*. 94th Cong., 1st sess., 1975.

United States. Department of Defense. *The Entry of the Soviet Union into the War against Japan: Military Plans, 1941–1945*. Washington, D.C.: 1955. Mimeographed.

United States. Department of State. *Foreign Relations of the United States* (FRUS), 1942, I: *General; The British Commonwealth; The Far East*. Washington, D.C.: Government Printing Office, 1960.

———. *Foreign Relations of the United States, 1942, III: Europe*. Washington, D.C.: Government Printing Office, 1960.

———. *Foreign Relations of the United States, 1944, V: The Near East; South Africa; The Far East*. Washington, D.C.: Government Printing Office, 1965.

———. *Foreign Relations of the United States, 1945. VI: The British Commonwealth; The Far East*. Washington, D.C.: Government Printing Office, 1969.

———. *Foreign Relations of the United States, The Conference of Berlin (Potsdam), 1945*. 2 vols. Washington, D.C.: Government Printing Office, 1960.

———. *Foreign Relations of the United States, The Conferences at Cairo and Teheran*. Washington, D.C.: Government Printing Office, 1961.

———. *Foreign Relations of the United States, The Conferences at Malta and Yalta, 1945*. Washington, D.C.: Government Printing Office, 1955.

———. *Foreign Relations of the United States, The Conference at Quebec, 1943*. Washington, D.C. : Government Printing Office, 1972.

U.S. Department of War. Strategic Services Unit History Project. *War Report of the OSS*, II: *The Overseas Targets*. New York: Walker, 1976.

U.S. Manhattan Engineering District (MED). *The Atomic Bombings of Hiroshima and Nagasaki*. Washington, D.C, 1946.

United States Strategic Bombing Survey (Pacific). *Effects of Air Attack on Osaka-Kobe-Kyoto*. Report No. 58. Washington, D.C.: Government Printing Office, 1947.

———. *Effects of Atomic Bombs on Hiroshima and Nagasaki*. Report No. 3. Washington, D.C.: Government Printing Office, 1946.

———. *Effects of Strategic Bombing on Japan's War Economy*. Report No. 53. Washington, D.C.: Government Printing Office, 1946.

———. *Japan's Struggle to End the War*. Report No. 2. Washington, D.C.: Government Printing Office, 1946.

———. *Summary Report*. Report No. 1. Washington, D.C.: Government Printing Office, 1946.

———. Naval Analysis Division. *Interrogations of Japanese Officials*. Report No. 72. 2 vols. Washington, D.C.: Government Printing Office, 1946.

Uyehara, George E. *The Political Development of Japan, 1867–1909*. New York: Dutton, 1910.

Vandenberg, Arthur H., Jr., and Joe Alex Morris, eds. *The Private Papers of Arthur Vandenberg*. Boston: Houghton Mifflin, 1952.

Weil, Martin. *A Pretty Good Club*. New York: Norton, 1978.

Weiner, Charles. "Retroactive Saber Rattling?" *Bulletin of the Atomic Scientists* 34 (April 1978): 10–12.

Welles, Sumner. *Where Are We Heading?* New York: Harper, 1946.

Wilson, George M., ed. *Crisis Politics in Prewar Japan*. Tokyo: Sophia University Press, 1970.

Zacharias, Ellis M. "The A-Bomb Was Not Needed." *United Nations World* 3 (August 1949): 25–29.

———. *Secret Missions: The Story of an Intelligence Officer*. New York: Putnam, 1946.

Index

Library of Congress Cataloging-in-Publication Data

Sigal, Leon V.
   Fighting to a finish : the politics of war termination in the United States and Japan, 1945 /
Leon V. Sigal.
       p.   cm.—(Cornell studies in security affairs)
   Bibliography: p.
   Includes index.
   ISBN 0-8014-2086-5 (alk. paper)
       1. World War, 1939–1945—Peace. 2. World War, 1939–1945—Diplomatic history. 3.
United States—Foreign relations—Japan. 4. Japan—Foreign relations—United States. 5.
United States—Politics and government—1933–1945. 6. Japan—Politics and govern-
ment—1926–1945. I. Title. II. Series.
D821.U6S54 1988   940.53'2—dc19   87-24876

CORNELL STUDIES IN SECURITY AFFAIRS

edited by Robert J. Art *and* Robert Jervis